FAREWELL AMERICA

The Plot to Kill JFK

JAMES HEPBURN

Introduction by William Turner

191 - no presemptive war
276 - domestic
      tranquility
294 - CIA organized
321 - why Oswald
343 - T.O.P.
344 ignored

Penmarin Books

For Walter,
the first born of a New America

Editorial Offices:
Penmarin Books
1044 Magnolia Way
Roseville, CA 95661
(916) 771-5869

Sales and Customer Service Offices:
Midpoint Trade Books
27 W. 20th Street, Suite 1102
New York, NY 10011
(212) 727-0190

"The *Farewell America* Plot" by William Turner appeared in *Rearview Mirror: Looking Back at the FBI, the CIA and Other Tails*, copyright © 2001 by William Turner. Reprinted with permission.

Farewell America was originally published in 1968 by Frontiers Publishing Company, Voduz, Liechtenstein, copyright under the International Copyright Convention. All efforts to contact Frontiers Publishing Company regarding reproduction have proved fruitless.

Penmarin Books are available at special discounts for bulk purchases for premiums, sales promotions, or education. For details, contact the Publisher. On your letterhead, include information concerning the intended use of the books and how many you wish to purchase.

Visit our Website at www.penmarin.com for more information about this and other exciting titles.

Printed in the United States of America
1 2 3 4 5 6 7 8 9 10   06 05 04 03 02

Library of Congress Control Number: 2002115235

Contents

PART III DESTINY

PART IV REVIVAL

*The soft, the complacent, the self-satisfied societies will
be swept away with the debris of History.*

JOHN FITZGERALD KENNEDY

*That whenever any Form of Government becomes destruc-
tive of Life, Liberty and the pursuit of Happiness, it is the
Right of the People to alter or to abolish it, and to institute new Government, laying its foundation on such principles and organizing its powers in such form, as to them
shall seem most likely to effect their Safety and Happiness . . . when a long train of abuses and usurpations,
pursuing invariably the same Object evinces a design to
reduce them under absolute Despotism, it is their right, it
is their duty to throw such Government and to provide
new Guards for their future security.*

DECLARATION OF INDEPENDENCE

Introduction:
The *Farewell America* Plot

WILLIAM TURNER

It had to be one of the most intrigue-ridden publishing ventures ever, more so than Che Guevara's diary or the memoirs of Stalin's daughter Svetlana. The story of *Farewell America* may have begun with a visit to the KGB in Mexico City; it progressed to the office of French President Charles de Gaulle in Paris. And it most certainly was aimed at advancing the 1968 presidential campaign of Robert F. Kennedy in America. In the doing, *l'affaire Farewell*, which was so convoluted it seemed borrowed from a John Le Carré novel, somehow liberated the famous Zapruder film from the *Life* magazine vault in which it had been sequestered.

My involvement in this international adventure was set up when I shifted from being a student of the Warren Commission Report to a critic. The more I learned, the more obvious it became that there was more to the JFK assassination than Lee Harvey Oswald, who allegedly had occupied a sniper's perch in the Texas School Book Depository building. Remembering that Dallas police officer Welcome Eugene Barnett had told me a woman ran up to him to report a shot from the now-famous grassy knoll, I found that, despite the FBI's attempts to keep the wraps on, there were scores of spectators in Dealey Plaza who heard at least one shot from the knoll (including, it came out years later,

1

Kennedy aides Kenneth O'Donnell and David Powers). I was particularly swayed by the fact that a dermal nitrate test on Oswald's cheek by the police detected no blowback of nitrate residues as would be expected if he fired a rifle (although residues were found on his right hand, which suggested he fired the handgun that killed Officer J. D. Tippit). Testifying before the Warren Commission, an FBI ballistics technician had explained the absence of cheek residues as the result of a tightly sealed chamber on the old Italian Army rifle supposedly fired by Oswald, which didn't sound right. I called Dr. Vincent Guinn, head of the General Atomics project in San Diego, which had developed an ultrasensitive process called nuclear activation analysis (NAA). He and Raymond Pinker, director of the Los Angeles Police Department crime lab at the time, also had been puzzled by the technician's explanation. As I wrote in *Invisible Witness: The Use and Abuse of the New Technology of Crime Investigation* in 1968, the pair "ordered an Italian Carcano rifle such as Oswald supposedly fired from the same mail order house in Chicago. They fired the obsolete weapon a number of times—some gun experts think it is likely to blow up—and tested their cheeks by NAA. Nitrates were present in abundance." Nor could the Carcano be put in Oswald's hands that day by fingerprints—none were found on the weapon.

Flaws in the official version kept piling up. Jack Ruby's mob ties and gunrunning operations belied his assertion that he had shot Oswald to spare Jacqueline Kennedy the ordeal of a trial. I found suspicious the fate of the Zapruder film taken by a spectator standing on the grassy knoll, which showed the entire assassination sequence. *Life* bought it from Abraham Zapruder and, instead of putting it to commercial use, squirreled it away. Not even Warren Commission members viewed it as a motion picture. The magazine published staggered still frames in a cover story endorsing the Warren Report when it was issued in September 1964, putting captions under each frame. The caption under frame 313, where Kennedy's head explodes, said it was from a shot from the front. But that meant Oswald couldn't have fired it. When *Life* realized its "error," it stopped the presses and rewrote the caption as a shot from the rear. The film also graphically demonstrated that the president and Texas Governor John Connally, sitting in the jump seat in front of him, were struck by bullets within three-quarters of a second of each other, dictating two weapons. The Warren Commission disposed of this quandary by inventing the Magic Bullet Theory, which held that one bullet zig-zagged completely through the president and the governor, smashing bones, emerging unmutilated. The theory was absurd, and over the years John and Nellie Connally, who also were in the limousine, insisted that there were two bullets (although, as political creatures, they didn't think this meant a conspiracy).

In February 1967 I received a call from Jim Garrison, the New Orleans District Attorney, whose probe into the JFK assassination had broken into the news a few weeks earlier. "Bill, I need your help," he said. "The paramilitary right and Cuban exiles are figuring prominently in the investigation." He had pegged me as an expert on the subject after reading a *Ramparts* article I had done on the Minutemen, a forerunner of today's ultraright militia units. I had interviewed the national leader of the Minutemen, Robert B. DePugh, in his Missouri redoubt, venturing there with some trepidation since a California unit had warned that time was short for *Ramparts* editors to "change our nefarious ways." But DePugh was surprisingly cordial. He boasted, "We have the most sophisticated and best-equipped underground army movement this world has ever seen." His membership harbored specialists not only in firearms but electronics, demolition, and chemical and biological warfare. And he added, out of the blue, that he suspected a couple of his members were on the shooting team at Dallas, using ammo encased in plastic sleeves so it could be fired from a larger caliber weapon without being matched to that weapon. DePugh knew that in 1962 one of his "patriots" named John Morris cooked up a plot to assassinate Senator J. William Fulbright because he wasn't "voting American" (he opposed the Vietnam War). When DePugh got wind of it, after money had actually changed hands, he squelched it, he said, in order to head off a massive federal probe of his organization. In researching the article, I picked up information that a Minutemen cell in Dallas threatened to "snuff" Stanley Marcus of the upscale Nieman-Marcus department store chain because he was Jewish and liberal (I called Marcus to inform him of the danger).

When Garrison phoned, I was familiar with him through the legal press, for which I wrote forensic science articles. Such was his reputation in the law enforcement field that he had been asked to write the foreword to *Crime, Law and Corrections*, a collection of criminology essays. It was haunting. As an army officer, Garrison had helped liberate the Nazi concentration camp at Dachau, and he had witnessed its horrors. Allegorizing on an extraterrestrial being descending onto a self-desolated world, he asks, "What happened to your disinterested millions? Your uncommitted and uninvolved, your preoccupied and bored? Where today are their private horizons and their mirrored worlds of self? Where is their splendid indifference now?"

In conferring with Garrison on the boilerplate of his investigation, it occurred to me that the Russian KGB probably had a thick file on Lee Harvey Oswald, who remained an enigma as to which side he was on. He had resided in the Soviet Union from 1959 to 1962 as an ostensible defector, staging a bit of guerrilla theater by slashing his wrists to persuade the Russians to allow him to stay. The KGB perforce would have been intensely curious about this ex-Marine radar expert who had been stationed at Atsugi, Japan, where there was a U-2 spy plane base.

After repatriating from the U.S.S.R., Oswald found work at a Dallas photographic and graphic arts firm, where he conversed in Russian with a fellow employee, Charles Ofstein. As Ofstein testified before the Warren Commission, Oswald disclosed, "All the time I was in Minsk I never saw a vapor trail," a suggestion that he was watching for high-flying aircraft such as the U-2. Oswald also talked about the dispersion of Russian military units, saying "they didn't intermingle their armored divisions and infantry divisions and various units the way we do in the United States, and they would have all of their aircraft in one geographical location and their tanks in another geographical location, and their infantry in another. . . ." The putative defector went out of his way at some risk to pick up intelligence on the Soviet armed forces. He told Ofstein that he journeyed from Minsk to Moscow one May Day to observe the huge parade of military units. On one occasion Oswald asked Ofstein to enlarge a photo that he explained was of "some military headquarters and that the guards stationed there . . . had orders to shoot any trespassers." Oswald displayed a more than casual interest in analyzing the Russian military.

But how to approach the Russians? As I told Garrison, "The press wolves out there would never stop howling if they caught us asking the time of day of the KGB." I thought of a plan. I would act as cut-out, isolating the DA's office from a third man who would make the contact. The person I had in mind was an ex-CIA contract pilot who had flown bombing raids against Cuba from Guatemala. He was tall and angular, with tousled sandy hair, cobalt eyes and a magnetic personality. He had appeared on the doorstep of Stanley Scheinbaum after the Michigan State University exposé appeared in *Ramparts*, offering to do "volunteer work" to redeem himself for his checkered stint with the Agency. Scheinbaum turned him over to me.

When I first met with him in January 1966, he was clutching a clipping from the *Fresno Bee* of March 7, 1965, from which he had carefully excised his name with a razor blade. It was in a way an obituary. It quoted Dr. Orlando Bosch, chief of the anti-Castro action group Insurrectional Movement for the Recovery of the Revolution (MIRR) in Miami, as saying, "His B-26 fighter-bomber was last seen by one of our patrol boats in flames. He was on his way back from a fire bombing mission in the Pinar Del Rio Province in western Cuba. The last radio transmission was that he was too low to bail out and could not maintain altitude." Bosch disclosed that the missing-in-action pilot "was first introduced to us as a reserve pilot for the Bay of Pigs invasion. He has done volunteer work for our organization and other anti-Communist organizations since 1959." In fact, he had bailed out of the anti-Castro movement, forcing the CIA-backed Bosch to kill off his identity. I gave him the nom de paix Jim Rose because it was the Rose Bowl time of year. Rose was the ideal candidate to approach the KGB—they would understand each other perfectly.

They did. I squeezed some travel money from a bemused Warren Hinckle, bought an airline ticket in cash so it could not be traced, and dispatched Rose to the Russian embassy in Mexico City, which was preferable to the one in Washington, the home turf of the CIA and the FBI. I instructed him to walk straight in and ask for the third secretary, usually a KGB *rezidentura*. Before long he was shaking hands with an owlish man with horn-rim glasses whom he would later identify from photos as Valery V. Kostikov, a KGB officer the CIA considered implicated in "wet affairs" (assassinations). Although Rose had no way of knowing it at the time, Kostikov was one of two KGB men who interviewed Lee Harvey Oswald when, in September 1963, he had desperately tried to secure a quick visa to reenter Russia via Cuba.

Kostikov asked Rose to turn over the camera dangling on a strap around his neck as a tourist prop; the KGB officer might have considered it something else, since the CIA laboratory had perfected camera guns that were aimed through the viewfinder. "I got it back later in better working order than when I gave it to him," Rose recounted. Rose explained the Garrison investigation to Kostikov and how there was a question of Oswald's true affiliation as well as increasing evidence of Cuban exile involvement with elements of the CIA in the assassination. Would it be possible, Rose delicately inquired, to obtain a "sanitized" version of the dossier on Oswald and whatever else might assist the investigation? "It will be necessary for you to stay in Mexico City for a few days," the Russian temporized. He asked the name of Rose's hotel, suggesting he stick close to it.

Rose was tailed from the embassy to his hotel, and remained under surveillance. He assumed it was the KGB, and that they were protecting him. That night at dinner, he observed a burly Russian-looking man sitting at a table across the room watching him without pretending to do anything else. Rose sent him a vodka neat, which prompted a smile and a salute. "They used a tail on a tail," Rose said. "It was very professional."

On the third day, one of his tails asked that he visit the embassy again. Kostikov was waiting. "What you request is not impossible," he said, choosing his words carefully. "But it is not necessary that it will happen. The only way that it could possibly occur is in a way that would be most unexpected, and untraceable to its source. Something might be left in your hands, for instance, by a visitor to your country." After this guarded answer, which Rose guessed came from Moscow, Kostikov changed the subject. "Do you like books?" he asked. He handed Rose two Soviet books, *West-East Inseparable Twain* and *USSR Today and Tomorrow*, apologizing that they were on the only ones translated into English. As a further gesture, he invited Rose and me to be guests at the forthcoming fiftieth-anniversary Red Army Ball at the embassy. Neither of us owned a tuxedo, so we didn't attend.

Eight months later, in April 1968, Jim Garrison phoned to report that he might have the Russian response (he always insisted that I go to a "neutral" phone to discuss sensitive matters). He had just received a call from New York from someone identifying himself as a representative of Frontiers Publishing Company of Geneva, Switzerland. The representative said his firm had an important work in progress on the Kennedy assassination that would soon be published in Europe, and he wondered if Garrison would be interested in taking a look. Within days the DA's mailbag brought three black-bound volumes of manuscript specklessly typed on an IBM machine. It was titled simply *The Plot*. Garrison dispatched a copy to me via courier.

The Plot manuscript, which would eventually be brought out as *Farewell America*, had a note attached saying that a fourth volume was being written. The author of record was James Hepburn, whose name was not to be found in the *Writer's Directory*. A brief biography stated he had attended the London School of Economics and the Institute of Political Studies in Paris, "where he prepared for the public service." It claimed that Hepburn had lived for a short time in the United States, making the acquaintance of Jacqueline Bouvier (Kennedy) and Senator John Kennedy. The text was sprinkled with European metaphors, such as the description of the Kennedy limousine swinging into Dealey Plaza: "Then the leaves began to fall, and soon the traces disappeared."

The immense breadth of knowledge contained in the manuscript dictated that Hepburn, whoever he was, was the beneficiary of a network of sources. Although borrowing liberally from published critics of the Warren Report, the manuscript displayed tremendous scope in the sections about the roots of the Cold War, the interlinkage between the large American corporate and banking interests and the ever-growing U.S. intelligence apparatus, and the international petroleum cartels. Brought alive by sinister portraits of CIA spymaster Allen Dulles, the cantankerous Dallas oilman H. L. Hunt, Roy Cohn and a bevy of military brass and Mafia chieftains, it advanced the theory that JFK was killed by an ad hoc amalgam of powerful interests, public and private, which had nightmares about a Kennedy dynasty that might extend through a Teddy presidency. The amalgam was called The Committee. It sponsored and carried out the assassination of JFK at both the supervisory level and the "gun" level— possibly recruiting professional assassins from the ranks of Cuban exiles embittered by Kennedy's failure to supervene with military force at the Bay of Pigs and to invade Cuba during the missile crisis. The bottom line was that JFK's enemies, collaborating with the CIA and other interested parties, moved to exorcise the Kennedy curse.

The manuscript bristled with such restricted information on the CIA that it could only have come from an inside source, and the author ventured cryptically, "In the domain of pure intelligence, the KGB is superior to the CIA." The social side of the Kennedys did not escape notice. One of the early chapters, entitled simply "King," dealt with the elegance of John and Jackie's White House. The gossips, it noted, complained that "the Kennedys spent $2000 on the food for one of their parties, neglecting to add (or perhaps they didn't know) that the President donated his entire salary to charity." Just how close to the White House the book's creators got is revealed in a paragraph about JFK's love life: "The President was discriminating in his affairs. . . . There were models of all nationalities, local beauty queens, society girls and, when he was really in a hurry, call girls. A Secret Service agent whose code name was 'Dentist' was in charge of the President's pleasures." The manuscript went on to lecture about sitting in judgment on such matters: "Puritanism is so widespread in this world, and hypocrisy so strong, that some readers will be shocked by these passages. . . . Why should a nation tolerate a President who is politically corrupt, but not one who is physiologically normal?" This was scabrous stuff for the time, when there was a gentlemen's agreement in the media not to bare the sex life of public officials. But it didn't survive *Farewell America*'s publication, having been scissored out by some phantom censor.

Before long, Jim Garrison called to say, "You know that fourth volume? It just walked in the door." But the messenger from Frontiers Publishing didn't have the final volume with him—a representative would have to be sent to Geneva to read it. I couldn't go because I was tied up with a political campaign, so the DA sent one of his corps of volunteer investigators, Steve Jaffe, a professional photographer. Jaffe went to the given address of Frontiers in Geneva, only to find that it was the office of a large law firm, Fiduciaire Wanner, specializing in Swiss banks. Frontiers was incorporated in Liechtenstein, he was told, but its editorial suite was in Paris. In the City of Light he again found himself in Fiduciaire Wanner offices, but this time his visit produced a man who gave his name as Hervé Lamarr, the publisher of *Farewell America*, née *The Plot*. Regretfully, Lamarr said, the author, James Hepburn, was not available. In fact, the Frenchman confessed over Pernods, Hepburn didn't exist as such.

Lamarr had concocted the name out of flaming admiration of
Audrey Hepburn. The James had come from *j'aime*—I love. A
nice French touch.

As they bistro hopped, Jaffe discovered that Lamarr's background was every bit as exotic as his taste in actresses. He had
been in the French army, attended Harvard, edited a women's
magazine, served in the French diplomatic corps in Indochina—
and was connected to French intelligence. This last item was
confirmed when Lamarr took Jaffe to the Elysée Palace to see
André Ducret, the chief of the secret service, whose office ad-
joined that of General Charles de Gaulle, the president. Ducret
told the young American how vital his mission and Garrison's
investigation were, and how France appreciated their efforts. He
disclosed that his secret service had indeed furnished information for certain parts of *Farewell America*. Then he ducked into
de Gaulle's office and returned with the general's personal calling card, on which he inscribed, "*Je suis très sensible à la
confiance que vous m'exprimez.*" (I am very moved by the confidence you have expressed in me.) The book now bore the
imprimature of the highest councils of the French government,
which was not too surprising. The haughty president of the republic had very much admired Kennedy's style, and never believed that Oswald was a "lone nut." "You're kidding me!" he
scoffed to an interviewer when apprised of the Warren
Commission's verdict. "Cowboys and Indians!" he concluded.
De Gaulle himself had been the target of a conspiracy of military officers a year before Dallas; the conspirators, known as the
Secret Army Organization and opposed to de Gaulle's pullout
from Algeria, set up a cross fire ambush of his car, but he narrowly escaped when his driver sharply accelerated.

When Jaffe pressed for the book's principal sources, Lamarr
named, among others, Ducret; Interpol, the international police
clearing house; and Philippe Vosjoly, the chief French petroleum espionage agent in the United States, who assertedly infiltrated the CIA, the Texas oil industry, and anti-Castro action
groups in South Florida. Vosjoly, Lamarr said, had interviewed
a member of the paramilitary ambush team in Dealey Plaza, a
Cuban exile, in Mexico City. And there was another source:
Daniel Patrick Moynihan, an assistant secretary of labor in the
Kennedy administration (later a senator from New York). Lamarr
confided that on the day after the assassination, Robert Kennedy

called in Moynihan, one of the family's most trusted aides, and instructed him to quietly assemble a small staff to explore two possibilities: that mortal enemy Jimmy Hoffa was behind it, or that the Secret Service had been bought off. In due time, Moynihan handed RFK a confidential report that there was no evidence of Hoffa's involvement or of Secret Service culpability. Through "personal friendships" with Kennedy insiders, Lamarr said, the report was delivered into the hands of French intelligence.

This pretty well accounted for a cryptic passage in a *Farewell America* chapter called "Secret Service" that went, "Only Daniel P. Moynihan, a former longshoreman, had some idea of such things." The chapter detailed the "glaring errors" of the president's guards, even to the number of bourbons and water they downed the night before. But it also credited the Secret Service agents with professionalism in recognizing the work of professionals on the other side. "They were the first in the President's entourage to realize that the assassination was a well-organized plot," the chapter said. "They discussed it at Parkland Hospital and later during the plane ride back to Washington. They mentioned it in their personal reports to Secret Service Chief James Rowley that night. Ten hours after the assassination, Rowley knew that there had been three gunmen, and perhaps four, at Dallas that day, and later, on the telephone, Jerry Behn (head of the White House detail) remarked to Forrest Sorrels (head of the Dallas Secret Service), 'It's a plot.' 'Of course,' was Rowley's reply. Robert Kennedy . . . learned that evening from Rowley that the Secret Service believed the President had been the victim of a powerful organization."

As for Oswald, *Farewell America* portrayed him as a CIA contract agent who had been sent to the Soviet Union to exploit his particular knowledge of the U-2 spy plane—he had been trained for the mission, learning both the Russian language and U-2 technology at the U-2 base in Atsugi. This was solid information, Lamarr assured Jaffe, which came from a French intelligence agent in Japan, Richard Savitt, who had known the Marine during his hitch there. After "defecting" in Moscow, Oswald made his way to Minsk, which was under the path of U-2 overflights between Turkey and Finland. There, *Farewell* matter-of-factly declared, he "was in regular contact with the CIA through its Moscow station at the American Embassy. As a U-2 specialist, he may have used a special radio transmitter broadcasting on a 30-inch wavelength, which is undetectable on the ground but can be picked up at 70,000 feet by a U-2, which is equipped with an ultra-high-frequency recording system (5,000 words in 7 seconds)." Upon Oswald's repatriation to the United States, the book reported, the CIA would have entertained the possibility that he had been converted to a double agent by the Soviets.

Who was the real author? Lamarr promised Jaffe that his identity would be divulged upon publication of an American edition of the book. In the meantime the author was limned as one man— not famous, not an aide of Kennedy—but an established American writer. Not long after Jaffe left Paris, *Farewell* was published in France as *L'Amérique Brule* (America Burns). *L'Express*, the country's foremost news magazine, termed it "the hope of one America against another," and it sold briskly. German and Italian editions followed, and *Bild*, Germany's largest daily, serialized it with the teaser "explosive as a bomb." At the same time, Frontiers Publishing, in the person of Lamarr, was searching for an American publisher. Warren Hinckle was tempted, puckishly foreseeing a *Ramparts* cover story, "Who Killed Kennedy, by the KGB." But first he wanted to see that elusive fourth volume that hadn't been included in the European editions. Surely it would pack a punch, perhaps name players. While in New York, Hinckle decided to brace Patrick Moynihan about his report on Hoffa and the Secret Service. At first the amiable Irishman refused to talk, but a second call to his Cambridge home, in which the subject under review was broached, brought him rushing to Manhattan. Hinckle and Bob Scheer, who also was present, briefed him on what the French were saying. Although he denied knowing Lamarr, he did not deny his secret mission for RFK. Nor did he confirm it. Clearly on edge, he wanted to make some private phone calls. "I have to ask some people," he said. Some twenty minutes later, he emerged more composed to announce that he had nothing to say on the matter.

By this time, a one-page sequel had been added to the *Farewell* manuscript, which was headed "The Man of November 5th." It began, "The choice made by the people of the United States on November 5th, 1968, will have profound and far-reaching consequences for the life, liberty and happiness of the universe. The peoples of the earth are awaiting new decisions." The entire tone, mirroring the angst Europeans felt regarding Pax Americana, conveyed the hope that Bobby Kennedy would be successful in his presidential run that year. But then, as if the clack of the typewriter had been interrupted by a news bulletin, the text lapsed into the past tense.

There was another funeral. Once again the stars and stripes flew at half-mast. On an evening in June, Robert Kennedy joined his brother beneath the hill at Arlington, and those who pass by can bring them flowers. The tombs are splendid, but the scores have not been settled. Who killed them? And why?

When Bobby Kennedy was shot, the *Farewell* project seemed to die with him, as if its sole purpose had been to boost his candidacy. Three months later, Hervé Lamarr called long distance, saying he had to see me. He would be in San Francisco the following day and would be staying at the Fairmont Hotel on Nob Hill. I told him I had to catch a plane to New York but could stop by for an hour on the way to the airport. Lamarr was slight and fidgety, with a wispy mustache and fingertips yellowed by countless Gitanes. The conversation went nowhere, and I wondered what the great urgency was. The Frenchman talked aimlessly, deflecting questions about the project. Jim Rose was with me and drove me to the airport.

The punch line came that night when Lamarr called Jim Rose and said, "You're both professionals. There's an important package I want you to have." It could be picked up at the St. Francis Hotel, at the bottom of Nob Hill. Rose approached the bell captain, gave a password, and was handed a sealed film can. When I returned from New York we screened what turned out to be a motion picture rendition of *Farewell*. As a sonorous narrator chronicled John Kennedy's political career, still photos of the president with kings and kids, pols and everyday people rolled along with shots of his grim-faced enemies: Dallas right-wing oilman H. L. Hunt; the pro-Blue General Edwin A. Walker, whom Kennedy had cashiered; the Big Steel executives forced to rescind price hikes; J. Edgar Hoover, who considered Camelot subversive; Richard Nixon; and on and on. There were also digressive interludes, such as one in which Frank Sinatra was heard singing "It's the Wrong Face" while visuals suggested secret *amours*. Then the music turned dirgeful as actual footage showed John and Jacqueline Kennedy boarding Air Force 1 in Fort Worth for the short hop to Dallas. There was the motorcade to downtown spliced together from the home movies of spectators lining the route. And then . . . the Zapruder film.

I was not prepared for how horrifyingly graphic the film was in moving form. After his limousine slows at a sharp turn, Kennedy clutches his throat in reaction to the first shot. He slowly slumps forward. Then his head literally explodes, creating a halo of blood mist. The force of the hit knocks him backward so violently into the rear seat cushion that it is compressed. He rebounds forward as Jackie grabs for him. There is no mistaking that the kill shot was fired from a frontal zone, somewhere on the grassy knoll. The Texas School Book Depository was to the rear.

With the film can in hand, I flew to Los Angeles to try to verify that it was the genuine article. A colleague, CBS television newsman Pete Noyes, had the network's film expert thoroughly examine it. Noting that the frames were in perfect order, that the coloring was consistent, and that there were no signs of tampering or editing, the expert pronounced the film a genuine second-generation print. I offered it to CBS to show nationally, and the Los Angeles executives who watched a studio screening were excited at the prospect. But top executives in New York scotched it on grounds that *Life* held the property rights and would sue. ABC and NBC also declined. It was left to a small Los Angeles UHF channel to air the Zapruder film for the first time.

How the French laid hands on the film was possibly explained by Richard Lubic, a member of RFK's California campaign who was with him in the pantry the night he was shot at the Ambassador Hotel in Los Angeles. Lubic told me that very early in 1968, when he was a staffer at *Life*'s companion publication, *Time,* in Time-Life headquarters in New York, the film was missing from its vault for several days. When the absence was discovered, there was quite a stir. The FBI and the CIA investigated, and even Mayor John Lindsay came by to ensure that the New York police gave it their best Kojak try. Although it was patently an inside job, no suspect was ever fingered.

When an American edition of *Farewell* was finally printed, an afterword was a bit coy as to the method of purloining. "We were fortunate enough to obtain two copies of this film, from two different sources in the United States," it read. "One is a poor copy, the other of excellent quality." Pointing out that the stills *Life* had run when the Warren Report came out were retouched, the afterword stated, "The unedited version of this very moving film utterly demolishes the official version of the assassination put out by the Warren Commission. The Zapruder movie belongs to history and to men everywhere."

The American edition of *Farewell* was never displayed in the windows of Brentano's and Doubleday. At the Fairmont Hotel session, Lamarr had casually answered "Sure" when I asked him if there would be one. A few weeks later, a notice arrived from a freight forwarder that a consignment of books from a Montreal warehouse was ready to be picked up. The shipping bill of $282 had not been prepaid, but the money to settle it was on deposit in a Swiss bank branch in San Francisco. To the end Lamarr was playing at foreign intrigue. Frontiers Publishing vanished as suddenly as it had sprung up, and Lamarr slipped back into the intelligence shadows.

It was left to me to settle the historical account. There were six cartons of some one hundred hardcover books each, printed in Belgium, in the shipment, and I distributed them all to researchers, college bookstores and institutions. The Los Angeles public library has five, the Australian embassy one. The Library of Congress catalog card number is 68-57391.

I also took to the hustings to show the Zapruder film to groups across the country, mostly on college campuses. While the overwhelming majority of audience members gasped at the head snap and agreed that it was convincing evidence of a shot from the front, an occasional hand would be raised to ask about theories put forth by Warren Report supporters that Kennedy's head jumped towards Oswald's rifle due either to a neurological reaction or jet propulsion effect. When I showed the film to an SRO crowd at Texas A & M University, an ROTC cadet called my attention to an article in a medical journal by Dr. John Lattimer advancing the jet propulsion theory. By this time I had had enough of the fanciful hypothesis. "Dr. Cyril Wecht, the forensic pathologist who is coroner of Pittsburgh and has seen countless gunshot wounds, concludes the shot came from the front," I replied testily. "Dr. Lattimer's medical specialty is urology, and I am tempted to ask: isn't that a pisser?"

I also pointed out to the doubting cadet that the windshield of a motorcycle cop riding to the immediate left rear of the limousine was splattered with brain and bone debris, which substantiated that the fatal head shot was fired from the right front—the grassy knoll zone. In any case, the repeated showing of the Zapruder film placed it in the public domain, where it belonged in the first place. *Life* eventually returned the original to the Zapruder family, which in 1978 gave it to the National Archives for "storage." When Congress created the JFK Assassination Records Review Board in response to heightened public awareness of a conspiracy as a result of Oliver Stone's 1991 motion picture *JFK*, in which the Zapruder film was shown (I lent Stone my copy), the board accomplished a legal "taking" of the original to put it "in the custody of the American people." In 1999 an arbitration panel set the value of the original at $16 million, to be paid to the family.

After Frontiers Publishing vanished without a trace, questions lingered. Did Jim Rose's August 1967 visit to the Russian embassy in Mexico City trigger the *Farewell America* project? Valery Kostikov said that any response would be "in a way that would be most unexpected, and untraceable," as for example "Something might be left in your hands by a visitor to your country." That is what happened, but it leaves the puzzling question, how could the Russians have set French intelligence in motion? It was an open secret that the French foreign espionage agency, SDECE, was so penetrated by the KGB that in intelligence circles it was quipped that the SDECE drank more vodka than wine. Although the KGB connection remains ambiguous, the stamp of the fleur de lis is unmistakable, as evidenced by the project's endorsement by de Gaulle and Ducret. This suggests, as Lamarr indicated, that there was witting collaboration by members of the Kennedy inner circle, because it is doubtful that de Gaulle would have proceeded without it. Although the family consistently held the public position that the Warren Report was the final answer, privately Bobby Kennedy expressed a different opinion by words and action. Charging Daniel Moynihan with forming a task force to look into whether Hoffa was implicated and the Secret Service was bribed demonstrates that he was skeptical from the start. The Moynihan report found its way to French intelligence, with some of its findings appearing in *Farewell*. A decade ago, Toronto bookseller Al Navis, who had just stumbled upon boxes of *Farewell America* collecting dust in a Montreal warehouse, queried David Powers, the Kennedy adjutant who was curator of the John F. Kennedy Museum, about the book. "I can't confirm or deny the European connection," Powers replied, "but Bobby definitely didn't believe the Warren Report." RFK's press secretary, Frank Mankiewicz, recently confirmed that RFK was engrossed in the Garrison case. "When the Garrison investigation started," Mankiewicz told author Gus Russo, "Bobby asked me if he had anything. I said I didn't know. He asked me to learn everything I could about it. He said to me, 'I may need it in the future.'" In May 1968 RFK's California campaign aide, Richard Lubic, tracked me down by phone in Garrison's office to advise, "After he's elected, Bobby's going to go. He's going to reopen the investigation." On June 3, two days before he was shot, RFK said, "I now fully realize that only the powers of the presidency will reveal the secrets of my brother's death." Ever pragmatic, he understood that only by becoming president and controlling the Justice Department could he realistically undertake a new probe.

The most likely exegesis of *Farewell America* is that it was a clandestine project by the "European connection," aided by access to the Kennedy group, to independently promote RFK's presidential bid, at the same time setting the stage for a fresh investigation once he was in the White House. Probably the riddle of *Farewell America* will never be fully solved. But in its brief life span the project produced a vital legacy. As the book hopefully put it, "The Zapruder movie belongs to history and to men everywhere." That desire has now been realized.

1

The Man of November 5

The election of the new Prince of the Universe should have had profound and far-reaching consequences for the future of the American people and for the life, liberty and happiness of Mankind.

But in the summer or 1968, the legitimate representatives of the Republican and Democratic Parties decided to pick their candidates for the 37th President of the United States from among the merchandise on sale in the bargain basement.

In the decades and in history books to come, 1968 will be remembered as the year the lights flickered out—as a year of frustration, regressions and shattered myths.

These revisions to the past—Prague, the Vatican, Chicago—are the manifestations of political and economic forces seeking desperately to preserve situations of which they have long since lost control.

But the twilight descending upon the United States will have the gravest consequences of all, for it is America that sets the pace of the world, and often dictates its choices.

As the sixties draw to a close, the people of the earth, left to themselves without gods and without leaders, are awaiting new decisions. The Man of November 5 cannot escape the confrontations before him. By refusing these choices, he will leave the problems unsolved.

Two Americans, John and Robert Kennedy, had the courage to meet these problems head on and break down the doors to the future. They were stopped by the frightened accomplices of the traditions on which they infringed.

When John Fitzgerald Kennedy's head exploded, it was for some the signal for toasts. One November morning the cannon boomed, the Panama Canal was closed, flags everywhere flew at half-mast, and it is said that even Andrei Gromyko wept. Adlai Stevenson declared that he would bear the sorrow of his death till the day of his own, and the Special Forces added a black band to their green berets.

Almost five years passed, and another bullet shattered the brain and stopped the heart of another Kennedy who had taken up the fight.

There was another funeral. Once again the Green Berets formed the honor guard; once again the Stars and Stripes flew at half-mast. One evening in June, Robert Kennedy joined his brother beneath the hill at Arlington, and those passing by can bring them flowers.

"Happy Days Are Here Again," they sang at the Chicago Convention. But the scores have not been settled.

Who killed them?

And why?

This book sets out to answer these questions. But beyond the facts and the outcries, behind the assassins and their motives, other culprits appear. The responsibility of American civilization is no longer in doubt.

Europe sometimes speaks of taking up the American challenge. But do the forces of arms, the excesses of an economy and the abuses of a political system constitute an adequate example? Washington, Lincoln and the Kennedys are gone; never in two centuries have the virtues and hopes on which the young republic was founded been so gravely endangered as they are today.

By their meditations, by their decisions, by their rebellion, the citizens of the United States will bring about their Renaissance.

We dedicate this book to the youth of the seventies. Only they will know how to face the crises that lie ahead. May they find in these pages the strength to delay the redoubtable old men and revive the forgotten glories.

PART I

INVASION

It is a mistake to look too far ahead. Only one link in the chain of destiny can be handled at a time.

WINSTON CHURCHILL

2

Legacy

The worst fault of a highly-intelligent sovereign is to impose tasks on his subjects which are beyond their forces, for his aims go far beyond what they are capable of doing and, when he is in charge of an undertaking, he thinks he can foresee its consequences. His administration is therefore fatal to the people. The Prophet himself has said, ' Pattern your step on that of the weakest among you. Too great an intellect is a burden for the people.'

IBN KHALDOUN

Americans are the sons of Calvin. John Calvin preached that the pursuit of wealth and the preservation of property is a Christian duty. He taught that the temptations of the flesh demand a discipline as strict as that of the military profession. " He created an ideal type of man theretofore unknown to both religion and society, who was neither a humanist nor an ascetic, but a businessman living in the fear of God.[1] "

Two centuries later, this new type of man came under the

---

1. Herbert J. Muller.

influence of John Wesley.[2] " We exhort all Christians to amass as much wealth as they can, and to preserve as much as they can ; in other words, to enrich themselves." For President Madison, " The American political system was founded on the natural inequality of men." Correlatively, the moral philosophy of the United States is based on success.

At the end of the Eighteenth Century a Frenchman, the Chevalier de Beaujour, wrote on his return from North America, " The American loses no opportunity to acquire wealth. Gain is the subject of all his conversations, and the motive for all his actions. Thus, there is perhaps no civilized nation in the world where there is less generosity in the sentiments, less elevation of soul and of mind, less of those pleasant and glittering illusions that constitute the charm or the consolation of life. Here, everything is weighed, calculated and sacrificed to self-interest."

Another Frenchman, the Baron de Montlezun, added, " In this country, more than any other, esteem is based on wealth. Talent is trampled underfoot. How much is this man worth ?, they ask. Not much ? He is despised. One hundred thousand crowns ? The knees flex, the incense burns, and the once-bankrupt merchant is revered like a god. "

The British went even farther than the French. " They are escaped convicts. His Majesty is fortunate to be rid of such rabble. Their true God is power. "[3]

In an introduction to a series of articles by historian Andrew Sinclair, the *Sunday Times* wrote in 1967, " In the five centuries since Columbus discovered the New World, savagery has been part of American life. There has been the violence of conquest and resistance, the violence of racial difference, the violence of civil war, the violence of bandits and gangsters, the violence of lynch law, all set against the violence of the wilderness and the city. "

The opinion of these Europeans is subject to question, but George Washington, speaking of the future of American civilization, commented that he would not be surprised by any disaster that might occur.

The disasters began as triumphs. The conquest of the West, the rise of the merchants, the industrial revolutions were America's great crusades, and from them were issued her Titans and her gods. Every civilization has its ideal man, an archetype that stands as a model for the average citizen. Athens chose the philosopher and the artist ; for the Jews, it was the law-giving prophet ; for Rome, the soldier-administra- tor ; for China, the learned Mandarin ; for England, the empire builder ; for Japan and German, and professional soldier ; for India, the ascetic. For the United States, it was the businessman !

While other nations might have chosen wisdom, beauty, saintliness, military glory, bravery or ascetism as their popular divinities, the United States chose the civilization of gain. The true gods and the only Titans of America were Jay Gould, Daniel Drew, Jay Cooke, Andrew Carnegie, Charles T. Yerkes, Solomon Guggenheim and Irenee Du Pont.

Some of these men, like J. Pierpont Morgan, became gay, high-living nabobs. But most, like Henry Ford, were frugal and dreary puritans. All of them, even the most devout, even the most devoted, even the most sincere, had one thing in common : where business was concerned, they were tough. The churches approved of this attitude. In his book *Heroes of Progress*, the Reverend McClinock wrote :

" May he long enjoy the fruits of his work and promote the reign of Christ on this earth, not only through the Chris- tian use of the vast fortune with which God has favored him, but through the living example of his active and peaceful piety. " He was referring to Daniel Drew, who cheated his associates, bribed municipal governments, and took advantage of the credulity of the people.

The first American giants — Rockefeller, Vanderbilt, McKay, McCoy — whether they were oilmen, shipowners, prospectors or livestock dealers, made or consolidated their fortunes by smuggling arms and supplies during the Civil War. Today's Titans are often college graduates. Some are affable and well-bred. They constitute an oligarchy of directorial bureaucrats who, while lacking the personal fortunes of the old Titans, have preserved their power and conserved their practices. For them, and it is true, profit is " the remuneration

---

2. Founder of the Methodists.
3. Oliver Sharpin, *The American Rebels,* 1804.

of a decision made in conditions of uncertainty. "[4] But this equation has become the basis for a moral philosophy that takes neither the nation nor the individual into account.

" Men who spend every weekday making money, and every Sunday at the Temple, are not made to inspire the muse of Comedy ", wrote Alexandre de Tocqueville, and he was correct. The standards of American society have been raised to untouchability. The dollar remains the criterion of worth and success. Money is the only real measure of human beings and things, and American society, while classless, is nothing more than a graph of economic levels.[5] " That which a people honors most becomes the object of its cult ", wrote Plato. This is a democratic notion in so far as it offers everyone a chance, or at least appears to, but its rigidity leaves room for all kinds of excesses.

In other times and on other continents, these Titans would have been, if not scorned, at least gauged by their relative worth. But the Titans have become the pride of every American citizen. In no other society is the cult of the successful man so strong, and it is unwise to disregard it. " America has been built by individual effort and a recognition of individual responsibility... Government may guide and help its citizens, but it cannot supply talent to those who do not have it, or bestow ambition or creative ability on those who are not born with these qualities ".[6]

This morality demands the tolerance or the complicity of those who hold political power : Congress and the President.

Theodore and Franklin Roosevelt were accidents along the way, deviates from the American mythology. An American who enters politics for unselfish reasons is regarded with suspicion. His attitude can only conceal a lust for power or a senseless and dangerous devotion to the " public welfare. " Politics and the public welfare have little in common, and the activities of a politician are not considered normal or comprehensible unless they are pursued for selfish and material gain. President Jackson was condemned in 1831 by *Vincenne's Gazette* in these terms : " Ambition is his crime, and it will be his undoing. "

Harold Laski has written that " a strong President is a moral threat " to all those who have toiled to build an

American society whose prosperity is based on initiative, energy and efficiency, but also on what Europeans call corruption, an additional arm made available to those whose sole motivation is profit. America, wrote George Washington, is a country where political offices bear no proportion to those who seek them.

America accepted Franklin D. Roosevelt only because she had no other alternative. She found herself again in Harry Truman, a solid citizen with no perverse ambitions who declared that " the combined thought and action of a people always lead in the right direction. "[7] Eisenhower was the ideal President. A victorious commander, he dazzled the crowds. Inconsistent, he had no dangerous political philosophy. A petty bourgeois, he dared not oppose the Titans.

And suddenly Kennedy appeared, the first President born in this century, a millionaire, a liberal, and an intellectual. The Democratic candidate nevertheless made no attempt to conceal his aims.

" In the decade that lies ahead — in the challenging revolutionary sixties — the American Presidency will demand more than ringing manifestoes issued from the rear of the battle. It will demand that the President place himself in the very thick of the fight, that he care passionately about the fate of the people he leads, that he be willing to serve them at the risk of incurring their momentary displeasure. "

" We stand today at the edge of a New Frontier — the frontier of the 1960's — a frontier of unknown opportunities and perils — a frontier of unfulfilled hopes and threats. "

" Woodrow Wilson's New Freedom promised our nation a new political and economic framework. Franklin Roosevelt's New Deal promised security and succor to those in need. But the New Frontier of which I speak is not a set of promises —

---

4. Professor B.S. Keirstead.

5. " An American citizen is now worth $ 200,000 " (*Dallas Morning News*).

6. David Lawrence, *U.S. News and World Report,* January 18, 1965.

7. Harry Truman, *Mister President*.

8. In Washington, January 14, 1960.

it is a set of challenges. It sums up, not what I intend to offer
the American people, but what I intend to ask of them. It
appeals to their price, not their pocketbook — it holds out
the promise of more sacrifice instead of more security... [9]

" The Scriptures tell of a time when there were giants on the
earth, and that is what our country needs today. This is not
the time for futilities. This is not the time for petty complaints
and half-measures. This is the time for men of action, not
men of words — this is the time for giant hearts, not faint
hearts... "[10]

" We have no time for complacency, timidity, or doubt. This
is a time for courage and action. "[11]

" The old era has ended. The old ways will not do. "[12]

It was all so beautiful, so unreal, that no one believed it.
They even admired his inscrutability, his ingenuity in using a
metaphor borrowed from American folklore, from the myth of
the West, to mask a demogogy that was all the more inoffen-
sive because it seemed credible. Others, more cunning, grew
concerned when, in West Virginia, under the low roofs of a
forgotten America, the Senator from Massachusetts spoke to
the abandoned miners, to the unemployed, to the families
vegetating in the hills. America began to ask herself if Kennedy was speaking seriously when he bent towards the little
people and the forgotten.

Kennedy's socialism aimed at enriching the poor rather
than impoverishing the rich, but it was dangerous nevertheless. For one hundred million Americans, the gravest danger,
after bankruptcy, is that those just behind may catch up with
them. The nouveaux rich are only rich so long as no one
grows richer. The have-nots live in constant fear of the down-
and-outs, and the hate and fear of the little Puerto Rican
for New York are really no more than the hate and fear of
half of New York for the little Puerto Rican.

Millions of Amerians have risen from the proletariat to the
middle class with insufficient intellectual means. They or their
sons want to continue to climb the ladder of society. This new
American bourgeoisie, which has risen by its own toil, works

less today and lives better, and pays less taxes. It claims to be descended from the Pilgrim Fathers, but its origins go back to the washing machine. The Great Society is essentially sectarian and violent. Its mottos are " each man for himself ", " it's none of their business" and "woe to the vanquished. "

Today's American is at the mercy of his anxieties. The United States has grown so wealthy that she has lost touch with the rest of the world. America is neither here nor there, be it a question of power or of weakness. She no longer knows what is happening on this earth. Her universe exists in the third person.

The difference continues to widen between the American radicalism of the Thirties and the radicalism of today, whose ethical basis is possession. True, this basis can be traced far back into the American past, and finds its theme song in the ballads of the Far West, where men killed for a horse or a bottle of beer. But Jeffersonian tradition placed, or restored, human values above real estate values.

Hemingway's Americans saw the Spanish Civil War as a struggle for the preservation of spiritual as opposed to material values : the power of the Church, the domination of the Army, and the wealth of the big landowners. They were in sympathy with the other Spain, although to all appearances it was Red. But today, when a majority of Americans are landowners, what other insurgents scattered throughout the earth still have the sympathy, or at least the comprehension, of a sufficient number of Americans, of the men who nevertheless trace their origins back to the revolutionaries of the Thirteen States of the Union ? And let no man be mistaken about the struggle for civil rights. The Negroes too want to become landowners.

America is no longer a young nation. There is New York, of course, superlatively demanding, offering, in the absurd and the sordid, the crude atmosphere of youth and folly of a town in search of its identity. Its culture is centered on the Jew and

9. At Los Angeles, July 15, 1960.
10. At Anchorage, September 3, 1960.
11. At Detroit, September 5, 1960.
12. At Seattle, September 6, 1960.

the Negro. It is a young city, but it is not an American city. It rejects the provincialism, the racism, the folklore, the religion, and the superpatriotism of the ordinary small town, whose preoccupations are diametrically opposed to the policies of any progressive and imaginative government.

Imagination itself has become " unAmerican. " It is accepted, but with fear and distrust, when it embellishes a concrete experience, the story of how a fortune was made or a victory won. But where it exists solely for itself, when it becomes a culture or a dialectic, it is no longer tolerated. " Americans are insensitive to philosophical ideas. They need something tangible, something concrete, something that has been acted on the stage. Acted, that is, seen and felt. What is said is not important. We are not impressed by explanations, and verbal play leaves us indifferent. What we want is action. "[13]

It was to men without imagination that Kennedy addressed these words :

" Now the trumpet summons us again — not as a call to bear arms, though arms we need — not as a call to battle, though embattled are — but a call to bear the burden of a long twilight struggle... "

The message got through, but there was something suspicious about the style. Culture is a major threat to modern American society. A society fears its deserters more than its enemies, and in its mind intelligence is too often equated with leftism. Kennedy said, " Our nation cannot allow itself to be economically rich and intellectually poor. " And Steinbeck added, " What a joy that literacy is no longer prima facie evidence of treason. "

But a portion of American society instinctively understood that Kennedy was declaring war on its own. " High society ", like the middle classes, felt only suspicion or dislike for his university professors. The American upper crust tries in so far as possible to preserve itsef in a superb state of ignorance. For these people, brilliant men like Theodore C. Sorensen or Adlai E. Stevenson, the kind of men who are too poor to leave big tips and too proud to accept them, are intruders in a society that places no value on pure intellect, or accepts it only when it occurs in one of its sons.

These well-to-do, these profiteers, these weaklings, and these simple people had one thing in common : their fear of everything that Kennedy represented. His principal fault was that he was not like them. He did not share their desires and their complacency, their weaknesses and their intolerance. These citizens of the Twentieth Century had no conception of the responsibilities of a President whose role, in reality, is that of viceroy of the universe.

The United States has never faced the irreparable. She has never even experienced a catastrophe. She has known no Roman domination, no barbarian invasion, no feudal wars, no massive bloodbaths. In consequence, she finds it difficult to accept a dominant leader. On the contrary, she wants a President who is subject to the will of his constituents, and even of his adversaries.

The chances of becoming President of the United States are extremely slight, even for a man in the forefront of public life, and such opportunism is needed that the way is left open for a mediocre but crafty politician who knows how to please. With Eisenhower, the United States was content to spend eight years in an armchair. The intellectual emancipation and the agitation of the new generation succeeded at the beginning of the Sixties in defeating, by a narrow margin, the advocates of a placid administrator of a complacent nation devoted to the welfare of the majority — in other words, corrupt. It was the strength of his electoral organization that carried Kennedy to victory, with the help, perhaps, of the seasonal favor of an actual minority that suddenly tired of mediocrity or, like a woman, was momentarily seduced.

But, once he was President, Kennedy set out immediately to give the nation a sense of responsibility and of pathos. This was all the more disturbing in that it was abstract, and therefore unfamiliar. How many of the 185 million Americans in 1960 sensed that this man would betray their heritage, the American way of life, the established order ?

Often primitive, readily stubborn, and capable of sudden violence, the American character contains dangerous elements with which men like Jefferson, Lincoln, and Theodore and Franklin D. Roosevelt have had to contend. If, as Machiavelli

---

13. Arthur Miller.

wrote, men find it easier to forget the loss of their father than that of their patrimony, then " there is nothing more difficult, more dangerous, than to try to change the order of things. "

3

King

The only glory in public life is that which portends the future and blazes a path through the haze of the present.

DISRAELI

Senator Kennedy won the 1960 Presidential elections by an "exquisitely narrow" margin.[1] White, Protestant Americans can legitimately claim that he was not their President. Kennedy was elected with the votes of 70 % of the Negroes, 78 % of the Catholics, and 80 % of the Jews, not to speak of the women. For what American woman wouldn't have wanted to be the mother, the wife, the elector of this gracious young man who, while campaigning in Boston, invited the ladies to step up to the platform one by one so that he, his mother and his sister might have the pleasure of making their acquaintance and of taking tea with them afterwards ? [2]

For his father, Joseph P. Kennedy, one of the twenty richest men in the United States, wealthier than Rockefeller

1. *Daily Telegraph.*
2. *New York Times.*

31

or Henry Ford, richer than the Pews, the Harrimans or the Whitneys, there were no accidents in politics — only money and organization. John Fitzgerald Kennedy wanted to become President almost as much as his father wanted him to, no matter what road he had to follow.

And he followed it. During the Kennedy campaign, you couldn't take three steps without running into a Kennedy banner, a Kennedy poster, a Kennedy brother or an employee of the Kennedys. Kennedy was seen, Kennedy was heard, and in some cases it was even possible to sleep with Kennedy. Kennedy spoke several times a day, and everyone talked about Kennedy for the rest of the day. The Kennedys were a new breed of politician. They had as much money, or more, than the best of the professionals, and they developed an electoral machine more powerful and efficient than any before. If we are to believe Victor Lasky, old Joe Kennedy once declared, " Three things are needed to win an election. The first is money, the second is money, and the third is more money. " Lasky claims that with the millions he spent for his son John, Joe Kennedy could have had his chauffeur elected to Congress. Senator Humphrey's bus was no match for his opponent's Convair.

There is some truth in these sarcasms, but John Kennedy was the only Democratic candidate who could have beaten Richard Nixon in 1960, no matter what the sums involved. At that time, John Kennedy already had a remarkable knowledge of politics, the daily diet of his family. To his technique, perfected by fourteen years in Congress, he added a total faith in his destiny. During the 1960 Democratic Convention, three candidates arrived almost simultaneously at Los Angeles airport. Stevenson's first words were, " I do not want to be chosen, and I have come here almost incognito. " Johnson said, " I'm sorry to be late, but I've just been traveling all over the country. " Kennedy declared " I am here to receive the nomination. "

In Congress, no one could decide whether he was a liberal or a conservative. A member of the Democratic Party, he often voted with Harry F. Byrd, the leader of the economy bloc. His vote in June, 1960 with Senator Williams of Delaware on a matter as controversial as the oil depletion allowance was surprising, but Senator Williams' bill was rejected by a wide margin, and it was thought that Kennedy had only been employing clever tactics.[3] He had voted against a similar bill in the past, and everyone remembered that he had supported the Republicans in the House of Representatives by voting against statehood for Hawaii, and against the censorship of Senator McCarthy. In short, it was said that he was independent because he could afford to be. This reasonable explanation satisfied even his toughest critics. He was on friendly terms with everyone, and in particular with the committee chairmen, who appreciated his courtesy and his attention. He was not as experienced as Senator Anderson, or as good a speaker as Governor Clement, or as popular with the farmers as Hubert Humphrey, but he was John Kennedy, the handsomest man in the Senate, a veteran of the war in the Pacific, the winner of a Pulitzer prize. Another millionaire, Henry Cabot Lodge, had money, but not as much as Kennedy. The power of the Kennedys could work magic, as Edward Kennedy's election to the Senate in 1962 was to prove.

President Kennedy would probably have preferred that his younger brother wait two more years, but he yielded to family pressure and, in the best Kennedy tradition, the organization was set in motion. There was more to this organization than just dinner parties and beautiful women. With rigorous pragmatism, the Kennedy Brain Trust analyzed the problems at hand and determined the most effective action. The power of the Kennedys had become a political reality capable of upsetting the traditional electoral scales.

Certainly, America had known other dynasties in the course of its history. There had been the Adams, the Harrisons, the Roosevelts and the Tafts, but the potency of these families manifested itself only once in a generation. John Adams was elected President at the age of 61, and his son John Quincy Adams did not enter the White House until he was 57, and without having played a real role during his father's term in office. William Henry Harrison entered the White House at 68, and was followed only by his grandson at the age of 55. The Roosevelts, Theodore and Franklin, were only distantly related. As for the Tafts, they exercised their

---

3. See Chapter Eleven, *Oilmen*

power in different spheres : William Howard was President, Robert a Senator, and in 1962 Robert A., Jr. was only running for the House of Representatives.[4]

That same year Edward Kennedy, aged 30, took his seat in the Senate. Robert Kennedy, 36, occupied the post of Attorney General under his brother John, making the Kennedys the most powerful family in the history of the United States, and probably in the history of the world.

Chief of the most powerful nation in the world, Commander-in-Chief of her armed forces, alone responsible for the use of nuclear weapons, directing relations with more than one hundred foreign governments, distributing more than ninety billion dollars a year through 2.5 million federal employees, living in a 132-room mansion, traveling in two jet planes or in one of the ten helicopters in his personal fleet, John Fitzgerald Kennedy was the most powerful man in the world.

The voters liked the idea that John Kennedy was the great grandson of the owner of a barroom and accepted the fact that his father had made his fortune as a bootlegger and had played the stock market when he was Ambassador to London. The average American, raised in the belief that the way money is earned has nothing to do with morality, saw nothing frightening about this. The rise of the Kennedys was in the best American tradition. Joseph had been the first Kennedy to graduate from Harvard. His sons attended Choate before entering Harvard in their turn.[5] His daughters and daughters-in-law attended Radcliffe or Vassar and were polished in the finishing schools of Switzerland and France. The Kennedys, now better-dressed than the most respected brahmins of Beacon Street[6], were no longer obliged to hide behind tinted window panes. They were in a position to set the styles themselves.

The working American doesn't really like the kind of people who have never had to earn a living. The self-made man rejects the notion that man is, to a great extent, the result of his social position, and the fact that the wealth of a family like the Kennedys permits its sons to set forth in the pursuit of power with no financial worries, and with a treasury large enough to finance a war. Obviously, this represents a threat to a democracy, which wants nothing of the virtues of political Sybarites, and many Americans feared the power of the Kennedys.

The public was not fully aware of what had happened when, on January 20, 1961, a new administration that was really a new regime took over in Washington. Largely inspired by George Pope Morris, the Civil War poet, and by Abraham Lincoln, the new President's Inaugural Address was one of the finest pieces in the history of American literature. This long sermon in blank verse with key words that rhymed was the thunderclap announcing the birth of a new state. It was the advent, not of a dynasty, but of the intellect.

" We observe today not a victory of party but a celebration of freedom — symbolizing an end as well as a beginning. For I have sworn before you and Almighty God the same solemn oath our forebears prescribed nearly a century and three quarters ago.

" The world is very different now. For man holds in his mortal hands the power to abolish all forms of human poverty and all forms of human life. And yet the same revolutionary beliefs for which our forebears fought are still at issue around the globe — the belief that the rights of man come not from the generosity of the state but from the hand of God.

" We dare not forget today that we are the heirs of the first revolution. Let the word go forth from this time and place, to friend and foe alike, that the torch has been passed to a new generation of Americans — born in this century, tempered by war, disciplined by a hard and bitter peace, proud of our ancient heritage — and unwilling to witness or permit the slow undoing of those human rights to which this nation has always been committed, and to which we are committed today at home and around the world.

" Let every nation know, whether it wishes us well or ill, that we shall pay any price, bear any burden, meet any hardship, support any friend, oppose any foe to assure the survival and

4. Seth Taft, William Howard's grandson, was defeated in November, 1967 in the Cleveland municipal elections.
5. John graduated in 1940, Robert in 1948, and Edward (with help) in 1954.
6. The most elegant street in Boston.

the success of liberty.

" This much we pledge, and more.

" To those old allies whose cultural and spiritual origins we share, we pledge the loyalty of faithful friends. United, there is little we cannot do in a host of cooperative ventures. Divided, there is little we can do — for we dare not meet a powerful challenge at odds and split assunder.

" To those new states whom we welcome to the ranks of the free, we pledge our word that one form of colonial control shall not have passed away merely to be replaced by a far more iron tyranny. We shall not always expect to find them supporting our view. But we shall always hope to find them strongly supporting their own freedom — and to remember that, in the past, those who foolishly sought power by riding the back of the tiger ended up inside.

" To those peoples in the huts and villages of half the globe struggling to break the bonds of mass misery, we pledge our best efforts to help them help themselves, for whatever period is required — not because the communists may be doing it, but because it is right. If a free society cannot help the many who are poor, it cannot save the few who are rich.

" To our sister republics south of our border, we offer a special pledge — to convert our good words into good deeds — in a new alliance for progress — to assist free men and free governments in casting off the chains of poverty. But this peaceful revolution of hope cannot become the prey of hostile powers. Let all our neighbors know that we shall join them to oppose aggression or subversion anywhere in the Americas. And let every other power know that this hemisphere intends to remain the master of its own house.

" To that world assembly of sovereign states, our last best hope in an age where the instruments of war have far outpaced the instruments of peace, we renew our pledge of support — to prevent it from becoming merely a forum for invective — to strengthen its shield of the new and the weak — and to enlarge the area in which its writ may run.

" Finally, to those nations who would make themselves our adversary, we offer not a pledge but a request : that both sides begin anew the quest for peace, before the dark powers of destruction unleashed by science engulf all humanity in planned or accidental self-destruction.

" We dare not tempt them with weakness. For only when our arms are sufficient beyond doubt can we be certain beyond doubt that they will never be employed.

" But neither can two great and powerful groups of nations take comfort from our present course — both sides over-burdened by the cost of modern weapons, both rightly alarm-ed by the steady spread of the deadly atom, yet both racing to alter that uncertain balance of terror that stays the hand of mankind's final war.

" So let us begin anew — remembering on both sides that civility is not a sign of weakness, and sincerity is always subject to proof. Let us never negotiate out of fear. But let us never fear to negotiate.

" Let both sides explore what problems unite us instead of belaboring those problems which divide us.

" Let both sides, for the first time, formulate serious and precise proposals for the inspection and control of arms — and bring the absolute power to destroy other nations under the absolute control of all nations.

" Let both sides seek to invoke the wonders of science instead of its terrors. Together let us explore the stars, con-quer the deserts, eradicate disease, tap the ocean depths and encourage the arts and commerce.

" Let both sides unite to heed in all corners of the earth the command of Isaiah — to ' undo the heavy burdens... (and) let the oppressed go free. '

" And if a beach-head of cooperation may push back the jungle of suspicion, let both sides join in creating a new endeavor, not a new balance of power, but a new world of law, where the strong are just and the weak secure and the peace preserved.

" All this will not be finished in the first hundred days. Nor will it be finished in the first one thousand days, nor in the life of this Administration, nor even perhaps in the lifetime of our planet. But let us begin.

" In your hands, my fellow citizens, more than mine, will rest the final success or failure of our course. Since this country was founded, each generation of Americans has been summon-ed to give testimony to its national loyalty. The graves of young Americans who answered the call to service surround the globe.

" Now the trumpet summons us again — not as a call to
bear arms, though arms we need — not as a call to battle,
though embattled we are — but a call to bear the burden of a
long twilight struggle, year in and year out, ' rejoicing in
hope, patient in tribulation ' — a struggle against the common
enemies of man : tyranny, poverty, disease, and war itself.

" Can we forge against the enemies a grand and global
alliance, North and South, East and West, that can assure a
more fruitful life for all mankind ? Will you join in that
historic effort ?

" In the long history of the world, only a few generations
have been granted the role of defending freedom in its hour of
maximum danger. I do not shrink from this responsibility — I
welcome it. I do not believe that any of us would exchange
places with any other people or any other generation. The
energy, the faith, the devotion which we bring to this endeav-
or will light our country and all who serve it — and the glow
from that fire can truly light the world.

" And so, my fellow Americans : ask not what your country
can do for you — ask what you can do for your country.

" My fellow citizens of the world : ask not what America will
do for you, but what together we can do for the freedom of
man.

" Finally, whether you are citizens of America or citizens of
the world, ask of us here the same high standards of strength
and sacrifice which we ask of you. With a good conscience
our only sure reward, with history the final judge of our
deeds, let us go forth to lead the land we love, asking His
blessing and His help, but knowing that here on earth, God's
work must truly be our own. "

In the enemy camp people listened, people read, people
were moved and sometimes shaken, but they preferred to
voice their amazement that President Kennedy had invited
mostly writers, artists and scientists to the inauguration —
Hemingway, Faulkner, Steinbeck, Pearl Buck, William Inge,
Arthur Miller, Thornton Wilder, Tennessee Williams, John
Hersey, Robert Frost, Saint John Perse, Alexander Calder,
Stuart Davis, Edward Hopper, Ludwigmies Van der Rohe,
Eero Saarinen, Paul Hindemith, Igor Stravinsky, Leonard
Bernstein, Fritz Reiner, Eugene Ormandy, and one lone jour-

nalist, Walter Lippman. " There's nobody left at Harvard "
became a popular wisecrack when the composition of the
Presidential team was announced. But some only half-
laughed. In the months that followed, America, anaesthetized
by eight years under Eisenhower, awakened to discover that
she had a President with both a brain and a heart.

Kennedy sought in the history of the world the perspectives
of the art of politics and the role that he might play in it. He
introduced his favorite heros — Greek, Roman, English,
French, German, and even American — to the American
people. He declared, " I have read a great deal about the
Presidency. The President must be at the center of the action.
He alone must make the decisions. "

" We must, I want, we will... "

" I know no one who can do this job better than I "

" To remain free, the free world must display more intelligence than the unfree world. "

Like Thomas H. Benton, he could suddenly recite from the
Georgics of Virgil, the Thousand and One Nights, Herodotus
or Sancho Panza, the New Testament, the German Reformers
or Adam Smith, Fenelon or Hudibras, the financial reports of
Necca or the acts of the Cour.cil of the Thirty, the debates
that preceeded the adoption of the Constitution, or some half-
forgotten speech by a deceased member of Congress. In
Chicago he quoted from the Greek poet Alcaeus. When the
students of a girls' school translated his Inaugural Address
into Latin because the style reminded them of Cicero, he
answered them in Latin (with the help of one of his assistants). The letter began as follows :

*Johannes Filiusgeraldi Kennediensis, Respublicae Presidens,
puellis Scholae Daltoni salutem plurinam dicit.*

He quoted the Founding Fathers, Woodrow Wilson and Justice Holmes, but he also cited Shakespeare, Goethe and
Sophocles, and it was said that at candlelight dinners at the
White House he would read from Keats and Marlowe, whom
no one in Kansas City had ever heard of.

The abstract verbal intercourse at his press conferences was
often over the heads of his public. He juggled easily with the
salaries of the laundry workers, the average Social Security

payment, the proportion of high school graduates unable to go to college, the number of university graduates in India, or the average per capita income in Libya or the Congo. He also declared that " there is no point in sending astronauts into space if our minds remain earthbound. "

He reminded the country that in the period following the Declaration of Independence and again during the Civil War, the most capable men in America, the most outstanding citizens, had chosen a career in politics. From the Civil War until the Depression, and again after the death of Roosevelt, they preferred to go into business. Kennedy wanted to make politics once again the foremost career in America.

He put up signs in the State Department reading " Junk the Jargon. Improve your writing. " Which meant : write English. Kennedy himself set the example, but many Americans thought his speeches strange. They heard it said that the President's style was inspired by Gladstone, but who was Gladstone ? To them, English was another language, and this intellectual Kennedy thought too much and too fast. He cut the fine sentiments and noble aspirations into a series of cabalistic fulgurations that flared up and died out with the speed of light. People began to feel that this man who never stopped thinking thought too much. In the frontier days of the West, a man who stopped to think was a dead man. Not only did Kennedy think, but his dialectic was straightforward and direct :

First, it is more and more obvious.
Secondly, it is more and more obvious.
Third...

Dwight McDonald, who never met Kennedy, wrote : " Americans often imagine that facts are solid, concrete and distinct objects like marbles, but they are far from this. Rather, they are subtle essences full of mystery and metaphysics, which change form, color and sense according to the context in which they are presented. They must always be treated with scepticism, and the judgment must be based not on the number of facts that can be mobilized in support of an opinion, but on a skillful discrimination between them and the objectivity with which they are treated to arrive at the truth, which is something altogether different from the facts, although there is some connection between them. "

When someone asked Kennedy, " What kind of a President will you be ? Liberal or conservative ? ", he replied, " I hope to be responsible. " It was an extremely intelligent answer, but one hardly suited to a bipartisan nation. When De Gaulle wrote to him on the subject of Berlin, " *Sur quel terrain nous rencontrerons-nous ?* "[7], Kennedy exclaimed, " Isn't that superb ! " He well knew that in De Gaulle's mind there was no suitable terrain, but his first reaction concerned only the General's style.

The history of the Kennedy administration will be difficult to write because nearly all the President's discussions with his advisors or his visiters took place man-to-man, mind-to-mind. He was an intellectual.

He was not friendly to the extent that people felt close to him. His personality was witty and penetrating, and his language was as direct as the finger he so often pointed during his press conferences. Romain Gary said that never, in seven years in the United States, had he encountered a cerebral mechanism that functioned so perfectly. " He does not answer your argument, but immediately asks another question. Little by little, I felt as if I were no longer there ; he reduced me to an intellectual function. I felt both honored by this excessive attention paid to me by the President of the United States and a little dazed to be subjected to this sort of analysis. I would have liked at least to know what he thought about me. There was something curiously voracious about his need for information... After three hours of conversation, I had no idea which argument I had gotten across, which idea had impressed or convinced him. He listened to everything with equal attention, but when I had finished he did not tell me his conclusion and went on to something else. He did not for one minute forget that he was President of the United States, and although he encouraged me to speak as his equal, the equality stopped there. "

Kennedy told Romain Gary, " Your children live on streets like the Rue Anatole France, Boulevard Victor Hugo, Avenue Valéry. When they are still very young they begin to sense the importance of history and culture. Our streets all have num-

---

7. " On what ground shall we meet ? "

bers. We have enough great names to replace them : Hemingway Square, Melville Boulevard... I would like to see a twelve-year-old boy come home and tell his mother, when she scolded him for being late, ' I was playing baseball on William Faulkner Avenue. ' "

Such an extraordinary man, interested in everything ! He would sometimes rise at daybreak to gaze pensively out of a White House window at the streetcleaners on Pennsylvania Avenue.

Washington ! A sleepy little town under Truman, headquarters of a provincial garrison in Eisenhower's time, it became under Kennedy the true capital of the nation. America likes her President to come from a small town. " Our Town " is the seat of moral rectitude, and its inhabitants are known to lead exemplary family lives. Past Presidents of the United States had always felt obliged to live simply and virtuously. The Roosevelts were well off, but Eleanor reigned with austerity. The Trumans had only the President's salary to live on, and their receptions offered nothing but cookies, lemonade, and good cheer. The Eisenhowers lived modestly in the company of a few tired old friends. The White House was not the hub of Washington society, which gathered weekly at a few lustreless diplomatic receptions and dull private parties, the most fashionable of which were given by a couple of old ladies who had become the moral arbiters of the town, and once a year at the Dancing Class.

That was Washington.

Then suddenly everything changed. Suddenly, Carolyn Hagner Shaw (Callie to her friends), whose *Green Book* with its roster of V.I.P.s could make or break a reputation, found herself dethroned. Dethroned also was Perle Mesta, former United States Ambassador to Luxembourg, a hostess who liked to dabble in politics. The generals' and senators' wives on Kalorama Road became suddenly conscious of their age. When they heard what was going on at the White House, they were reminded of Margaret Mitchell's Atlanta, that wide-open city that made no effort to hide its sins. They read in the papers that Shakespeare and ballets were performed at the White House, where the finest dishes and the most exquisite wines were served while an orchestra played at dinner.

American society confuses elegance with extravagance. For the jealous matrons of Washington, the elegance that reigned at the White House naturally meant a waste of money. They gossiped that the Kennedys easily spent $ 2,000 on the food for one of their parties, neglecting to add (or perhaps they did not know) that the President donated his entire salary to charity.[8] The Washington upper-crust was dying for an invitation to the White House, but it either wasn't invited, or wasn't automatically invited. The White House receptions — the only ones that really counted — were open only to the personal guests of the Kennedys. Even the " cliff dwellers " and Mesdames George Garrett, Sidney Kent Legare, John Newbold and Benjamin Thoron (" we're not snobs in the usual sense ") were ignored.

The big, fashionable embassies — the British, the French, the Chilean, the Mexican, the Peruvian — followed suit. By giving preference on their invitation lists to those already honored by the Kennedys, they practiced a sort of social segregation patterned largely on that of the White House. It was a little like a royal court. Only the oil magnates, celebrating noisily at the Carroll Arms Hotel, did not feel left out.

Washington was a new city. Certain Senators changed their ties, and under the scrutiny of the cold rationalists of the New Frontier, visiters to the White House learned not to spit. The spitoons, for that matter, had been removed. The lobbyists moved their parties to Miami or Las Vegas. If, when they stopped by the Jockey Club, they noticed someone who looked like Salvador Dali or Pablo Casals, it really was that " degenerate " Dali or that " Communist " Casals. The clothes of the Kennedy clique came from Dior, Balenciaga or Chanel, and in their dresses from Saks Fifth Avenue or Garfinkels, the best-dressed women in the city suddenly felt very provincial.

" King Jack " and his court and the *dolce vita* at the White

---

8. Since his election to the House of Representatives in 1947, Kennedy had always donated his salary and the royalties from his books to charity. As the President's salary is $ 100,000 and his personal income amounted to $ 400,000, his critics pointed out that, after taxes, his generosity cost him only $ 9,524.

House were on the tip of every tongue, and many people felt
that Sodom and Gomorrah had been destroyed for less.
America became suddenly conscious of the fact that there
were 72 servants in the White House, although the Eisenhowers had had as many. Had the Kennedys, these fabulously
rich Kennedys, with their limousines, their jewels, their long
gowns and their impassive air of the well-to-do, forgotten that
the President and the First Lady are supposed to set an
example of piety, sobriety and moral respectability ?

This book is not intended as a censure of Jacqueline
Kennedy, but everything associated with the image of a President contributes to his strengths and his weaknesses. His wife
is destined to play a part in history. John Kennedy was a man
with a strong personality. He had no need of a strong wife. A
President's wife assumes new responsibilities and the obligation to renounce certain of her former prerogatives. The
American people, with their common sense and their strong
moral principles, want a First Family that is simple and
respectable. Since the President is essentially a political figure,
it falls to the First Lady to symbolize the American family.

Jacqueline Kennedy was bored by the White House. To
her, the traditional social obligations of the First Lady were
only a nuisance. She disliked the atmosphere of Washington
politics — the party rallies, the womens' clubs, and the
company of the Congressional wives. Her disdain for the
" hurly-burly and the vulgarity of politics " won her some
powerful enemies. Washington — and even New York — were
too small for her. Nor was she made for " the citadel,
the impregnable refuge of the family. "[9] The Republican press
referred to her as a " desert princess ", a " dark-haired
beauty ", a " Parisian nymph "[10].

Spite and jealousy had their part in the gossip and scandals
that circulated, and continue to circulate, about President
Kennedy's wife, but there is generally an element of truth in
the ugliest of rumors. " The people are sometimes mistaken in
their cheers, but never in their jeers. "[11] Jacqueline Kennedy
had chosen " to live in the cream of the cream and to swim in
it "[12], and that is a dubious position for the wife of a President.

Doubt leads to suspicion. In little time, Jackie's slips overshadowed her virtues. Her popularity faded as her egoism and

her indiscretions became public knowledge.[13] Americans condemned Jackie for " putting on airs. " European aristocrats,
who disdain " café society ", scoffed at her " mauvais genre. "
Both were mistaken.

Jacqueline Kennedy had, perhaps, an " unfortunate passion
for the nobility "[14], but above all she wanted to LIVE — as
much and as well as possible. Such is the desire of most
modern young women, but the American public expects
something more from its First Lady. The voters had dreamed
of a young queen with democratic ideals. Instead, they got a
star.

Her biggest mistake was probably in considering John
Kennedy first as a husband, secondly as a Kennedy, and

---

9. John Steinbeck.

10. *Time* magazine, September 25, 1963.

11. Richard Cromwell.

12. Porfirio Rubirosa, an international playboy and personal
friend of Jackie's.

13. In September, 1962, George Gallup published the results
of a poll on Jacqueline Kennedy's public image. Heard by the
Gallup poll reporters were the following criticisms :

1. Travels too much away from family
2. In the limelight too much
3. Her hair-do
4. Her taste in clothes
5. Undignified
6. Her voice, the way she talks
7. Spends too much money, wastes money
8. Pictures in the paper in a bathing suit
9. Doesn't wear right attire to church
10. Too much social life, parties.

Also heard were : show-off, snobbish, too fun-loving, unaware of
common people, etc.

14. On several occasions she expressed her dislike for Princess
Grace of Monaco, who is, on the contrary, a noteworthy example of nobility, dignity and simplicity.

The night of President Kennedy's funeral, his widow curtsied
to Prince Philip of Edinburgh, who had come to present his
condolences on behalf of Queen Elizabeth. The curtsy was quite
out of place, but Jackie probably thought it would look chic.
Prince Philip was so embarrassed that, back in London, he
remarked that for a minute he thought he was at the Royal
Variety Performance.

never as President of the United States. She was wrong.[15] The American Constitution and the tradition of the Presidency assign no special role to the President's wife. She must rely on her good sense, her discretion, and her heart. Remarkable First Ladies like Abigail and Louisa Catherine Adams attracted little notice. Dolly Madison was a ravishing beauty, and Frances Folsom was only 21 when she married President Cleveland, but all remained in the shadow of their husbands and on the inside pages of the newspapers. The reputation of President Lincoln was hurt by the superficial frivolities of his wife, but when Mary Todd Lincoln died insane, public opinion remained indifferent.

The civilization of modern communications, with its idols and its popular myths, has turned the spotlight on the President's wife. A wife who can make or break the career of a private citizen has her part in the destiny of a President. The energy, the tact, and the intelligence of Lady Bird have done much for Lyndon Johnson. Governor Rockefeller's divorce and remarriage have hurt his political career. " Jackie " tarnished the image of the Kennedys. They accepted her only because she was the wife of one of them. She had stolen John's heart, and she had married him. That was the limit of their affinity. With her French and (although she denies it) Jewish blood, her high society upbringing and her finishing school education, she was about as far removed from the tradition of American womanhood as Pat Nixon or Ethel Kennedy are close.

Spite and envy had their part in the attacks on the President and his wife. " Calumny is a necessary ingredient of every authentic glory "[16], and no one, not even the President of the United States, is immune. It was said that Franklin Delano Roosevelt had syphilis, and that Eisenhower was a German Jew. Women had always been the weak spot of the Kennedys. " It runs in the family ", people said. President Kennedy liked to relax, and he needed to. A Secret Service agent whose code name was " Dentist " was in charge of the President's pleasures.

Puritanism is so widespread in this world, and hypocrisy so strong, that some readers will be shocked by these passages. But why should we feign to ignore such matters, when they have already passed into history ? Why should a nation tolerate a politically corrupt but not a physiologically normal President ?

The pastimes of great men are of very little importance. Too intelligent, in too much of a hurry, too hard-working, too enthusiastic, too generous, John Kennedy also had too much vitality and too much heart. The national interest requires that the state be a cold monster. The weakness and the hypocrisy of its citizens demand the same attitude of a Chief of State. Kennedy was treated with cortisone, but he hid this from the public, and he was wrong. Eisenhower had suffered a heart attack and a serious operation, and the details were known to

---

15. Jacqueline Kennedy's style of living shocked not so much because of her " immorality " or her " European elegance " as because of her disregard for the traditions and regulations of the American government and the political policies of her husband the President.

She hired Stephane Boudin, Director of Jansen's in Paris, to redecorate the White House. The new curtains, rugs, upholstery, the wood paneling and even the woodwork and some of the furniture were ordered from France, from the workshops of Saint Sabin and the Gobelins in particular, but Jacqueline Kennedy arranged to have the bills sent from Jansen's New York branch. The White House is prohibited by law from purchasing furnishings abroad when the equivalent can be purchased in the United States.

When she declared to the press in 1962, on her return from a trip to India and Pakistan (a trip that was filmed in color by the U.S. Information Agency at a cost of $ 78,104) that she had " left $ 600 in a bazaar where she hadn't intended to spend more than $50 ", did she forget that the American balance of payments was $ 2,203 in deficit, and that President Kennedy had just signed a bill limiting the free entry privileges of Americans returning from abroad to $ 100 ?

When she accepted the gifts of jewelry presented her by President Ayub Khan of Pakistan and King Hassan of Morocco, did she realize that Pakistan received $ 323 million in American aid (in 1962), and Morocco $ 56 million (in 1963) ? To our knowledge, these diamonds and emeralds were not among the objects she left behind, as tradition dictates, when she left the White House.

16. Edmund Burke.

every American. Ordinary men take comfort in the illnesses of the great. Kennedy took several baths a day and slept on a horsehair mattress with a bedboard, but he would have walked if he were half dead. People distrust those who are not like themselves.

It is difficult to abolish prejudice in those bereft of ideas. The more hatred is superficial, the more it runs deep.

4

Crowd

All statecraft is founded on the indifference of most of those concerned. Otherwise, no statecraft is possible.

DISRAELI

Presidents are not destined to be loved. Virtue does not excite admiration. There is no better way for a President to attract a growing number of enemies than to express himself too explicitly on the multitude of subjects with which he is concerned. It is the little things that divide a nation.

For Kennedy, " power without justice is meaningless. " But politics is not concerned with morality or fine sentiments, and it was for his cold logic and his sincerity that Kennedy was contested, and even detested, throughout his lifetime. Resentment surrounded him on all sides. Not only the hate of the Far Right, the big businessmen, the oilmen or the military ; not only the fanaticism of the extremists of the John Birch Society or the Ku Klux Klan. Organizations and corporations with little in common, be they financial, ideological, or simply mediocre or faint-hearted, joined in a common front against the invader. His adversaries included doctors and lawyers, churchmen and speculators, the American Legion, govern-

49

ment officials, professional diplomats, and trade unionists.[1] To maintain the balance, the Far Right even joined forces with the utopian left to oppose him. The civil rights President, this intelligent and compassionate President, even counted Negroes, poor people, and intellectuals among his enemies.

Many anguished intellectuals felt that he had taken advantage of his position to seduce their brothers into betraying their vocation. For them, the professors from Harvard were putty in the hands of the professional politicians. They saw the President's interest in philosophy and the arts as a ruse designed to neutralize their opposition by absorbing it. They thought it a shame to exchange first-class intellectuals like those in the vanguard of the New Frontier for second-class politicians, and for them a politician could only be second-class. They also claimed that Kennedy, like Carl Sandburg, was too progressive for the United States. Others, far above in their ivory towers, considered that the respect of the intellectual had nothing to do with the tragic problems of the times, the practical aspects of which very often eluded them. As for the liberal intellectuals, they criticized Kennedy for not launching an ideological crusade. They found the President too timid. They would have liked to see more lost causes, more big deficits, more lofty designs. They wanted him to eliminate the conservatives. The fact that Kennedy became almost as popular as Eisenhower reinforced their suspicions. They were unable to accept the idea of a popular President. For them, his popularity was enough to disqualify him as a intellectual or a liberal.

The utopian left went even further. It thought that the President should adopt a policy of strict neutrality in the Cold War. It felt that a really liberal President should follow in the footsteps of Switzerland, Sweden, or even India. It was totally opposed to nuclear dissuasion, be it preventive or coercive, and its creed was " better Red than dead. " The lowliest of the intellectuals accused Kennedy of " subversion, sabotage, corruption, blackmail and treason. " Revilo P. Oliver[2] was later to write in *The Conspiracy* : " As long as there are Americans, he will be remembered with disgust. If the United States is saved by the desperate efforts of her patriots, a grand and glorious future can be ours. But we shall never forget how close we came to total destruction in the year 1963. "

Had Kennedy set out to " destroy " the United States when, on April 27, 1961, he expounded his ideas on government service ?

" No responsibility of government is more fundamental than the responsibility of maintaining the highest standards of ethical behavior by those who conduct the public business. There can be no dissent from the principle that all officials must act with unwavering integrity, absolute impartiality and complete devotion to the public interest...

" Of course, public officials are not a group apart. They inevitably reflect the moral tone of the society in which they live. And if that moral tone is. injured — by fixed athletic contests or television quiz shows — by widespread business conspiracies to fix prices — by collusion of businessmen and unions with organized crime — by cheating on expense accounts, by the ignoring of traffic laws, or by petty tax evasion — then the conduct of our government must be affected. Inevitably, the moral standards of a society influence the conduct of all who live within it — the governed and those who govern.

The ultimate answer to ethical problems in government is honest people in a good ethical environment. No web of statute or regulation, however intricately conceived, can hope to deal with the myriad possible challenges to a man's integrity or his devotion to the public interest. Nevertheless formal regulation is required — regulation which can lay

---

1. Although he was pro-labor and a personal friend of trade union leaders like George Meany, the trade unions turned against Kennedy when he tried to put an end to some of their abuses. There was, for example, his conflict with the railroadworkers unions. The Administration wanted to eliminate the firemen on diesel engines and cut down on the number of crews because of automation. The regulations dating back to the time of steam engines were no longer justified now that diesel engines were in use. The train from Chicago to Denver, which covered 1,034 miles in 16.5 hours, changed crews eight times, every 130 miles, and each crew received 1.25 days of pay for each two hours of work.

2. Professor of Classical Languages at the University of Illinois.

down clear guidelines of policy, punish venality and double-dealing, and set a general ethical tone for the conduct of public business. "

At the end of his speech, the President declared that he was issuing an order :

a) prohibiting federal employees from accepting gifts ;

b) prohibiting federal employees from using information not available to the public for private gain ;

c) prohibiting federal employees from using their authority to induce others to provide them with things of value ;

d) prohibiting federal employees from accepting outside employment when such employment was considered " incompatible " with their government service.

He added that he intended to issue more detailed regulations concerning the conduct of Presidential appointees. Finally, he announced that a member of the Cabinet would be designated to coordinate all questions concerning morality in government.

Obviously, this exordium was greeted with little enthusiasm by certain federal employees. Still, they had the moral satisfaction of rereading what Kennedy had already said about them on January 30, 1961 :

" I have pledged myself and my colleagues in the Cabinet to a continuous encouragement of initiative, responsibility and energy in serving the public interest. Let every public servant know, whether his post is high or low, that a man's rank and reputation in this Administration will be determined by the size of the job he does, and not by the size of his staff, his office or his budget. Let it be clear that this Administration recognizes the value of dissent and daring — that we greet healthy controversy as the hallmark of healthy change. Let the public service be a proud and lively career. And let every man and woman who works in any area of our national government, in any branch, at any level, be able to say with pride and with honor in future years : ' I served the United States government in that hour of our nation's need. "

The " initiative ", the " sense of responsibility " and the " energy " of the State Department became one of the President's immediate preoccupations when he took office. " Foggy Bottom " was an enigma to Kennedy. " The State Department is a bowl of jelly full of people who are constantly smiling ", he told Hugh Sidey of *Time*. He felt that no one really ran it, and his directives and remonstrances to Dean Rusk had little effect. The only solution was a thorough-going reorganization, and had the White House had the opportunity, it would have undertaken the job. Instead, the President's assistants confined themselves to acid comments like the following : " This is only the latest and worst in a long number of drafts sent here for Presidential signature. Most of the time it does not matter, I suppose, if the prose is tired, the thinking banal and the syntax bureaucratic, and occasionally when it does matter, State's drafts are very good. But sometimes, as in this case, they are not. "

Kennedy and his advisers wanted a complete renovation of American foreign policy — not only of its style and its methods, but also of its orientation. The old hands at State considered this activist crusade as totally naive. The " striped-pants set " at Foggy Bottom had little confidence in this Platonic empire in modern dress. They regarded the New Frontier as closer to illusion than to hope. They believed that the wisdom of a policy is less important than its continuity, and that the mark of an amateur diplomat is his inability, or his refusal, to see that any change in policy, even for the better, implies a recognition of past error and is consequently detrimental to the national prestige. The professional diplomat thrives on routine and avoids making waves. He replaces a forceful expression with a milder phrase. He dissimulates the realities of this " seething planet of revolutionary violence, ferocity and hate " with euphemisms like " this great struggle for freedom ", the " free world ", and " national sovereignty ".[3]

Dean Rusk is certainly a *good* man, but as Secretary of State he lacked purpose. He bitterly resented the impertinent and welcome interference of the White House in the affairs of the Department of State. Like most of his subordinates, he felt that the capacity of words, phrases and style to dominate the political or economic realities of the modern world should never be underestimated — that a press conference is no substitute for foreign policy.

President Kennedy wanted to be his own Secretary of State.

------

3. Arthur Schlesinger.

He had always been interested in foreign affairs, and if he didn't always know where he would end up, at least he always knew where he was heading. At the White House, he was surrounded by a team of advisers known as the " Little White House ", the pillars of which were McGeorge Bundy and Robert Kennedy.[4] A British liberal magazine, the *New Statesman*, wrote in 1963 : " America has not one Secretary of State but half a dozen ", and added, " American diplomacy as a result has the improvised flavor of a touch football game on the White House lawn. " The author might as well have been talking about United States foreign policy in the pre-and post-Kennedy eras. American diplomacy has never been equal to the power of the United States and its international objectives.

In 1962, the State Department was beset by anxiety and apprehension. There was a noticeable thinning in the ranks of the old guard. The rules provided for the annual retirement of 3 % of the upper grades. A Presidential directive increased this figure to 5 %. Instead of 60 career diplomats, 100 were retired that year. When Kennedy took office, 13 out of the 21 highest positions in the State Department were occupied by career officers. In 1962, only 6 were career men ; the other 15 were administrative appointees. He named 80 new ambassadors, 35 of whom were political appointees.[5] Nevertheless, the people at State recalled that Kennedy had declared during his campaign, " The key arm of our foreign policy is our ambassadorial and Foreign Service staff. In my travels to every continent, I have often been impressed with the caliber of the men and women in the Foreign Service. "

Kennedy placed men in key ambassadorial positions whom the State Department considered, and continued to consider, as amateurs. He appointed a General as Ambassador to France, university presidents to Chile and the Philippines, lawyers to Denmark, NATO, and the Ivory Coast, a publisher as Ambassador to Guinea, writers to Japan and Brazil, and professors to Egypt and India. In the State Department hierarchy itself, young men found themselves suddenly promoted, and more experienced diplomats were recalled to Washington. At the Geneva conference on Laos, Averell Harriman took the daring step of appointing William H. Sullivan, Grade 3, over the heads of men in Grades 1 and 2 simply because he considered him more capable.[6]

Kennedy ordered all United States Ambassadors to supervise and coordinate the activities of all American agencies in their respective countries (with the exception of the military). This measure was hardly welcomed by the Central Intelligence Agency. With a budget half again as large as that of the State Department, better-paid and better-qualified personnel, political bureaus, military planning groups, naval and air units, landing forces, and the privilege of not having to account for its activities to Congress, the CIA considered the Presidential decision as an attack on its basic prerogatives. In the days of the Dulles brothers, Allen (Chief of the CIA) had always reported directly to his brother Foster (Secretary of State). But by 1961 John Foster Dulles was no more than a distant memory, and after the Bay of Pigs disaster, Allen Dulles fell into disfavor and was replaced by John McCone.

Wishing to inject new blood into the senior ranks of the administration, Kennedy conceived the idea of drafting corporation vice-presidents for a year of government service. But the vice-presidents found it hard to adjust to government ways, and they reacted too often with " That's not the way we do it at Proctor and Gamble. " The Kennedy style was no more suited to big business than it was to old-guard diplomacy.

John Kenneth Galbraith, Kennedy's Ambassador to India, declared, " A dollar or a rupee invested in the intellectual improvement of human beings will regularly bring a greater increase in national income than a dollar or a rupee devoted to railways, dams, machine tools or other tangible goods. "

The President gave most high officials and department heads the impression that they were behind the times. He was not preoccupied with the official hierarchy, nor with unanimous decisions. At the highest level, Kennedy had decided to

---

4. Also known as the " Tuesday group. " Other members were George C. McGhee, Paul H. Nitze, and Walt W. Rostow.

5. During Eisenhower's term in office, only twenty United States Ambassadorships were held by non-career diplomats.

6. Unlike the Civil Service, Foreign Service grades begin at 8 and run to 1.

abandon the tradition that all decisions of the Cabinet and the National Security Council be approved by the majority. He abolished the weekly meetings of the Cabinet, the Cabinet Secretaries, the administrative body of the National Security Council, the Coordinating Committee for Operations, and dozens of inter-departmental committees. He called it " doing away with bureaucracy ", and he justified his actions by saying that he saw no reason why the Postmaster General should be concerned with problems in Laos.

A few officials resigned, but most decided to stick it out. Administrations pass, but the civil service remains. They were only going through a difficult period. Many members of the American Legion agreed. They had opposed Kennedy ever since he had declared, in 1947, that " the leaders of the American Legion haven't done anything good since 1918. "[7]

Kennedy the ex-journalist gave the journalists complexes, and they criticized the way he " managed " the news.[8] Mark S. Watson of the *Baltimore Sun* complained that " every journalist is a weapon in government hands ", and Arthur Krock, the veteran *New York Times* columnist, wrote in *Fortune* :

" On the strength of almost 50 years of reporting, executive editing, and editorial commentary on the news, most of it in Washington, I would make two general judgments on the management of the news by the present President and — on its understanding of his will and attitude — by his Administration as a whole :

1. A news management policy not only exists but, in the form of direct and deliberate action, has been enforced more cynically and boldly than by any previous Administration in a period when the U.S. was not in a war or without visible means of regression from the verge of war.
2. In the form of indirect but equally deliberate action, the policy has been much more effective than direct action in coloring the several facts of public information, because it has been employed with sublety and imagination for which there is no historical parallel known to me...

Management of the news by indirection, though pursued for the same purpose as active management, requires a far wider definition. One principal form it takes in the present Admi-

nistration is social flattery of Washington reporters and commentators — many more than ever got this ' treatment ' in the
past — by the President and his high-level subordinates. "

The press had flattered the handsome candidate and the
photogenic First Family. The new President's policies were
received with less enthusiasm. Journalistic deception is part of
politics, but it irritated the President. His staff was also known
to blunder, and he made a few mistakes himself, as for
example when he cancelled the White House subscription to
the *New York Herald Tribune*.

Kennedy often displayed more virtue than wisdom in his
eighteen months in office. His bungling with regard to the
press was typical of the aristocratic and plutocratic conception
of the writer and journalist that is one of the dominant traits
(although they deny it) of the Kennedy family.

The emissaries of the Lord were hardly more favorable.
The churches attacked the diabolical private lives of the
President and the First Lady. But that was not all. The
Protestant churches had been unhappy at the nomination of a
Catholic candidate. The Reverend W. A. Criswell, pastor of
the First Baptist Church of Dallas (with an annual budget of
$195,000) declared in 1960 : " Kennedy's election would be
the death of a free church in a free state. " Later, he was to
add : " The abolition of segregation is as ridiculous as it is
foolhardy ", and " The judgment of the Lord will strike down
those who court scandal. "

When he took his oath of office, Kennedy was attacked for
not laying his hand on the Bible. He had (although the
Constitution does not require it), but the television cameras
missed it, and had he not, no one would have been surprised.
The Reverend Norman Vincent Peale spoke for many Protes-

---

7. In 1964, the American Legion held its annual convention
at Dallas. It paraded past the spot at Dealey Plaza where
Kennedy had been killed, and no one even stopped.

8. Statistics record that in October, 1961, there were 8,150
people involved in the information activities of the federal government (as opposed to 3,632 in 1952), and that 3,515 of these
specialists were working in Washington, obscured behind a variety of official titles.

tants when he said, " Kennedy is unfit to hold Presidential office. Our American civilization is at stake. I do not say that we will not survive the election of Kennedy, but we will no longer be the same. "

When one of its members was elected to the Presidency, the American Catholic Church was hardly more enthusiastic. Catholics were critical of President Kennedy's " leftist " advisers. Why, the President even bragged that he had attended public schools ! The late Cardinal Spellman, spiritual leader of American Catholicism, a comfortable and active Republican and a vehement anti-Communist, lost the influence that he had enjoyed at the White House in the days of John Foster Dulles. He made no secret of the fact that he found it displeasing, not to say scandalous, that the first Catholic elected to the Presidency was also the most secular President the United States had ever known. The Catholic review *America* wrote in its editorial of January 13, 1962 :

" In view of his peculiar position, Mr. Kennedy is not expected to make excessively friendly overtures to anyone connected with his Church. Indeed, he has hewed carefully to a line which enables him to live up to these negative expectations. He rarely finds himself in positions in which he might have to be photographed with Cardinals or other Church dignitaries.

It is significant, for instance, that there were no photographers present for the relatively little-publicized visit of the Cardinal Secretary of State to the White House early in December.

Every published photograph of that brief meeting would have cost Mr. Kennedy 10,000 votes in the Bible Belt in 1964, and Mr. Kennedy, who is an experienced politician, can scarcely be asked to overlook such hard facts of public life in America.

These calculations are not very courageous but, after all, John Kennedy is not the first U.S. President who has had to plot his course by means of opinion polls from the Protestant heartland of this nation.

Photographs of the President with Protestant spokesmen like Evangelist Bill Graham, on the other hand, are pure 14-karat gold, to be laid away at 5 percent interest till the day of reckoning in 1964. "

The leaders of American Catholicism also attacked Kennedy for refusing to appoint an Ambassador to the Vatican, for rejecting the idea of a " holy war " against the Soviet Union, and for favoring birth control. They even criticized him for not holding Mass at the White House.[9] When, in 1961, Kennedy submitted a Bill to Congress authorizing federal aid to primary and secondary schools but withholding it from parochial and other church-controlled schools as stipulated by the Constitution, protests poured in from Jews and Protestants as well as Catholics. The reaction of the combined churches was so vehement that the bill was rejected. The following year, the ecclesiastics returned to the charge when Kennedy proposed, as part of his tax reform bill, to modify the system of tax deductions for contributions to charity (which had reached the truly " divine " annual figure of $7.5 billion annually).

In the camp of hate there were also the wealthy. Not only those, in the majority, who feared for their privileges, but also those who were irritated by the refinements of the Kennedy style of living. The American aristocracy had learned that the Kennedys never discussed money at the table, that they considered it out of place and of no interest. Instead, they talked about politics, and, when there were women or guests present, about art. Did these people really imagine that there was no connection between politics, or art, and money ? Or had they left the money-making to their father, so that they could continue to live for their ideas alone, in ignorance of the " secret of the governor " ? [10] What did these Kennedys think they were doing, asking their brother-in-law[11] to set up a system providing legal assistance for the poor ?

The poor, too, were often reticent. Thirty million white Ame-

---

9. The only Mass ever celebrated at the White House was held on November 23, 1963, the day after the President's death.

10. " The poor man thinks he is a friend of the poor, and the rich man knows that he is not. "

11. Sargent Shriver, dubbed by *Time* the " anti-poverty Czar. "

ricans[12], half of them in the South, earn less than $3,000 a year. Under-qualified and under-paid, many of these have-nots are also incompetent and lazy, and while they are conscious of being exploited by their southern employers, they also realize that they could not continue to live without them. " *Republicans are good for business...* " There were also the twelve thousand Americans who, without their white skins, would have nothing. These poor whites could always look down on the Negroes, those nobodies whom Kennedy wanted to turn into somebodies.

No region in the United States could identify completely with John Fitzgerald Kennedy. The average American, and not only in the Middle West, is a man of habit — one might even say of prejudice. He likes his food plain and his religion straightforward, and he prefers American-made products. He disapproves of short-term love affairs and people who are overly-critical. He regards foreigners as good-for-nothing if not downright inferior, and the American system as the great-est in the world.

The average American probably didn't go as far as those banners in Mississippi that called on the voters to " Knock Out the Kennedys. " The *Kennedys* : not only the President, but his wife, his brothers, his children, and even his ancestors. But he had little in common with the First Family, and he judged the President in terms of the threat to his way of life.

The medical profession provides an interesting example of this phenomenon, for its hate surpassed all others. Its target was a man who believed that doctors should still remember Esculapus and devote themselves to healing *all* the ill. But the doctors were more anxious about the changes that Kennedy wanted to make in the Social Security laws, initiatives that would be considered timid in comparison with the systems already existing in most European nations.[13] Doctor Fishbein, the official spokesman of the American Medical Association, had declared in 1939 :

" Indeed all forms of security, compulsory security, even against old age and unemployment, represent a beginning invasion by the state into the personal life of the individual, represent a taking away of individual responsibility, a weakening of national caliber, a definite step toward either communism or totalitarianism. "

As soon as he entered the White House, Kennedy turned his attention to the health problems of children, the aged, and the poor. They were the subject of the speech that he never got to deliver at Austin. He wanted not only to establish government medical insurance for the aged and the unemployed, but to outlaw tax deductions for unjustified or exagerated medical expenses. He wanted the federal government to care for invalids, feeble-minded and retarded children, and to cover the cost of exceptionally high surgery bills in low-income families. He noted also that 40 % of all college students came from the 12 % of American families with incomes of more than $10,000 a year. He wanted, if not to reform the medical schools, at least to help the " talented young people without money who are unable to bear the cost of medical school. "[14] He proposed to create 40 new medical and dental schools. He was already thinking of the country's needs in 1970.[15]

But the AMA dubbed Kennedy's Social Security proposals the " Cruel Mystification ". To which Kennedy replied, in private (but it was repeated and even appeared in print) that this " mystification " was only " cruel to some of their ukases, their exclusivities, and their rackets. " Their visceral hate for him is exemplified by the Oklahoma doctor cited in Manchester's book who, on learning of Kennedy's assassination, cried, " Good, I hope they got Jackie ", and the other doctor who yelled to a colleague, " The joy ride's over. This is one deal that Papa Joe can't fix. "

---

12. By 1963, this number had dropped to 25 million.

13. In 1962, doctors in Saskatchewan, Canada, went on strike for the same reason.

14. It costs an average of $ 1,750 a year to send a child to college. Families with an income of less than $ 6,000 a year have difficulty in meeting these expenses. The average scholarship aid for a medical student is $ 500, as against $ 1,600 for a biology major. Medical schools are reluctant to admit women.

15. His proposal for medical care for the aged (Medicare), which would have added an additional 0.25 % to the Social Security deductions, was adopted in 1967.

John Kennedy continued to cherish the dream of that America for which he was responsible. On April 9, 1963, he spoke at length to his fellow-Americans of " Random Village ", a hypothetical village of 100 citizens, ten of whom are Negroes and six of whom live alone.

Half the families in Random Village own their own homes. The local newspaper is Republican, but the majority of its reporters are Democrats. When they leave school, the sons of the citizens of Random Village will have twice as much chance of being unemployed as their fathers. The wives of these citizens know that there are six times as many visitors to the country's national parks than there were when they were young (half the village likes to swim in the summer), but every year they see more of their favorite beaches and wilderness spots swallowed up by commercial establishments. Most of the adults never finished high school, but they all want their children to have an education, and would even like to see them go to college so that they can earn higher salaries and have less chance of being unemployed.

Nevertheless, only 16 of their 24 children will finish high school, and only 9 will go to college. For the 7 others, college is too expensive ($1,500 a year in a state university, and $2,000 in a private institution), or there is simply no room for them.[16] The large numbers of postwar babies are approaching college age. There will be twice as many college students in 1970 as there were in 1960.

The inhabitants of Random Village are mythical, but they are also mortal. One of them will die during the year, but two new babies will be born. Each citizen will see a doctor five times and a dentist once or twice. Eleven will be hospitalized. But many will wonder why there are not enough doctors, dentists, and hospitals. For, as Kennedy noted, " there are no doctors or dentists in Random Village. " Fifteen years ago, there were 10 doctors in the region for 10,000 inhabitants. Today, there are only 9. In ten more years, this number will have dropped to 8.

Ten inhabitants of the village will require treatment for mental illness or behavior disorders. Three of them are mentally retarded (if the village were Swedish, only one would be mentally retarded.) Many could be cured who will not have the chance to be.

Nine of the villagers are over 65, and one of them is over 80. Ninety percent of them will be hospitalized at least once before they die, and for twice as long as when they were young. Nevertheless, their incomes are now only half as great, and only five of the nine have any kind of private health insurance.

And Kennedy continued his parable by emphasizing that the adoption of his new federal aid programs would in no way affect the independence or the vitality of the people of Random Village. He emphasized the need to continue the housing program for the village, where one house out of five is in poor condition or dilapidated. Welfare payments must also be continued, he said, for one family in eight in the village has a weekly income of less than $35.

A program of vocational retraining was needed because one-third of the unemployed in the village had been out of work for more than 15 weeks this year and would be unable to find work for which they were suited. The government must pursue its efforts in the field of civil rights, for the Negro families in the village were twice as likely to be poorly housed as the whites, and earned only half as much. Their children had only two-thirds thirds as much chance as their white neighbors to finish school, and were twice as likely to be unemployed. " Neither injustice nor crime nor disease nor slums can be confined to one group in the village ", Kennedy insisted.

But in 1962 the majority of the citizens were preoccupied less with the pleasures and difficulties of life in the village than with the stock market trend. The Black Monday crash was felt throughout the country. Few stockholders were ruined, but many were hit. The value of the national portfolio diminished by 137 billion dollars on June 21, 1962. The two million stockholders of the American Telephone and Telegraph Company lost eight billion dollars. The shareholders of Du Pont and General Electric, U.S. Steel and General Motors lost more than three billion dollars per company. Those of

---

16. 1963 statistics.

Sears Roebuck, Minnesota Mining and Manufacturing and the Ford Motor Company lost more than two billion, while the securities of the Aluminium Company of America, American Home Products, Bethlehem Steel, Eastman Kodak, General Telephone and Electronics, Reynolds Metal, R. J. Reynolds Tobacco, Texaco, Union Carbide and Westinghouse dropped more than a billion dollars.

As a result of slow inflation and the depreciation of Treasury Bonds and other fixed-revenue securities, the United States has become a nation of stockholders. Many Americans had invested in the stock market to cover the cost of a house, a college education for their children, or a trip to Europe. The average stockholder was not the only one to be hurt. The employees of firms with profit-sharing schemes and the retired people who had invested 21 billion dollars in the stock exchange also saw their investments dissolve.[17]

The statements of the mutual funds and the reports of the security analysts circulated these figures among the worried stockholders. But eighteen months later, the computers refrained from reporting with equal clamor that the Dow Jones average was once again positive. It is true that the President had just been buried. At that time, the Administration was preoccupied with the farm problem,[18] and it is probable that most of the shareholders have a clearer recollection of their great fright of 1962 than of the subsequent recovery of the market. " We'll vote for Goldwater in 1964, and if Kennedy is re-elected we'll buy an island in the Indian Ocean, " many vowed.

Kennedy was a frail little boy who liked to read in bed. He doted on the tales of the Knights of the Round Table and the exploits of the Duke of Marlborough. He chose to follow in their footsteps, and set out on his own Crusade. At each new dawn, he sounded the trumpet and summoned the nation to arms. " The country was awakened and restless. But the wicked had risen along with the good, the idle with the industrious, the heartless with the merciful, the poor with the rich, the enemies with the friends, the profiteers of the dark night with the men of the clear morning. "[19] It sometimes seemed as though only children accepted him without reservation. The daughter of Supreme Court Justice Byron White said to her father on the evening of November 22, " Daddy, when are we going to be happy again ? "

The people, to excuse their egoism, believe that they are right because they are the people, forgetting that they are only a moment of the people. Winston Churchill spoke of the " weakness of the good ", but was it weakness to participate fully in the problems of the times, and to assume the responsibility for the people of the moment, but also for the generations to come ?

One day, despite all the barriers, despite all the gunmen, will kindness and justice enter Random Village ?

The crowd counted a certain number of important people. Roy Cohn, for instance. For those to whom this name is unfamiliar, Roy Cohn is the son of a judge, a graduate of Columbia Law School, who was an assistant to Attorney General James McGranery before joining the staff of Senator Joseph McCarthy.

Cohn was long considered one of the most brilliant young men in the United States. " He got more notoriety, more fame, more material success, and more enemies than most men manage to do in all of a lifetime. " Others remarked that he had always been fascinated by puzzles, and that he was somewhat of a puzzle himself. An anti-communist investigator, later a financial consultant, he was accused of furnishing false witnesses and using informers.

From the moment they met, Roy Cohn and Robert Kennedy knew that there was much that separated them.[20]

---

17. It has been calculated that a person who invested $ 10,000 in the stock market in January, 1961, at the beginning of the Kennedy era, had only $ 7,900 left after the 18.8 % drop in the Dow Jones average in June, 1962.

18. Farm prices in 1963 had dropped to 86 from the 1960 index of 100, but the portion of the family budget devoted to food had dropped from 26.9 % in 1947 to 20 % in 1960, and to 18.8 % in 1963.

19. Hans Habe.

20. Robert Kennedy also served on Senator McCarthy's staff when Roy Cohn was his chief legal adviser. He wrote later that the Senator's biggest mistake had been his confidence in Roy Cohn and his acolyte G. David Shine.

Robert Kennedy was a Kennedy. Cohn was a Jew and nearly penniless. He set out to make money, fought to get ahead, moved carefully and plotted his revenge. His rash initiatives, McCarthy's miscalculations and his growing vendetta with Bob Kennedy were very nearly the end of him.

Cohn's personal motto is, " It's profitable. " It's not a very original idea, but the man has energy and talent, and he is a remarkable gambler. He would have liked to have been the head of a large corporation. As his political career was temporarily in jeopardy, he turned his attention to other things. A specialist in business promotions, he speculated in some highly diverse operations that stretched from New York to Central America and even to Hong Kong, and carried off some remarkable feats. He wanted to transform the Lionel Corporation, an old-fashioned manufacturer of toy trains, into an electronics giant. He bought it up for $ 900,000 and appointed a General[21] to head it, with the idea that he would prove an ideal negotiator with the Pentagon. But Roy Cohn, while an excellent speculator, is no businessman, and he soon tired of the game. He also had a powerful enemy in Washington — Attorney General Robert Kennedy — who was watching his every move, just waiting for him to make a mistake.

Cohn lost $ 500,000 in Lionel, and his life began to cave in around him. In 1961, certain companies for which he served as a consultant lost $ 2.5 million dollars, and $ 4 million the following year. The Attorney General's crusade against organized crime concerned him indirectly. A lawyer or legal consultant does not always choose his clients, and he has no control over their actions.

An ascetic playboy and unlucky gambler, Cohn was often seen at Las Vegas, where people like Moe Dalitz, who had been one of the targets of the Kefauver Committee, and oilman Sam Garfield were the most innocuous of his acquaintances. It's a long way from the world of crime to the world

---

21. Brigadier General John B. Medaris, former Commander of Redstone Arsenal.

22. Fortunately for him, there is some justice in the world. The matter was straightened out in 1964 after a series of negotiations and interventions.

of oil, but Cohn was consulted on several occasions by the executives of large oil corporations, and in particular by Haroldson Lafayette Hunt (whom he had known when he worked for Mc Carthy) and by some of Mr. Hunt's acquaintances, who had awkward problems involving complex legal questions.

Roy Cohn was never consulted in vain on a question of financial speculation. His talent lay in analyzing the problems involved, in drawing the ideas together and in proposing solutions. Others were left to carry them out. Speaking of himself, he said, " I am a younger man dealing with older men. "

But time was running out for Roy Cohn. In September, 1963, his speculative activities brought him before the Grand Jury of the State of New York.[22] Today, five years later, it is doubtful whether Mr. Cohn remembers all of the matters that he dealt with in 1963. As *Life* magazine pointed out, " He deals with so many people that he may get a bit confused about whom he has seen and whom he has not. " Nevertheless, Roy Cohn swung a big deal that year.

5

Negroes

To me, the President's legislative proposals (on civil rights) are clearly destructive of the American system and the constitutional rights of American citizens. I shall oppose them with every means and resource at my command.

SENATOR RICHARD B. RUSSELL

The racial problem, America's canker, burst under Kennedy.

In 1960 Dr. Martin Luther King had called on his fellow Negroes to vote for the Senator from Massachusetts, and 78 % had responded to his appeal. A 1962 pool revealed that the Negroes chose Dr. King as their favorite hero, followed closely by John Fitzgerald Kennedy. Kennedy inspired respect and enthusiasm among many of them. But most saw him, if not as their redeemer, at least as the best card in their very weak hand.

A few days after President Kennedy's inauguration, on February 1, 1961, James Farmer, President of CORE[1], in-

---

1. The Congress of Racial Equality, founded in 1942, has a membership 80,000. After supporting a policy of non-violence throughout the Fifties, it rallied to the Black Power movement in 1966.

augurated the Freedom Riders' movement. Hundreds of militant integrationists, trained in passive resistance and prepared to confront the brutality of the local police, were sent to test segregation facilities in the South. In the month of May alone, there were 24 marches and demonstrations. Kennedy, who at the time was engrossed in international problems, chose not to attack the Negro problem head on during his first two years in office, but to act through the intermediary of the federal agencies, and in particular through his brother, the Attorney General.

In November, 1961, the Supreme Court ruled against segregation in hotels and restaurants. There was some local resistance, but the real problem lay elsewhere, in the fields of employment, education and housing. In 1961, unemployment was twice as high among Negroes as among whites. It was particularly difficult to enforce equal employment in industry. The problem was far more complex than it appeared. It involved vocational training and re-training, and depended on population migration and the attitude of the trade unions.

The Kennedy Administration stepped up the recruitment of Negro employees by the federal government.[2] Federal agencies such as the Veterans and Housing Administrations were required to show why they employed such a low percentage of Negroes. The Committee on Equal Employment Opportunity was empowered to cancel government contracts where it was established that the contracting firms practiced racial discrimination in their employment. This measure affected 38,000 companies. The Committee's authority extended even to the building firms employed on federally-financed construction projects. It was not long before the federal government was accused of employment discrimination in favor of Negroes. When a federal official hired a white person, he was asked to show why he had not chosen a Negro instead. Federal agencies were required to show why they employed white people in certain positions for which there were qualified Negroes available.

Three Negroes were promoted to supervisory positions at the Dallas Post Office in June, 1963. The first of the Negroes ranked 54th on the official promotion list. The United Federation of Postal Clerks and the National Association of Letter Carriers lodged a formal protest. " Why take the exam at all ? ", asked Owen Murphy, head of the Letter Carriers' local. " They'll just pass you by. " Post Office officials insisted that the three Negroes were highly qualified, and that it was wrong to assume that the 53 whites ahead of them were any more so. The Assistant Postmaster General, Richard J. Murphy, suggested that their previous low rank might have been the result of racial discrimination.

Critics claimed that there were two categories of typists employed by the Labor Department : white girls, who were required to type at least 40 words a minute, and Negroes, for whom 20 was considered sufficient. Similar discrepancies with regard to professional qualification appeared to exist in the Social Security and the Veterans Administrations.

Nevertheless, officials of the Kennedy Administration denied the existence of a quota for Negro employment. On July 9, 1963, in New York, a member of the Human Rights Commission demanded that sanctions be taken against Anne M. Kelly, a New York City Board of Trade official who had expressed her preference for a white secretary.

This kind of pressure brought results. Although Negroes represented only 10.5 % of the population during the fiscal year ending June 30, 1962, they accounted for 17 % of the 62,633 civil service jobs during the same period.[3] Between June, 1961, and June, 1963, the percentage of Negroes em-

---

2. The desegregation of federal employment began under Roosevelt. Between 1932 and 1937, he appointed Negroes to his " Black Cabinet ", doubled the number of Negroes employed by the federal government, and, on June 25, 1941, outlawed racial discrimination in defense industries. Segregation disappeared from the Army in 1950, during the Korean War. In 1954, the Supreme Court outlawed segregation in the schools, and in 1956 in public transportation facilities. In 1957, the Civil Rights Act, which outlawed voting discrimination, was passed by Congress. But while the problem of segregated transportation was solved, the problem of school segregation remainde : there were serious riots in Tuscaloosa in 1956, and in Little Rock in 1957. Trouble broke out in Nashville in 1960 over restaurant desegregation, and Negro voting rights were often obstructed by local authorities.

3. This percentage was as high as 25 % in the Veterans Administration, and 20 % in the Post Office Department.

ployed in the middle grades of the civil service increased by 35.5 %, and in the upper grades by 88.2 %. Attorney General Robert Kennedy appointed 40 Negro United States attorneys.

Reactions were vehement. Senator John Stennis of Mississippi declared in the Senate, " If federal employees are to be appointed solely because they are members of the Negro race, not only will the civil service laws be violated, but it will discourage and prevent qualified white people from taking the trouble to apply. "

Negro publisher S.B. Fuller stated that Negroes should seek positions only as fast as they were qualified to hold them, and Representative Huddleston of Alabama declared, " Favoritism is the rule and complete disregard of the merit system is the attitude now prevailing. "

The President of the U.S. Civil Service Commission, John W. Macy, Jr., rejected these attacks, saying : " What we are trying to do is to give all citizens an equal opportunity to compete for federal positions. What we are saying is that the Negro has had a long time to wait, and he is welcome in the federal service if he meets the proper qualifications and standards. " And he added, " The Government can't very well sell private employers on the idea of hiring more Negroes if the Government itself doesn't set a good example. "

The federal government had no legal authority to oblige employers to hire Negroes. The administration, therefore, attempted to act by other means, for example through the vocational training centers that were partially subsidized by the federal government. The AFL-CIO counted 1.5 million Negroes among its 13.5 million members, but many trade unions refused to admit Negroes, and the union rules constituted a major obstacle to the government's efforts. Many of the unions were concerned about the preferential treatment given to Negroes. They considered that any favors accorded the Negroes could only be to the detriment of the whites.[4]

Simultaneously, Washington intervened directly in the integration of schools and colleges. On the very day of Kennedy's inauguration, January 20, 1961, James Meredith, a Negro, requested admission to the University of Mississippi. In September, 1962, Mississippi went to battle behind its Governor, Ross Barnett, against the admission of Meredith.

Many people were wounded, and two were killed. An anonymous member of the Harvard Law School faculty declared in the report of the Civil Rights Commission (1962) that in Mississippi " Citizens of the United States have been shot, set upon by vicious dogs, and otherwise terrorized because they sought to vote... Students have been fired upon, ministers have been assaulted... children, at the brink of starvation, have been deprived of assistance by the callous and discriminatory acts of Mississippi officials administering Federal funds. "

Meredith entered the University of Mississippi under the protection of 16,000 federal troops. The people of the South, but also many other Americans, felt that this was not integration, but the pressure of a minority. In Mississippi and throughout the South as far as the Mexican border, people were suddenly conscious that their way of life was ending. William Faulkner had written, " If I have to choose between the United States government and Mississippi, then I'll choose Mississippi, even if it means going out into the street and shooting Negroes... "

With Kennedy's support, the tide of the Negro Revolution swept through Nashville, Raleigh and Greensboro, Cambridge, Albany, Selma... Waves of Negroes marched, prayed, staged sit-ins and voting registration drives, knowing that they had the backing of the federal government. During the school year 1962-63, only Alabama, Mississippi and South Carolina, of all the southern states, continued to maintain totally segregated schools.[5] Private schools and colleges presented another

---

4. In 1963, while white unemployment continued to rise (from 5.6 % to 5.7 %), Negro unemployment dropped from 11 % to 10.9 %.

5. The percentage of integration in the 8 other southern states was very slight :
Arkansas : 0.25 %
Louisiana : 0.04 %
Virginia : 0.56 %
Florida : 0.53 %
North Carolina : 0.27 %
Texas : 2.16 %
Georgia : 0.01 %
Tennessee : 1.13 %

and altogether different problem.[6]

But the Negro problem had passed beyond the local or regional level. Not only had it become a nationwide concern, but it had shifted geographically. The North, in the broadest sense of the term — all of the states except the eleven of the South — now contained the majority of the Negro population[7], and the Negro migration towards the big cities of the North increased from year to year.[8] In New York City alone, the Negro population (more than a million) was greater than that of the seven largest cities in the South. The city with the highest percentage of Negroes in 1950 had been Jackson, Mississippi. In 1960, it was Washington, D.C.[9] In the decade between 1950 and 1960, 1.5 million Negroes migrated to the North. The Negro always dreams of another town than his birthplace. Today, the experts estimate that before the end of this century, with the exception perhaps of New York City, most of the 50 largest cities in the United States will be more than 50 % Negro.[10] This is one of the most important racial migrations in the history of mankind, and it is certain

---

6. In 1962-1963, there were 270,000 Negroes among the 4.2 million students in colleges and preparatory schools. Some examples :
Private colleges :
  Columbia : 20 Negroes out of 700 undergraduates.
  Princeton : 15 out of 3,045.
  Yale : 75 to 90 out of 8,350.
State Universities
  University of Illinois : 1,200 to 1,500 Negroes out of 23,490.
  University of Pennsylvania : 800 to 1,000 out of 10,350.
  Michigan State University : 300 to 500 out of 24,000.
Private Preparatory Schools
  Georgetown (Maryland) : 1 out of 276.
  Groton (Massachusetts) : 3 out of 200.
  Lawrenceville (New Jersey) : 0 out of 630.
  Horace Mann (New York) : 16 out of 600.
7. In 1950, 60 % of the Negro population (9,053,000) lived in the eleven states of the South, the remaining 40 % (4,989,000) in the North. In 1963, only 10,100,000 Negroes (49 %) remained in the South. 51 % of the Negro population (10,400,000) lived in the North.
8. This migration was encouraged by the southern segregationists, who financed the departure by bus of tens of thousands

that if civil war ever breaks out again in the United States, this time it will be in the North.

As fast as the Negroes moved into the cities, the whites fled to the suburbs. In the South, integration was resisted in nearly every domain : schools, stores, theaters, hotels, restaurants. In the North, Negroes had always, in theory at least, been admitted to these facilities on the same basis as whites, but the important increase in the Negro population created a pressing problem in the schools. Educational facilities in the North were theoretically integrated,

---

of Negroes towards the North. The New Orleans Citizens Council inaugurated these " shipments " on April 21, 1962.

9. For other northern cities, the population figures are as follows :

	1950	1960
Washington	35 %	54.8 %
Newark	17.1 %	34.4 %
Baltimore	23.7 %	35 %
Detroit	16.2 %	29.2 %
St. Louis	18 %	28.8 %
Chicago	13.6 %	26.7 %
Philadelphia	18.1 %	23.7 %

10. Between 1950 and 1960

994,000 whites left	New York City and	172,000 Negroes entered
678,000	Chicago	153,000
344,000	Philadelphia	63,000
542,000	Detroit	82,000
211,000	Washington	134,000

During the same period :

Mississippi lost	323,000	Negroes and California gained	354,000
Alabama	224,000	New York	282,000
South Carolina	218,000	Illinois	189,000
North Carolina	207,000	Ohio	133,000
Georgia	204,000	Michigan	127,000
Louisiana	92,000	New Jersey	112,000
Virginia	70,000	Florida	101,000
Tennessee	57,000	Pennsylvania	77,000
Hawaii	52,000	Dist. of Col.	54,000
W. Virginia	40,000	Indiana	45,000
Texas	27,000	Connecticut	39,000
Oklahoma	26,000	Maryland	36,000
Kentucky	15,000	Wisconsin	29,000
Arizona	10,000	Missouri	28,000

(Statistics from the U.S. Publishing Corp., 1962).

but the white children left the schools as fast as the Negro children entered.[1]

Negro leaders demanded that pupils be transported by bus to other neighborhoods to maintain a racial balance in the schools, and the Kennedy administration at first supported their demands. The Negroes wanted proportional representation everywhere. But the bussing of pupils was practical only over short distances, and it drew strong protests from the white suburbs. Civil rights leaders protested that this amounted to *de facto* segregation.[12]

Deserted by their white inhabitants, certain city neighborhoods became 100 % Negro. Negroes who wanted to get away from these ghettos tried to buy homes in white neighborhoods, but often the white owners or real-estate agents refused to sell to them, or they were unable to obtain the necessary mortgage. The restrictive covenants by which the home owners in one neighborhood pledged not to sell to Negroes were declared illegal in certain states.

The federal government fought discrimination on every front. Its principal weapon was the 70 to 80 billion dollars in federal aid funds. On June 11, 1963, Kennedy addressed the nation on the subject of civil rights. The following week, he sent his civil rights bill to Congress.

This civil rights legislation was not simply, as many foreigners assumed, a new Declaration of Human Rights. To many Americans, it appeared more as a threat to their traditional system of free enterprise and to the balance of society itself. In July, 1963, *U.S. News and World Report* headed one of its articles " The Civil Rights Plan and Your Business. " The southerners were not the only ones to protest.[13] Reactions were swift throughout the country, even in regions where the Negro population was virtually nonexistant. Not only the President, but Governors, Senators, and Representatives became targets for criticism. Several members of Congress were caught in the cross-fire from their white constituents, the various ethnic minorities — Poles, Italians, Jews — and the trade unions. America asked itself, " Where is this going to stop ? ".

Some hoped that the Kennedy Bill would be completely rewritten by Congress, and many felt that civil rights would be for Kennedy in 1964 what his Catholicism had been in 1960.

Political analysts calculated that he would automatically lose not only all of the South, but also Illinois, New Jersey, Missouri, and Michigan.[14] It was sometimes felt that "civil rights" constituted an infringement of the rights of white people, particularly of those who, unlike the Kennedys, did not have the money to send their children to private schools[15], to stay at the Carlyle[16], to live in a wealthy neighborhood, or to own a second home.[17]

For the average citizen, open housing laws constituted a violation of his personal liberty. He demanded the freedom to choose his own tenants and neighbors. Under the new laws, a federal court could issue an injunction forcing the owner of a hotel or motel to admit Negroes to his establishment, and he was liable to arrest if he refused. The country clubs which made their facilities available to the guests of a neighboring hotel would be obliged to admit *all* guests, regardless of color. Hotel beauty parlors, swimming pools, dress shops, bars, dentists and doctors no longer had the right to refuse Negro clients. Anyone who felt he was the victim of discrimination in any place whatsoever could henceforth lodge a complaint with the federal courts. If found guilty, the offender would be

---

11. Englewood, New Jersey, a suburb of New York City, is a typical example. Its schools had always been integrated. But when the Negro population increased to 27 % (in a town of 26,000 inhabitants), one elementary school became 98 % Negro, another 65 %, while the others remained 90 % white.

12. In Washington, three-quarters of the public schools are not really integrated : 27 are completely Negro, and 88 others are 90 to 99 % Negro. Seventeen are 90 to 99 % white, and three are all white.

13. An Atlanta, Georgia newspaper editor had written in 1962 : "Now it's relatively fashionable to be for integration !"

14. Nevertheless, the Civil Rights Act was voted in 1964, the Voting Rights Act in 1965, and in 1966 a law was passed making the obstruction of civil rights a federal crime punishable by life imprisonment.

15. Choate, Kennedy's prep school, had one Negro student out of 550 in 1963.

16. A luxurious Manhatten hotel where the Kennedys often stayed.

17. The Kennedys had a winter home at Palm Beach, a segregated winter resort.

required to pay court costs, and might even be sent to prison.

The implications of this legislation were many. If a bank refused to grant a mortgage to a Negro who wished to buy a house in a white neighborhood, for example because it feared that the value of the house would drop if the neighborhood became Negro, it could be prosecuted for racial discrimination, and the Federal Deposit Insurance Corporation could withdraw its insurance guarantee. The federal government could cut off all federal aid, for the construction of a state highway, for example, if any one of the contractors on the project was found guilty of racial discrimination. If, in any firm employing more than 15 persons, an employee complained that he was fired because of his race, the case could be taken up by the Committee on Equal Employment Opportunity which, if it found the company guilty, could force it to re-hire the employee. In certain cases, the legislation could even be used to enforce " fair " promotion practices within a company. Federal aid to housing construction carried the same restrictions.[18]

This apparently fair legislation, with the reservation that it hurt the middle and lower-class whites most of all, in fact left the way open for all sort of abuses. Many Americans felt that it went too far — even Jews, who themselves were often the victims of discrimination in country clubs, hotels and private schools. It called into question the sacrosanct principle of the respect of the individual and free enterprise by the federal government.

Kennedy's choice was clear, although he must have known that legislation alone could not solve the Negro problem. To restore the Negroes ' identity, it was necessary to reform the very structures of American society.

Economics was an important part of the problem, but it was not the only part, nor was it the most essential. Those who opposed the Kennedy Bill produced statistics to show that, from the international standpoint, the economic position of the American Negro was actually very satisfactory, and that the Negroes were progressing with a speed unequaled in other parts of the world.[19] There is reason to question whether civil rights did not conceal, or at least delay, the recognition of the real problem, the problem on which the success of such legislation depended.

But the Negro problem is not, primarily, a problem of economics. As long as they remained in the South, the Negroes, penned up though they were, constituted an ethnic family which lived its own life and had its own culture. It was a subordinate society, but it was homogeneous. This Negro society even practiced internal segregation. At Atlanta there was a Negro church where very dark-skinned Negroes were not welcome, and similar forms of discrimination were not uncommon elsewhere.

In the North, there was no large ethnic family — only a series of Negro ghettos or Negro residential neighborhoods. The Negro in the North in 1963 was far more disheartened than his brother in the South, for, if he was not confronted

---

18. Of the 5,905 building and construction firms questioned about the repercussions of this legislation, 41.2 % declared that they would lose 50 to 75 % of their business, 1.3 % that their business would increase, 34.9 % that it would not bring about any change, and 22.6 % that they had no opnion.

(Statistics from *U.S. News and World Report*).

19. In 1930, 3 out of 4 Negroes were employed on cotton plantations or as unskilled laborers. In 1963, this number had dropped to 1 in 3, and 20 % held skilled jobs.

The average income of a white American had increased by 475 % since 1940, from $ 1,112 to $ 5,287. The Negro average for the same period had risen by 555 %, from $ 460 to $ 3,015, and the discrepancy between white and Negro incomes was growing smaller every day.

The average per capita income of an America Negro was 40 % higher than that of a Soviet citizen, and three times as great as that of the average Japanese.

This average ($ 1,100 per year) fell halfway between the average per capita income in Australia ($ 1,200) and West Germany ($ 1,040), and was equal to the average per capita income in Great Britain.

The per capita average of some of the other dark-skinned peoples of the world was (in comparison with the $ 1,100 of the American Negro) :

Mexico : $ 300
Ghana : $ 200
Haiti : $ 100
Congo : $ 70
India : $ 60

with legal segregation, he nevertheless encountered discrimination everywhere he turned. Little by little, his soul was destroyed. The American Negro became a psychological cripple. What could civil rights mean to the unemployed misfits wandering aimlessly through the streets of Harlem or Watts, or to the neglected adolescents who had strayed into the world of drugs and prostitution ?[20].

Many Negroes sensed that John Kennedy, like his brother Robert, was neither for them nor against them — that their actions were based solely on a respect for the Constitution and a belief in justice. They were reminded of that phrase of Mark Twain's, " Negroes are not only Negroes, they are also men ". What they sought was not simply a recognition of their right to exist. Nor did they want civil rights to appear as a gift. Already, they regretted that the emancipation of the slaves had not come about as a result of their own insurrection. They tried to convince themselves that the first slaves had reached America with the pilgrims on the Mayflower, and that the father of emancipation was not Abraham Lincoln, but Frederick Douglass, a Negro from Maryland. But wherever they turned, they came up against the Wall.

The Wall, for a Negro, is the need to be loved. Negroes want love, particularly from those who scorn them — and not a condescending love because they are black. But even love is denied them. James Baldwin is right when he says, " Power, that's all the Negro asks today from a white man. " Negroes don't want a white Lincoln, but a black Lincoln. Unintentionally, Kennedy reminded them that they are, for the moment, incapable of producing a black Kennedy. Stokely Carmichael was later to say, " I don't trust whites who are interested in Negroes. "

Kennedy's legislation was aimed at the whites, but it could not give the Negroes power, nor did it. They would have to win that themselves. That is the way revolutions start.

Was Kennedy right to open the gates of a revolution that could, in the long run, destroy America ? Is it possible to maintain a minority in oppression ? Could it have been done any differently ?

That is not the question. At least, it is not our purpose to answer it. The Kennedys did not invent, or even inflame, the

Negro problem. But they were the first to fully recognize it, and to appeal to the wisdom not only of the whites, but also of the Negroes.

During the riots in Detroit, the National Guard had the impression that it was " at war with another country ", and Governor Hughes of New Jersey was probably closer to the truth than many suspected when he declared, " These people claim that they hate the whites, but actually, it is America that they hate."

A century of misery, of disappointments, of humiliations, of brutality and hate have turned black America into a foreign body in the flesh of the nation. The Negroes ' hate is so strong that they have ceased to hate themselves. Negro girls have learned to wear their hair kinky, and Negroes have taken a new interest in their culture. Even the African dialects are coming back. After dreaming of integration in the great American melting pot and realizing that they are only a gray scum on its surface, locked in its borderless ghettos, the Negroes inevitably chose independence. And when they set out to win it in earnest, even Rap Brown, who summoned them to " Kill ! ", will have been superseded.

Martin Luther King declared that " Kennedy is doing his best, but the best is not enough. " For the majority of Americans, the best was too much.

Kennedy envisaged his civil rights reform as part of a vast moral, social, intellectual and economic transformation of the United States. He knew that " All this will not be finished in the first hundred days. Nor will it be finished in the first thousand days, nor in the life of Administration, nor even perhaps in our lifetime on this planet. " But he added that that was no reason not to begin. On October 9, 1962, over the Voice of America, Robert Kennedy had proclaimed the belief and the hope that he shared with his brother : " What the world has seen in Mississippi is a democratic nation putting its house in order. It is the proof of our intention to

---

20. Three out of 4 needy Americans are Negroes. In 1963, the percentage of the population earning less than $ 300 a year (considered the threshold of poverty in the U.S.) was 15.9 % among whites and 43.1 % among Negroes.

live not under the rule of men, but under the rule of law. "

Kennedy's reforms were, and could only be, half-measures. They turned people against him without bringing him support.[21]

The Negro revolution was, and is probably, inevitable. It would have occurred even without civil rights, and without Kennedy. It is written in the statistics of the migration, in the rumbles of other, more distant, revolutions, in the complexes that come from oppression, and especially in the indelible skin color of 20 million Americans. The law cannot turn black into white. The Negroes are still American Negroes, and not Negro Americans.

The civil rights reform was probably no more than a medicine that served to delay the operation, and no one can tell whether surgery will save the patient, whether the " white problem " can be solved. At the time, however, Kennedy's legislation disturbed America and increased her anxieties.

In a statement issued after a conference of eighteen southern Senators on June 12, 1963, Senator Richard B. Russell, key spokesman for the South, declared :

The President's speech (on June 11th) appealed eloquently to the emotions but completely disregarded reason, human experience and true equality under the Constitution. The fact that every citizen has the same right to own and operate a swimming pool or dining hall constitutes equality. The use of federal power to force the owner of a dining hall or swimming pool to unwillingly accept those of a different race as guests creates a new and special right for Negroes in derogation of the property rights of all of our people to own and control the fruits of their labor and ingenuity.

" The outstanding distinction between a government of free men and a socialistic or communistic state is the fact that free men can own and control property, whereas statism denies property rights. 'From each according to his ability and to each according to his need' may have greater emotional appeal than 'work hard to acquire property and the law will protect you in its enjoyment.' However, Marxism has not worked and can never work because it does not take human nature into account. To rebut the emotional appeal, we have the hard, undeniable fact that in our free-enterprise system we have plenty, whereas the Marxists — though they have never

*been able to apply literally their avowed creed — all suffer
from scarcity and privation.*

" *Our American system has always rejected the idea that one
group of citizens may deprive another of legal rights in
property by process of agitation, demonstration, intimidation,
law defiance and civil disobedience.*

" *I do not believe that the American people will be easily
frightened into discarding our system for adventures into
socialism that have been discarded wherever tried.*

" *The highest office of the land should symbolize respect for
law, whether it be legally enacted ordinances of the meanest
hamlet in the land or the written word of our national charter
— the Constitution.*

" *I was, therefore, shocked to hear the President justify,
if not encourage, the present wave of mass demonstrations,
accompanied by the practices of sitting or lying in public
streets and blocking traffic : forming human walls before the
doors of legal businesses and assaulting with deadly weapons*

---

21. On June 10, only a day after the President's civil rights
address, the Alabama National Guard was called out to halt
racial disturbances, and on June 19 in Savannah, 3,000 Negroes
rioted against the whites. Panic spread throughout the South at
the perspective of a Negro invasion of white schools and white
residential districts. In the southern states, hate for President
Kennedy was at its apogee.

At the same time, Negro militants and extremist leaders, who
had already attacked Robert Kennedy on May 28 for being " too
soft ", multiplied their threatening declarations. In August, 1963,
James Meredith took his final examinations. On August 28 the
Civil Rights march took place in the capitol to the strains of
" We Shall Overcome. " The Washington march marked a
change in the strategy of the civil rights leaders. John Lewis,
chairman of the Student Non-Violent Coordinating Comitt-
ee, prepared a speech that contained such statements as : " We
will not wait for the President, the Justice Department nor the
Congress, but we will take matters into our own hands and
create a source of power outside of any national structure... We
will march through the South, through the heart of Dixie, the
way Sherman did. " (Mr. Lewis deleted these passages after the
Catholic Archbishop of Washington objected).

On November 9, 1963, Richard Nixon declared that President
Kennedy's " extravagant campaign promises " were largely responsible for the racial crisis facing the United States.

officers of the law whose only offense was undertaking to maintain order and protect private property.

" *The South has its shortcomings as well as other areas. But a calculated campaign waged by the metropolitan press, television and radio has magnified the unfortunate occurrences in the South while crimes of violence in other areas have been minimized. This has generated bitterness and hatred against the white people of the Southern states almost amounting to a national disease. It is also encouraging a condition bordering on anarchy in many communities. These terrible conditions are sure to further deteriorate with increasing disorder unless the President of the United States desists from using threats of mass violence to rush his social-equality legislation through the Congress.*

" *No American citizen has the right to select the laws he will obey and those he will disobey. The President of the United States has a higher call to leadership than to use threats of mass violence and disregard of reasonable local laws as a means of securing action in the courts and Congress, however desirable he may regard it to be...*

" *I believe in equality before the law for every American. In equal measure, I reject the idea that federal power may be invoked to compel the mingling of the races in social activities to achieve the nebulous aim of social equality. Every Negro citizen possesses every legal right that is possessed by any white citizen, but there is nothing in either the Constitution or Judeo-Christian principles or common sense and reason which would compel one citizen to share his rights with one of another race at the same place and at the same time. Such compulsion would amount to a complete denial of the inalienable rights of the individual to choose or select his associates.*

" *I hope that the American people will not be swept further down the road to socialism by the present unprecedented wave of propaganda. To me, the President's legislative proposals are clearly destructive of the American system and the constitutional rights of American citizens. I shall oppose them with every means and resource at my command. I do not believe a majority of the Congress will be frightened by thinly veiled threats of violence.* "

6

Gangs

I believe (that this nation) is the only one
where every man, at the call of the laws, would fly
to the standard of the law, and would meet in-
vasions of public order as his own personal concern.

THOMAS JEFFERSON

" It's like Chicago in the Al Capone days ", declared John
Irwin, first assistant District Attorney of Middlesex County,
Massachusetts, in 1967, noting that in the past six years there
had been 45 gangland murders in the Boston area alone.
Writing in the *Saturday Evening Post*[1], Bill Davidson added,
" On an even higher level, the New England Mafia has
contacts among a group of millionnaire pillars of the community ", and Charles Rogovin, head of the Organized Crime
Section of the Massachusetts Attorney General's office, remarked, " Since I came here from President Johnson's Crime
Commission, I feel as if I've been watching old gangster
movies. The other families of the Mafia have become much
more subtle in their killing. Their victims mostly just disap-

---

1. November 18, 1967.

pear — and there's no heat, no hue and cry. But here they brazenly shoot them down at high noon on a busy street. "

Despite theses remarks, Massachusetts is not first among the criminal states, and neither Boston nor Worcester nor Springfield figure among the key cities in the industry of crime, the foremost industry in the United States. The vigorous action taken by the Justice Department and the FBI agains the New England Mafia in the past two years was inspired more by political than by technical considerations. The Empire of Crime remains intact. The annual budget of the private government of organized crime was estimated in 1960 at $ 60 billion, more than the budget of the Department of Defense ($ 47.5 billion)[2].

Organized crime could never have survived and developed on a large scale without the " protection of the law-enforcement agencies ".[3] Face-to-face with organized crime, or rather side-by-side, stands a police force that often ignores its existence, and sometimes even supports it. On June 15, 1961, Attorney General Robert Kennedy declared, " The problem of organized crime will not really be solved as long as the attitude of the American people remains what it is — acceptance of crime and corruption ", and as long as Americans are only interested in " getting a bigger TV set, a bigger car, and earning an extra buck. "

Robert Kennedy's career began in 1951 as a lawyer in the criminal division of the Justice Department. In 1953, he became one of the five assistants of Roy Cohn, chief legal counsel for Senator McCarthy, chairman of the Investigations Subcommittee of the Senate Committee on Government Operations. He took over Cohn's job when Senator McClellan[4] replaced McCarthy in 1954. In 1957, with a staff of 65, he became chief counsel of the Senate Rackets Committee, also headed by Senator McClellan. There, he encountered men like Antonio Corallo, who had been hired by a factory manager simply to keep his eye on the workers ; dubious business consultants like George Fitzgerald and Eddie Cheyfitz[5] ; industries like Kohler, Inc., a Sheboygan, Wisconsin manufacturer of plumbing fixtures, which in 1897 had cut its employees' salaries by 50 % and given each a bathtub, and pursued much the same policies in 1958. He exposed corruption in the labor unions — primarily in the Bakers and Confectioners Union, but also in the Mechanics, the Carpenters, the Hotel Employees, the New York Postal Workers, the Textile Workers, and even the Garbage Collecters unions. He became an expert on labor racketeering. In November, 1957, he received the first annual award as " Outstanding Investigator of the Year " from the Society of Professional Investigators.

When he became Attorney General, Robert Kennedy already had a good idea of the importance of organized crime in the United States. The kingpins of crime, some of them survivors of the Chicago era, others more recent arrivals, had left the gangs for the big cities. The gambling industry alone supported 50,000 potentates, employed the services of 400,000 petty bookmakers, and ruined one million families every year. Gambling had become so big that it was capable of disturbing the national economy. There was also prostitution, the narcotics traffic and commercial pornography, not to speak of hold-ups and murders. This industry of vice, which had already contaminated the trade unions, was also active among the youth of the country. In the decade, between 1950 and 1960, crimes doubled and juvenile delinquency tripled, although the population increased by only 18 %.[6]

The war against crime cost the United States $ 22 billion a year, or $ 120 per citizen. " Crime pays if it is well-organized. American gangsters have become specialists ", noted C.

---

2. Gambling alone accounts for $ 20 billion.

3. *Report of the Commission of Inquiry of Massachusetts,* 1957.

4. Democrat from Arkansas.

5. George Fitzgerald represented James Hoffa. Eddie Cheyfitz was Dave Beck's attorney.

Several firms of business consultants furnish information not only on legal questions, but also on labor problems, and can even provide informers if the need arises. Nationally-known companies such as Macy's, General Electric, and Republic Aircraft employ such techniques.

6. It has been estimated that 800,000 Americans have been murdered since the turn of the century. Two million firearms are sold to private citizens in the United States each year.

Wright Mills. An export on the question, Donald R. Cressey[7], wrote : " The situation is more dangerous than the situation in the 1920's and the 1930's when the monopolies controlled by organized criminals were primarily monopolies on only the distribution of illicit goods and services. The real danger is that the trend will continue to the point where syndicate rulers gain such a degree of control that they drive supporters of free enterprise and democracy out of ' business ' and then force us to pay tribute in the form of traditional freedoms. Syndicate rulers are among the most active monopolizers in the American economy. " And Cressey continued, " We agree with Senator Kennedy who... became convinced that if we do not on a national scale attack organized criminals with weapons and techniques as effective as their own, they will destroy us. " He wrote this in 1967, when organized crime, more prosperous than ever, was still in control of the empire that Robert Kennedy had tried to defeat five years before.

In 1951, the Kefauver Commission had concluded that organized crime, which it referred to as the Mafia, was run by Costello-Adonis-Lansky (the New York Syndicate) and Accardo-Guzik-Fischetti (the Chicago Syndicate). But between 1951 and 1961, the Kefauver Commission found it difficult to obtain reliable information about the nature of the Mafia and the extent of its activities. In 1957, it disclosed that 58 crime lords had met at the Appalachin Conference in upper New York State, but in 1960 the federal government and the Justice Department had little information about what had transpired at the meeting, and many of the participants were unknown to them.[8]

When Robert Kennedy was appointed Attorney General, the Crime and Rackets Section of the Justice Department employed only 17 people. They worked individually, without illusions, and received no comprehensive information on international and organized crime. By 1963, their number had swelled to 60, and they were able to draw on information which was available to the press and the public, but which had never been officially brought to their attention.

Robert Kennedy opened federal investigative bureaus in six large cities outside of Washington. These bureaus were charged with gathering information on 1,100 notorious racketeers. In 1961 and 1962, Congress approved seven anti-crime laws authorized by the Attorney General, the most important anti-criminal legislation voted since 1954. The first result was the dismantling of the nationwide telegraphic betting system. In November, 1962, a gambling and prostitution establishment in Detroit which had been doing a $ 20 million-a-year business was raided and closed down. In 1963, the illegal gambling organizations were obliged to cease their activities in many different parts of the country. In the first six months of 1963, 171 racketeers were indicted, as against 24 in 1960.[9]

In October, 1963, Robert Kennedy persuaded Joseph Valachi, a member of the crime syndicate who had requested government protection in 1962 and who had been imprisoned since that date for second-degree murder, to testify. The Attorney General revealed that the crime syndicate, known to its members as Cosa Nostra, was directed by a board of between 9 and 12 active members whose names were known to him, and to whom the representatives in the various cities were responsible. On October 19, 1963, he declared to the *New York Times* that these racketeers were only able to

---

7. Chairman of the Criminology Section of the American Sociological Association — Task Force on Crime — Administration of Justice (Washington, 1967).

8. Among the participants at this conference, held at the home of Joseph Barbara, 19 were in the clothing business, 7 owned trucking firms, 9 slot-machines, and 17 restaurants. Eleven were importers of olive oil and cheese, 4 were funeral directors, and the others were involved in car sales, coal companies, and show business. One was an orchestra leader.

In 1967 this Board of Directors of organized crime (founded in 1931 by Al Capone and Lucky Luciano) included 4 New Yorkers, Vito Genevose .(in Leavenworth federal prison), Carlo Gambino, Joe Colombo, and Joe Bonnano ; Sam Giancanna of Chicago ; Joe Zerilli of Detroit ; Steve Maggadino of Buffalo ; and Angelo Bruno of Philadelphia.

9. Kennedy declared in January, 1963, that he had evidence against : Mickey Cohen on the West Coast, Frankie Carbo of New York, Alfred Sica of Los Angeles, Buster Wortman of St. Louis, Kid Cann, who had controlled Minneapolis for 30 years, and Trigger Mike Coppola of Miami.

Mickey Cohen, typical of this type of gangster, had declared an income of $ 1,200 in 1956 and $ 1,500 in 1957, but he owned an armored car worth $ 25,000, silk pyjamas that cost $ 275,300 suits, and 1,500 pairs of socks !

operate by buying the protection of those in whom the communities placed their confidence. He denounced hired killers and the wall of silence surrounding them.

Joseph Valachi was the first member of Cosa Nostra to reveal the activities of this " cruel and calculating " organization. Since 1960, there had been 37 gangland murders in the city of Chicago alone, and 70 bombings in the region of Youngstown, Ohio. Kennedy named the principal ringleaders of the organization and declared that he was determined to put them out of action or in prison. He praised the Los Angeles and New York police departments for their cooperation, but he also cited the example of Newport, Kentucky, the type of American community where crime and corruption prevailed with the consent of the Mayor, several members of the city council, and the local police force.[10] He added that there were many Newports throughout the country, that organized crime had become particularly subtle, that it made the most of modern communications techniques, and that it had tremendous resources at its disposal to circumvent the law. It used extortion not only as a source of revenue, but also to take over control of businesses. It had infiltrated the clothing industry, bowling alleys and liquor stores, juke box companies, vending machines and the construction business. These rackets were often run by telephone, and from outside the state.

The Attorney General declared that he would ask Congress to vote new laws authorizing the use of wire-tapping devices and guaranteeing the immunity of witnesses. " Fighting organized crime is like working a jugsaw puzzle ", he said. He emphasized that organized crime affected the entire community, that it was the concern of every citizen. " There is an old saying, " he concluded, " that every society gets the kind of criminal it deserves. It is equally true that every community gets the kind of law enforcement it insists on. "

The McClellan Committee decided that the term " American Confederation " represented the best definition of Cosa Nostra, which might be considered as a sort of private government, and not only as an economic cartel. The Confederation of Crime has its own Code of Ethics. Each member is expected to :
- Be loyal to members of the organization.

- Be rational. Be a member of the team.
- Be a man of honor. Respect womanhood and your elders.
- Be a stand-up guy. Keep your eyes and ears open and your mouth shut.
- Have class. Be independent. Know your way around the world.

The Confederation is founded on the following principles :

1) Organized crime is a business venture that seeks every opportunity to corrupt or have influence on anyone in government who can or may in the future be able to do favors for organized crime.

2) Insulation serves to separate the leaders of the confederation from the illegal activities which they direct.

3) Members are subject to discipline of a quasi-military nature.

4) The public relations of the organization are of the utmost importance.

5) The structure of the organization must be such that it does not appear to be and cannot be attacked as an organization.

6) Job specialization is essential. The organization counts among its members the corrupters, the corruptees, the enforcers, the executioners, the money-movers, and the button men, representing the lowest echelon of the confederation. The corrupters are as essential to the organization as the negotiators to a trade union. The money movers are assisted by other specialists, who invest the funds of the organization in legal enterprises. The button men carry out the orders passed down through the hierarchy. The organization also has its own " accountants " and " lawyers ".

The work of the confederation is greatly facilitated by the structure of the police. There are 420,000 police officers in the United States attached to 40,000 police stations, 50 of which are federal, 200 adjuncts of the state police, and

---

10. As a result of these revelations, the voters recalled the County Sheriff, and the chief detective of the local police force was fired.

39,750 under the control of the local police.

The Task Force report entitled " The Police ", published in 1967 by the Justice Department, acknowledges that in several cities in the United States a large proportion of police officers are engaged in various forms of criminal or immoral activities, and that a few dishonest policemen may spread corruption throughout the force. Such was the case in Denver, where it was discovered in 1961 that a small group of corrupt police-men had implicated dozens of other officers throughout the city in their criminal activities. The majority of those involved were not, in fact, active accomplices, but their oath and regulations required them to report any suspicious actions, and prohibited them from taking part in any illegal activity.[11] The report acknowledges that corrupt police chiefs may set a dangerous example for younger officers. " Corruption then becomes an element of promotion, and the existence of this corruption at the highest level of authority may influence all of the members of the police. "

In Chapter 7, " The Integrity of the Police ", the report recalls that the Mayor and Sheriff of Phenix City, Alabama, were forced to resign in 1955, but that political corruption allied with organized crime and vice had continued to spread to several other cities in the state. The Justice Department discovered in 1961 that the head of the gambling syndicate in Syracuse, New York, had been living in that city for 25 years and had never been bothered by the local police.

The state police are no more trustworthy than the local police. Governor Claude Kirk of Florida preferred to hire a private detective agency to investigate crime and corruption in his state. The local police in certain states, California for example, are to all appearances fairly honest, but in other states, for instance Texas, they are thoroughly corrupt.

Many police departments refuse to acknowledge the exis-tence of organized crime and concern themselves only with local and isolated criminal offences. This attitude has the effect of guaranteeing the immunity of the crime syndicates. Other police departments even cooperate with the confedera-tion by exchanging information with its local representatives.

There are substantial differences in the quality of police personnel in the United States. A white-collar worker earns an average of $ 7,124 a year. The average salary of a

policemen is only $ 5,321.[12] In Seattle, a policeman earns
$ 375 a month less than a cable splicer. In Nashville, an
electrician makes $ 3.22 an hour, a policeman only $ 2.55.
The disparity is even greater in the upper echelons. The
salaries offered college graduates by the police are rarely
competitive with those offered by private industry. The salary
of a municipal police chief varies between $ 7,054 and
$ 17,600 a yaer (in cities with a population of more than
500,000). Only eight out of the 38 cities with a population of
between 300,000 and a million pay their police captains more
than $ 11,000 a year. In only nine of these cities does a
sergeant earn more than $ 9,600. In certain other cities with
more than a million inhabitants, Dallas for example, the
salaries paid police officers are even lower than these average
figures. Nor is there much room for promotion within the
official hierarcy. The maximum salary of a San Francisco
patrolman is only $ 600 a year more than the minimum he
received when he entered the force.

The excessive decentralization of the police, the dilution of
its responsibilities and the diversity of its efforts also created
numerous problems with regard to criminal arrests.[13] The

---

11. Section 310.71 of the police regulations states :
" Members and employees shall not accept either directly or
indirectly any gift, gratuity, loan, fee, or any other thing of value
arising from or offered because of police employment or any
activity connected with said employment. Members and
employees shall not accept any gift, gratuity, loan, fee, or other
thing of value the acceptance of which might tend to influence
directly or indirectly the actions of said member or employee or
any other member or employee in any matter of police business ;
or which might tend to cast any adverse reflection on the
department or any member or employee thereof. No member or
employee of the department shall receive any gift or gratuity
from other members or employees junior in rank without the
express permission of the Chief of Police. "
12. Unless otherwise indicated, all of these statistics date
from 1966. In general, the financial situation of the police was
even less favorable in 1963.
13. The national average for criminal arrests is 22 % for
thefts and 59 % for crimes, but these figures should be regarded
with suspicion, and they exclude most of the crimes imputable to
the Confederation of Crime.

leaders of the Confederation of Crime are " represented, in one form or another, in legislative, judicial and executive bodies all over the country ".[14] The late Chief William H. Parker of the Los Angeles police added, " Despite the most aggressive and enlightened leadership, law enforcement cannot rise above the level set by the electorate. "

There are three varieties of official corruption : *nonfeasance* (failure to perform a required duty at all) ; *malfeasance* (the commission of some act which is positively unlawful) ; and *misfeasance* (the improper performance of some act).

Where does the FBI come into this paradise of crime ? J. Edgar Hoover[15] controls the only police organization existing on the national level. In the 38 years that he has occupied this position, he has known seven Presidents and out-lasted 13 Attorney Generals[16]. As of August 31, 1962, the Federal Bureau of Investigation employed 14,217 people, including more than 6,000 federal agents. Congress has always granted Hoover's budgetary requests. J. Edgar Hoover has become something of a national monument. No one dares to contradict " the Director ", nor to suspect him.

The FBI has two principal functions : it investigates violations of federal law, and it presents its conclusions to the Attorney General and the federal attorneys. It is concerned with investigation, not law-enforcement. All of the so-called " federal " crimes fall within its jurisdiction, but the list of these, although it covers some 165 subjects, is limited. The FBI has no jurisdiction over tax violations, narcotics, customs, the mails, or the protection of the President. On the other hand, it is concerned with kidnapping, bank hold-ups, stolen cars that have been driven across state lines, and other interstate infractions of the law. Theoretically, organized crime does not fall within its jurisdiction, since it thrives on gambling, frauds, rackets, and other crimes that constitute violations of state rather than federal law, but the FBI's highly-developed intelligence sources keep it informed about the Confederation of Crime and its activities.[17]

Attorney General Robert Kennedy ordered the FBI to investigate the inter-state activities of the confederation, but this assignment irritated Mr. Hoover, who was nevertheless instructed by President Kennedy to defer to the Attorney General's wishes and to report directly to him.[18] When, in

1962, Robert Kennedy ordered the FBI to investigate the steel corporations, Hoover consented only reluctantly, and there is some indication that the order was carried out with " misfeasance "[19].

The Attorney General would have liked to create a National Crime Commission to bring together and coordinate all the available information on the confederation, its activities, and the movements of its members, but J. Edgar Hoover wants no competition, and he has his own ideas about how a federal law-enforcement agency should be run.

The FBI has 55 main offices and 500 branch offices throughout the country, but it prefers not to work with the state and local police unless they are considered " honorable " (which singularly limits the possibilities for cooperation). Moreover, " honorable " in this case has a very special meaning.

Mr. Hoover, a puritan Presbyterian and a bachelor who is active in the Boy Scout movement (he is an honorary member of its National Council) has repeatedly declared, " I am opposed to a national police force. I have a total respect for the sovereignty of the states and the local authorities, to whom we furnish a considerable amount of information which helps them to solve local crimes. " Hoover believes the FBI should devote itself first and foremost to its original function, that of protecting the nation against subversion and treason, both on the inside and from the outside.

In 1937, Franklin D. Roosevelt charged the FBI with the surveillance of the Nazi agents and sympathizers in the United

---

14. Donald R. Cressey.

15. Director of the FBI since 1924.

16. Hoover speaks slightingly of the " various Attorney Generals under whom I have served. "

17. In 1967 Bill Davidson wrote, " So many FBI plants have infiltrated the Mafia organization that you can hardly tell the Mafiosi from the informers.

18. Something that had probably not happened to Mr. Hoover since 1928.

19. He is said to have ordered federal agents to wake up journalists in the middle of the night to ask them questions that could just as well have waited until morning, a procedure that was severely criticized by the public.

States. When the war broke out in 1941, it coordinated the internal security measures against spies and saboteurs and found its true vocation. When the Second World War gave way to the Cold War, the FBI turned its attention to the Communists. Hoover was charged with the task of " unmasking and dismantling Soviet espionnage activities. "

On October 19, 1960, Hoover declared, " We are at war with the Communists ".[20] Certain generals had been forced to resign for similar statements, but even Kennedy hesitated to replace " the Director. " Eleven days after Kennedy's assassination, on December 3, 1963, Hoover reaffirmed his creed. A month earlier he had declared, " President Kennedy's closest advisers are either Communists or Communist sympathizers. " Hoover repeatedly emphasized the essential role played by the FBI in the struggle against Communism and in the protection of the " American way of life. " Since the advent of Castro, the Caribbean area had taken on a special importance for the FBI, which showed a sudden interest in the Cuban exile groups. Hoover considered that " it is more important to prevent or circumvent espionnage, sabotage, and other subversive activities than to prosecute the individuals who engage in this type of activity... " Such a rationale can have far-reaching consequences.

A self-appointed judge of what is good for the United States, Hoover refused to send FBI agents to Little Rock in 1957. Despite the injunctions of Robert Kennedy, he refused to engage his agents completely in the enforcement of civil rights legislation. It was a known fact that local FBI agents in several southern states cooperated with the segregationist local police force. When, on September 15, 1963, a bomb exploded in a Negro Baptist church in Birmingham, Alabama, killing four Negro children, the FBI learned who was guilty, but failed to pass on this information officially, thereby becoming the passive accomplice of the local police.

Robert Kennedy had been aware of Hoover's power since entering the Justice Department in 1953, but he needed him, and he was obliged to postpone his retirement, although Hoover was 65. In August, 1962, he even defended the FBI chief against the attacks of Wilbur H. Ferry, vice-president of the Fund for the Republic, declaring, " Let's leave that to the experts. Mr. Hoover is my expert. "[21]

It has been written that Bob Kennedy was " too politically sophisticated to clash openly with the honors-encrusted FBI Director. " Serious criticism of Hoover or the FBI is still regarded in the United States as something close to treason, and it is tantamount to political suicide. Hoover's sources of information, and the files at his disposal, are in fact more important than those available to comparable organisms in totalitarian states, where the heads of the intelligence services have the power to dismiss the Chief of Police.[22] The FBI has files on 200 million people, only 20 % of whom have ever been arrested. It keeps up-to-date dossiers on all the leading political and business figures. A great many Americans have reason to fear the FBI, which has confidential information about the lives and activities of the most diverse and the most insignificant citizens.

To the icy courtesy of the Attorney General, Mr. Hoover replied in October, 1962, before his favorite audience, the American Legion, that " the Communists have infiltrated every sector of our society. "[23] Why this obsession with the Communist bugbear ? Ever since its creation by Theodore Roosevelt, the FBI has been at war with what it calls " the forces of evil. " By this is meant not so much the overall category of doers of evil, and in particular high-class crim-

---

20. In 1968, the word " Communist » has lost a great deal of its impact. The traditional American Communist Party has become a " revisionist bourgeois clique ", and the authentic Marxists have switched their allegiance to the Communist Party U.S.A. (Marxist-Leninist), a splinter group of Stalinist-Maoists who divide their energies between Watts and Harlem.

21. He had previously declared that Hoover's assistance was " unmatchable. "

22. In the Soviet Union, Beria was eliminated in this fashion. In France, Roger Wybot, the director of the Office of Territorial. Security, who had kept his job through 12 successive governments in the Fourth Republic because he had files on numerous political figures, was dismissed when General de Gaulle came to power. Mr. Wybot had no file on the General.

23. James Meredith, the " black communist " (as the FBI has called him) had been admitted to the University of Mississippi in September, 1962, and the Kennedy administration seemed in no hurry to respond to " the Cuban menace. "

inals, but liberals. Hoover himself once said, " This term liberalism should not be taken lightly... " The obsession with Communism has the effect of maintaining the American people in a state of tension. The FBI knows perfectly well — at least we assume that its directors are sound of mind — that it has little to fear from a Communist Party of only 10,000 members, all of whom are known to the FBI and under constant surveillance, and which has been infiltrated by more than 1,000 FBI informers. The FBI is represented on the Central Committee of the American Communist Party, and at one point it even appointed its security chief. It has been estimated that the FBI, through the dues paid by its agents, is the most important single contributor to the Communist Party in the United States.

Hoover's attitude is based more on morality than on politics. When *U.S. News and World Report* asked him, " Some people say that the Communist Party cannot possibly represent a danger for the United States, " he replied, " Emphatically ' No '. Members of the Communist Party, U.S.A. are active participants in the international criminal conspiracy which is totally alien to our way of life and completely dedicated to enslaving the world. " He was thus expressing the point of view not of the government he was supposed to represent, but of the anti-Kennedy faction. Hoover's extremism, his puritanism and his technical competence had the effect of placing, in a passive way at least, the efficient machinery of the FBI at its disposal.

Hoover is a perfectionist as far as the efficiency and the quality of his employees are concerned. The FBI recruits highly-qualified men and women whose integrity is above reproach. Carefully screened before they are hired, they are well-paid[24] and thoroughly trained. Each is a specialist, and his responsibilities are narrowly defined and rigorously supervised. The autonomy of an FBI man is strictly limited, even in technical areas. When the principal objective is security or secrecy, each subordinate must control all of the details in his area or activity, and each supervisor must control all of his subordinates. The FBI encourages its employees to inform on one another not only for professional misconduct, but also for deviations from the exemplary moral standards to which every member of the bureau is expected to adhere.[25] FBI employees are bound by a multitude of rules and regulations, some of which even concern their mode of dress. If he wants to stay on the good side of the Director, the well-dressed G-man must wear a dark suit, a shirt with French cuffs, and a handkerchief in his pocket.[26]

The FBI hierarchy is strictly observed. FBI agents are totally subordinated to their superiors, and through them to the Director. Carlos Marcello, one of the leaders of the Confederation of Crime, was arrested in New Orleans on September 22, 1966 and charged with striking a federal agent, Patrick J. Collins, Jr. Marcello declared that he could hardly have known that Collins was an FBI agent, since he was in shirtsleeves.[27] Such a violation of bureau regulations could only have been committed with the knowledge of the

---

24. FBI agents earn from $ 8,421 to $ 16,905 a year, exclusive of overtime pay and bonuses. The Director's salary is $ 30,000 a year.

25. Thomas Henry Carter, an FBI clerk and a bachelor, was fired in August, 1965 after he was denounced by his FBI colleagues for having spent the night with a woman.

26. Hoover's moral principles are as good as law in the FBI. An FBI agent does not go out at night without his wife. He does not read *Playboy*. He does not have pimples. He does not drink. He does not wear his hair too short (it is considered a sign of immaturity). He wipes his hands (and *not* on his pocket handkerchief) before entering the Director's office (the Director does not like sweaty hands). He does not smoke in front of the Director (the Director does not like the smell of tobacco). He is expected to read the Director's book, *Master of Deceit,* and Don Whitehead's *The FBI Story*, and to pass them along to his friends.

27. Marcello is one of the richest men in Louisiana. His fortune has been estimated at $ 40 million, and he owes it to political graft and police corruption. He controls casinos in Jennings, Lafayette, Bossier City, West Baton Rouge, and Morgan City, Louisiana, the government of Jefferson Parish (county), which he has made his headquarters, the Jefferson Music Company, which operates juke boxes and coin machines, and a system of bookmakers. He owns gambling places and houses of prostitution in Bossier City, across from Shreveport, a company called Sightseeing Tours in New Orleans, a night club in Dallas, and other concerns. In 1963 he was in contact with certain politicians and oilmen in Texas and Louisiana.

hierarchy. Even J. Edgar Hoover is capable of making an exception to the rules if there is sufficient justification. There have been other slip-ups. A crime is a federal offense for the FBI only when the Director deems it such. The FBI only intervenes in the affairs of the local police when they do not share the Director's views about " Communists " and " degenerates. "

Does the honorable Mr. Hoover, we wonder, ever adorn his French cuffs with the cuff links that his Attorney General in the Kennedy years, another man with an eye for detail, gave him one year for Christmas — simple gold cuff links inscribed with the Seal of Justice ?

PART II

FORTRESSES

If your Majesty asks, "What must be done for the benefit of my kingdom?," the high officials will say, "What must be done for the benefit of our families?," and the minor functionaries and the common people will say, "What can be done for our benefit?" The former and the latter will attempt to snatch these advantages from one another, and the kingdom itself will be endangered. In a kingdom of ten thousand chariots, the sovereign's assassin will be the head of a family with one thousand chariots. In a kingdom of one thousand chariots, the prince's assassin will be the head of a family with one hundred chariots. To own one thousand chariots out of ten thousand, or one hundred out of one thousand, may not seem like such a bad lot, but if gain is put before justice, men will not be satisfied until they have everything.

MENG-TSEU

7

Politicians

But the Senate, despite its decline in power and public esteem during the second half of the Nineteenth Century, did not consist entirely of hogs and damned skulking wolves.

JOHN KENNEDY
PROFILES IN COURAGE

" Whether I am on the winning or losing side is not the point with me. It is being on the side where my sympathies lie that matters. "

This disinterested creed was acceptable coming from a Senator, but a President is supposed to leave his heart behind. " Deceit, dishonesty and duplicity are the dominant characteristics of most national leaders. "[1] There were few exceptions among the American political leaders of the Sixties. These professionals had nothing but contempt for the author of *Profiles in Courage*, this amateur who preached indulgence. They underestimated the future of this uncommon admirer of the rational and courteous Whigs of the beginning of the

---

1. Frederick II.

Nineteenth Century. They were somewhat astonished at the organization of this candidate who set up his headquarters in a nine-room suite in the Esso Building in Washington, kept a card file of the 30,000 most influential Democrats in the country, and flew around in a $ 270,000 Convair cheered by red-headed hostess Janet des Rosiers.

Kennedy covered a million miles, the equivalent of 40 times around the globe, introducing the voters to his sophisticated Messianism, his heroic speeches, and his movie-star smile. " We love you on TV. You're better than Elvis Presley... ", the students of Louisville told him. Like Woodrow Wilson, he kept repeating, " The hearts of men await our acts. " He even declared that the President should be in the thick of the fight. The professionals just laughed. They knew that there are neither friends nor enemies in politics, only colleagues and competitors — that virtues are nil and tactics are everything. They were sure he would lose, but he won by a hair[2], and they were surprised. They were even more surprised to learn that the ignorant and obstinate Protestants of West Virginia and the backwoods farmers of Minnesota, fervent supporters of Hubert H. Humphrey, had voted for him.

Once they had recovered, the professionals took a second look at his platform. They noted that Kennedy had taken stands or made promises 150 times on matters of national defense, 54 times on foreign policy, 21 on agricultural problems, 35 on administration and justice, 41 on employment, 14 on business, and 16 on economic policy. They realized that he had managed to rally the Negroes while winning votes on the theme of white supremacy[3], and that although he claimed to be a liberal he had, on October 4, 1960, accused Eisenhower and Nixon of weakness and failure to act on the Cuban problem. At Evansville, he had even promised to overthrow Castro. He had affirmed his opposition to Communism and promised to strengthen national defense and initiate an anti-missile missile program. At Columbus, Ohio in 1959, Kennedy had described himself as not only a liberal, but a " strong liberal ", but conservative Republicans scoffed at the liberal notions of this millionaire, and liberal Democrats regarded him with suspicion.

Realizing that they had been beaten on their own ground,

been overlooked, and that the opposition groups the President needed to reconcile had no Cabinet representation. The Secretary of Agriculture did not come from the Farm Belt and wasn't known for his support of the farmers, and the Secretary of Labor was not one of the names backed by the unions. The job of Postmaster General went not to a politician or to the head of the party, but to an experienced administrator. Nevertheless, Kennedy named Douglas Dillon Secretary of the Treasury rather than J. Kenneth Galbraith in an attempt to reassure the Republicans.[4]

Kennedy's initial legislative proposals were moderate. He needed support on Capitol Hill, and he handled Congress like a wild animal that has to be treated with caution. He knew that there is nothing men like less than the truth, and that politics is a continual struggle, but he was as yet unaware of the burden of the Presidency. It had taken Harry Truman eighteen months to develop his own personal style. Kennedy was later to comment that " The first months are very hard... "[5] He had difficulty in adapting his way of thinking to that of the politicians. Speaking before the cameras of CBS television in hommage to poet Robert Frost, he remarked :

" There is a story that, some years ago, an interested mother wrote to the principal of a school : Don't teach my boy poetry. He is going to run for Congress.

" I have never taken the view that the world of politics and the world of poetry are so far apart. I think politicians and poets share at least one thing, and that is that their greatness depends upon the courage with which they face the challenger of life. "

When Lyndon Johnson was Senate Majority Leader, he had described the Senate in quite another way :

" *The Senate is a wild animal that has to be tamed. You can stimulate it by pricking it lightly, but if you sting it too hard it may yield, or it may go after you. You have to approach it in just the right way, and you have to know what kind of a*

---

4. Galbraith, a liberal Democrat and Harvard professor of economics, was named Ambassador to India.

5. To William H. Lawrence of ABC television in December, 1962.

mood it's in. "

Lyndon Johnson had also said : " *They told me when I came to Congress that the best way to get along with your fellow Congressmen is to follow along.* "

A Congressman has only two things to worry about : his fellow Congressmen, who can ruin his career, and his constituents, who can end it. A Senator who fails to support the interests of his state is taking a big risk. Kennedy knew that the Founding Fathers had conceived of the Senate as " a body which would not be subject to constituent pressures " and of Senators as " ambassadors from individual sovereign governments to the Federal Government, not representatives of the voting public. "[6] But things hadn't turned out that way. The ambassadors " were very often subject to corruption. Tradition and the law govern the conduct of the members of the executive branch, but the legislators are accountable to no one. Apparently it is impossible to legalize the relationship between money and politics in public life.[7] Three members of the Kennedy administration were millionnaires, but they could

---

6. *Profiles in Courage.*

7. The Citizens' Research Council of Princeton, N.J. estimated total campaign expenditures (reported and unreported) at $ 200 million in 1964. *Time* has suggested that the actual figure may be closer to $ 400 million. Barry Goldwater's unsuccessful Presidential campaign cost $ 19.3 million, John Lindsay's campaign for Mayor of New York $ 2,000,000, and Nelson Rockefeller's Governorship race $ 5,000,000. It can cost $ 100,000 to run for a seat in the House of Representatives. The result is to rule out office seekers with modest means. As *Time* points out, " A candidate must now be rich or have rich friends or run the risk of making himself beholden to big contributors by accepting their big contributions. "

A further consequence of the financial pressures on political candidates is to open the way to corruption. *Time* calls political contributions " the basic nourishment of democracy. " California Democratic boss Jesse Unruh says, "'Money is the mother's milk of politics. " Yet the laws governing the sources and the use made of political contributions are considered a joke, a " swiss cheese " full of loopholes.

The 1925 Corrupt Practices Act, the consequence of a reform that originated with Teddy Roosevelt, prohibits contributions from national banks, corporations, labor unions and Government

account for their fortunes, something which the majority of
the 40 millionaire Congressmen (18 Representatives and 22
Senators, or one out of 3) would have found it more difficult
to do.[8] His vicuna coat cost Sherman Adams, Eisenhower's
right-hand man, his White House job, but the shady dealings
of Oklahoma Senator Robert Kerr, the uncrowned king of the
Senate, were common knowledge[9]. Walter Lippman once said
that : " With exceptions so rare they are regarded as miracles
of nature, successful democratic politicians are insecure and
intimidated men. They advance politically only as they placate,
appease, bribe, seduce, bamboozle, or otherwise manage to

---

contractors, and limits individual contributions to $ 5,000 a year
per candidate. It sets a limit on spending of $ 5,000 for a House
candidate, $ 25,000 for a candidate for the Senate, and
$ 3,000,000 for any political committee — yet in 1960 the Demo-
cratic National Committee reported a $ 3,800,000 *deficit.* In
1964, 10 Senate and 77 House candidates reported no expenses
whatsoever. Presidential and Vice-Presidential candidates and
intrastate committees are entirely exempt from these provisions.
One way used to get around the $ 3,00,000 limit is to create a
number of different interstate committees, each authorized to
spend $ 3,000,000 a year, and which secretly channel funds to
the unreporting state committees. Public cynicism is such that
only 10 % of the voters make political contributions. Even the
nation's greatest political figures flout the laws. Senate leaders
feel that detailed information about campaign contributions is
" none of the public's business ", and many legislators are afraid
the truth would shock the voters. None are prepared to permit
their challengers to benefit from new and stricter codes.

In 1962, President Kennedy appointed a committee that
recommended a modest string of small reforms : tax relief for
small donors, repeal of limitations on individual donations and
interstate committee expenditures, tighter reporting and a registry
of election finance to help enforce the rules. Congress ignored it.

8. In this regard, *U.S. News and World Report* comments :
" Many of the fortunes were amassed by the Senators and
Representatives themselves... " (February 25, 1963).

9. On October 7, 1963, Bobby Baker, secretary of the Senate
Democratic Caucus and known as the 101 st Senator, resigned
from his post following accusations of irregular financial manipulations and influence-pedding. Baker, a former Senate page who
had served as " a sort of valet to some of the most powerful men
in America ", had been recommended for his job by Lyndon
Johnson. In a few years he had amassed a small fortune.

manipulate the demanding, threatening elements in their cons-
tituencies. The decisive consideration is not whether the proposition is good but whether it is popular — not whether it will
work well and prove itself, but whether the active-talking
constituents like it immediately. "[10]

Once Kennedy was installed in the White House and his
style of living became apparent, the politicians realized that
he had little in common with them. As a rural Congressman
remarked in 1962, " All that Mozart string music and ballet
dancing down there and all that fox-hunting and London
clothes... He's too elegant for me. " Representative Edward
Hebert of Louisiana referred to the New Frontiersmen as
" a bunch of striplings who are geniuses in the intellectual
community but have never fired a shot in anger. "
Many politicians were so accustomed to addressing ignorant
audiences that their vocabulary never advanced beyond a
grammar-school level.[11] The American as opposed to the
English language is keyed to the lowest common denominator.
Kennedy's English was incomprehensible to them :

" Would you have counted him a friend of ancient Greece
who quietly discussed the theory of patriotism on that hot
summer day through those hopeless and immortal hours
Leonidas and the 300 stood at Thermopylae for liberty ?
Would you count anyone a friend of freedom who stands
aside today ?[12]

" Thucydides reported that the Peloponnesians and their allies
were almighty in battle but handicapped by their policy-
making body — in which, they related, ' each presses its own
ends... "[13]

Who on earth was Thucydides ? Where was the Pelopon-
nesos ? And what was Thermopylae ?

But there was more to it than that. In matters of religion
Kennedy maintained a strict neutrality, but he had a Catholic

---

It appears that when he found himself in financial difficulty
in 1962, he appealed, at Johnson's suggestion, to Senator Kerr,
who promptly opened a $ 300,000 bank account in Baker's name
in Oklahoma City.

In January, 1966, Baker was indicted for income tax evasion.
He was brought to trial in January, 1967, but went free on
$ 5,000 bail. Senator Kerr died on January 1, 1963.

conception of the Presidency. While Protestant theory bases political authority on the mandate of the people and a respect for the individual, Catholics regard authority as stemming directly from God. " I have tried to give my government a tone and a style that will serve as a inspiration for perfection ", said Kennedy. " Perfection " is a foreign word on Capitol Hill, and Congressmen don't·like to be preached at. The American Constitution places legislative power ahead of the executive. The President may request, suggest or advise the Congress, but that is the limit of his formal powers. Congress alone controls federal spending. The President is like a cat on a hot tin roof. His program is entirely dependent on the will of Congress.

" A President who wants to make the most of his office must learn to weigh his stake of personal influence — power in the sense of real effectiveness — in the scales of every decision he makes. He must always think about his personal risks, in power terms not merely to protect himself — that's the least of it — but in order to get clues, insight about the risks to policy. His own position is so tenuous, so insecure, that if he thinks about it he is likely to learn something about unknowns and uncertainties in policy alternatives. "[14]

Only twice in American history has the Senate unanimously backed the President : in 1930 after the Wall Street crash, and after the attack on Pearl Harbor. The Constitution stipulates that the Congress makes policy and the President executes it, but history and the rapid development of the United States have shifted the initiative to the White House. Nevertheless, the legislative system is such that Congress has the power to block not only revolutionary changes, but also needed re-

10. As a Senator from Massachusetts, John Kennedy voted in favor of the St. Lawrence Seaway and freer trade. Both of these bills ran counter to the interests of the New England shipping and textile industries.

11. The same Congressmen could be seen slipping furtively away from a White House dinner in order to light a cigar.

12. Farewell remarks to the participants in the Summer Intern Program, August 28, 1962.

13. Frankfurt, June 5, 1963.

14. Professor Richard E. Neustadt.

forms. Its structure is unsuited to the requirements of modern government. With its negative powers, it is an anachronism.

It is true that by 1960 the Constitution was no longer followed to the letter. Congress retained the right to make policy, but the problems of a modern nation are so complex and so extensive that its members preferred to confine themselves to representing the interests of their constituents and blocking the initiatives of the administration. America is not adequately represented on Capitol Hill. The nervously conservative majority of the House of Representatives is continually in opposition to the more relaxed and open majority in the Senate. The members of the House, whose electoral districts are smaller, are absorbed by local problems. Because of their two-year term, they are constantly preoccupied with getting re-elected, to the detriment of their legislative duties.

Most Congressmen shy away from the real problems facing the nation, those that can only be solved by federal intervention.[15] Under Eisenhower, the power of the federal government diminished, to the benefit of the states. Washington and Dallas are worlds apart. " Many people in this country speak of Washington as if it were somewhere overseas ", says Senate Democratic leader Mike Mansfield.

The states are willing to accept favors from Washington. State highway construction, for example, is financed 93 % by the federal government, and federal education subsidies are equally high. But they refuse to accept the obvious — that the United States are becoming more and more united. Even the regional accents are blending into one, but the cotton planters of the South still don't share the interests of the wheat farmers of the Middle West.

Simultaneously with the development of the Presidential powers since the end of the Second World War, Congress has extended its control over the administration. The federal agencies are at the mercy of the committees on Capitol Hill. What great power today can afford the luxury of an omnipotent legislature ?

In reality, neither the President nor the Congress have clearly-defined powers. Their spheres of action overlap. But Kennedy's legislative proposals were more carefully planned and minutely detailed than those of any other President, even Roosevelt during the New Deal. Then, the future of the nation was at stake. The legislators knew it, but they grumbled about the " Roosevelt dictatorship " nevertheless, and 25 years later they still had not forgotten.

Few Senators, even Democratic Senators, shared Kennedy's outlook. They voted in favor of his bills because a Senator is expected to support the President when his party is in power, or in some cases because they feared reprisals.

Lyndon Johnson's accession to the Vice-Presidency in 1961 had weakened the majority group in Congress. The Democratic Party is the only true national party, but in the Congress it is split by conflicting local and regional interests. In 1961, the Southern Democrats allied with the conservative Republicans against the remainder of the Democrats, who were supported by a few liberal Republicans. But on important votes the latter returned to the fold. Such party discipline was rarely in evidence among the Democrats.

The pressure of the lobbyists further confused the issues. In 1961, they were responsible for the House rejection of the Federal Education Bill that had already passed the Senate, and in 1962 in the Senate they succeeded in blocking the trade bill already approved by the House. With the 64 Southern Democrats generally voting against him, Kennedy was forced to rely on the votes of the dissident Republican

---

15. Certain Congressmen didn't hesitate to take advantage of their position. Newspaper stories in 1962 revealed that federal funds were made available to U.S. Congressmen traveling abroad.

In Paris, for example, " He (the Congressman) decides how much — the Embassy doesn't question it. After that, he is on his own conscience. For all the Embassy knows, the money could go for night clubs or gambling or perfume, as well as for hotels and meals. The Embassy also stands ready to give him whatever other help he asks — a car, driver, reservation for dinner, night club or theater. ' Anything except women', says an official of one Embassy in Europe. ' We draw the line there. " (*U.S. News and World Report*, September 24, 1962).

In the years after World War II, these distractions were paid out of " counterpart funds " (local currency deposited by a foreign government in counterpart of U.S. dollar aid), but in Europe these funds are nearly exhausted, and the money now comes from other sources, for example the Department of Defense.

Representatives. The fate of the New Frontier rested in the hands of a few aging Southern Senators, most of whom had been born before the turn of the century and represented rural interests in an urban nation, or hung on the ephemeral support of the nonconformist Republicans.

The traditions and peculiarities of the Congressional system further complicated the situation.[16] The vote on the budget was once delayed for four months because Representative Cannon (Missouri), aged 83, and Senator Hayden (Arizona), aged 84, were not on speaking terms. Other Senators like Richard Russell (Mississippi) or Harry F. Byrd (Virginia), who once declared that " the Social Security Administration is bankrupt ", were centuries away from President Kennedy in their thinking. The antediluvian rules governing the Congress gave them all the help they needed. Kennedy himself acknowledged that :

" The Constitution and the development of the Congress all give advantage to delay. It is very easy to defeat a bill in the Congress. It is much more difficult to pass one. To go through a committee, say the Ways and Means Committee of the House subcommittee and get a majority vote, the full committee and get a majority vote, go to the Rules Committee and get a rule, go to the floor of the House and get a majority, start over again in the Senate, subcommittee and full committee, and in the Senate there is unlimited debate, so you can never bring a matter to a vote if there is enough determination on the part of the opponents, even if they are a minority, to go through the Senate with the bill. And then unanimously get a conference between the House and Senate to adjust the bill, or if one member objects, to have it go back through the Rules Committee, back through the Congress, and have this done on a controversial piece of legislation where powerful groups are opposing it, that is an extremely difficult task. So that the struggle of a President who has a program to move it through the Congress, particularly when the seniority system may place particular individuals in key positions who may be wholly unsympathetic to your program, and may be, even though they are members of your own party, in political opposition to the President — this is a struggle which every President who has tried to get a program through has had to deal with. After all, Franklin Roosevelt was elected by the largest majority in history in 1936, and he got his worst defeat a few months afterwards in the Supreme Court bill. "

And he added : " No President's program is ever put in. The only time a President's program is put in quickly and easily is when the program is insignificant. But if it is significant and affects important interests and is controversial, therefore, then there is a fight, and the President is never wholly successful. "[17]

Kennedy's legislative proposals encroached upon traditional doctrines and attacked vested interests. It was not often that he emerged victorious from the battle. In less than 3 years, he sent 1,054 bills to Congress. During his first 100 days in office, he made 277 separate proposals concerning anti-recession measures, health, housing, education, foreign aid, Latin America, the highway program, taxes and agriculture. There were too many ideas and they came too fast. His proposals were presented too coldly and analytically, and they implied too critical a view of American society. Congress began to feel uncomfortable. Many legislators felt personally threatened. This was *their* society. Would there be anything left after the storm ?

Then suddenly they remembered that this President had won the election by only 120,000 votes, that 27 of the 50 states had voted against him, and that without the votes of his home state of Massachusetts he would never have entered the White House. They realized too that the majority of the Protestants, the businessmen, the liberal professions, the farmers, and the small town people were against him.

True, Kennedy breakfasted every Tuesday morning with the Congressional leaders and met regularly with party representatives. True, too, he had great respect for Capitol Hill, and when he accompanied a Congressman to his state he went all out to support him. The problem lay elsewhere. Kennedy was on good personal terms with the members of Congress, but he failed to discuss matters with them often enough, and he didn't believe in committees. In their eyes,

---

16. The chairmanships of Congressional committees are awarded on the basis of seniority.
17. December 17, 1962.

he spoke too frankly and refused to dodge the issues[18], and they didn't like the idea that he intended to govern the United States himself. " The executive branch of the government even wants to control the farmers ", exclaimed Senator Dirksen.

In 1961, Congress approved the budgets for national defense and the space program and voted in favor of the Peace Corps and the Alliance for Progress, but it rejected Kennedy's most important proposals, those aimed at helping the poor, the elderly, the unemployed, the students, the Negroes, and the farmers, and it voted down the measures that posed a threat to the medical profession, the businessmen, the stockholders, and the states.[19] The bills voted by Congress dealt

---

18. One evening at the White House, a Latin American political figure drew President Kennedy aside and started talking about the desperate position of his country, threatened, he claimed, by " political agitators and Communists. " The President thought for a moment and then replied, " That's a very nice dress your wife is wearing. " Coming from anyone else, this remark would have been considered a clever ploy, but Kennedy left the United States perplexed.

19. Rejected by Congress were proposals for :
- hospital and mdical care for the aged under Social Security ;
- an Urban Affairs Department ;
- stand-by power for the President to cut taxes ;
- withholding of taxes on dividends and interest ;
- aid to public schools and colleges ;
- an overhaul of the unemployment pay system, with more federal controls ;
- a curb on literacy tests used to block Negro voters ;
- public power from the U.S. Atomic plant ;
- federal scholarships for college students ;
- repeal of the 4 % dividend credit and of exclusion for first $ 50 in dividends in federal income tax returns ;
- broader powers for the Federal Trade Commission over business practices ;
- aid to medical schools ;
- rigid controls over grain farmers ;
- a permanent Civil Rights Commission ;
- pay for teachers' education ;
- schooling for illiterate adults ;
- changes in expense-account rules ;
- new tax rules on overseas earnings ;
- aid for migrant farm works, etc.

with problems which, while in some cases urgent, were of secondary importance, and which had only minor political and economic repercussions.[20] The coalitions re-formed on every issue, against an Urban Affairs Department one day, against the extension of Social Security the next. The 87th Congress will be remembered less for what it did than for what it did not do.

But if the Congress was dissatisfied with Kennedy's domestic program, it was even more concerned about his foreign policy. His second State of the Union Message, in January, 1962, did nothing to reassure them :

" Our overriding obligation in the months ahead is to fulfill the world's hopes by fulfilling our own faith...

" A strong America cannot neglect the aspirations of its citizens — the welfare of the needy — the health care of the elderly, the education of the young. For we are not developing the Nation's wealth for its own sake. Wealth is the means — and people are the ends. All our material riches will avail us little if we do not use them to expand the opportunities of our people. Last year, we improved the diet of needy people — provided more hot lunches and fresh milk to school children — built more college dormitories — and, for the elderly, expanded private housing, nursing

---

20. Approved by Congress were measures to :
- raise the minimum wage from $ 1 to $ 1.25 an hour ;
- appoint more federal judges ;
- tighten federal drug laws ;
- finance about $ 5 billion worth of public works, including $ 900 for emergency projects in depressed areas ;
- raise postage rates 1 cent ;
- raise federal wages ;
- authorize the Justice Department to subpoena company records in civil antitrust cases ;
- enlarge national parks ;
- start a $ 435 million plan for retraining the unemployed ;
- empower the President to call up 150,000 reservists and endorsing any needed action in Cuba ;
- adopt new laws on crime and gambling ;
- provide additional help for small businesses ;
- approve a higher debt ceiling ;
- cut the duty-free allowance for travelers returning from abroad.

homes, health services, and social security. But we have just begun.

" To help those least fortunate of all, I am recommending a new public welfare program, stressing services instead of support, rehabilitation instead of relief, and training for useful work instead of prolonged dependency.

" To protect our consumers from the careless and the unscrupulous, I shall recommend improvements in the Food and Drug laws — strengthening inspection and standards, halting unsafe and worthless products, preventing misleading labels, and cracking down on the illicit sale of habit-forming drugs...

" These various elements in our foreign policy lead, as I have said, to a single goal — the goal of a peaceful world of free and independent states. This is our guide for the present and our vision for the future — a free community of nations, independent but interdependent, uniting north and south, east and west, in one great family of man, outgrowing and transcending the hates and fears that rend our age.

" We will not reach that goal today, tomorrow. We may not reach it in our own lifetime. But the quest is the greatest adventure in our century.

" We sometimes chafe at the burden of our obligations, the complexity of our decisions, the agony of our choices. But there is no comfort or security for us in evasion, no solution in abdication, no relief in irresponsibility.

" A year ago, in assuming· the tasks of the Presidency, I said that few generations, in all history, had been granted the role of being the great defender of freedom in its hour of maximum danger. This is our good fortune ; and I welcome it now as I did a year ago. For it is the fate of this generation — of you in the Congress and of me as President — to live with a struggle we did not start, in a world we did not make. But the pressures of life are not always distributed by choice. And while no nation has ever faced such a challenge, no nation has ever been so ready to seize the burden and the glory of freedom. "[21]

A man is revealed more by what he writes than by what he says, and even more by what he does than by what he writes. The Senators took inventory of the year 1961:

- on March 9, the Communists prepared to seize power in Laos ;
- on April 12, the Soviets sent a man into space ;
- on April 19, Castro repulsed the timid American invasion at the Bay of Pigs ;
- on May 1, Hanoi predicted that it would control South Vietnam before the end of the year ;
- on May 30, Trujillo was assassinated in the Dominican Republic ;
- on June 4, Khrushchev told Kennedy in Vienna that the West would be driven from Berlin ;
- on June 21, Khrushchev announced his intention of signing a separate peace treaty with East Germany ;
- on July 4, Khrushchev and Breznev sent a message of congratulations on the occasion of the 185th anniversary of American independence ;
- on July 8, Khrushchev announced that the Soviet Union was obliged to postpone the reduction of her armed forces ;
- on July 26, President Juan Qudros of Brazil re-established diplomatic relations with the Soviet Union ;
- on August 13, work began on the Berlin Wall ;
- on September 1, the Soviet Union resumed nuclear testing ;
- on September 25, in a speech to the United Nations on the subject of Berlin, Kennedy quoted a Russian author[22] ;
- on October 27, the United Nations General Assembly requested the Soviet Union not to explode a 50-megaton bomb, and on October 28 the Soviets exploded it anyway ;
- on November 25, President Kennedy granted an interview to Aleksei Adzhubei, Khrushchev's son-in-law.

Adlai Stevenson, Kennedy's Ambassador to the United Nations, had declared : " The problem is not power, but moral righteousness. Foreign Chiefs of State regard United States foreign policy with astonishment, hilarity, or disdain. " He

---

21. January 11, 1962.
22. " One recalls the order of the Czar in Pushkin's ' Boris Godunov ' : ' Take steps at this very hour frontiers be fenced in by barriers... that not a single soul pass o'er the border, that not a hare be able to run or a crow to fly. ' "

was speaking, of course, of the foreign policy of the previous administration. Seventeen years after the end of World War II, the Congress noted that the only real allies the United States had left were the Germans, the Japanese, and the Spanish. While Representative Otto Passman of Louisiana was denouncing what he called the " internationalists ", Kennedy was saying : " In urging the adoption of the United States Constitution, Alexander Hamilton advised his fellow New Yorkers to ' think continentally '. Today, Americans must learn to think intercontinentally. "

" Acting on our own, by ourselves, we cannot establish justice throughout the world ; we cannot insure its domestic tranquility, or provide for its common defense, or promote its general welfare, or secure the blessings of liberty to ourselves and our posterity. But joined with other free nations, we can do all this and more. We can assist the developing nations to throw off the yoke of poverty. We can balance our worldwide trade and payments at the highest possible level of growth. We can mount a deterrent powerful enough to deter any aggression. And ultimately we can help to achieve a world of law and free choice, banishing the world of war and coercion. "[23]

In April, 1962, a Gallup poll revealed that a majority of the American people approved of what Kennedy was doing. He was as popular as Eisenhower. He grew more and more sure of himself. Congressmen and their wives were invited to the White House. They were forced to admit that he was much more accessible on the telephone than Ike, and that, unlike Franklin D. Roosevelt, who refused to receive his Congressional enemies, Truman, who cold-shouldered the Senators who had ignored him as Vice-President, and Eisenhower, who had kept his distance, Kennedy was on good terms with everyone. But his Congressional adversaries regarded his smiles as nothing more than clever tactics, and their committees continued to block his proposals.[24] They knew that they were up against an activist, a President who thought in broad strokes, not in terms of petty administrative details, an ultra-liberal who was on good terms with the unions and the Negroes, but whose strong point was not administration.

He made maximum use of public relations and his direct

access to the people to win popular support for his programs. Certain Democrats noted that his actions were more judicious than his words. They concluded that he was a persuasive, but not a dominant, President. The Republicans were less indulgent. They were wary of his intelligence, his generosity, and his ambition. The Republicans in the House were more vehement in their criticism. " *He's a clever politician* ", they said. " *He's only popular with the press. There's not a quarter of the people in my district who approve of his program.*". The President was labelled an opportunist and egocentrist. " *He talks like Churchill and acts like Chamberlain* ", they cried. " *For him, a Southern Democrat is the devil himself.* "

The Congressional elections of 1962 were a disappointment to the Republicans, who gained few seats, probably because of Kennedy's vigorous stand during the Cuban missile crisis.[25] But the Democratic majority was only a chimera. Kennedy's legislative program still hung on the votes of three or four Democrats, and most of his proposals were still pending before Congress.

In January, 1963, Kennedy went on the offensive.[26] In the first six months of 1963, Congress approved 29 of his bills, but not the most important of them.[27] He re-introduced the tax cut proposal aimed at stimulating the economy, and his measures providing aid to students, old people, and the poor.

The Congressmen were more concerned about their mail. Their constituents urged a renewed offensive against Cuba and a decrease in federal spending, and they opposed any

---

23. July 4, 1962.

24. The proposal for a tax cut and the bill establishing a withholding tax on dividends and interest. The Southern Democrats blocked a bill outlawing the literacy tests used in voter registration.

25. The composition of Congress following the 1962 elections was as follows : Senate — 67 Democrats and 33 Republicans ; House of Representatives — 256 Democrats and 178 Republicans.

26. See Chapter 12, *Condemnation*.

27. In the first six months of 1963, Congress voted to raise the ceiling of the national debt and approved a plan for controlling agricultural production.

agreement with the Soviet Union. Legislative egoism is always a reflection of that of the voters. In the first days of the new administration, the Republican as well as the Democratic Congressmen had tried to steer the flow of federal dollars towards their states, but now the floors of the Capitol groaned under the burden of increased federal spending.[28]

On June 19, 1963, Kennedy introduced his civil rights bill, The temperature of Congress shot up ten degrees and the debate was lively, but civil rights was holding up the whole legislative program. Many Democrats disagreed with Kennedy about the urgency of this law. Many more Americans agreed with the Southern Senator who declared, " Kennedy's in a trap and I think he's beginning to realize it more and more.[29]" They doubted that the administration could control the civil rights leaders, and when the President declared that this control depended on the passage of the civil rights bill, they accused him of blackmail. A breath of revolt swept through Capitol Hill.

The Republicans proclaimed that this was the most political administration they had ever known. They refused to vote his tax cuts without comparable cuts in federal spending, and they opposed his foreign aid program.[30] In the last days of his administration, Congress sank into lethargy. Not only the major projects of the administration, but also the bill increasing taxes to provide funds for unemployment relief and urgent measures such as those concerning the Export-Import Bank and the regulation of cotton and milk prices were being held up at the Capitol. On May 25, 1961, Kennedy had told Congress :

" I believe that this nation should commit itself to achieving the goal, before this decade is out, of landing a man on the moon and returning him safely to earth... in a very real

---

28. The 1962-1963 budget totaled $ 92,6 billion, as against $ 87.7 in 1961-1962, and $ 81.5 in 1960-1961.

29. *U.S. News and World Report,* August 12, 1963.

30. United States foreign aid had totaled $ 5.1 billion in 1962-1963. Kennedy managed, nevertheless, to maintain the requested level for 1963-1964, a total of $ 4.7 billion. (Foreign aid in the last year of the Eisenhower administration totaled $ 4.2 billion.)

31. *U.S. News and World Report,* August 12, 1963.

sense, it will not be one man going the moon... it will be an entire nation. "

But in 1963 the majority of the voters were prosperous and self-satisfied. They weren't interested in the future. A Representative just back from his constituency declared. " My people don't want a lot of legislation. They are fat, dumb, and happy. They don't know what is going on in Washington, and don't want to know. They think there are too many laws. Maybe we ought to go on a repealing spree and get rid of some we already have on the books.[31]

Machiavelli had written, " We see by the experience of our times that those princes have become great who have paid little heed to faith, and have been cunning enough to deceive the minds of men. In the end, they have surpassed those who relied on loyalty. " And Richard Nixon, a man who understands American politics, remarked, " *Kennedy's weaknesses are to be found in his successes — both in domestic and in foreign policy.* "

America was fat, dumb and happy.

8

Warriors

There is little in the education, training or experience of most military officers to equip them with the balance of judgment necessary to put their own ultimate solutions... into proper perspective in the President's total strategy for the nuclear age.

SENATOR J. WILLIAM FULBRIGHT

Three days before Kennedy entered the White House, on January 17, 1961, President Eisenhower, in his farewell address to the nation, issued a warning to the American people :

" Threats, new in kind or degree, constantly arise... Our military establishment today bears little relation to that known by any of my predecessors in peacetime... Until the latest of our world conflicts, the United States had no armaments industry. American makers of plowshares could, with time and as required, make swords as well. But now we can no longer risk emergency improvisation of national defense ; we have been compelled to create a permanent armaments industry of vast proportions. Added to this, three and a half million men and women are directly engaged in the defense establishment. We annually spend on military security more than the net income of all United States corporations.[1]

" This conjunction of an immense military establishment and a large arms industry is new in the American experience. The total influence — economical, political, even spiritual — is felt in every city, every State House, every office of the Federal government...

" In the councils of government, we must guard against the acquisition of unwarranted influence, whether sought or unsought, by the military-industrial complex. The potential for the disastrous rise of misplaced power exists and will persist.

" We must never let the weight of this combination endanger our liberties or democratic processes... "

During Eisenhower's two terms in office, federal military expenditures reached a high of $ 350 billion, $ 182 billion more than defense expenditures under Truman, despite the fact that his term coincided with the end the Second World War and the Korean conflict.[2] If the cost of veterans' benefits and the portion of the national debt attributable to military expenses are added to this figure, it can be said that 77 % of the United States budget in 1960 was devoted to paying for the wars of the past and preparing those of the future.

The Pentagon was not only the most important buyer of arms in the world, but also the world's largest corporation. In 1960, the Pentagon had assets totalling $ 60 billion.[3] It owned more than 32 million acres of land in the United States, and 2.5 million overseas. Its holdings were twice as large as those of General Motors, U.S. Steel, A.T. and T., Metropolitan Life, and Standard Oil of New Jersey combined. Few states in the union — and few countries in the world — have a budget as large as that of the Defense Department, and one-third have a smaller population.[4]

In 1941, Secretary of Defense Charles Wilson had declared that the war economy should be a permanent institution, and not the result of an emergency situation. Defense industries, he said, should not have their activities restricted by political witch hunts, nor sacrificed to the handful of isolationists who had dubbed them " dealers in death. " With the return of peace in 1945, James W. Forrestal, Secretary of the Navy in 1944, founded the " Association of Industry for National Security. "

The 1960 military budget included $ 21 billion for the purchase of goods. Three-fourths of this amount went to less than one-hundred corporations. The Pentagon's largest contractors at that time were General Dynamics ($ 1.26 billion in 1960)[5], Lockheed and Boeing ($ 1 billion each), General Electric and North Aviation ($ 900 million each). Eighty-six percent of these defense contracts were not awarded on bids. The Boards of Directors of the most favored contractors included several high-ranking retired military officers. General Dynamics, the Army's top contractor, counted 187 retired military officers, including 27 Generals and Admirals, among its personnel.

The public relations activities of the arms manufacturers were particularly agreeable to the Pentagon. In 1959, the Public Relations Department of Martin Aviation of Baltimore offered a " long weekend of relaxation " with appropriate recreational activities (known as Operation 3B, for Bathing, Blondes and Bars) to 27 high-ranking officers, including General Nathan F. Twining, Chairman of the Joint Chiefs of Staff. In 1960, Martin Aviation was awarded $ 800 million

---

1. In 1957 *Fortune* wrote : " We must obtain a reduction in the amount spent on highways, aid to the Negro community, and other non-military extravagances. "

2. On July 1, 1944, the United States military budget totalled $ 81.3 billion. Three years later it had dropped to $ 11.8 billion, but private industry was expanding rapidly to supply the needs of the civilian sector of the economy — automobiles, homes, household appliances, and all sorts of gadgets.

The Korean War took up the slack, and in 1953 the military budget swelled to $ 50.4 billion. By 1954, this figure had dropped to $ 40.7 billion, but tax cuts provided another boom in 1955, which marked a record demand for new cars and a record high in buying. Since the beginning of the recession in 1960, the military budget had risen from $ 47.5 billion (1960-1961) to $ 51.1 (1961-1962) and $ 52.7 (1962-1963).

3. General Motors' assets in 1966 totalled $ 12.9 billion.

4. In December, 1967, the Defense Department controlled a budget of $ 76 billion, and employed 4,500,000 people.

5. In the first nine months of 1967, General Dynamics did $ 1.57 billion worth of business, an increase of 24 % over 1966. This rise is indicative of the boom in the aviation industry resulting from the Vietnamese War.

worth of defense contracts. Companies like Hughes Aircraft, Sperry Gyroscope, and Chesapeake and Potomac Telephone employed similar techniques.

Since the end of the Korean War, the existence and the expansion of the arms industry in general and the aeronautical industry in particular had been closely connected with the continuation of the Cold War, which was vital to numerous industrial concerns.[6] ' Vice-President Nixon had declared : " Rather than allow the Communists to nibble us to death in little wars all over the world, in the future we shall rely on our power of massive and mobile retaliation " The Pentagon was prepared for all contingencies. It had even made a detailed study on " how to preserve a viable society after a nuclear conflict. "

In the course of his electoral campaign, John Kennedy had promised an increase in military expenditures. The Democratic candidate declared after his election to the Presidency that he had been ill-informed at the time about the actual ratio of American and Soviet forces. He had believed the fanciful information put out by the Air Force and the Pentagon and reprinted in the newspapers that the Soviet Union possessed 500 to 1,000 intercontinental nuclear missiles (in actual fact, it had 50). Once he was in the White House and had access to the more accurate (but still inflated) estimates of the Central Intelligence Agency, he discovered that Soviet strength had been exaggerated, but that this exaggeration was part of the strategy of the Pentagon.

On March 28, 1961, Kennedy declared before Congress, " In January, while ordering certain immediately-needed changes, I instructed the Secretary of Defense to reappraise our entire defense strategy, capacity, commitments and needs in the light of present and future dangers. The Secretary of State and others have been consulted in this reappraisal, and I have myself carefully reviewed their reports and advice. "

This new policy required the cooperation and control of the men responsible for carrying it out. Kennedy's new Defense Secretary, Robert McNamara, had just completed a successful reorganization of the Ford Motor Company. " America produces few men of McNamara's caliber... A man of diamond-hard will and titanium physique ", *Time* wrote about him. McNamara was 45, seldom socialized, took an interest in racial problems and urbanism, and enjoyed mountain climbing and poetry (Yates, Frost and Yevtochenko). He arrived at his office at 7:15 a.m. and worked until after 8 in the evening. At the Pentagon he had " an almost Calvinist horror of emotion, an almost mystical reverence for reason. He was the first Secretary of Defense with the ability, experience, and just plain guts to bring the vast, sprawling, hideously bureaucratic U.S. Defense establishment under effective civilian control.[7] "

As early as January 21, 1961, the Joint Chiefs of Staff understood that henceforth they were to be ruled. In his first week at the Pentagon he asked 96 basic questions. He let it be clearly understood that from that time forward, basic strategy would be defined by the President and himself. He abolished 500 committees (out of 4,000) and coordinated the activities of those that he maintained. He overcame inertia and incompetence with the aid of computers, contingency planners, and coordinators. His aim was to relieve the military men of the need to be intelligent. He and his deputies would provide the intelligence, at the necessary times and places. " War is a simple art, and everything is in the execution ", Napoleon had said. The military officers and even the high-ranking civilians in the Pentagon were obliged to learn a new three-dimensional language for which they were not at all prepared.

The new Defense Secretary substituted revolution for evolution. The concept and practice of systems analysis was introduced. The goal : scientific evaluation of major weapons developments and other expensive projects to determine as objectively as possible the return on a proposed investment, a compared with its alternative. McNamara wasn't interested in the opinions, the recommendations, or the conclusions of the officers in the Pentagon. He demanded written answers to specific questions. Concerning any administrative problem

---

6. After the failure of the Kennedy-Khrushchev meeting in Vienna in the spring of 1961, the Los Angeles *Mirror News* ran a full-page advertisement that began, " The summit meeting has failed. What does that mean for you ? A fantastic electronics boom. Billions of dollars, a healthy industry in Southern California employing 110,000 people. "

7. Stewart Alsop.

with political or financial repercussions, he asked only one thing : " What is the alternative ? What are the choices ? " He forbade the Generals to attend meetings in uniform (a two-star General is somewhat cowed before a three-star General, especially when he is wearing his stars). In 1961 he drew up a list of 131 urgent measures and presented it to his subordinates. By the end of the year, 112 of his suggestions had been carried out. Never before had the Generals been called upon to answer so many questions. The Pentagon stood behind the Air Force postulate, " The extermination of the Soviet system must be our primary national ojective, our obligation to the free people of the world. We must begin the battle at once. "

After the Bay of Pigs disaster, McNamara let it be known that the Pentagon would no longer play the role of passive accomplice of the CIA and the State Department. He had appointed Charles J. Hitch and Paul H. Nitze as his deputies. In 1960, Hitch had written a book entitled *The Economics of Defense in the Nuclear Age*, which introduced a new concept of military strategy. He suggested that the army and defense requirements should be subordinated to the national economy on a long and short-term basis. Paul H. Nitze, former director of the Policy Planning Staff at the Department of State, felt that the President should consider his Secretary of State as the managing director of a foreign policy " where diplomatic, military, economic, and psychological aspects need to be pulled together under a basically political concept. "

This theory became the basis of Kennedy's policy. He intended to replace John Foster Dulles' strategy of massive retaliation with a strategy of flexible response. He ordered a review of all existing plans and all the sacrosanct strategic concepts. Kennedy felt that the strategy of nuclear warfare should be based on something more than intuition. He told Congress :
" Our arms must be subject to ultimate civilian control and command at all times, in war as well as peace. The basic decisions on our participation in any conflict and our response to any threat — indeed all decisions relating to the use of nuclear weapons, or the escalation of a small war into a large one — will be made by the regularly constituted civilian authorities. This requires effective and protected organization, procedures, facilities and communications in the event of

attack directed toward this objective, as well as defensive measures designed to insure thoughtful and selective decisions by the civilian authorities. This message and budget also reflect this basic principle...

" The primary purpose of our arms is peace, not war — to make certain that they will never have to be used — to deter all wars, general or limited, nuclear or conventional, large or small — to convince all potential aggressors that any attack would be futile — to provide backing for diplomatic settlement of disputes — to insure the adequacy of our bargaining power for an end to the arms race. The basic problems facing the world today are not susceptible to a military solution. Neither our strategy nor our psychology as a nation — and certainly not our economy — must become dependent upon the permanent maintenance of a large military establishment. Our military posture must be sufficiently flexible and under control to be consistent with our efforts to explore all possibilities and take every step to lessen tensions, to obtain peaceful solutions and to secure arms limitations. Diplomacy and defense are no longer distinct alternatives, one must be used where the other fails — both must complement each other...

" Our arms will never be used to strike the first blow in any attack. This is not a confession of weakness but a statement of strength. It is our national tradition. We must offset whatever advantage this may appear to hand an aggressor by so increasing the capability of our forces to respond swiftly and effectively to any aggressive move as to convince any would-be aggressor that such a movement would be too futile and costly to undertake.

Kennedy proposed an increase of $ 650 million in military expenditures, but his new budget was tailored to eliminate " waste, duplication, and outmoded or unjustifiable expenditure items. " The President justified his thinking in the following words :

" This is a long and arduous undertaking, resisted by special arguments and by interests from economic, military, technical and other special groups. There are hundreds of ways, most of them with some merit, for spending billions of dollars on defense, and it is understandable that every critic of this Budget will have a strong preference for economy on some expenditure other than those that affect his branch of the service, or his plant, or his community.

" But hard decisions must de made. Unneeded facilities or projects must be phased out. The defense establishment must be lean and fit, efficient and effective, always adjusting to new opportunities and advances, and planning for the future. The national interest must be weighed against special or local interests. "[8]

Nevertheless, Kennedy asked Congress to approve the construction of ten more nuclear submarines, and he requested considerable expansion of the Polaris program, which he described as " a wise investment for the future. " He also recommended the development of the Minuteman strategic missile, the continuation of the Skybolt airborne missile, an increase in the budget of the Strategic Air Command, the expansion of military research projects and aeral transportation to abolish obsolete equipment (the Titan, the B 47, the Snark), and he requested the cancellation of the projects for the B 70 intercontinental bomber and the Eagle naval missile. Both programs were already out-of-date, but their manufacturers as well as the Pentagon had reasons for wanting them continued.[9]

The Pentagon was in favor of the Nike-Zeus anti-missile missile program, which was to be carried out by Western Electric. The Eisenhower administration had already ordered a freeze on the funds voted by Congress, and when they were voted again the Kennedy administration did the same. He also froze the funds for the B 70 bomber.[10] But the Pentagon had alfready spent $ 1 billion on this project, and the most cautious estimates at the time placed the total cost at something close to $ 10 billion.[11]

These Presidential policies, and the intelligence and efficiency with which McNamara and his team intended to carry them out, constituted a revolution at the Pentagon. " In establishing civilian control of the Pentagon as a fact of life as well as a theory, McNamara perhaps went too far in alienating service officers. He not only out-thought and outmaneuvered such potentates as General Curtis LeMay, but he sometimes humiliated them as well, " wrote *Time*.

" With a computer's mind and a martinet's will power, McNamara remolded the U.S. war machine from the spasmic rigidity of massive nuclear retaliation to the exquisite calibration of flexible response. He cut costs, knocked heads beneath brass hats, bullied allies into line, cowed Congressional satraps, made enemies nearly everywhere, " added *Newsweek.*

The days and the months passed feverishly. Faced with imperious orders from the top, the Generals and the Admirals yielded at first, then revolted. A sort of guerilla warfare broke out among the 7,000 offices, 18 miles of corridors and 150 staircases of the Pentagon. Anti-administration declarations by high-ranking officers multiplied in the spring of 1961. General Edwin Walker declared, " We must throw out the traitors, and if that is not possible, we must organize armed resistance to defeat the designs of the usurpers and contribute to the

---

8. March 29, 1961.

9. In 1967, 17 top military experts estimated that the nuclear forces of the United States and the Soviet Union would evolve in the following manner in the coming decade :

United States	Soviet Union
1962 : 25 to 50,000 megatons	1962 : 6 to 12,000 megatons
1971 : 6 to 15,000 megatons	1971 : 30 to 50,000 megatons

The experts used these figures to back up their plea for an increase in the American nuclear potential, but they also noted that under Kennedy American nuclear superiority was on the order of 4 to 1.

10. On February 25, 1962, the Air Force and the Boeing Corporation presented the B 70 bomber to the press once again, although Kennedy persisted in his refusal to release the blocked funds.

11. This system would be obsolete before it was operational, as has been the case up to now with all the anti-missile missile programs.

In 1967, identical arguments and industrial pressure led the Pentagon to reinstate a project for the construction of ABM antiballistic missiles. Mc'namara tried to reduce this program, knowing that the Russians themselves admitted that their Tallin system of Galosh and Griffon antiballistic missiles was already obsolete. Due to progress in electronics and the techniques of ultra-miniaturized micro-circuits, the American system, which will not be operational until 1974, and which the Pentagon considers insufficient, is also already obsolete. The new LSI (for large-scale integrated circuits) technique makes possible an assemblage ten times more dense and multiplies the sensitivity (reaction speed) of missiles by five. *Electronics* writes that " the radars and computers that will guide our anti-missile missiles will be as old-fashioned as a Ford next to the latest Ferrari. "

return of a constitutional government.[12] " He was backed by General P.A. del Valle and Admiral Arthur Radford.

" Some of the advisers now surrounding the President have philosophies regarding foreign affairs which would chill the average American ", declared Admiral Chester Ward (retired). " World War III has already begun and we are deeply engaged in it ", stated Admiral Felix B. Stunny. Admiral Ward accused the White House advisers of giving priority " not to freedom, but to peace " and added, " I am not in favor of preventive warfare, but I am in favor of a preventive strike " (sic).

General White, chairman of the Air Force Chiefs of Staff, declared, " I am profoundly apprehensive of the pipe-smoking, tree-full-of-owls type of so-called professional defense intellectuals who have been brought into this Nation's capital. I don't believe a lot of these over-confident, sometimes arrogant young professors, mathematicians and other theorists have sufficient worldliness or motivation to stand up to the kind of enemy we face. "

The *New York times*[13] wrote, " The Pentagon is having its troubles with rightwingers in uniform. A number of officers of high and middle rank are indoctrinating their commands and the civilian population near their bases with political theories resembling those of the John Birch Society. They are also holding up to criticism and ridicule some official policies of the U.S. Government. The most conspicuous example of some of these officers is Maj. Gen. Edwin A. Walker... "

Senator Stuart Symington of Missouri rose in the Senate to condemn the extra-curricular activities of certain military officers, and Senator J. William Fulbright of Arkansas declared that by proclaiming that the United States was engaged in a desperate struggle and that its sole objective in the Cold War should be not peaceful coexistence, but total victory, the military leaders were giving support to the most irresponsible elements of the Far Right. As a result of these denunciations, General Walker was relieved of his duties for extremism and propaganda in the Army.

McNamara was strong enough to resist the combined pressures of his military advisers and Congress. With Kennedy's approval, he opted for the expansion of the intercontinental ballistic missile program at the expense of the conventional bombers so dear to military and industrial circles.

The Pentagon had been its own master for twenty years —
in the aftermath of World War II, during the Korean Conflict,
and finally under the sympathetic administration of General
Ike. The warriors realized now that the good years were gone.
Not only did they fear for their priviliges, but they considered
it their duty to try and " save the nation. " During the Korean
War, the Army had been shaken by the success of the brain-
washing techniques applied to American prisoners of war.
With Eisenhower's benediction, the National Security Council
had set up a civilian education program to arouse the public
to " the menace of the Cold War " and the necessity for
nuclear survival. Feeling persecuted by the President and his
Secretary of Defense, the warriors decided to avail themselves
of this forum to inform the civilian public about the anti-
American conspiracy of the men of the New Frontier. In the
spring of 1961, the " public alerts ", the " freedom forums ",
the " strategy for survival conferences " and the " fourth
dimensional warfare seminars " proliferated. The stated aims
of these programs were " to alert all in attendance to the
specific objectives of international communism, " " to reveal
areas of Communist influence upon American youth ", " to
re-orient American thinking toward un-American ideas ", and
to " identify public officials and policies displaying a ' soft-
ness ' toward communism. " The featured addresses bore titles
like " What You Can Do in the Fight Against Communism, "
and " No Wonder We are Losing. "

Admiral Ward was the featured speaker at a fourth dimensional warfare seminar held on April 15 in Pittsburgh. On
April 14 and 15, " Strategy for Survival " conferences sponsored by Major General William C. Bullock, the area com-

---

12. General Walker began his political career in the Arie
Crown Theatre in Chicago on February 9, 1962 before a crowd
of 5,000 people. He had spent three decades in uniform, and had
been decorated as a hero of the Korean War. In 1959 he joined
the John Birch Society. Walker liked to say, " In patriotism,
loyalty and combat, there are no moderates. " He advised his
audience to " attack on all fronts " and to " man your weapons
and speak boldly. "

13. June 18, 1961.

mander, were held in several cities in Arkansas. The invitations to an " Education for American Security " seminar in Illinois were sent out in officially franked envelopes. " Project Alert " in Pensacola, Florida was endorsed by local Navy headquarters, and out-of-town participants in " Project Action ", held on April 28-29 in Minneapolis, were offered overnight accommodation at the Naval Air Station. A seminar organized by anti-Communist crusader Dr. Fred Schwarz was sponsored in New Orleans by Rear Admiral W.S. Schindler, and at Corpus Christi Admiral Louis J. Kirn, Chief of Naval Air Advanced Training, sat on the platform.

Senator Fulbright charged that, " the content no doubt has varied from program to program, but running through all of them is a central theme that the primary, if not exclusive, danger to this country is internal Communist infiltration. The thesis of the nature of the Communist threat often is developed by equating social legislation with socialism, and the latter with communism. Much of the administration's domestic legislative program, including continuation of the graduated income tax, expansion of social security (particularly medical care under social security), Federal aid to education, etc., under this philosophy would be characterized as steps toward Communism.

" This view of the communist menace renders foreign aid, cultural exhanges, disarmament negotiations, and other international programs, as extremely wasteful, if not actually subversive... There are many indications that the philosophy of the programs is representative of a substantial element of military thought, and has great appeal to the military mind... There is little in the education, training, or experience of most military officers to equip them with the balance of judgment necessary to put their own ultimate solutions... into proper perspective in the President's total strategy for a nuclear age... " And he concluded with a warning :

" The radicalism of the right can be expected to have great mass appeal. It offers the simple solution, easily understood, scourging of the devils within the body politic, or, in the extreme, lashing out at the enemy.

" If the military is infected with this virus of rightwing radicalism, the danger is worthy of attention. If it believes the public is, the danger is enhanced. If, by the process of the military educating the public, the fevers of both groups are raised, the danger is great indeed.

" Perhaps it is farfetched to call forth the revolt of the French Generals[14] as an example of the ultimate danger. Nevertheless, military officers, French or American, have some common characteristics arising from their profession, and there are numerous military ' fingers on the trigger ' throughout the world. "

In July, a Defense Department order went out restricting the right of military officers to express their political opinions in public and participate in such information programs.[15] There was a violent reaction from the conservatives. Senator J. Strom Thurmond, a North Carolina Republican and General in the Army Reserve, attacked the move as an " infamous attempt to intimidate the leaders of the United States Armed Forces and prevent them from informing their troops about the exact nature of the communist menace.[16] "

On July 8, Khrushchev announced that the government of the USSR was obliged to postpone the reduction of its armed

---

14. A reference to the French Generals' putsch of April, 1961 in Algiers.

15. McNamara was called before the Senate Armed Services Committee to explain his action. When he arrived at the Capitol, he was greeted by 70 housewives wearing John Birch Society buttons.

16. Senator Barry Goldwater wrote :

" There exists today a new literature of military strategy which is in no manner the work of career officers, but of nuclear philosophers, as they have recently begun to call themselves, and who expose their humanitarian dislike for the bomb in all their writings.

" Today's Generals and Admirals are not bloodthirsty pirates with black patches over their eyes and cutlasses between their teeth. They are intelligent, competent, well-educated men who are trying as hard as our diplomats to find peaceful solutions to international problems. Our Generals and our Admirals are strategists of peace as well as experts on military questions.

" I believe that something both new and old is happening in our country, and that the great traditions of American history will find their true place. "

forces. Kennedy was sufficiently concerned by the information he received from the CIA to make a televised address on July 25, 1961 asking the country to be prepared to defend freedom in Berlin and elsewhere. He announced a supplementary defense build-up that included doubling and tripling the draft calls and calling up reservists to active duty. Finally, he recommended the construction of atomic shelters. These pessimistic declarations raised the spirits of the military men, but frightened the American people. The federal government printed pamphlets describing how to build a family-sizestet atomic shelter. The newspapers and television discussed the consequences of a nuclear attack. Atomic scientist Dr. Edward Teller stated, " If we don't prepare, 100 million Americans could die in the first days of an all-out nuclear war. Thirty to 40 million more could die from starvation and disease. The United States would cease to exist... " A Jesuit priest, Father McHugh, declared for his part that shelter owners had the moral right to keep out their panicked neighbors. A brochure published by the Office of Civil Defense advised all boat owners to head for the open sea as soon as the alert was sounded.

Congress demanded an expanded arms program, the money for which was to come from the aberrant projects of the welfare state. Senators Jackson and Keating declared that Congress would grant the President and the armed forces all the money they requested, and in particular $ 500 million for the Boeing B 70. The Pentagon was once again optimistic. The Generals and the Admirals multiplied their inflammatory statements. But on August 2, Senator Fulbright again spoke out :

" Military officers are not elected by the people and they have no responsibility for the formulation of policies other than military policies. Their function is to carry out policies formulated by officials who are responsible to the electorate. This tradition is rooted in the constitutional principle that the President is the Commander in Chief of the Armed Forces and that, therefore, military personnel are not to participate in activities which undermine his policies. "

On November 16, 1961 in Seattle, President Kennedy declared, " We must face the fact that the United States is neither omnipotent nor omniscient — that we cannot impose our will upon the other 94 percent of mankind — that we cannot right every wrong or reverse each adversity — and that therefore there cannot be an American solution to every world problem. "

For the first time in the history of the United States, a President had dared to attack the myth of the national infallibility. Three days later, at a Democratic Party banquet in Los Angeles, Kennedy continued, " Let us concentrate more on keeping enemy bombers and missiles away from our shores, and concentrate less on keeping neighbors away from our shelters. Let us devote more energy to organizing the free and friendly nations of the world... and devote less energy to organizing armed bands of civilian guerillas that are more likely to supply local vigilantes than national vigilence. "

This remark was aimed at the paramilitary organizations such as the John Birch Society, the Minutemen and the Ku-Klux Klan.[17] At the time that Kennedy spoke, these extremist groups were made up largely of visionaries, profiteers,

---

17. The John Birch Society, founded by Robert Henry Winborne Welch, Jr., born in 1899, an alumnus of the Annapolis Naval Academy and Harvard Law School, vice-president of a candy factory in Belmont, Mass., favors, among other things, the immediate liberation of Cuba, the abolition of foreign aid, and the reinstitution of generalized segregation. In 1961, the society claimed a membership of 100,000. It kept files on " Comsymps " (anyone whose ideas were considered too liberal) and attempted to infiltrate universities and the government. It had genuine influence in the army.

The society is named after Captain John Morrison Birch, a young missionary who was killed at the age of 27 by the Chinese Communists while on a mission in Northern China 10 days after the end of World War II. According to Welch, Birch was the first victim of World War III.

The Minutemen, a clandestine combat militia, is headed by Robert Bolivar DePugh, who runs a $ 400,000 a year pharmaceutical business. Its 25,000 members hold daily drills with everything from pistols to antitank guns to be ready to check a Communist invasion, and organize guerilla warfare seminars throughout the country. Although it is loosely organized, several hundred of its groups are armed and dangerous and capable of doing anything in support of their ideology or the interests of their leaders. Their motto is " Action Now " and their program calls for the assassination of dangerous Communists.

and fanatics. But General Walker and other highranking officers began training new leaders in 1962. The organizations gained strength, and by 1963 they and other groups such as the Friends of General Walker and the Patrick Henry Association had become forces to reckon with.

The Far Rightists dreamed of a world without communism, without foreign imbroglios, without the United Nations, without the federal government, without trade unions, and without Negroes. Their goal was an America with no Supreme Court which would invade or destroy Cuba, abolish the graduated income tax and stop importing Polish hams. For these people, even Eisenhower was an active agent of the Marxist conspiracy. When Kennedy moved into the White House, they were certain the Russians had landed. " God, I miss Ike. I even miss Harry ", one man from Cincinnati told *U.S. News and World Report* in 1962.

The rightist movements not only had the benefit of military leadership, but also of important private funds. Harding University in Arkansas [18] furnished most of the speakers for the extremist forums. Its President, Dr. George S. Benson[19], had the financial backing of companies like Lockheed, Boeing, U.S. Steel, Lone Star Cement, Olin Mathison Chemical, American Iron and Steel Institute, and Acme Steel. In 1961, these companies contributed more than $6 million to Harding. General Electric and the CIA were among its most important benefactors.

Nevertheless, the international situation continued to deteriorate. In August, the Berlin Wall was constructed, and in September, the Soviets first, and then the United States began nuclear testing again. On October 28, the very day the U.N. General Assembly requested it not to, the Soviet Union

---

The KKK, headed by Robert Shelton, a former air-conditioner salesman, accepts as members only " loyal citizens born in the United States, Christian, white, with high morals, of the Protestant faith, believing in Americanism and the supremacy of the white race. " But behind this relatively moderate creed lies a plethora of folklore and a group of savage people.

18. Which received its first gift, $ 300,000 from General Motors, in 1949. The decision was made by Alfred P. Sloan, who was President of GMC at the time.

exploded a 50-megaton bomb. On October 31, Senator Jackson criticized Kennedy for taking risks in national defense by delaying construction of the Boeing B 70, rebaptized the RS 70 to enhance its image. That same month, the Army sponsored a " Project Alert " in San Francisco, and in December the Navy did the same.

Kennedy attempted to thaw the Gold War by diplomacy [20], but the exaggerated statements of the warriors of the Pentagon were hardly calculated to help him. McNamara, who was now " constantly scrapping " and who was loathed by Congress, which found him " arrogant and even supercilious ", continued to wield his authoritarian power, to demonstrate his aversion to favoritism[21], and to construct a rational system of defense. He declared, " Technology has now circumscribed us all with a conceivable horizon of horror that could dwarf any catastrophe that has befallen man in his more than a million years on earth. Man has lived for more than 20 years in what we have come to call the atomic age. What we sometimes overlook is that every future age of man will be an atomic age. If, then, man is to have a future at all, it will have to be

---

19. Dr. Benson once declared, " If you want to force Washington to do what needs to be done, you must first reach public opinion. My goal is to strike it deep down in the roots so as to orient it towards piety and patriotism. "

He also proclaimed that " Any American who loves freedom and is willing to work, work, work to protect it can find intelligent direction and companionship in a John Birch Society group. "

20. On November 25, Kennedy granted an interview to Aleksei Adzhubei, editor in-chief of Izvestia, who told him, " Your election brought great hope to the people of our country ". On November 28, the nuclear test ban conference, which had been adjourned since September 9, re-opened in Geneva. On December 21, Kennedy met with MacMillan at Bermuda to examine Western relations with the USSR.

21. In October, 1963, Secretary of the Navy Fred Korth was asked to resign by McNamara. He was accused of showing favoritism towards the Continental National Bank of Fort Worth, of which he had been President prior to his appointment in 1961. (The Continental National Bank was one of 20 banks that had lent $ 200 million to General Dynamics to enable it to begin construction of the TFX, now the F 111).

a future overshadowed with the permanent possibility of thermonuclear holocaust. About that fact, we are no longer free. Our freedom in this question consists rather in facing the matter rationally and realistically and discussing action to minimize the danger. No sane citizen ; no sane political leader ; no sane nation wants thermonuclear war. But merely not wanting it is not enough. We must understand the difference between actions which increase its risk, those which reduce it, and those which, while costly, have little influence one way or another. Nuclear strategy is exceptionally complex in its technical aspects. Unless these complexities are well understood, rational discussion and decision-making are simply not possible. "

The Cuban missile crisis of October, 1962 was the turning point in the Gold War. On October 22, Kennedy declared, " I call upon Chairman Khrushchev to halt and eliminate this clandestine, reckless and provocative threat to world peace and to stable relations between our two nations. I call upon him further to abandon this course of world domination, and to join in an historic effort to end the perilous arms race and to transform the history of man...

" We will not prematurely or unnecessarily risk the costs of worldwide nuclear war in which even the fruits of victory would be ashes in our mouth — but neither will we shrink from that risk at any time it must be faced...

" The path we have chosen for the present is full of hazards, as all paths are — but it is the one most consistent with our character and courage as a nation and our commitments around the world. The cost of freedom is always high — but Americans have always paid it. And one path we shall never choose, and that is the path of surrender or submission.

" Our goal is not the victory of might, but the vindication of right — not peace at the expense of freedom, but both peace *and* freedom here in this hemisphere, and, we hope, around the world. God willing, that goal will be achieved. " The Soviets backed down.

By 1963 the *détente* had become a reality, and the Pentagon knew it had lost the game. That spring, the Navy Chief of Staff, Admiral George W. Anderson, handed in his resignation.[22] President Kennedy declared on March I that the Admiral would continue to serve the country in an important post.[23] On July 26, 1963, the President announced the imminent signature of the Treaty of Moscow : " This treaty is not the millennium. It will not resolve all conflicts, or cause the Communists to forego their ambitions, or eliminate the danger of war. It will not reduce our need for arms or allies or programs of assistance to others. But it is an important first step — a step towards reason — a step away from war. "

Noting the public's satisfaction, the Pentagon switched its tactics. It employed retired Generals such as ex-Major General Johnson to express its point of view in new and softer terms. General Johnson foresaw no other issue than " retreat or defeat " until the leaders of the administration had " determined their goals. " He noted that the United States had treaty obligations to defend 45 nations[24] around the world,

---

22. Mainly because McNamara had gone over his head to enter into direct communication with the commanders of U.S. naval units during the Cuban crisis. In addition, the Admiral disapproved of the fact that the Defense Secretary had gone against the advice of the Navy and Air Force and awarded the TFX contract to General Dynamics rather than Boeing. The Air Force was also highly displeased with the cancellation of the Skybolt projet in May, 1962. Eisenhower had signed an agreement to supply 100 Skybolt air-to-air missiles to Great Britain, but as a result of the NATO crisis, Kennedy decided to cancel this project, which he considered too costly and superfluous.

23. On July 30, Admiral Anderson was named Ambassador to Portugal, " a maritime country, a country of great importance in the year 1963 and the years to come ", in the words of the President. Before he took up his post, the Admiral made the headlines again by declaring that things were going badly at the Pentagon and recommending that the members of the Joint Chiefs of Staff be appointed for a period of 4 years rather than 2. Kennedy refused, and the Admiral departed for Lisbon, where Lyndon Johnson left him.

24. Canada, Iceland, Denmark, Norway, West Germany, Belgium, Netherlands, Luxembourg, United Kingdom, France, Portugal, Italy, Greece, Turkey, Iran, Pakistan, Haiti, Costa Rica, Dominican Republic, Panama, Venezuela, Ecuador, Colombia, Peru, Bolivia, Paraguay, Brazil, Chile, Argentina, Uruguay, Nicaragua, El Salvador, Guatemala, Mexico, Honduras, Australia, New Zealand, Philippines, Thailand, Formosa, Japan, South Korea, Cambodia, Laos, South Vietnam, etc.

and that the country needed not only to continue the Cold War, but to " win the hot war " if it should occur. He expressed his regret that at no spot in the world was the nation taking the initiative, not even in Cuba, where every month that passed saw Castro more deeply entrenched in power. He remarked that the size of the army had decreased by more than a million men since the end of the Korean War. He estimated that an invasion of Cuba alone would require 22 divisions, more than there were stationed on U.S. soil, and concluded that the United States was not prepared for either a very limited (such as Vietnam)[25] or a limited war (such as Cuba or Berlin). He acknowledged that the United States was relatively well " covered " for a total war, with stocks of 40,000 nuclear weapons of 30 different types which were very costly to maintain, but that as the " civilians in government continue to place their faith in talk ", the utility of this atomic arsenal was yet to be proved. The ex-Major General frankly admitted that he was afraid the industrialists " would not be satisfied with the indefinite maintenance of this atomic stock-pile. "

To the latter, the Kennedy administration replied that dis-armament would be limited and progressive, and that the reductions would be partially compensated by civilian uses for the atom and the space programs of NASA. It added that it planned to fight the consequences of too rapid a conversion of the economy by reinforcing unemployment insurance, increas-ing information about new employment opportunities, orga-nizing vocational re-training programs, establishing new indus-tries, and re-orienting research programs towards chemistry, space exploration, illness, urban transportation, construction, education, water purification, population control, tropical diseases and the exploitation of ocean resources.

But this program would be long in getting started, and it would not be enough. The critics of the administration predict-ed a recession : consumers were burdened by their credit obligations, international competition was becoming tougher, and the dollar remained weak. Peace brought with it the risk of serious perturbations, if not a reversal, of the economy.[26] Already in 1962, when Republic Aviation threatened to close its Long Island plant, putting 20 000 people out of work, the President had released $ 1.3 billion of the defense funds voted

by Congress, although the Air Force and the House Armed
Forces Committee had requested $10 billion.

On March 30, 1963, McNamara decided to close 52 military installations located in 25 different states, plus 21 bases
overseas. This reorganization was to be spread over a three-
year period. His announcement had important repercussions
throughout the country. The merchants of Del Rio, Texas
contributed $50 apiece to send a delegation to Washington to
protest the closure of Laughlin Air Force Base. The delegates
pointed out that the base was the only important industry in
Del Rio (18,612 inhabitants), that the military and civilian
salaries paid by the base totalled $ 10.5 million per year, and
that 1,700 families from the base did their shopping in Del
Rio.

At Benecia, California (6 000 inhabitants), the town council
learned that the military depot there was to be closed. It

---

25. This, of course, was in 1962. At that time General Har-
kins was predicting that the Vietnam war would be won by the
end of the following year and described the local opposition as
made up of " neutralist intellectuals and a few members of the
Vietcong. "

26. Eight months earlier, the U.S. Arms Control and Disarmament Agency had published its predictions of what would
happen to the economy if the Cold War should end. It forecast
an increase in military expenditures until 1965, followed by a
progressive but important reduction until 1977 :

1962-63	1963-64	1964-65	1968-69	1971-72	1974-75	1977-78
$ 52.7	$ 54.0	$ 56.1	$ 38.9	$ 27.0	$ 17.3	$ 10.2

(in billions of dollars per fiscal year)

In 17 years, the share of the budget devoted to airplane
construction would drop from $ 6.9 to $ 0.5 billion. The amount
spent for missiles would drop from $ 5.1 to $ 0.1 billion, the
military space program would be reduced from $ 0.5 to $ 0.0
billion, naval construction would drop from $ 1.9 to $ 0.2
billion, and the amount spent on various other equipment would
decrease from $ 3.6 to $ 0.7 billion (*Economic Impact of
Disarmament*, 1962).

In February, 1962, the magazine *U.S. News and World Report*
published a chart showing the percentage of military contracts in
industrial sales. For aviation and aeronautical equipment, this
percentage was 94 %, for naval contruction 61 %, for radio and
telecommunications equipment 38 %, for electrical equipment
21 %, for iron and steel 10 %, and for oil 10 %.

estimated that the town stood to lose more than $200 000 a year in sales taxes, gasoline and liquor sales, as well as the business of the 2,400 employees of the depot, while the sewage system had just been renovated at a cost of $ 1.6 million. Representative John Baldwin (Republican) protested to Washington, pointing out that the Benecia depot was the very type of military installation that the country needed if it was to have (as Kennedy had promised) a trained army capable of facing up to any situation.

At Tacoma, Washington, a shoe salesman had just sold a pair of shoes. The customer handed him a $20 bill and a leaflet that stated, " *You have just made a sale to an employee of the Mount Rainier depot. How much money will you lose when the $14 million in salaries paid by the depot is transferred to Utah? Write to your Congressman, to your Senator, to your Governor.* " And America wrote.

In addition to the three and a half million people directly employed by the Defense Department[27], seven and a half million others owed their jobs to defense contracts. The consequences of disarmament would affect the entire country. Studies made by the U.S. Disarmament Control Commission revealed that national defense industries accounted for more than 10 % of the total national product, and employed nearly 10 % of all the workers in the country. An annual reduction of $ 5 billion in the military program might slow down the national economy by $ 10 or $ 12 billion a year.[28]

---

27. 4,600,000 in 1968.

28. California, Texas, Florida, Alaska, Hawaii, the District of Columbia, New Mexico, New Hampshire, Georgia, Alabama, Oklahoma, Maryland, New York State, Ohio, New Jersey and Massachusetts would not be the only states to suffer. Defense manufacturing accounted for 30 % of all factory jobs in Kansas, 28 % in the District of Columbia, 24 % in New Mexico, 23 % in California, 21 % in Connecticut and Arizona, 20 % in Utah, 18 % in Colorado, 14 % in Florida, 12 % in Maryland, and 10 % in Missouri and Texas. Ten states accounted for two-thirds of all military contracts (for a total of $ 17 billion) : California $ 5.8 billion, New York $ 2.5 billion, Ohio $ 1.3 billion, New Jersey $ 1.2 billion, Massachusetts, Texas, Washington and Connecticut $ 1.1 billion each, Pennsylvania $ 0.9 billion, and Missouri $ 0.7 billion.

The President of Standard Oil of California, the company most directly concerned by the Korean War, had declared in 1953 : " Two kinds of peace can be envisaged. One would enable the United States to continue its rearmament and to maintain important military forces in the Far East ; it would have very little effect on industry, since the maintenance of a peace-time army requires almost as much oil as in time of war. But if there should be a great improvement in the relations between the United States and the Soviet Union, and in particular a disarmament agreement, the blow to the oil industry and the rest of the economy would be terrific. "

Neither the industrialists nor the military were prepared in 1963 to bow before political, or simple reasonable, decisions. The Generals realized that the test ban treaty constituted a step towards general disarmament. General Thomas D. White, former head of the Army chiefs of Staff, remarked, " *True security lies in unlimited nuclear superiority.* " Admiral Lewis Strauss added, " *I'm not sure it's necessarily a good thing to cut down on tensions.* " Admiral Radford, former head of the Joint Chiefs of Staff, declared, " *I join with all my former colleagues in expressing my anxiety concerning our future security.* " General Thomas Power, Commander of the Strategic Air Command, even attacked the test ban treaty before the Senate Armed Services Committee.

On April 4, 1962, General Walker testified before the committee. As he left the hearing room, journalist Tom Kelly of the Washington *Daily News* asked if he had any comment. The General's reply was a punch in the nose.

9

Businessmen

...the President's action points inevitably to a federal dictatorship over business.

DAVID LAWRENCE, *U.S. News and World Report*

The American people will find it hard, as I do, to accept a situation in which a tiny handful of steel executives whose pursuit of private power and profit exceeds their sense of public responsibility can show such utter contempt for the interests of 185 million Americans.

PRESIDENT KENNEDY, April 11, 1962

Engraved over the entrance to the Business School of Columbia University is a motto which exhorts the nation's businessmen to a " high sense of duty. "

Since the death of Roosevelt, whose very name they re-

149

viled[1], the businessmen had been left to their own devices. Truman and Eisenhower had been modest petty bourgeois, and Nixon would certainly have followed in their footsteps. The businessmen were wary of President Kennedy, who as a young Senator from Massachusetts had opposed the Taft-Hartley law and neglected the industrialists of his state. Kennedy did not regard profitmaking as the most esteemed of vocations. Brought up in a family of millionnaires and a millionnaire himself, he was not impressed by other millionnaires, nor did he consider the successful businessman the most admirable of beings. He liked to quote from Dr. Johnson : " A merchant's desire is not of glory but of gain ; not of public wealth, but of private emulument ; he is therefore rarely to be consulted on questions of war or peace, or any designs of wide extent and distant consequence. " He was well aware of their power, but he did not trust the Titans. When he became President he declared, " Taken individually, labor leaders are often mediocre and egotistical, but labor as a whole generally adopts intelligent positions on important problems. On the other hand, businessmen are often individually enlightened but collectively hopeless in the field of national policy. "

Eisenhower sought out the Titans, respected their advice, and treated them as they thought they deserved to be treated — in other words, as representatives of the most influential body in the nation. Kennedy kept his distance. Prior to his election he had had little contact with industrial circles, and once he was in the White House he saw even less of them. Businessmen were generally excluded from the Kennedys' private parties. Not only did he " snub " them (in the words of Ralph Cordiner, President of General Electric), he also attacked them. Kennedy did not consult the business world before making his appointments. The men he placed at the head of the federal regulatory agencies were entirely new.[2] Since the end of the war, the businessmen had become accustomed to considering these bodies as adjuncts of their own professional associations. They were more indignant than surprised. They attempted to intervene, but in vain. The President had a mind of his own.

In January, 1961, the nation seemed stable and prosperous.

The economy was suffering from a slight recession, but the level of unemployment was considered acceptable[3]. But in his first State of the Union Message on January 30, Kennedy spoke of the changes needed in terms that seemed to echo the words of Franklin D. Roosevelt as he inaugurated the New Deal, at a time when the economy of the United States had struck bottom and the Titans were nearly asphyxiated. " The present state of our national economy is disturbing ", he began. He called for " urgent increases in federal expenditures in the fields of housing, urban renewal, school construction, medical research, and juvenile delinquency. He proposed a new plan for the economic, social and cultural development of foreign countries.

The President's policy towards Latin America alarmed the businessmen even more than it worried the Pentagon and the diplomatists. The business world foresaw the economic consequences of the President's foreign policies. In *Strategy of Peace*, he had written :

" Just as we must recall our own revolutionary past in order to understand the spirit and the significance of the anticolonialist uprisings in Asia and Africa, we should now reread the life of Simon Bolivar, the great ' Liberator ' of South America... in order to comprehend the new contagion for liberty and reform now spreading south of our borders...

" Fidel Castro is part of the legacy of Bolivar, who led his men over the Andes Mountains, vowing ' war to the death ' against Spanish rule, saying, ' Where a goat can pass, so can an army '. Castro is also part of the frustation of that earlier revolution which won its war against Spain but left largely

---

1. In 1902, Teddy Roosevelt had designated the Administration (later to become the Pentagon), the lobbyists, and organized finance as " public enemies of the nation ". Franklin D. Roosevelt declared that " Private enterprise is a public service. "

2. William Cary was appointed to head the Securities and Exchange Commission, Newton Minow as Chairman of the Federal Communications Commission, Frank McGulloch to the National Labor Relations Board, Joseph Swidler to the Federal Power Commission, and Paul R. Dixon as Chairman of the Federal Trade Commission.

3. 3.9 million unemployed in 1960 ; 4 million in 1961.

untouched the indigenous feudal order...

" But Cuba is not an isolated case. We can still show our concern for liberty and our opposition to the status quo in our relations with the other Latin American dictators who now, or in the future, try to suppress their people's aspirations. "

Later he added, " Our differences with Cuba do not concern the impulse that drives the people of this country toward a better life. The economic and social reforms undertaken in Cuba must be encouraged.

One of his closest advisers, historian Arthur Schlesinger, wrote : " All across Latin America the ancient oligarchies — landholders, Church and Army — are losing their grip. There is a groundswell of inarticulate mass dissatisfaction on the part of peons, Indians, miners, plantation workers, factory hands, classes held down past all endurance and now approaching a state of revolt. "

Near Recife, Schlesinger had seen poverty-stricken villages full of starving children covered with scabs. He recalled that before Castro came to power Havana had been nothing but a giant casino and brothel for American businessmen over for a big weekend. " My fellow countrymen reeled through the streets, picking up fourteen-year-old Cuban girls and tossing coins to make men scramble in the gutter "[4], he wrote.

The policies of the President and his advisers were certain to have economic repercussions. In April, 1962, a year after the inauguration of the Alliance for Progress, Latin America, in the eyes of the conservatives, appeared headed for chaos. In Argentina, President Frondizi had just been overthrown by a military coup, and rioting had broken out in Guatemala and Ecuador. There was no country to the South that could be considered politically and economically stable.[5] Capital flowed back into the United States, frightened by the spectre of castroist revolution.

But the effect on the American economy threatened to be even worse. The businessmen could not accept concepts like those of Schlesinger, who declared that the essential thing was not, as Nixon had suggested, to stimulate the cosmetics industry[6], but to build hospitals and to invest in sectors that affected the strength of the nation and the welfare of the people.

Kennedy and his team called themselves " liberals ", but

the most intelligent of their adversaries, like economist Milton Friedman, questioned their right to use this term. " As a supreme, if unintended compliment, the enemies of the system of private enterprise have thought it wise to appropriate its label ", Friedman wrote.

To his adversaries, President Kennedy's economic policies appeared to be inspired entirely by a concern for public welfare to which they were fundamentally opposed. They quoted the words of Jefferson, " The government is best which governs least. " Many of them preferred the freedom to make a million or go bankrupt to the governmental planning and regulation that diminished the range of these alternatives. Senator Barry Goldwater was a good example of this mentality. The little people considered the cowboy-grocer as one of their own, and the big men knew that, regardless of his political destiny, they had nothing to fear from him. For Goldwater, a General in the Air Force Reserve, intelligence was nothing but the " *extremism of imbeciles* ". Turning his back on this kind of extremism, Goldwater expressed himself in vague definitions of the great problems of the day, asserting that unemployment was but " *an excuse for the lazy* ", and the government " *the end of individualism* ". But he turned serious when he wrote : " Welfare is a private concern... The current instrument of collectivism is the Welfare State. The

4. On August 16, 1961, Richard Goodwin, another of Kennedy's advisers, met at Montevideo with Ernesto " Che " Guevara, then " czar " of the Cuban economy.

The late journalist Lisa Howard was in the process of arranging a meeting between Bob Kennedy and Guevara at the time of President Kennedy's assassination.

5. In April of 1962, *U.S. News and World Report* published a round-up of the Latin American situation which concluded, " Clearly, after one year of the Alliance for Progress, Latin America is in worse trouble than it was before the program started. Experts warn that the situation will get worse before it gets better.

6. Since 1964, the cosmetics industry has expanded rapidly. Between 1964 and 1967, Avon Products, with 190 different branches, tripled its international sales. In 1966, the combined profits of its American and International Divisions totalled $ 55.5 million, or 13.5 % of its turnover ($ 408 million).

collectivists have finally realized that it is possible to institute socialism through a policy of welfare as well as by national-ization. Welfare socialism is much more difficult to combat. It takes an individual and changes him from a spiritual creature, proud, hardworking and independent, into a depen-dent and animal creature.

" We must reject this false notion that Communism is brought about by poverty, illness, and other similar social or economic conditions. Communism is brought about by the communists, and by them alone. Communism is internat-ional conspiracy, and its goal is to re-establish slavery through-out the earth.

" The advent of a reign of freedom, justice, peace and prosperity is impossible until Communism has been defeated. The victory over Communism must be the principal and immediate goal of American policy. All other objectives are secondary. We must take the offensive. American civilization is man's greatest achievement in the history of the world...

" In *Strategy of Peace*, Kennedy actually described Fidel Castro as the ' heir of Bolivar, the great liberator of South America '... the same Bolivar who led his men across the Andes after declaring all-out war on Spain. We must fight Communist subversion throughout the Western Hemisphere, within our borders as well as in Central and South America, with all the weapons at our disposal. It is inconceivable that Castro, that show-off puppet, that lackey of Kennedy be allowed to make fun of us and jeer at our freedom only a few minutes ' flying time from our closest city... Financial circles have been deeply disturbed by the recent events in Guate-mala, Bolivia, and particularly in Cuba...

" In the last analysis, the choice is not between surrender or nuclear war. It is between winning or fighting a nuclear war. We must cut out extravagant and useless domestic prog-rams and stop wasting our money on utopian foreign aid projects "

As if in answer, Kennedy declared on March 13 : " For the first time we have the capacity to strike off the remaining bonds of poverty and ignorance — to free our people for the spiritual and intellectual fulfillment which has always been the goal of our civilization...

" This political freedom must be accompanied by social

change. For unless necessary social reforms, including land
and tax reform, are freely made — unless we broaden the
opportunities for all our people — unless the great mass of
Americans share in increasing prosperity — then our alliance,
our revolution, our dream, and our freedom will fail. But we
call for social change by free men — change in the spirit of
Washington and Jefferson, of Bolivar and San Martin and
Martin — not change which seeks to impose on men tyran-
nies which we cast out a century and a half ago. Our motto is
what it has always been — progress yes, tyranny no —
progreso si, tirania no ! "

Caracas[7] and then Bogota gave the President of the United
States a warm welcome. In Mexico in June, 1962, he paid
tribute to the Mexican revolution, and in March, 1963 in
Costa Rica he defended the rights of the peasants to land and
an education and called for an end to " the ancient institutions that perpetuate privileges. " His enemies saw the Kennedy Administration as the ally of the " agitating popular
forces " of the continent south of the border, " working
towards progress and a better life for the masses by evolution
if possible, or by revolution if that is the price that must be
paid. "[8]

Revolution ! Many people thought that it had already invested
the White House, despite the reassurances of the President.
On February 13, 1961, he told the National Industrial Conference Board : " There is no inevitable clash between the
public and private sectors — or between investment and
consumption — nor, as I have said, between Government and
business. All elements in our national economic growth are
interdependent. Each must play its proper role — and that is
the hope and the aim of this administration...

" We will not discriminate for or against any segment of
our society, or any segment of the business community. We

---

7. Where rocks and tomatoes had been thrown at Nixon in
1958.

8. On November 16, 1963, Argentinian President Illia cancelled the agreements signed with foreign oil companies in 1958
and 1959.

are vigorously opposed to corruption and monopoly and human exploitation — but we are not opposed to business. We know that your success and ours are intertwined — that you have facts and knowledge that we need. Whatever past differences may have existed, we seek more than an attitude of truce, more than a treaty — we seek the spirit of a full-fledged alliance. "

His tone annoyed his business audience, who thought they perceived a hint of paternalism, and who were somewhat less than eager to cooperate with the federal government. The Business Advisory Council discontinued its meetings and decided to break off relations with the Commerce Department. The members of the Council noted uneasily that the Kennedy virus had spread to Commerce Secretary Luther Hodges, a man they had thought they could count on.

The Democrats had inherited a rather mediocre economic situation from the Eisenhower Administration. 1961 was not a very good year. True, the national income had increased 19.6 % between 1958-1961 as compared with its 1954-1957 level, corporate sales had risen 18.7 %, and salaries had climbed 18.9 %. But the prosperity of an economy is written in the balance sheet, and during the same period business profits had risen only 3.3 % after taxes.[9] Critics also noted that the federal and state governments were steadily expanding, and that their expenditures equalled one-third of the gross national product.[10] Retail prices had remained stable, and wholesale

---

9. In 1961 the gross national product, which had grown by 4 % in 1960, increased by only 3.3 %, but rose to 68 % in 1962.

10. In 1963, one out of every six workers was employed by Washington or the state governments. These governments absorbed 35 % of the gross national product (but Kennedy's critics forgot to add that there were 2,548,000 federal employees, as compared to 7,188,9000 in the state and local governments).

11. Retail Price Index :
1960 : 100.7
1961 : 100.3
1962 : 100.6
1963 : 100.3

12. A comparison between the earnings of 515 top businessmen in 1960 and 1961 revealed an increase in income for 243 and a decrease for 161. 71 reported no change. Frederick G.

prices had dropped 1 %[11], but the personal incomes of some
of the Titans had also dropped.[12]

Things looked better at the beginning of 1962. The automobile industry, the economic thermometer of the nation,
predicted an annual sales figure of 7 million cars, an increase
of 1,500,000 over the previous year.[13] 1962 promised more
than a recovery and less than a boom. In January Bradford B.
Smith, an economist for U.S. Steel, told the National Industrial Conference Board, " I have said to this group many
times that as the nation goes, so goes the steel industry, only
twice as fast. I would say the steel production in the first half
of 1962 could look pretty good. "

A month later, however, Roger Blough, Chairman of U.S.
Steel[14], noted that overall industrial profits, which should have
reached the figure of $ 35 billion in 1961[15], were only $ 23
billion, and added that over the past three years hourly
salaries in the steel industry had increased 40 cents (between
12 and 13 %), while profits had been the poorest ever

Donner, Chairman of General Motors, with gross earnings of
$ 557.725 (including $ 405.324 in taxes) earned $ 16,300 less
(before taxes). J.W. Schwab, Chairman of United Merchants and
Manufacturers Textile, earned $ 384,505 in 1960 and $ 324,400
in 1961. In the steel industry, Thomas E. Millsop, President
(later Chairman) of National Steel, earned $ 285,100 in 1960
and $ 260,100 in 1961. Roger W. Blough, Chairman of U.S.
Steel, earned $ 283,333 in 1960 and $ 300,000 in 1961 (all of
these figures indicate income before taxes. Mr. Blough received
$ 3,000 of his 1960-1 increase ; the remaining $ 13,000 went
for taxes).

13. Automobile sales :
1960 : 6,675,000
1961 : 5,543,000
1962 : 6,933, 000

14. The largest steel corporation in the world. In 1966 it
produced 29 million tons of steel.

15. Mr. Blough based this figure on 1947 statistics, a questionable procedure at best. He might also have noted that profits
during the Eisenhower administration had hardly moved at all :
$ 22.8 billion in 1950, $ 23.0 billion in 1955, $ 22.7 billion in
1960, $ 23.3 billion in 1961, and that they had climbed to
$ 25.9 billion the first year the results of the Kennedy administra-
tion were felt.

recorded in the history of steel. In 1961, 85 % of these profits, he claimed, had been used to pay dividends. He declared that an economy should not be judged solely by its prices, which always depend on costs, but rather by the comparative level of costs and profits. Blough told *U.S. News and World Report* that the President might understand businessmen, but that he certainly didn't like them. He recalled that President Kennedy had sent a letter to steel industry leaders in September, 1961 warning them against any increase in prices. " The steel industry, in·short, can look forward to good profits, without an increase in prices. Since 1947, iron and steel common stock prices have risen 397 % ; this is much better performance than common stock prices in general ", the President had written.

On April 6, 1962, the Steelworkers Union agreed, at the request of the federal government, to limit its wage demands to a 10-cent-an-hour increase beginning on July 1, 1962.[16] On April 10, the steel industry announced a price increase of $ 6 a ton[17], placing the President, the consumers, and the unions before the *fait accompli*. In the course of its history, the steel industry had often defied American Presidents, but it had forgotten what it was like to be thwarted. The following day at his press conference, the President declared : " ...the American people will find it hard, as I do, to accept a situation in which a tiny handful of steel executives whose pursuit of private power and profit exceeds their sense of public responsibility can show such utter contempt for the interests of 185 million Americans. "

This denunciation of the Titans stunned the nation. It marked the birth of a legend. The President's remarks made headlines throughout the world and were even quoted in *Pravda*, which expressed its surprise and satisfaction. The businessmen were disconcerted by the violence of his reaction and by the apparent extent of his public support, but Roger Blough maintained that his decision had been made " in the interest of the stockholders " and that the profits of the largest steel producers were 33 % lower in the first quarter of 1962 than they had been in 1959.[18]

The administration replied that the dividends paid to the stockholders of the steel corporations in 1958-61 were 17 % higher than those paid in 1954-57. The steel industry rejoined that profits had exceeded $ 1 billion in 1959, but that they had fallen to $ 807 million in 1961, endangering investment possibilities, the future of the steel corporations, and consequently the future of American industry. But, faced with FBI investigations, the pressure of public opinion, and the cancellation of government contracts, it yielded and revoked the increase.[19]

On May 7, 1962, *U.S. News and World Report wrote : " What happened is frightening not only to steel people but to industry generally... President Kennedy had the public interest at heart in acting as he did, but the results may not in the long run be what he intended them to be. "*

The following day at Atlantic City, speaking before the United Auto Workers Convention, Kennedy declared : " This administration has not undertaken and will not undertake to fix prices and wages in this economy. We have no intention of intervening in every labor dispute. We can suggest guidelines for the economy, but we cannot fix a single pattern for every plant and every industry... This is a competitive economy...

---

16. David McDonald, President of the Steelworkers Union, declared that the cost of steel production had decreased by 1 % since 1958.

17. This represented an increase of 3.5 %, while the 10-cent-an-hour wage increase represented a rise of only 2.4 %. The administration claimed that the price increase would cost the Pentagon $ 1 billion (Mr. Blough lowered this figure to $ 20 million). Blough added that profits per ton of steel had dropped from $ 12.19 in 1958 to $ 79.70 in 1961.

18. Effects of the crisis on the revenue and the number of persons employed by U.S. Steel from 1960 to 1965 :

Employees	Revenue
1960 : 225,081	$ 600,500,000
1961 : 199,243	$ 387,096,059
1962 : 199,044	$ 337,403,081
1963 : 187,721	$ 410,069,357
1964 : 199,979	$ 493,388,130
1965 : 208,838	$ 550,384,380

19. Comparative profits of American industry as a whole and the steel industry were as follows :

	1947	1950	1955	1959	1961
Industry as a whole	15.1 %	15 %	12.3 %	10.2 %	8.7 %
Steel Industry	11.7 %	13.8 %	13.1 %	8.0 %	6.1 %

We believe it has served us well, the free enterprise system. "

The preceding day, May 7, Roger Blough had told the stockholders of U.S. Steel : " *This concept is as incomprehensible to me as the belief that Government can ever serve the national interest in peacetime by seeking to control prices in competitive American business, directly or indirectly through force of law or otherwise.* " And he added that since 1950 wages had doubled, revenues from taxes on business had increased by 68 %, the profits of storeowners and farmers had risen by 70 %, while corporation profits had only increased by 2 %. He remarked that in recent years the prices of many industrial products had increased, and that he did not see why there should be any discrimination against steel.

Replying to President Kennedy's remarks at Atlantic City on May I, Walter Reuther, President of the United Auto Workers, declared that what the economy needed was " to increase demand, and therefore salaries. " That same day Dr. Charles E. Walker, Executive Vice President of the American Bankers Association, made a speech at New Brunswick attacking increased federal expenditures and the concepts of the President's economic advisers.

May 28, 1962 was the blackest day on Wall Street since the 1929 crash. Steel holdings fell to 50 % of their 1960 level. " *This could become total war* ", declared Avery C. Adams, Chairman of Jones and Laughlin Steel, to the stockholders of his company. The unions began to wonder whether the consequences of the President's intervention might not prove more serious for them than for the corporations.[20] Allan Sproul, ex-President of the Federal Reserve Bank of New York, declared that " although there was no panic by stockholders after the stockmarket crash of May 28, 1962, another May 28 might have different consequences .[21]

In July, 1962, the steel industry at Pittsburgh was working at only 55 % of capacity, as compared to 70 % in April. The steel companies noted that this crisis hit them just when they were faced with competition from foreign producers favored by lower costs and cheaper labor, and from related industries (plastics, aluminium, cement, glass, wood) that were becoming more and more diversified and more and more powerful. One of the paradoxes in the arguments of certain businessmen was the fact that, while rejecting any notion of federal intervention in their affairs, they called for greater protection against foreign competition.[22]

Business reaction was unanimous. Ralph Cordiner, President of General Electric, declared that Kennedy ought to reread his Lincoln[23], and David Lawrence[24] wrote :

" *The heavy hand of government has just won a pyrrhic victory... Economic facts cannot be changed merely because politicians dislike them. Nor can America's private enterprise system survive very long if the Federal Government itself engages in the mudslinging of class warfare and, in effect, tells an industry it must disregard profits, disregard dividends, and pay labor whatever the Administration says shall be paid even if, as in this case, it costs the industry an additional $ 100*

---

20. In 1961, there had already been 64,500 job cuts in the steel industry.

21. On December 26, 1962, the stockmarket situation was as follows (as compared with the preceding year) :
Greatest rise
international oil (up 13.2 %)
shipping (up 12.3 %)
Greatest drop
vending machines (down 50.6 %)
cigarettes (down 43.3 %)
speciality machinery (down steel (down 35.9 %)
Other notable drops
motion pictures (down 33.0 %)
food chains (down 30.9 %)
publishing (down 0.8 %)
tires, rubber goods (down 27.3 %)
electronics (down 25.7 %)

22. A true market economy, as defined by Milton Friedman, suffers as much from the interior and exterior protectionism of many industrial leaders as from governmental controls and restrictions. But, as Galbraith notes, Friedman is a romantic, and his concepts are far removed from those of the true conservatives.

23. Lincoln had declared before Congress on December 3, 1861 :

" Labor is prior to and independent of capital. Capital is only the fruit of labor and could never have existed if labor had not first existed. Labor is the superior of capital, and deserves much the higher consideration. Capital has its rights, which are as worthy of protection as any other rights. "

24. Editor of *U.S. News and World Report*, April 23, 1962.

million a year.

" *Apparently (Mr. Kennedy) believed that the Administration could coerce the industry into submission. For what else was meant by Mr. Kennedy's statement that the 'Department of Justice and the Federal Trade Commission are examining the significance of this action in a free, competitive economy ?... This implied a threat of criminal prosecution. It was a move designed to terrorize those who disagreed with the Administration... While denying any inclination toward state socialism, the President's action on steel prices points inevitably to a federal dictatorship over business. "*

And he concluded, " *Socialism (is) often a forerunner of Communism. "*

Analyzing the battle underway, Richard E. 'Neustadt[25] wrote, " As far as I can observe it from abroad, the steel case was a classic demonstration of two things : of the tenuousness and uncertainty of presidential power — one might almost say the weakness of the President's position — coupled with almost incredible political naivete on the part of the U.S. Steel Corporation. "

Some months later, Kennedy explained his reaction :

" I think it would have been a serious situation if I had not attempted with all my influence to try to get a rollback, because there was an issue of good faith involved. The steel union had accepted the most limited settlement that they had since the end of the second war... in part, I think, because I said that we could not afford another inflationary spiral, that it would affect our competitive position abroad, so they signed up. Then, when their last contract was signed... steel put its prices up immediately. It seemed to me that the question of good faith was involved, and that if I had not attempted... to use my influence to have the companies hold their prices stable, I think the union could have rightfully felt that they had been misled. In my opinion it would have endangered the whole bargaining between labor and management, which would have made it impossible for us to exert any influence from the public point of view in the future on these great labor-management disputes which do affect the public interest. "

In June, 1962, at the height of the crisis, business circles in the United States were much more concerned about the

President's style and personality than by the decline in the stock market, which it knew to be artificial, or the state of the economy, which it considered hopeful.[26] Kennedy's speech at Yale[27] on June 11 confirmed the worst fears of the businessmen :

" The great enemy of the truth is very often not the lie — deliberate, contrived, and dishonest — but the myth — persistent, persuasive, and unrealistic. Too often we hold fast to the cliches of our forebears. We subject all facts to a prefabricated set of interpretations. We enjoy the comfort of opinion without the discomfort of thought...

" We cannot understand and attack our contemporary problems in 1962 if we are touched by traditional labels and wornout slogans of an earlier era. But the unfortunate fact of the matter is that our rhetoric has not kept pace with the speed of social and economic change. Our political debates, our public discourse — on current domestic and economic issues — too often bear little or no relation to the actual problems the United States faces...

" (These problems) cannot be solved by incantations from the forgotten past. But the example of Western Europe [28] shows that they are capable of solution — that governments, and many of them conservative governments, prepared to face technical problems without ideological preconceptions, can coordinate the elements of a national economy and bring

---

25. Columbia University professor and author of the book *Presidential Power, the Politics of Leadership.*

26. The expansion had resumed in March, 1962, then slowed down in the second quarter and stopped in the third, but a new expansion was forecast for the month of October, and the forecasts proved correct.

27. When Kennedy returned to New Haven on October 19, 1962, at the height of the Cuban crisis, a group of Yale students greeted him with a sign that read, " Be more courageous and less photogenic. "

28. Here, the President was praising the interventionism and even the state socialism of European countries such as Great Britain, France, Italy and Sweden.

about growth and prosperity...

" Some conversations I have heard in our own country sound like old records, long-playing, left over from the middle thirties. The debate of the thirties had its great significance and produced great results, but it took place in a different world with different needs and different tasks. It is our responsibility to live in our own world, and to identify the needs and discharge the tasks of the 1960's...

." Nearly 150 years ago, Thomas Jefferson wrote, ' The new circumstances under which we are placed call for new words, new phrases, and for the transfer of old words to new objects. ' New words, new phrases, and for the transfer of old words to new objects — it is truer today than it was in the time of Jefferson, because the role of this country is so vastly more significant... As we work in consonance to meet the authentic problems of our times, we will generate a vision and an energy which will demonstrate anew to the world the superior vitality and the strength of the free society. "

This was a serious seech. Not only did he attack the Titans, but also those of his fellow-citizens who took pride in their traditional stereotypes, their worn-out slogans, their old records, their ancestral cliches, their imaginary problems, and their prefabricated interpretations, and of whom Kennedy said that they were 150 years behind and understood nothing of the real problems of their times.

It was already late when he announced on television on August 13 that since he had entered the White House the gross national product had increased by 10 %, industrial production had risen 16 %, disposable personal income had gone up 8 % ($ 30 billion), the unemployment rate had dropped by 1 million, and that in Carbon County, Pennsylvania, George Demart, aged 52, was finally able to support his family. He added that corporate profits had risen 26 %, but those concerned were probably no longer listening when he concluded :

" We have to move ahead, and I know that there are those who oppose all these moves as they opposed moves in other days much as they opposed a ban on child labor and, more recently in the Senate, medical care for the elderly.

" This country would still be in the dark ages economically
if we permitted these opponents of progress and defenders of
special privileges to veto every forward move. But the President of the United States, I believe, and the Congress and
all of us must be committed to action in our time. "

The fever fell somewhat in the fall. Business was good, and
1963 looked better still. The increase in federal expenditures,
defense contracts, and urban renewal projects acted as a
stimulus on the economy. But businessmen remained pessimistic and distrustful. At the American Bankers Association
Convention at Atlantic City on September 23-26, 1962, it was
predicted that automobile production would drop by 500,000
units in 1963.[29] Most financial experts in New York and
Chicago warned of a new recession.

There was no recession. On the contrary, the United States
was in the midst of an industrial expansion.[30] But the federal
government remained vigilant. In July, 1962, it had protested
to the banks, which were predicting inflation and deforming
the financial market. In November it denounced unjustified
price increases in the pharmaceutical industry. In 1963, its
antitrust suits multiplied.

The tendency towards corporate mergers was accentuating.[31]
Pursuing its traditional anti-trust role, the Justice Department
opened investigations into price-fixing conspiracies and other

---

29. Instead, it rose by 705,000.

30. In 1960, the gross national product was $ 502.6 billion. In
1961 it rose to $ 518.7 billion, in 1962 to $ 556.2 billion,
and by 1963 it had reached $ 583.9 billion.

The incomes of most of the nation's top businessmen rose in
1962 : F.G. Donner climbed to $ 643.975 a year and J.W.
Schwab to $ 367,613, but steel industry leaders weren't so
fortunate. Roger Blough remained at $ 300,000, and Thomas E.
Millsop dropped from the list of those earning more than
250,000 a year.

31. There were 1,400 mergers in the first half of 1967.

John Kenneth Galbraith believes that anti-trust procedures
should be invoked not only against General Motors (which
controls 54.5 % of the market), but also against the Ford Motor
Company, the big oil companies, U.S. Steel, General Electric,
and several other large corporations.

illegal activities. This action brought positive results (prices of electrical equipment dropped 30 %), but it infuriated industry. " Mergers arouse acute suspicion of the Government's trustbusters ", wrote *U.S. News and World Report.*[32]

In January, the Justice Department asked a federal court to force the General Motors Corporation to dispose of its locomotive business and break up its merger with the Euclid Road Machinery Company. In a third case, it charged General Motors with monopolizing the manufacture and sale of intercity buses.

In the face of such attacks, businessmen began to ask themselves what would happen when large companies attempted to grow or diversify through mergers. Was this the end of all corporate mergers ? The Federal Trade Commission opened an inquiry into the relationships between 1,000 of the nation's largest companies. It was particularly curious about " joint ventures " and " reciprocity ", or the extent to which big companies bought from their own best customers. To what extent did a steel company order its machinery from the machinery manufacturer who regularly bought its steel ? How far did a truck manufacturer go in favoring a steel company that purchased its trucks ?

General Dynamics was ordered to dispose of a division dealing in industrial gases that it had acquired five years before, and a merger of Consolidated Foods with a firm producing dehydrated onions and garlic was broken up after the FTC charged that the food firm had required some of its suppliers to buy the products of its new division. The FTC suggested that any merger might be judged illegal if it tended to promote reciprocal business.

The government brought price-fixing charges against a long list of industries, including milk, baked goods, silver products, copper tubing, pulpwood, brass-mill products, macaroni, sewing machines, etc., and in many instances won easy victories. In 1963, the Justice Department's Antitrust Division won 45 out of 46 cases.

Big business grew more and more concerned about the tendencies of the Kennedy administration, and industrialists aren't the type of people to sit around and chew their fingernails. Employers complained that they were continually placed at a disadvantage in their relations with the labor unions, which were backed by Washington. They felt that the National Labor Relations Board had abandoned the neutral position it had occupied under Eisenhower. " *The NLRB is also affected by the spirit of crusade* ", declared Joseph L. Block, Chairman of Inland Steel. J. Mack Swigert added, " *The financial power of the unions is so great that many employers can't risk a strike* ".[33]

Kennedy stated over and over again that he was opposed to government control of salaries and prices, but his administration intervened more and more often in labor disputes. Washington appointed mediators who stressed the " public interest ", which was generally interpreted as favoring the unions. Federal pressure was exerted on numerous corporations, especially in the missile and space industry, which had not yet adopted the union shop. The regulatory commissions available to the President wielded considerable power.[34] The National Labor Relations Board ordered that workers fired for union activities, or who had lost their jobs because their employer refused to negotiate with their union, be reinstated

---

32. April 1, 1963.

33. The percentage of working time lost during the three years of the Kennedy administration was the lowest in a decade :

Eisenhower	*Kennedy*	*Johnson*
1958 : 0.22 %	1961 : 0.14 %	1964 : 0.18 %
1959 : 0.61 %	1962 : 0.16 %	1965 : 0.18 %
1960 : 0.17 %	1963 : 0.13 %	1966 : 0.19 %
		1967 : 0.30 %, or 41 million man days

34. The Interstate Commerce Commission is the oldest of these bodies, followed by the Atomic Energy Commission, the Federal Reserve System, the Export-Import Bank, the Federal Housing Administration, the Securities and Exchange Commission, the National Labor Relations Board, the Federal Trade Commission, the Federal Power Commission, the Federal Communications Commission, etc.

The Securities and Exchange Commission, which regulates the stock exchange and overseas stock market transactions, went into action on the day of President Kennedy's death. That afternoon, 6 million shares .changed hands on Wall Street, In 30 minutes, the Dow Jones average fell 21.16 points (on May 28, 1962, it had fallen 35.95 points). At 2 : 09 p.m. the Stock Exchange was closed (wich didn't prevent some people from making a killing).

with their back pay plus 6 % interest.

The businessmen feared that the federal government would somehow take control of wages[35], and their fears were voiced at the gatherings of the American Management Association, the National Association of State Labor Relations Boards, and the American Mining Congress. The Vice President for Labor Relations of the Ford Motor Company declared that the Kennedy administration appears to be " seeking some sort of halfway house between private bargaining and Government compulsion that will give it the degree of influence or control over the results that it conceives to be needed... it is prepared to go past the point of relying simply on reason and persuasion. "

Others went much further. *U.S. News and World Report* charged that " *the machinery for a true socialist economy already exists* " and quoted one financier who added, " *The pension funds give considerable room for maneuver. By acting in a certain direction, they could be used to destroy the capitalist framework.* "

1963 could be considered a good year for business. But the businessmen didn't think so. The gross national product, wages, taxes, and prices had progressed satisfactorily, but the steel industry was still working at only 50 % of capacity, and profits were lower than what businessmen thought they ought to be, and proportionally lower than what they had been in 1950.[36]

Speaking at the University of Chicago, Henry Ford declared, "How high are profits ? By any relative measure, profits are now at about the same level as they were during the 1954 recession. *Today, after 3 full years of rising prosperity for the rest of the economy, profits have finally climbed back up until they are as high as they were at their lowest point in the decade after the end of World War II. The reduction of federal income taxes is an important step in the right direction* "[37].

Industrialists noted that the growth rate of the American economy in 1963 would be the lowest of all the industrialized countries, and emphasized that this lag could have " dramatic " consequences. They forecast that the Soviet Union would have caught up with the United States in terms of industrial production by, 1975-80.

Kennedy responded to these predictions by pointing out that the exceptional growth rate of the Soviet Union was due in large part to its huge crop — three times larger than that of the United States — of students in all branches of learning, future researchers, and future technicians, and he cited this as one more reason for assuring equal educational opportunities for all students and breaking down the financial barriers surrounding the universities.[38] He was especially concerned

---

35. When, in December, 1967, U.S. Steel, followed by other producers, announced a price increase of $ 5 a ton, President Johnson stated simply that steel industry leaders had been informed of " his feelings " on the matter, and that he did not exclude the idea of government control of prices and salaries in the future. Industrial circles took this threat calmly.

At the end of July, 1968, he again permitted the steel industry to raise its prices.

36. Between · 1950 and 1955, profits averaged 3.6 % of sales. From 1955 to 1959, they averaged only 3.1 % (a drop of 14 %), and between 1960 and 1963. 2.6 % (a futher drop of 16 %).

Since 1950, while the gross national product had increased 106 %, employees' and, workers' wages 70 %, investments 90 %, taxes 56 %, prices 33 % and federal expenditures 179 %, profits (which totalled $ 23 billion in 1950) were only $ 27 billion in 1963, or $ 20.5 billion in terms of 1950 values, 10 % less than in 1950.

The dividends paid by American industrial corporations had averaged 11.4 % from 1955 to 1959. Between 1960 and 1963, they averaged only 9.4 % (a decline of 18 %).

37. The Ford Motor Company had been prosecuted in November, 1961 under the Clayton Antitrust Act for having absorbed the Electric Autolite Co. in April. The Justice Department claimed that this merger would reduce competition in the production and sales of spark plugs, noting that in 1960 Electric Autolite and General Motors had produced 90 % of the spark plugs sold in the United States.

Ford expressed its surprise and retorted that its principal competitor, General Motors, manufactured spark plugs and batteries through its subsidiary company, A.C. Sparkplugs.

38. In 1967, there were 4,000 universities or higher technical institutes in the USSR. Four million Soviet citizens attended college. Five million young workers and farmers took university correspondance courses. There were approximately 400,000 young researchers working in Soviet research centers, and the nation had nearly ten million engineers, five times more than the United States.

about unemployment : in 1963 there were 4,166,000 people out of work, as compared to 4,007,000 in 1962.[39] The businessmen were more concerned about federal deficits and expenditures.[40]

In 1962, Kennedy had elected to pursue a new economic and financial policy based on the potential gross national product.[41] To bring this potential into being, it was necessary to create " fiscal drag " — in other words, to reduce taxes on individuals and corporations. On December 14, 1962, speaking to the members of the Economic Club at the Waldorf Astoria Hotel in New York, the President upset the traditional economic thinking not only of the businessmen, but also of the members of Congress. Many Congressmen were violently opposed to any increase in federal spending, which they blamed for weakening the dollar, and considered the budget deficit as an evil in itself which should be reduced by all possible means. But Kennedy felt differently.[42] He began by reassuring them : " To increase demand and lift the economy, the Federal Government's most useful role is not to rush into a program of excessive increases in public expenditures, but to expand the incentives and opportunities for private expenditures. "

But he went on to declare, " Our practical choice is not between a tax-cut deficit and a budgetary surplus. It is between two kinds of deficits : a chronic deficit of inertia... or a temporary deficit of transition, resulting from a tax cut designed to boost the economy, increase tax revenues, and achieve... a budget surplus. "

The President planned to apply P.P.B.S., which had been used so successfully at the Defense Department, to the federal budget[43], but in 1963 the primary problem was that of balancing the budget. Kennedy proposed a Keynesian program of budgetary deficit designed to encourage economic expansion.[44] This classic plan consisted of alleviating fiscal pressure without a corresponding decrease in public expenditures. A tax cut, investment tax credit, and a simultaneous increase in public spending would increase demand and stimulate consumption.

On January 17, 1963, President Kennedy presented both his 1963 budget and his proposals for a tax cut and tax reform to Congress. Senator Harry F. Byrd and Representative Wilbur D. Mills, respectively chairman of the Senate Finance Committee and the House Ways and Means Committee, voiced their opposition to the plan. " Power feeds on power. Big government is too big "[45], said Senator Byrd, who

---

39. The Council of Economic Advisers (Walter Heller, John P. Lewis and Gardner Ackley) did not believe that unemployment was structural (the result of technological advances), and could therefore be cured by adapting the workers to changing job conditions. Instead, they felt that it was necessary to increase the level of demand.

40. Since 1950, federal expenditures had increased by 179 %. The 1960 budget (the last of the Eisenhower administration) included a deficit of $ 1.2 billion. In 1961 (in the first year of the Kennedy administration), the budget deficit was $ 3.9 billion. In 1962, it was $ 6.4 billion. The 1963 deficit was estimated at $ 6.8 billion in July, 1963.

41. This formula has been employed in Europe for many years, but the term often covers unorthodox financial manipulations.

42. David Brinkley reported on September 9 : " Harry Truman was out for his walk this morning and he said he did not think we should have a tax cut until we get the budget balanced, and the other day Senator Humphrey was saying in the Senate that what the American people think is true is very often more important than what is actually true. "

43. In 1968, the increasing use of the Planning, Programming, Budgeting System, or P.P.B.S., has proved President Kennedy's foresight correct. This system, which has already been instituted in New York State and Wisconsin, and which is under study by Colorado, Michigan and Vermont, was developed by the Defense Department in 1961.

P.P.B.S., which constitutes a first step in public planning, is an overall examination (on the national, state or local level) of the objectives, the available resources and the basic principles of public spending, which were formerly dealt with in separate studies.

44. Milton Friedman claims that Keynes is as out-of-date as Marx, and that his doctrine is based on the situation in Great Britain after the 1929 crash, when the nation was faced with falling prices and underemployment. Friedman does not believe that the Keynesian serum can be applied to an expanding economy, as it speeds up inflation.

45. The budget for fiscal year 1960 will be around $ 150 billion ($ 190 billion using the new method of calculation). In President Johnson's defense, however, it should be noted that around $ 40 billion of this is accounted for by exceptional Defense costs.

added that in his opinion confidence was not reassured by expanding federal domination and control, or judicial usurpation of power, or excessive federal spending, and that he was feeling the oppression of all three.

What Kennedy wanted was not simply a temporary tax cut, but a thorough revision of the American fiscal system. The tax reform sealed his fate.

Some Americans were opposed to it on principal, like the Florida businessman who found himself in the same plane with Douglas Dillon one day in 1962. The Treasury Secretary spent some time explaining the tax reform in terms of this man's corporate outlook and income, and the businessman was most impressed. Finally, as the plane landed at Miami, he turned to Secretary Dillon and said, " I am grateful to you for explaining the bill. Now tell me just once more : why is it I am against it ? "[46].

The answer came from Barry Goldwater :

We have been persuaded that the government has an unlimited right to appropriate the wealth of the people. The government has the right to demand an equal percentage of the wealth of every man, and no more. This is as valid for incomes as it is for gifts and inheritances. Taxes should be the same for everyone, as they are for cigarettes. Progressive taxation is a confiscation.

It is scandalous that a man who earns $ 100,000 a year contributes 90 % of his revenue to the national budget, while a man who earns only $ 10,000 contributes only 20 %. It is a penalty for success. "

But taxes weren't the same for everyone. The President was astounded to learn that of the 19 Americans whose income exceeded $ 5 million a year, 5 paid no income tax at all in 1959, and none of the 14 others had been taxed in the $ 5 million a year bracket, and that in 1954 one American with an income of $ 20 million a year had not paid a cent of taxes. Similar examples abounded. In most cases, these scandalous exemptions were the result of the multiple deductions and loopholes that the tax system offered to certain corporations, notably in the oil industry.[47]

Kennedy was determined to put an end to these abuses. Already, on April 20, 1961, the day he learned of the failure of the Bay of Pigs invasion, he declared before Congress :

" A strong and sound Federal tax system is essential to America's future... The elimination of certain defects and inequities as proposed below will provide revenue gains to offset the tax reductions offered to stimulate the economy... Special provisions have developed into an increasing source of preferential treatment to various groups. Whenever one taxpayer is permitted to pay less, someone else must be asked to pay more. The uniform distribution of the tax burden is thereby disturbed and higher rates are made necessary by the narrowing of the tax base. Of course, some departures from uniformity are needed to promote desirable social or economic objectives. But many of the preferences which have developed do not meet such a test and need to be reevaluated in our tax reform program. "

And he added, " The war on poverty is not over. It has just begun. "

The 1963 tax reform was aimed at : 1) relieving the hardships of low-income taxpayers and older people, and encouraging economic growth ; 2) revising the tax treatment of capital gains to provide a freer and fuller flow of capital funds ; and 3) broadening the base of individual and corporate income taxes so as to remove special privileges, correct defects in the tax law, and provide more equal treatment of taxpayers.

But the most important aspect of this reform focused on the tax provisions which " artificially distort the use of resources ". The President declared that " no one industry should be permitted to obtain an undue tax advantage over all others " and called for the correction of defects in the tax privileges granted the mineral industries, the oil industry first of all.

As they read through the 24 pages of Document No. 43, the President's Tax Message to Congress, certain businessmen

---

46. Quoted by Kennedy at Tampa on November 18, 1963.
47. See Chapter 10, *Oilmen*.

had good reason to be against it.[48] They were far less interested in the health of the American economy[49] than in the
rate of their profits.

On November 18, 1963, three days before his death, President Kennedy presented his economic report to the Florida
Chamber of Commerce :

" For the first time in many years, in the last 18 months,
our growth rate exceeds that of France and Germany. It is
because, as *Fortune* magazine recently pointed out, corporate
profits in America are now rising much faster than corporate
profits overseas...

" By next April, with the indispensable help of the pending
tax cut bill, the United States will be sailing with the winds of
the longest and strongest peacetime economic expansion in
our Nation's entire history. "

And he concluded :

" I realize that there are some businessmen who feel they
only want to be left alone, that government and politics are
none of their affairs, that the balance sheet and profit rate of
their own corporation are of more importance than the
worldwide balance of power or the nationwide rate of unemployment. But I hope it is not rushing the season to recall to
you the passage from Dickens ' ' Christmas Carol ' in which
Ebenezer Scrooge is terrified by the ghost of his former
partner, Jacob Marley, and Scrooge, appalled by Marley's
story of ceaseless wandering, cries out, ' But you were always
a good man of business, Jacob '. And the ghost of Marley, his
legs bound by a chain of ledger books and cash boxes,
replies, ' Business ? Mankind was my business. The common
welfare was my business. Charity, mercy, forbearance and
benevolence were all my business. The dealings of my trade
were but a drop of water in the comprehensive ocean of my
business. '

" Members and guests of the Florida Chamber of Commerce, whether we work in the White House or the State
House or in a house of industry or commerce, mankind is our
business. And if we work in harmony, if we understand the
problems of each other, and the responsibilities that each of
us bears, then surely the business of mankind will prosper.
And your children and mine will move ahead in a securer
world, and one in which there is opportunity for them all... "

But many businessmen were indifferent to harmony, the problems of mankind, the future of their children, and Charles Dickens. Four days later, President Kennedy landed at Dallas. There is no stronger hate than that of the robber barons.

On February 26, 1964, Congress approved Public Law 88-272, which amended the Internal Revenue Code of 1954. Nowhere in the 128 pages of this act, however, will you find the provisions concerning the " removal of certain inequities " requested by President Kennedy.

In April, 1964, now that they had a President " who

---

48. The tax reform favored the 450,000 businesses (out of 585,000 in the country) with a net revenue of $ 25,000 per year, and which benefited from a 27 % reduction in their taxes.

Other proposals favored : child care deductions, older people, contributions to charity and medical facilities, and research and development activities. An amendment defining certain medical and drug expenses was designed to prevent abuses in tax deductions.

49. On January 21, 1963, President Kennedy informed Congress that during the 1961-62 expansion :

1) Private income had increased by $ 46 billion to reach a high of $ 450 billion, or 12 % more than the maximum attained during the previous expansion. The net revenue per farm had increased by $ 330, while the net income of the farmers from agricultural activities had increased overall by $ 800 million. The total income of American consumers, after taxes, had risen by 8 %, which represented an annual increase of $ 400 in the standard of living (in terms of 1962 prices) for a family of four ;

2) The number of civilian non-agricultural jobs had increased by 2 million, while the average work week in the factories had risen from 39.3 to 40.3 hours ;

3) Company profits had attained a record high of $ 51 billion in 1962 ;

4) Wholesale prices had remained remarkably stable, while consumer prices had risen by only 1.1 % a year (the best record of price stability attained by any important industrial nation with the exception of Canada) ;

5) The improving competitive situation had led to a marked improvement in the balance of payments deficit, which had dropped from $ 3.9 billion in 1960 to $ 2.5 billion in 1961, and to around $ 2 billion in 1962.

The President added that prospects for continued moderate expansion in 1963 were favorable.

understands business ", in the words of W.B. Murphy, President of the Campbell Soup Company, the businessmen interviewed by *U.S. News and World Report* declared, " *All the business news is good — profits up, sales climbing, output rising. Everything is breaking out on the upside. "*

The Great Society had begun.

It was at the height of its glory when, on July 4, 1967, President Johnson told a cheering crowd :

" *We own almost a third of the world's railroad tracks, almost two-thirds of the world's automobiles, half the trucks, half of all its radios, a third of all the electricity, a fourth of all the steel... half of its wealth. "*

" *And bear in mind* ", continued the President (who had forgotten to include half the world's oil) " *that the rest of the world would like to exchange places with us. "*

10

Oilmen

" The American Beauty Rose can only be coaxed to that degree of splendor and fragrance that enchants us by sacrificing the other buds growing around it. In the business world, the same operation is the result not of an unhealthy trend, but simply of a law of nature and of God. ".

JOHN D. ROCKEFELLER, Jr.

Oil is the lifeblood of modern civilization. It provides the fuel for our planes, our ships, our trucks, and our 180 million automobiles, and it is the source of some 300,000 petrochemical products. Oil accounts for more than half of the maritime freight tonnage, and furnishes more than 60 % of the world's energy. It is the number one industry in the world today.

The budget of the oil industry is larger than the budget of the United States government. The annual revenue of the largest oil company in the world, Standard Oil of New Jersey, is greater than the revenue of the government of Canada.

Directly or indirectly, through American domestic production[1]
as well as overseas holdings, the American oil industry controls 80 % of the world market [2].

Through their overseas domination and the steady growth
of the oil market in the past fifty years, the big companies
have grown increasingly bigger.[3] Their interests, however, do
not always coincide with those of the continents and the
peoples they control. Europe, which consumes 25 % of the
oil produced in the world today, accounts for only 0.7 % of
world reserves, and for only 1.4 % of world production. In
the coming decade and probably until the end of the century,
Western Europe's major problem will be how to obtain
enough oil.[4]

Oil is no longer an exclusive capitalist commodity. The
International (mainly American) Consortium that dominates
the world market, after attempting unsuccessfully following
World War I to gain control of Russian resources, saw them
pass under Soviet control. In 1962 the Soviet Union (with an
annual production of 1.3 billion barrels) had little surplus oil
to export, but since then the situation has changed. Soviet
production in 1968 is estimated at more than 2.1 billion
barrels.

Simultaneously with its ideological and political transformation, the USSR is converting its coal-burning industry (including its armaments industry) into an oil-burning consumer
industry. In a few years it will have the same proportion of
consumer to heavy industry as the countries of Western
Europe. Its desire for international commercial expansion and
its need for foreign currency have led the Soviet Union to
abandon its socialistic oil policy. The consequences of this

---

1. The evolution of world oil production between 1860 and
1966 was as follows :

	1860	1930	1966
U.S.A.	476,000 b	861 million b	2.9 billion b
U.S.S.R.		135 million b	1.9 billion b
Venezuela		140 million b	1.2 billion b
Middle East		42 million b	3.3 billion b
Rest of the world	21,000 b.		2.2 billion b

change are three :
- an increase in production, in order to export more oil ;
- the creation of a distribution network which, because the USSR has relatively few tankers, is largely dependent on the

2. Of the 20 largest oil companies in the world with an annual turnover in the neighborhood of $ 57 billion, 14 are American ($ 42 billion), one is Anglo-Dutch and another British ($ 1 billion), and one is Belgian ($ 700 million). But American influence extends even to these foreign companies.

Company	Country	Turnover (in millions of dollars)
Standard Oil (N.J.)	U.S.A.	$ 12,191
Royal Dutch Shell	G.B.-Holland	7,711
Mobil Oil	U.S.A.	5,253
Texaco	U.S.A.	4,427
Gulf Oil	U.S.A.	3,781
Shell Oil	U.S.A.	2,789
Standard Oil (Ind.)	U.S.A.	2,708
Standard Oil (Calif.)	U.S.A.	2,698
B.P.	G.B.	2,543
Continental Oil	U.S.A.	1,749
Phillips Petroleum	U.S.A.	1,686
Sinclair Oil	U.S.A.	1,377
Union Oil California	U.S.A.	1,364
C.F.P.	France	1,140
E.N.I.	Italy	1,093
Signal Oil and Gas	U.S.A.	847
E.R.A.P.	France	806
Petrofina	Belgium	704
Ashled Oil and Refining	U.S.A.	699
Industry Oil	U.S.A.	695

3. In the period between 1930 and 1966, energy consumption doubled every 15 years, and oil consumption rose from 19 to 60 %. %.

In 1938, the world consumed only 2.1 billion barrels of petroleum products. By 1971 it will be consuming 14 billion barrels per year, and by 1980 28 billion barrels.

4. In Europe, despite the increasing use of natural gas (which in 1965 provided 4 % of all the energy consumed, as compared with 0 % in 1950) and the advent of atomic energy (0.4 % in 1966), oil consumption has risen steadily, (from 10 % in 1945 to 45 % in 1965), while coal consumption has steadily dropped (38 % in 1965, as compared with 75 % in 1945).

COMECOM pipeline which runs to the heart of Western Europe[5] ;

- the adjustment, with certain exceptions (barters such as that practiced with Italy, or agreements based on political considerations, as with Cuba) of Soviet prices to bring them into line with the prices of the Consortium.

At the present time, the USSR is feeling its way into the world petroleum market. This has led to a change in its Middle East policy following a series of instructive failures in the area. The neo-Soviets have come to understand the ground rules of the petroleum industry, and Soviet influence in the Middle East is steadily rising.

By 1980, Soviet oil production is expected to exceed 3.5 billion barrels. Through the pipeline, it will provide an increasing percentage of Western European consumption. But before that date the conflict of interests between the Soviet Union and the International Consortium will either be resolved or will come to a head. In the latter event, there will be economic warfare ; in the former, the United States and the Soviet Union will set revolutionary principles aside to carve up the world oil market among themselves.

If Soviet expansion continues at its present rate, the oil market in the 1980's will be dominated by a Communist-capitalist cartel that will swallow up Western Europe while continuing to juggle with the Middle East. For beneath the golden sands of the Persian Gulf lie the most important oil reserves on the globe, $300 billion worth (in terms of current prices), on which the Consortium hopes to earn $75 billion at its usual rate of commission.

About one-fourth of the price of refined oil goes to the companies of the Consortium in the form of clear profits. In the Middle East, another fourth goes to the countries that own the concessions. The remaining half not only covers the cost of production, transportation and refining, but provides profits comparable to those earned in other industries.

Oil as an industry is in a class by itself. No other economic activity offers such high profits, to the detriment of the consumers and the producing countries. In the Middle East, the people gain nothing from the riches extracted from their soil. The royalties paid by the Consortium go to the rulers and their relatives, the ruling classes, high government officials, and a few local businessmen. By supporting the emirates of the Persian Gulf and protecting their rulers, Great Britain, now supplanted by the United States, has contributed to the preservation of archaic social structures and paved the way for revolution.[6]

In 1968, the overseas investments of American oil companies total more than $30 billion (nearly 40 % of all American investments abroad.)[7] The giants of the oil industry not only control the world market, but governments and foreign and military policy as well. In the United States, the Republican and a portion of the Democratic Party get much of their financial backing from the oil industry. The State Department

---

5. The temporary outlets of the COMECOM pipeline are located at Neutspils and Klaipeda in the Baltic states, East Berlin, Most (Czechoslovakia), Vienna, Budapest, and Trieste (Italy).

6. 95 % of the population of Saudi Arabia is still illiterate. The country has 750,000 slaves. Trade unions are prohibited by law, and the death penalty is inflicted with the bastinado.

If the royalties paid to the Sultan of Kuwait were divided equally among his people, each Kuwaiti citizen would have an annual income of more than $ 1,500, giving Kuwait one of the highest standards of living of any underdeveloped country. Instead, the average annual income in Kuwait is $ 100. 98 % of the population is illiterate, and 85 % suffers from tuberculosis.

An exception to this rule is the Sultan of Bahrein, who contributes a large portion of his royalties to the state treasury. In his territory, most dwellings have running water, sanitary conditions are satisfactory, and public education is developing rapidly. Nevertheless, the Sultan of Bahrein is the poorest of the Middle East rulers. In 1955 he received only $ 8.5 million in royalties, as compared to $ 36 million paid to Qatar, $ 84 million to Iran, $ 223 to Irak, and $ 280 each to Saudi Arabia and Kuwait. Iran is relatively prosperous, but Irak is continually shaken by corruption, political intrigue and assassinations.

7. American investments abroad rose from $ 1.4 billion in 1943 to $ 10 billion in 1958 ($ 5.1 billion of which was reported) and to $ 28 billion in 1967 ($ 15 billion of which was reported). In 1967, American investments in Europe totalled $ 10 million in the mining industry, $ 290 million in miscellaneous industries, $ 640 million in the chemical industry, $ 795 million in the machinery industry, and $ 1,200 million in the oil industry.

and the White House and a substantial portion of the press give systematic support to the industry. Even college graduates in quest of jobs are warned of the danger of opposing it.[8]

Four oil companies were classed in 1966 among the ten largest American corporations : Standard Oil of New Jersey, which ranked third (after General Motors and Ford), Socony Mobil, fourth, Texaco, seventh, and Gulf Oil, which ranked tenth. But this list is open to question. It fails to take account of the most important factor in economics, profits.

Although the combined personnel of these four oil companies totalled only 346,846 (388,016 persons are employed by General Motors alone), their net profits, $2,661,684,000, exceeded those of the entire automobile industry ($2,603,638,000) — in other words, the combined profits of General Motors, Ford, and Chrysler, which together employ four times as many people. But General Motors, Chrysler, and Ford, together with deficit-ridden American Motors, comprise almost the entire American automobile industry. The fourteenth, fifteenth, and sixteenth places on the list of the top 500 companies are held by Shell Oil, Standard Oil of Indiana, and Standard Oil of California, whose combined net profits exceed $1 billion, and further down the list are 15 other oil companies whose profits add another million to industry profits. It can be said that the combined profits of the American oil industry (which in addition to these 22 top companies include several thousand smaller ones) are greater than the annual turnover of General Motors.[9]

---

8. Frank W. Abrams, past President of Jersey Standard, jointed with General Motors, U.S. Steel and several other corporations to form a committee for economic aid to education in an effort to stave off what he considered a future threat to industrial investments.

In 1955 Senator Fulbright cited a brochure edited by Socony Mobil for job-hunting students which warned them that their "'personal opinions'" could cause them difficulties in their career. His criticism, together with a protest from the Princeton Alumni magazine, caused the brochure to be withdrawn, but the paternalistic and totalitarian attitude of the oil companies continued unchanged.

Standard Oil of New Jersey is symbolic of the oil industry. It is also its moral leader. At first glance, it looks like just another corporation. In theory, it is what is left of the empire created by John D. Rockefeller, which was broken up by anti-trust legislation in 1911.[10] But half a century later Jersey Standard, which theoretically neither produces nor refines nor transports nor sells any oil, controls one-fifth of the world market. It owns the largest private tanker fleet in the world (126 ships totalling 5,096,000 tons), ranking 12th in 1967 on the world list of fleets, along with the national fleets of Panama, Sweden, Denmark and Spain. It has a security department eight times larger than the security department of General Electric, employing about 30 special agents who are graduates of the CIA or the FBI. Its 14 top executives control more than 300 subsidiary companies, one-third of which rank among the largest corporations in the world.[11]

The history of Standard Oil is the history of the oil industry, which was born a little more than a century ago at Titusville,

---

9. Figures released by the Chase Manhatten Bank show that be-tween 1934 and 1950, the 30 largest oil companies moved more than $ 121 billion, with net profits of $ 12 billion and taxes of $ 4 billion. These companies had taken out so few loans that only $ 700 was paid out in interest. $ 12 billion appeared on the balance sheets in the form of stock depreciations, amortizations, and reserves. Of the $ 12 billion in profits, $ 7 billion was reinvested and $ 5 distributed to stock-holders.

10. The Rockefeller family's holdings are now limited to 15 %, but the 100 most important stockholders (out of a total of 300,000), most of whom are descendents of John D. Rockefeller and his partners, own more than 40 % of the shares.

11. One of its " little sisters ", Socony Mobil (actually Stan-dard Oil of New York) has assets of nearly $ 5 billion, and Standard Oil of Indiana has nearly $ 4 billion in assets. In 1966 Jersey Standard earned $ 1,090,944,000 in profits, two-thirds of which came from its overseas subsidiaries. Of the latter, Creole of Venezuela, for example, generally earns profits of around 30 %. Creole and Lago, Standard's second Venezuelan subsidiary, to-gether with Imperial of Canada, Imperial Petroleum in Latin America, Esso Standard, and its other foreign subsidiaries, earned more than $ 800 million in profits in 1966.

Pennsylvania in 1859.[12] Oil, however, has always existed. In ancient times it was used for eternal flames and torches, but no one ever thought of commercializing it. Until the 19th Century commerce was based on grain, and it was there that personal fortunes were made and power won.

Standard Oil was founded in 1860, and for nearly half a century the oil industry and the life story of John D. Rockefeller were one. During 51 years Standard eliminated its competitors by every means at its disposal, corrupting public officials and violating or getting around the laws, until it was dissolved in 1911.

Around 1890, its world monopoly began to slip. The Russo-Swedish Nobel group inaugurated operations in the Caucasus, and between 1891 and 1901 Russian production actually exceeded that of the United States. The British Rothschilds, realizing the future possibilities of oil, in particular with regard to modern shipping, aided the Royal Dutch Company to escape the control of Standard and conquer some of Rockefeller's markets in the Far East.[13] In 1907 Royal Dutch merged with the Shell Transport and Trade Company, which until then had specialized in mother-of-pearl. With the backing of the Foreign Office and the privileges it enjoyed in the British and Dutch colonies overseas, the Anglo-Dutch company, headed by Henry Deterding, expanded rapidly. Contrary to Standard, which had patterned its commercial policies after the isolationist principles of Theodore Roosevelt and Taft and sought only markets abroad, Royal Dutch Shell carried out explorations and extended its operations throughout the world[14]. In 1912 it began operating in the United States and soon controlled half of American production. It also forced its way into Mexico, where it bought out the Pearson group that owned the No. 4 well at Potrero del Llano, with a production of 91 million barrels. By 1921 Mexican production equalled 40 % of United States produc-

---

12. The first oil well was drilled by Edwin Laurentine Drake, better known as Colonel Drake, who discovered oil at 69 feet at Titusville on September 8, 1859. Nevertheless, he was fired in 1864 by his employer, Seneca Oil, and given the paltry sum of $ 731 in compensation. The state of Pennsylvania showed its gratitude by granting him an annual pension of $ 1,500.

tion, but foreign companies (British and American) sacrificed everything to the present and devastated the Mexican reserves. Gas pressure was wasted and the Golden Way oilfield near Tampico was invaded by salt water. By 1930 Mexican production had dropped far behind, and she was soon eclipsed by her neighbor to the south, Venezuela. In 1963, Mexican production equalled only 4 % of American and 20 % of Iranian production.

In the Middle East, where oil reserves are at least 100 times greater than those of the United States, a British adventurer, William Knox d'Arcy, obtained a concession from the Shah of Persia in 1901 covering five-sixth of his lands. In 1908 the Anglo-Persian Oil Company (later the Anglo-Iranian Oil Company, and later still British Petroleum or B.P.) was founded. The British Navy had just switched to oil-burning ships, and Winston Churchill, First Lord of the Admiralty, persuaded His Majesty's government to purchase a majority share in the new company.[15] At that very moment, America and Europe discovered the automobile. In 1908 Henry Ford began producing his famous Model T. The rush was on. In 1911 there were 619,000 automobiles. By 1914 there were 2 million, and by 1924 there were 18 million cars on the road, 16 million of them in the United States. That year the United States alone consumed more oil than Europe consumed in 1960.

The war revealed the strategic importance of oil. Not only did it contribute heavily to the allied victory, but it became part of the stakes of the game. Wilhelm II wished to destroy British oil domination and give Germany a share in Mesopotamian oil. He built the Berlin-Bassorah railway (via Cons-

---

13. Today, Royal Dutch Shell is the most important private industrial concern in Western Europe, and perhaps in the world (with the exception of the United States).

14. Shell has a policy of forming a national company in every country where it operates.

15. The British government invested approximately two and a half million pounds, and got back several billion pounds on its investment. It was represented on the Board by two administrators and exercised its veto only on political and naval questions, never interfering with commercial policies.

tantinople and Bagdad) to compete with the route of the
Indies. Once Germany had been defeated, the British and the
French divided up the oil of the former Turkish Empire.[16] In
1920, Royal Dutch Shell circled the globe. It had subsidiaries
in the United States, Mexico, Venezuela, Trinidad, the Dutch
East Indies, Ceylan, Roumania, Egypt, the Malay Peninsula,
North and South China, Siam, the Philippines, and Burma. In
association with other British companies it acquired concessions in Colombia and Central America, and it was trying to
establish itself along the Panama Canal. Soon it would extend
its activities to Honduras, Nicaragua, and Costa Rica. It also
bought out the Rothschild holdings in Russia for far less than
they were worth. Banker Sir Edward Mackay declared that
" all of the known, probable or possible oilfields outside the
territory of the United States were either British property,
under British direction or control, or financed by British
capital ", and added that " the world was solidly barricaded
against an attack from American interests "[17].

Jersey Standard realized that Woodrow Wilson's policy of
isolationism and pacifism represented a threat to its future.
A.C. Bedford, President of Jersey Standard, declared, " What
we need is an agressive foreign policy ", and the Interstate
Commerce Commission recommended that the United States
give diplomatic support to the acquisition and exploitation by
American companies of oil properties overseas. The State
Department dispatched a series of diplomatic notes, the tone
of which grew more and more violent, demanding that the
United States be given a share in the Turkish and German
holdings.

In 1922 talks opened between Bedford and Sir Charles
Greenway, President of Anglo-Iranian. They dragged on for
six long years, but Gulf in the meanwhile had obtained a
concession on the island of Bahrein (which it later ceded to
Standard of California) which the British geologists had
somehow overlooked. At the same time Socony Mobil (which
when Standard Oil was dissolved in 1911 had inherited most
of its Asian interests) and Shell were engaged in a struggle to
the death in India. Their price war brought prices down all
over the world. In 1928 Sir Henry Deterding (founder and
promoter of Royal Dutch Shell) invited Sir John Cadman of
Anglo-Iranian and Walter C. Teagle, new President of Jersey

Standard, to his home in Scotland. At the conclusion of what has since been known as the Achnacarry Conference, it was agreed that outright competition had resulted in excessive overproduction. The Big Three decided :

1. to maintain the status quo of 1928 (in other words their respective positions) on the world market ;

2. to fight overproduction and the waste of new, non-competitive installations ;

3. to fix uniform production prices ;

4. to supply markets from their closest source of supply through a series of reciprocal agreements between companies ;

5. to avoid producing in excess of demand.

The companies signing the agreement explained that these measures were designed to protect the consumers from price hikes resulting from a multiplicity of separate operations. In actual fact, they laid the foundations for an arrangement by which the members of the international cartel would cooperate in the most profitable exploitation of world oil reserves. They brought the war between Shell and Socony to an end by making it possible to fix prices in India, and prevented a new price war in Mexico. A sort of line of demarcation was drawn between the British and American zones of influence. It was nothing short of a monopoly.

American anti-trust legislation was no problem. It was

---

16. The Turkish Petroleum Company (which wasn't Turkish at all) owned oil fields in Mesopotamia. Before World War I it was divided up between Anglo-Iranian (50 %), Royal Dutch (20 %), and the Deutsche Bank, whose share of 25 % was seized by the British at the start of the war. For having allied itself with Germany, Turkey was dismembered in 1918, and Britain appointed the rulers of the former Ottoman colonies. But the war booty was divided up under the cover of the League of Nations mandates. Germany's share of 25 % was handed over to the Compagnie Française des Pétroles in exchange for an indemnity and French permission to install a pipeline across its Syrian and Lebanese mandates.

17. It is difficult for us today to imagine a time when United States foreign policy was based on the rivalry between Shell and Standard, when Shell was refused the right to participate in bids for federally-owned concessions, and when writers prophesied war between Great Britain and the Union.

expressly stipulated that the Achnaccary Agreement did not apply within the United States. But in 1929 17 companies joined to form the Oil Exporters Association, which set quotas and established prices, which were aligned with the highest costs in the country, those prevailing in Texas and the Gulf of Mexico. The British had no objection to this arrangement, as it enabled them to make high profits on their low-cost crude from Iran and Irak. As for the American companies, which were already making good profits from domestic production, they intensified their overseas explorations, which would earn them even higher profits.

The " Red Line " agreement concluded in 1929 consecrated America's entry into the Middle East. The holdings of Turkish Petroleum were divided up again, this time between four partners which joined to form the Irak Petroleum Company : Anglo-Iranian (still controlled by the British government), Royal Dutch Shell, the Compagnie Française des Pétroles, and Standard Oil of New Jersey (in association with Socony Mobil). Each was given a 23.75 % share in the venture.[18] The Red Line agreement stipulated that the four associates undertook to maintain the same percentages in all of the countries that lay within a red line on the map. The red line ran all the way around the Middle East.

At the time that the Irak Petroleum Company was founded, Irak was the only oil-producing country in the region. But Standard of California discovered oil at the edge of the sea on the concession it had acquired from Gulf at Bahrein. As it had no distribution network in the Orient, it signed an agreement with the Texas Company (becoming Caltex in 1936). Standard of California also began operating in Saudi Arabia, on the territory of El Hasa which King Saud had seized from the bedouin princes. With Texaco it formed the Arabian American Oil Company (Aramco).

Caltex and Aramco soon proved to Standard and Socony that the reserves on their concessions far exceeded those of Irak. The latter two companies regretted having signed an agreement to share their future discoveries with the French and the British. But American solidarity and Jersey's power soon overcame that obstacle. Jersey Standard, Caltex and Socony joined with Aramco, excluding Royal Dutch Shell, Anglo-Iranian and the Compagnie Française des Pétroles.

Great Britain already controlled sufficient resources in Iran, Venezuela, the Malay Peninsula, and Burma. France was traditionally a non-commercial country, and she had no petroleum policy. Like Gulbenkian, she was given an indemnity.

The Irak Petroleum Company faced the difficult problem of income taxes. In order to benefit to the maximum from American and British tax provisions that favored the overseas activities of their companies, it was decided that any profits earned would not go to IPC, but would appear instead on the balance sheets of the constituent companies. Obviously, this was contrary to the interests of the government of Irak. IPC sold oil to Iraqi consumers at its usual Texas-based prices, and the company was not eager (or perhaps unable) to calculate its actual net cost, which would have brought its excessive profits to the attention of the Iraqi government.[19]

By the time of the Second World War, the world had been divided up between the Big Seven (Jersey Standard, Royal Dutch Shell, Socony, Texaco, Gulf Oil, Standard of California, and BP). The war caused a few minor annoyances, and there was concern as the Germans neared the Caucasus and Egypt, but the oil business was booming.[20]

---

18. The remaining 5 % went to the broker, Gulbenkian.

19. Moreover, the companies mixed the Iraqi oil with oil from Iran and Saudi Arabia, making it difficult to determine the actual cost.

In 1939 Jersey Standard felt that it had gotten back all of its original Iraqi investment. Nevertheless, Iraqi production was held back in favor of production in Saudi Arabia and Iran, where the raoyalties paid were very low (4 shillings per ton of crude in Iran, plus 20 % of the profits).

20. At the beginning of the war, the difficult position of the Allies in the Middle East led Roosevelt to consider government participation in Aramco, in the same way that the British government had held a majority in Anglo-Iranian since 1914. But Standard of California and Texaco kept delaying the talks, and once Rommel was defeated, the two companies even refused to consider admitting the government as a minority stockholder. They felt, and there was little evidence to contradict them, that they already enjoyed government protection.

The companies of the Aramco-Caltex group managed to avoid American taxes on their wartime profits by founding new companies in the Bahamas and Canada.

The requirements of the war nevertheless led the Allies to impose quotas on raw commodities throughout the world, and even the distribution of oil was controlled. The experts on the War Production Board demanded that the United Nations be given the power to administer world stocks of raw materials, and in Britain the Labour Party proposed a similar plan. In 1945 at the Washington Conference, Sir Anthony Eden and Secretary of State Cordell Hull legalized and completed the old Achnacarry Agreement that divided up the world's oil reserves between Great Britain and the United States. Highly displeased, the Soviet Union that same year signed the Moscow Agreement with France.

In 1947 the International Cooperative Alliance proposed that the petroleum industry in the Middle East be nationalized in order to eliminate the nascent rivalry between Russia and the West, raise the living standards of the Arabs, and diminish the price of oil to the consumer. It proposed that the United Nations create a special agency to control the' petroleum resources of the Middle East and admit all buyers on an equal footing, in accordance with the Atlantic Charter. But when the United Nations Economic and Social Council voted on the measure on August 12, 1949, only Norway and Colombia supported it. Eight member countries abstained (including the Communist states), and eight others voted against it, including the United States, Great Britain and the Netherlands.[21]

The international oil cartel was in greater danger when, in December, 1952, the Economic and Financial Commission of the U.N. approved a joint Iranian-Bolivian resolution in favor of the right of nationalization. The United States was the only country to vote against it.

Iran was Britain's private preserve. Sinclair (42nd largest American corporation in 1966, with $1,377 billion in sales) and Standard had carried out some explorations there, but had withdrawn at London's insistence. In 1959 Iranian Prime Minister Mossadegh demanded an increase in royalties, the rate of which had remained unchanged since before the war, as well as a 50-50 split in profits. Anglo-Iranian refused, whereupon Mossadegh nationalized the company[22], and the crisis was on. The American firms profited from the opera-. tion. Aramco's production rose from 196 to 280 barrels, that of Kuwait from 126 to 266 million. In 1955 Iran began to export oil in small quantities and at reduced prices to non-producing countries such as Italy and Japan. But the Consortium regarded Iran as an ominous sign. To its great relief, the CIA went into action, and Mossadegh was replaced by Zahedi.[23]

The American intervention aroused a storm of ill-feeling against the United States that has not yet been dissipated. The Iranians claimed they had been exploited by Anglo-Iranian for forty years.[24] John Foster Dulles turned the Iranian problem over to Herbert Hoover, Jr., who formed an alliance of five big companies (Jersey Standard, Socony, Texaco, Gulf, and Standard of California) which formed a common front in

---

21. Royal Dutch Shell is richer and more influential than the government of the Netherlands. Two other Dutch companies, Philips and Unilever, have international standing. These three firms make it difficult for the government of the Netherlands to pursue an independent economic policy.

22. The Iranian assets of Anglo-Iranian have been estimated at $ 1 billion.

23. The CIA's action is accounted for not only by the singular nature of the American intelligence agency (see Chapter 15, Spies), but also by the fact that the Pentagon and the administration in Washington feared that with the Abadan refinery closed down, the Air Froce might run short of fuel in the event of Third World War. Such a shortage had already occurred during the Korean War.

24. They estimated Anglo-Iranian's gross profits since 1914 at $ 5 billion, $ 500 million of which had gone to the Admiralty in the form of low-cost fuel oil, $ 350 million to the stockholders, $ 1.5 million to the British treasury, and $ 2.7 million to the corporation for depreciations and new investments.

To these sums they compared the royalties paid to Iran : before 1920, none ; from 1921 to 1930, $ 60 million ; between 1931 and 1941, $ 125 million, mainly in the form of military equipment which was later used against them by the British and the Russians.

In 1951 Iran received 18 cents on every barrel of oil (a barrel equals 42 gallons and weighs an average of 306.6 pounds). In comparison, Bahrein received 35 cents, Saudi Arabia 36 cents, and Irak 60 cents.

The Iranians also complained that nearly all the gas from their wells was burned by Anglo-Iranian, when it could have been put to use for the benefit ot the population.

the interminable negotiations with the British and demanded that the Iranian holdings be divided equally between Anglo-Iranian and themselves. The new company was called Iranian Oil Participants, Ltd. The British (who received an indemnity of $ 510 million) kept their majority with 54 % of the shares (40 % went to Anglo-Iranian, now BP, and 14 % to Shell), while the five American concerns got 8 % each.[25] The new agreement was signed on October 21, 1954 and ratified by the Iranian Parliament, which recognized the validity of the new Consortium for a period of 40 years.[26]

But the American independent companies were annoyed. They felt the Big Five were deliberately shutting them out from their overseas treasure chests, while continuing to benefit from domestic sales prices for their low-cost crude from the Middle East and Venezuela.[27] The Consortium, however, was more concerned about the reaction of the other oil-rich states, which were carefully scrutinizing every clause of the agreement signed with Iran. The latter country had obtained nothing more than a 50 % share of the profits, the same accorded the other producing states, plus the promise of a gradual increase in production. This new agreement raised the American share in the oil production of the Persian Gulf to 55 % in 1955 (as compared to 14 % in 1938). The British and the Dutch were declining in power.

In 1956 came the Suez crisis. On July 26, Egypt nationalized the canal. Since that date, the Middle East has become a battleground of vested interests[28] where the member countries of the Consortium, the United States, Britain and France, struggle for predominance under the interested gaze of the Russians, whose problems are simpler because, unlike the French, they have enough oil for their own needs, unlike the

---

25. The Compagnie Française des Pétroles, which by the terms of the Red Line agreement had a right to its share, was granted 6 %.

26. In 1966 the Consortium was forced to yield to new demands from the government of Iran and surrender one-fourth of its concessions (the 1954 agreement provided for the surrender of one-fifth in 1979). It was also obliged to increase production by 13 % in 1967 and 1968. The Arab blockade in June, 1967 enabled it to go well over this figure.

British their power does not depend on their position in the
Persian Gulf, and unlike the United States they are not
subjected to private industrial pressures.

The USSR is content to sit back and watch as the cracks
grow wider between the Western powers, between the Western powers and the Arab states, and between the Arab states
themselves. In 1956 half the oil consumed in Europe was
imported from the Persian Gulf, and 60 % of it was shipped
through the Suez Canal.[29] Britain and France risked a war to
ensure control of their oil supplies, and only the intervention
of the United States stopped them. During the winter of 1956-
1957, American companies took advantage of the European
shortage to raise the price of fuel oil $ 1.50 a ton, and the
price of crude $ 2 a ton. The price hikes affected American
consumers as well. They cost the Americans $ 1.25 billion
and the Europeans $ 500 million. Suez brought Jersey Stan-
dard $ 100 million in additional profits. The Big Five beat all
records for profits during the first quarter of 1957. Jersey

---

27. The Big Five managed to pacify the most voracious of the
independents by each sacrificing 1 % of their shares. The 5 %
distributed was sold in April, 1955 to the following companies :
Atlantic Richfield, Tidewater Oil, Aminoil, Atlantic Refining,
Getty Oil, Continental Oil, Signal Oil and Gas, Standard Oil
(Ohio), and American Independent Oil. Harvey O'Connor states
that each company paid $ 1 million for its shares, which a few
years later were earning them $ 850,000 a year. Such a good
investment was also a kind of indemnity, but the independents
continued to demand a share for themselves in the Middle East.

In 1947 Aminoil (American Independent Oil Company), an
association of independents made up of Phillips Petroleum, Han-
cock, Signal, Ashland, Deep Rock, Sunray, Globe, J.S. Abercrom-
bie and the promoter, Ralph K. Davies, had been given a bone
to gnaw in the form of a neutral zone between Arabia and
Kuwait theoretically reserved for the nomads. But the Sultan
demanded high royalties, and 10 years later the reserves were
estimated at only 50 million tons. It looked like the independents
were stuck with the leftovers, but in 1966 this neutral zone was
producing 133 million barrels.

28. Biafra is the latest battleground of the oil companies —
American, British and French.

29. Twelve years later, giant tankers of up to 1 million tons
designed to detour around the Cape have apparently condemned
the Suez Canal to a position of minor importance.

Standard's profits rose 16 % (compared to the last quarter of 1956), Texaco's 24 % and Gulf Oil's 30 %.[30]

The Persian Gulf brought the Consortium more than $ 1 billion a year. Continuing the policy followed by the Department of State since 1920, John Foster Dulles lent his support to the big American oil companies, and when necessary the intelligence services and the military backed him up. The Middle East was almost completely encircled, and Britain was losing her foothold. In 1957 the King of Jordan, hitherto subsidized by the British, switched his allegiance to the Americans. Saudi Arabia's King Saud renewed his country's agreement with the U.S. Air Force and the Strategic Air Command in exchange for $ 10 million in weapons. The London *Times* wrote, somewhat maliciously, that " The bizarre combination of a large American company (Aramco) and an ancient feudal kingdom constitutes a real threat to Anglo-American cooperation in the Middle East. "

The growing demands of the Saudi Arabian King were not the only problem the Consortium had to face. It had managed to gain a foothold in the Sahara[31], but it was deeply concerned when the Italian firm ENI (Ente Nazionale Idrocarburi) proposed an agreement giving the government of Iran a 75 % share of profits (at a time when a 50-50 split was still the rule in the Middle East).[32] ENI's President, Enrico Mattei, had the courage to defy the Consortium. He declared : " The oil companies have built their power by concentrating control of production and distribution in a few hands, by maintaining a relationship of supplier to client with the consumers in a closed and rigid market, by refusing to grant compensation other than tax revenues to the countries owning the reserves, by excluding all agreements and arrangements between states for a more rational organization of the market, but they have also created the conditions for a breaking up of the system or its transformation under the pressure of new forces and new problems... The price of crude oil is based not on production costs in the Middle East, but on the much higher costs in the United States... As a result of the rivalry between the various nations and the Western oil companies, oil has become an element of disorder and instability that gives rise to nationalist demands in the oil-rich countries and arouses the jealousy of those states that have none.

" Italy, France, Belgium, Germany and Japan are anxious to free themselves from their subserviance and that of the consumers to the traditional organization of the oil industry... For the first time in a century we have the possibility of substituting a buyers' market for a sellers' market. An orderly market is necessary if we are to change the order established by the big international companies. The supremacy of what is known as the international cartel is not ' taboo ', and Italy is not obliged to respect it when this supremacy is breached on all sides by public and private initiatives.

" Oil is a political resource par excellence. What must be done now is to see that it is made to serve a good policy which is free, in so far as possible, from all imperialist and colonialist reminiscences, devoted to the preservation of peace, to the welfare of those whom nature has provided with this resource, and of those who make use of it in their industry. " A short time later, in 1962, Enrico Mattei was killed in the crash of his private plane.[33]

At the beginning of the Sixties, the Consortium's problems multiplied. The evolution of the market revealed growing competition[34], but what was even more serious was the wave

---

30. Gulf and Jersey Standard increased their Venezuelan production, while Texaco expanded its operations in Indonesia and Canada. In this way, they were able to sell their oil at higher prices while maintaining stable production costs.

31. Jersey Standard was admitted to the Sahara, then French territory, following a request from French Premier Guy Mollet for a $ 100 million loan from Washington which was eventually granted by the Chase Manhatten Bank (Jersey Standard is a member of the Chase group).

32. On the surface, ENI continued to respect the 50-50 rule, but by associating with an Iranian company, INOC, it actually granted 75 % of the profits to Iran. In the midst of the negatiations concerning ENI's concession in the rich Koum basin, the Iranian Prime Minister was overthrown.

33. In 1932 André Maginot, a French Minister who had founded the Union Petrolière Latine, was poisoned. His death was also the death of the UPL.

34. Between 1950 and 1962, the American share in world production dropped from 69.8 % to 57.9 %, and its share in refining from 65 % to 52.1 %. Jersey Standard, which in 1958 accounted for 10.8 % of all production, had dropped to 10.3 % in 1961.

of popular revolts. Fortunately, for every Mexico[35] there were
two or three Venezuelas[36], but nations all over the world were
suddenly becoming conscious of the importance of the min-
erals in their soil. Those that had been by-passed by nature
realized that the balance of their economy depended on the
security of their supplies. The Consortium knew that the
Italian ENI, the French ERAP, the Mexican Pemex, and the
Argentinian YFP could easily be copied elsewhere. It began
to pay special attention to its sources of supply in the Middle
East and to its principal clients in Western Europe.[37] Their
hatred of the foreigners who depleted their soil, however, was
not strong enough to forge the peoples of the Middle East
into a powerful and united community.

In January, 1968, the principal oil-exporting countries of
the Middle East — Saudi Arabia, Kuwait, Iran, Iraq, Qatar,
Syria and Libya — joined with Indonesia and Venezuela to

---

35. In 1938 Mexico expropriated Royal Dutch Shell, Standard
Oil, and several other foreign companies which refused to grant
wage increases demanded by the oil workers union (which
amounted to $ 1.7 million per year). Mexican President Car-
denas founded Pemex, a state company which was boycotted at
first by its powerful neighbors. The British government even
broke diplomatic relations with Mexico. It was not until the
Second World War that the Consortium forgave the Mexicans.
Today Pemex pays the Mexican government nearly a billion
pesos a year in taxes, while before the nationalization the
amount paid by private companies operating in Mexico never
exceeded 44 million.

In 1963 Mexico, once considered incapable of exploiting her
own resources, was producing 115 million barrels (16 million
tons), and oil was her most important source of revenue. These
expropriations ensured her prosperity if not her economic independence for the Mexican economy is still closely bound to that
of the United States.

36. Shell was the first oil company to operate in Venezuela.
In 1922 it was joined by Standard of Indiana, followed by Gulf.
In 1932 Standard of New Jersey took over Standard of Indiana's
operations at Maracaibo and began offshore drilling. In 1937
Venezuela accounted for 40 % of world production. Gulf was
obliged to make concessions to Jersey, whose local subsidiary
Creole became the giant of Venezuela. In 1938 Jersey, Gulf and
Shell formed a pool to exploit their reserves and naturally
applied Texas prices. In 1943 the companies were obliged to split

form an organization to commercialize the oil of its member states, to defend their economic and commercial interests, and to examine ways to develop the oil industry and its derivatives. The principal object of this agreement was to raise prices and create a fleet of tankers and a petrochemical industry under the control of the producing countries themselves.

The Consortium is fighting every foot of the way, but it is beginning to realize that its days in the Middle East are numbered. On the other hand, it has sufficient political power to maintain its position for the moment in Venezuela. Cau-

---

their profits 50-50 with the Venezuelan government. In 1948 the " Democratic Action " government that had come to power in 1945 demanded a revision of this agreement, but was overthrown by a military junta backed by the United States. Between 1949 and 1954, Creole reduced its personnel from 20,500 to 14,400 persons while increasing its production by 35 %. In 1949 the company earned net profits of $ 336 million.

The revenue paid by the oil companies covered three-quarters of the Venezuelan national budget (the government's revenues from other sources were lower in 1956 than Creole's profits). But Venezuela produces only half the grain, milk and meat, and only one-third of the vegetables, that she consumes. The wide plains of Orinico support fewer cattle today than during the revolution of 1812. From their mountain *conucos* or their huts on the latifundia, nine-tenths of the Venezuelan population can watch the distant lights of fabulous Caracas.

37. In January, 1957, Anthony Nutting, a member of the British Cabinet, suggested a form of internationalization — a kind of " Schuman plan " for Middle East oil.

In March, 1957, Walter J. Levy wrote in *Foreign Affairs* :

"...The demands and responsibilities which have devolved on our international oil companies go far beyond the normal concerns of commercial operations. Public and private responsabilities become increasingly interwined. Our existing arrangements for government-industry relationships in this new uncharted area appear to be inadequate to cope with the broad range of new problems."

On April 10, 1957, Lord Henderson suggested before the House of Lords that her Majesty's Government " take the initiative, through the United Nations, to get an International Oil Convention for the Middle East which would ensure a just distribution of oil to consumer contries, as well as a fair deal for the oil-producing countries. 'Oil politics' have been a disturbing factor in the Middle East situation over many years", the British peer added.

tion, however, has led it to concentrate its exploration efforts in South America and Africa, where the oil fields of Libya, the Sahara, Nigeria, and Gabon produce more than 700 million barrels. For Jersey Standard, the future lies in Africa.

The Consortium also had problems in Europe. In 1966 Western Europe consumed 2.9 billion barrels of oil, only 126 million of which came from her own soil. Britain is a member of the Consortium. Her oil policy is patterned after that of the United States, and despite the promise of important oil discoveries in the North Sea, she remains dependent on her concessions in the Persian Gulf and has not yet resolved her coal problem.[38] The Common Market is a bigger headache for the Consortium. Germany produces only 56 million barrels of oil a year, plus an additional 14 million barrels in Libya, but the distribution networks in Germany are almost entirely controlled by American concerns (Texaco was able to buy out DEA, an important Germany company, with only one-fourth of its annual profits).

Italy is less aggressive but just as realistic as France. Her oil policy is that defined by Enrico Mattei, and she is linked to the Soviet COMECOM pipeline at Trieste. The Italians have undertaken explorations in the Adriatic, Somalia, the Sinai, the Gulf of Suez, Tunisia, and the Persian Gulf. In December, 1967 they obtained a 12,000 square kilometer concession at Rub El Khali in Saudi Arabia, together with permission to construct a petrochemical complex.

In France the present Minister of Agriculture and former Prime Minister, Edgar Faure, wrote in 1939 that " If the government has an oil policy, the leaders of the oil industry

---

And Walter Lippman wrote in November of the same year :

"'We should, it seems to me, have it clearly in mind that we are on the threshold of a new situation in regard to the oil in the Middle East. This is often taken to mean that the Arab countries, infiltrated by the Soviet Union, may attempt to ruin Western Europe by depriving it of access to the oil.

"'Theoretically, that could happen if we take the simple view that Russia may conquer and occupy the oil countries. But in fact, this is not likely to happen, since it would precipitate a world war. What is likely to happen is that the Arab countries, using Soviet influence as a lever, will attempt to force the Western oil

will have a policy in the government. " Until 1939 France too
was dominated by the Consortium. Since De Gaulle's accession to power in 1958, and in particular since 1963, France
has stood in direct opposition to the interests of the American
oil industry. The French government already controlled a
portion of the third-largest non-American company in the
world, the Compagnie Française des Pétroles, and it spent
several billion dollars drilling for oil in the Sahara. When
political considerations forced De Gaulle to give the Sahara
back to the Algerians, the government, desirous of obtaining
oil independence, began looking in other directions. A state
oil company, ERAP, was created which today ranks 17th in
the world, and whose activities and policies in the Middle
East (notably in Irak and Iran) run contrary to the methods
and interests of the International Consortium.[39] Today,

---

companies to a radical revision of the existing contracts. The
Middle Eastern countries have no interest in cutting off the
export of oil to Europe. On the contrary, it is their vital interest
that the trade should continue. What they will seek, both the
oil-bearing countries around the Persian Gulf and the transit
countries like Syria and Egypt, is a bigger share of the profits of
tne oil business.

38. The British continue to work the unprofitable coal mines
of Wales, the Midlands, Yorkshire, Nottinghamshire, and Lan-
cashire, immobilizing some 700,000 workers, and British explorations in the North Sea area are carried out in collaboration with
the big American firms.

British fiscal legislation is far less favorable to the oil industry
than American legislation. Britain's energy policy consist of
penalizing the use of oil in order to protect her coal industry.
British tax legislation does not appear to have contributed signi-
ficantly to the overseas expansion of British oil companies, and
it offers no special privileges designed to stimulate new explorations by British firms.

39. On February 4, 1968, ERAP signed an agreement with
the Irak National Oil Company (INOC) giving the French company on-shore and off-shore exploration rights on a 10,000
square kilometer concession along the Persian Gulf. Mr. Jean
Blancard, Vice-President of ERAP, declared that the agreement
" follows in the footsteps of history. The era of traditional
concessions, when the oil power established their hegemony
over huge areas, is a thing of the past. "

At the same time, another French company, the Société Nationale

France is the most active supporter of the idea of a Common Market oil organization. Such a body is indispensable to Europe, but it is contrary to the interests of the Consortium — in other words, to the interests of the big American companies.[40]

In November, 1966, Walter J. Levy, an American expert, submitted a 52- page confidential report to the European Economic Community (Common Market). Levy noted that " eighteen percent of the oil importations of the Common Market are controlled by the companies of the Common Market.[41] As things stand now, this figure is destined to drop. " Levy recommended the adoption throughout the Common Market of fiscal measures of the type already existing in France, which are aimed at stimulating oil explorations. These measures are specifically directed at the oil industry and are nearly as favorable as the tax privileges granted oil companies in the United States, with the difference that in France any amount deductible from taxes must be reinvested within five years in explorations or related activities. Levy suggested that this provision be included in any fiscal measures adopted by the Common Market countries.

---

des Pétroles d'Aquitaine, was competing with the Freeport Co. for the right to work an Iraqi sulphur deposit which would make it the second largest producer of sulphur in the world.

Also in Iraq, the Compagnie Française des Pétroles was negotiating for the North Rumeila concession which the Iraqi government had seized from the Irak Petroleum Company.

The economic and political differences between France and the United States are partly the result of French oil policy.

40. The only company producing any significant quantity of oil in France thus far has been an American firm, Esso Rep, which is 90 % controlled by Jersey Standard (Esso Standard 89 % ; Finarep 1 %). Esso Rep has an annual production of 21 million barrels.

The most important French oil company, the Compagnie Française des Pétroles, founded by Raymond Poincaré, is not a state concern. Mr. Jeanneney, French Minister of Industry, declared in 1960 that "'state control of the CFP is extremely theoretical " and that " the interests of the ' oil franc ' are not always given priority. " In actual fact, according to well-informed sources, control is held by a number of different companies acting for Royal Dutch Shell.

This report, which was submitted to Dr. Walter Hallstein, was an indication of the Common Market's preoccupation with the development of the oil industry of its member states in order to be able to compete with the Consortium.[42]

This orientation of the oil policy of the Common Market was hardly welcomed by the Consortium. The battle was on.[43] The measures proposed by France and Walter J. Levy to enable the Common Market to regain its oil independence were identical to those that had enabled the United States to gain control of the market.

The oil industry has dominated the American economy for

. ERAP, the state-owned company, has not quite caught up with the CFP, but it already holds first place among the state-owned companies in continental Europe, and it is evident that the French government is anxious to see it expand.

41. The European companies concerned by this report were : Ente Nazionale Idrocarburi (ENI, Rome), Entreprise de Recherches et d'Activité Pétrolières (ERAP, Paris), and several German companies belonging to the Deutsche Mineraloel-Explorationsgesellschaft MBH (DEMINEX).

42. Ten European companies (ERAP, ENI, C. Deilman Bergbau GmbH, Preussag AG, Deutsche Schachtbau und Tiefbohr GmbH, Saarbergwerke AG, Schlolven Chemie AG, Union Rheinische Braunkohlen Kraftstoff AG, Wintershall AG and Gelsenkirchener Bergwerks AG) followed up this report with one of their own that was nothing less than a declaration of war on the Consortium. It conclued :

" If the Common Market is to have an energy policy, the oil and natural gas sector, which constitutes the most important element in this policy, must not escape the action of the Common Market. To prevent this from happening, the Common Market must create conditions which enable this policy to exist through legislation and regulations adapted to the circumstances, and it must safeguard the instruments of this policy, in other words the companies of the Common Market. "

43. A German, firm, Saarwerke, and an Italian company, ENI, have received permission from the French government to install a distribution network in France. Other measures and agreements are currently under discussion.

This new European energy policy explains a great deal, and in particular De Gaulle's position with regard to the Israeli-Arab conflict of 1967. De Gaulle is neither pro-Arab nor pro-Zionist ; he is merely a realist.

nearly 40 years.[44] The 1930 crisis enabled it to eliminate the independent prospectors and made possible the establishment of federal and especially state controls the likes of which existed in no other industry, and which had the effect of maintaining artificially high prices for petroleum products. You will find no mention of price fluctuations for crude oil and gas in any financial publication. Almost all of the world's raw commodities are quoted on the stock exchange, with the exception of oil.[45]

The oil market is no freer in the United States than it is in the rest of the world.[46] The rules that govern the activities of the Oil Empire within the United States are particularly advantageous for prospectors and land owners[47], which explains why there are more than a million oil wells on U.S. territory, and why 400,000 of them produce, or are permitted to produce, only 10 barrels a day (while one well in Mexico has an annual production of 7 million barrels, and several wells in Irak produce more than 500,000 barrels a year).

Mackay, the British oilman, once remarked, " The Americans are plundering their natural resources ". Under the rules that have governed the American oil industry for nearly 40 years, two-thirds of the United States reserves have been wasted. Henry M. Bates, Dean of the University of Michigan Law School, remarked in 1935 that " the losses resulting from the rule that any oil discovered belongs to the property owner can be evaluated at several billion dollars and constitute the most ruthless and the most unjustifiable destruction of our

---

44. Twenty-two companies account for 65 % of all the oil produced and 87 % of all the oil refined in the United States. Nine thousand other compagnies account for the rest.

In 1963, oil and natural gas provided 75 % of all the power consumed in the United States (as compared with 60 % in 1950). Their combined value was eight times that of all the ferrous and non-ferrous metals (iron, copper, lead, zinc, gold, silver, bauxite, manganese, tungsten, titanium, and uranium) mined in the United States.

45. An Oil Exchange did exist in the 19th Century, but in 1895 Standard Oil of New Jersey announced that henceforth it would set its prices itself. At that time, Jersey Standard was buying 80 % of all the oil produced in Pennsylvania and controlled all of the pipelines (which enabled the companies to

natural resources ever perpetrated by the American people. "

Nevertheless, the oil industry justifies its privileged position by pointing to the need to conserve American oil reserves, a major part of the wealth of the nation and a strategic necessity in time of war. But, as Harvey O'Connor remarks, the word " conservation " must be taken with a grain of salt. When oilmen talk about conservation, they are speaking of the conservation of their profits.

The problem emrged for the first time in 1930, when the immense reserves of the East Texas oilfields upset the balance of the market. It was decided that production quotas would be established each month in accordance with the demand. A national quota was set, and in each oil-producing state a special body was established to see that it was respected.[48] In

---

enforce their production quotas and the quotas set by the states).

46. There are 200,000 sales outlets for petroleum products in the United States, mainly service stations. To all appearances there is open competition, but actually the big oil corporations control 85 % of the market. Service station managers are bound by contract to the big companies, which supply their gasoline and cover their operating and advertising expenses.

47. Contrary to what is true in Europe, in the United States any oil discovered belongs to the owner of the land on which it is found. Generally, the owners lease their rights to the companies. In 1963 the oil companies paid nearly $ 2 billion in leasing rights to property owners spread over one-tenth of the area of the United States, principally in Texas. Since 1859 these leases have cost the companies an estimated $ 40 billion.

48. Ninety percent of the American Oil Empire is concentrated in only seven states : Texas, Louisiana, California, Oklahoma, Wyoming, New Mexico, and Kansas. The combined production of Texas and Louisiana alone accounted for 55 % of American domestic production in 1963. Most of the oil companies based in Texas have important|investments in Louisiana, which is closer to the Eastern market.' Louisiana, where the most important oilfields since Spraberry Fields in the 1930's were discovered in 1956, is also favored by a larger "'acreage-to-well" ratio than Texas. The average well in Louisiana is currently allowed 79 % more oil daily than the average well in Texas.

Most of these oil wells produce only two or three weeks per month. In Texas, the number of production days was reduced from 171 in 1957 to 104 in 1960. During the second quarter of 1960, the oil wells in Texas were worked an average of only 9 days per month, and during these 9 days they were limited to

Texas, this task was assigned to the Texas Railroad Commission, which had been created in 1891 to regulate the railroads. In 1919 its authority was extended to the oil industry. Given the dominant position of the state of Texas in the Oil Empire, the Texas Railroad Commission serves as a model for the other state regulatory bodies. The annual variations in the quota bear no relation to scientific conservation techniques.[49] Nor are the consumers represented on these commissions. The system is, in effect, a monopoly, and it enables the oil industry to top all other American industries in sales per employee[50] and to maintain a steady rate of profits regardless of the national economic situation and international events.[51]

The system of " posted prices " is one of the pillars of the industry. These prices do not represent the net cost increased by a normal margin of profit. Instead, they are fixed by the Consortium. While it is difficult to determine the actual net cost of crude oil, it can be estimated at one-tenth the wholesale sales price. The companies of the Consortium and the company-backed local rulers (in Venezuela as in the Middle East) pocket most of the difference.[52] The Consortium's profits were and are excessive when calculated on

---

two-thirds of their maximum output. The producers estimated their loses at $ 6 million per year, but prices remained stable. On the other hand, the number of people employed was reduced by 25 % (from 164,904 in 1958 to 124,922 in 1963) and the corresponding expenses dropped from $ 967 million to $ 880 million   Nevertheless, despite this reduction in output, nearly 200 new wells are drilled every day (43,300 in 1950, 58,200 in 1956, and 43,600 in 1963).

49. Petroleum engineers have their own techniques of conservation, which can be resumed as follows :
1) the elimination of gushers and uncontrolled flows that waste gas pressure
2) the limitation of the number of wells to the minimum required by the geological structure of the oilfield. Too many wells reduce the gas and water pressure, while too few result in the loss of a certain amount of oil
3) the regulation of the output of each well so as to maintain a uniform pressure throughout the oilfield
4) the maintenance in each well of a sufficient proportion of gas to oil to ensure a continuous flow

(Harvey O'Connor, *The Empire of Oil*)

production costs in Texas, but the latter, which already include profits for the local operators, are four or five times higher than net costs in the Middle East, and three times higher than net costs in Venezuela.

The American independent producers are constantly urging higher production quotas for themselves. In 1954 twenty-nine companies were forced to lower production as a result of competition from foreign oil. Even Standard of Indiana

---

50. The figures given by *Fortune* for the year 1967 are :
Oil : $ 64,943
Mining : $ 54,023
Automobiles : $ 25,016
Aviation : $ 19,179
Textiles : $ 18,404

51. Standard Oil of New Jersey earned $ 758 million in 1961 and $ 840 million in 1962 ; Gulf Oil earned $ 338 million in 1961 and $ 340 million in 1962 ; Socony Mobil earned $ 210 million in 1961 and $ 242 million in 1962 ; Standard Oil of Indiana earned $ 153 million in 1961 and $ 162 million in 1962.

52. The net cost of oil as it comes out of the well in the Middle East is around 20 to 30 cents per barrel. The same oil is sold by the Consortium at between $ 2 and $ 3 a barrel.

Oil in Kuwait costs approximately 5 cents a barrel (0.12 cents a gallon) ; oil in Saudi Arabia costs 10 cents a barrel (0.24 cents a gallon) ; and oil in Libya costs 40 cents a barrel (1 cent a gallon). In March, 1965, Consortium prices for oil leaving these countries was as follows :

Kuwait :	$ 1.59 a barrel
Iran :	$ 1.78 a barrel
Saudi Arabia :	$ 1.80 a barrel
Iraq :	$ 1.95 a barrel
Sidon :	$ 2.17 a barrel
Libya :	$ 2.21 a barrel
Sahara :	$ 2.30 a barrel

The companies charge 60 to 70 cents a barrel for transportation. The considerable increase in the tonnage of today's oil tankers (100,000 and 200,000 tons, and soon even more) ensure even greater profits than those earned by the oilmen in the Fifties and Sixties (a 100,000 ton tanker earns approximately $ 500,000 gross per cargo).

Excluding these transportation charges (the companies generally use their own fleets of tankers), the profits per barrel of oil are 3 to 4 times higher for overseas than for domestic production.

complained that imports had increased by 35 % between 1951 and 1954, while at the same time its Texas production had been ordered cut by 35 %. (It was as a result of these complaints that the members of the Consortium agreed to sell the independents 5 % of the shares in their Iranian operations). But the independents' protests had little effect. The big corporations had friends in Washington. In 1952 a commercial treaty concluded with Venezuela set the import duty for Venezuela oil at 2 % of its value, rather than the 20 % requested by the American producers. The National Security Resources Board, backed by the Mutual Security Agency, recommended that import duties be abolished altogether " if necessary. "

In 1955 the government considered limiting oil imports to 10 % of national production, but the big corporations promised not to exceed their importation level of the preceding year, and this apparently satisfied Eisenhower. Actually, Jersey Standard and the other members of the Consortium had little to fear from any restrictions imposed by Congress. Their foreign market was growing steadily, and they had diversified interests within the United States. Their importations of foreign oil brought them super-profits, but they made money from their integrated operations in Texas, Oklahoma, and Louisiana as well.

Conflicting interests can rarely be reconciled. Texas and Venezuela seemed destined to clash, but the men from Jersey Standard were well versed in the art of the most profitable

---

The net cost to the companies of the Consortium has remained relatively stable since 1954. The retail sales price for gasoline in American service stations in November, 1967 was $ 9.51 a barrel (plus tax). This gasoline was sold at an average price of 33.33 cents a gallon (which included 10.68 cents in taxes). The break-down of this final price was as follows :

Retails profits :   approximately 20 %
Taxes :   approximately 30 %
Transportation, refining, refinery labor, miscellaneous costs and refining costs, transportation from the Gulf to the refinery, delivery to the retailer, storage, and wholesale profits : 20 %
Price of the crude :   20 %

compromise. The big integrated corporations make profits on all four sectors of their activities : extraction, transportation, refining, and retail sales. Distribution is sometimes run at a loss and pipeline profits are largely fictitious. Refining is an indispensable intermediate operation of which the independents are purposely deprived. Extraction is the main source of revenue, but it is the interlocking operations as a whole that provide the profits.[53]

The profit margins of small, strictly producing companies are extremely precarious, particularly in the case of the independent refineries, which are at the mercy of a slight increase in the cost of crude or a slight drop in the price of gasoline.[54]

(but the latter price already included the company's profits on production and transportation).

The United States is the only important industrial nation in the world where the oil industry makes more on a gallon of gasoline than the government (70 % as opposed to 30 %). In Europe in particular, these proportions are generally the reverse, to the benefit of the countries concerned.

53. Beneath the Big Five and the twenty-odd large companies are a multitude of independent producers. Concentration has been the rule in the oil industry for the past ten years. Between 1959 and 1963, the big corporations of the Chase Manhattan Group increased their production by 526,000 barrels per day, while the production of other companies dropped by 37,000 barrels.

In 1956 the ten largest companies in Texas produced 41 % of all the oil in the state ; by 1963 they were producing 51 %. The decline of the small producers was due in part to the quota system (proration) imposed by the States (actually by the big companies). In addition, a number of independent producers were bought out by larger companies.

The independents still accounted for half of national production, but pipeline fees considerably reduced their independence.

54. Oil cooperatives are virtually unknown in the United States. The first was the Consumers Cooperative Association of Kansas City, Missouri, founded in 1929 with a capital of $ 3,000. In 1962, however, the total production of the cooperatives equalled only 200,000 barrels, while a single unit at Baytown, Texas belonging to Humble Oil produced 300,000. The cooperatives own less than 1 % of the wells in the United States, and their refiners can handle only a fifth of the oil they produce. Nor do they have a pipeline or other organized means of transportation.

The independent, integrated producers and the small producers of crude are in a somewhat better position. They
benefit not only from the posted prices, but also from the
special tax privileges accorded the oil industry as a whole.
These fiscal privileges enable the Big Five to earn colossal
profits while guaranteeing super-profits to the big independent
and integrated companies. They also provide large profits for
the medium-sized concerns, particularly the producers, and it
is to them that the small producers, which in any other sector
of the American economy would have been swallowed up
long ago, owe their survival.[55]

A booklet entitled " An Appraisal of the Petroleum Industry of the United States ", published in 1965 by the Office of
Oil and Gas (headed by Rear Admiral Onnie P. Lattu)
devotes only one line in 96 pages to the depletion
allowance.[56] But Milton Friedman, who can hardly be accused of being a socialist, wrote a whole article on the subject
in the June 26, 1967 issue of *Newsweek* :

" Few U.S. industries sing the praises of free enterprise
more loudly than the oil industry. Yet few industries rely so
heavily on special governmental favors. These favors are
defended in the name of national security. A strong domestic
oil industry, it is said, is needed because international disturbances can so readily interfere with the supply of foreign
oil. The Israeli-Arab war has produced just such a distur-
bance, and the oil industry is certain to point to it as

Cooperatives do not aspire to control the market, but in
countries where they are sufficiently powerful (such as Sweden,
where they account for 12 % of the market), they serve as a
restraint on the conduct of the other companies.

55. As Walter J. Levy notes : " The companies which are
integrated from the well to the service station have obvious
competitive advantages over the strictly producing companies, for
they can temporarily do without their profits from one sector of
their operations."

Standard Oil of New Jersey, for exemple, is apparently content
with a profit rate of approximately 17 % which, taking into
account its superprofits from its foreign operations, necessarily
reduces its profits from its domestic operations and, given its
nearly complete control of the market, the profit margins of the
independent producers as well.

confirmation of the need for special favors. Are they right ? I believe not.

" The main special favors are :
" 1 - *Percentage depletion.* This is a special provision of the Federal income tax under which oil producers can treat up to 27.5 % of their income as exempt from income tax — supposedly to compensate for the depletion of oil reserves. This name is a misnomer. In effect, this provision simply gives the oil industry (and a few others to which similar treatment has been extended) a lower tax rate than other industries.

" 2 - *Limitation of oil production.* Texas, Oklahoma, and some other oil-producing states limit the number of days a month that oil wells may operate or the amount that they may

---

But the big oil companies conceal some of their profits in companies incorporated in privileged territories. Jersey Standard, for exemple, uses the International Corporation registered in Liechtenstein. (In the United States, the tax haven for H.L. Hunt and many other oilmen is the state of Delaware).

56. The depletion allowance is based on the notion that the more oil has been extracted from a well, the less there is left. This, of course, is nothing more than a special version of what is known in industry as depreciation.

If a $ 100,000 factory operates for ten years, its owner is entitled to deduct $ 10,000 a year from his gross profits for plant depreciation. In the oil industry, on the contrary, the rate of depreciation applied has nothing to do with the cost of running a well. A well which costs $ 100,000 and produces $ 500,000 worth of oil each year for ten years until it runs dry would normally justify a depreciation of $ 10,000 a year.

An oil company, however, is entitled to deduct 27.5 % per year from its gross income, which amounts, in the case cited above, to $ 137,500 per year, or to $ 1,375,000 in ten years, on an investment of only $ 100,000.

The Common Market has considered applying this system to its own industry, but with certain basic differences. Europe, contrary to the United States, needs first to find oil in her own soil. As a result, the Common Market measures would grant a tax reduction to companies carrying out explorations, on the condition that the amount of this deduction be re-invested within five years in new explorations (French P.R.G. system).

produce. The purpose of these limitations is said to be ' con
servation. ' In practice, they have led to the wasteful drilling
of multiple wells draining the same field. And the amount of
production permitted has been determined primarily by estimates of market demand, not by the needs of conservation.
The state regulatory anthorities have simply been running a
producers' cartel to keep up the price of oil.

" 3 - *Oil import quotas*. The high domestic prices enforced by
restriction of production were threatened by imports from
abroad. So, in 1959, President Eisenhower imposed a quota
on imports by sea. This quota is still in effect. Currently it is
slightly more than 1 million barrels a day (under one-fifth of
our total consumption).

" Foreign oil can be landed at East Coast refineries for
about $ 1 to $ 1.50 a barrel less than the cost of domestic oil.
The companies fortunate enough to be granted import permits
are therefore in effect getting a Federal subsidy of this amount
per barrel — or a total of about $ 400 million a year.

" These special favors cost U.S. consumers of oil products
something over $ 3.5 billion a year. (Gibert Burck, *Fortune*,
April, 1965). This staggering cost cannot be justified by its
contribution to national security.

" The following points indicate the basis for this judgment :
" 1 - Restricting imports may promote the domestic industry
but why pay a $ 400 million subsidy to oil importers ? A tariff
of $ 1.25 a barrel would restrict imports just as much — and
the U.S. Government rather than the oil importers would get
the revenue. (I do not favor such a tariff but it would be less
bad than a quota).

" 2 - Oil from Venezuela — after the U.S., the largest oil
producer in the world — is most unlikely to be cut off by
international disturbances threatening our national security.
Yet it too is covered by the import quota.

" 3 - Restrictions on domestic oil production at least have
the virtue that domestic production could be expanded rapidly
in case of need. But such restrictions are an incredibly expensive way to achieve flexibility.

" 4 - The world oil industry is highly competitive and far-
flung and getting more so. The Mideast crisis has let large

oil-producting areas undisturbed. Moreover, the Arabian countries themselves cannot afford to refuse to sell for long. Only World War III is likely to produce severe disruptions of supply — and then the emergency is likely to be brief.

" 5 - If all the special favors to the oil industry were abandoned, prices to the consumer would decline sharply. Domestic production also might decline — but then again, if the industry were freed of all the artificial props that raise costs and stifle initiative, production might rise rather than decline. In either event, a vigorous and extensive domestic industry would remain, protected by the natural barrier of transportation costs.

" If domestic production did decline, we might want to insure against an emergency by stockpiling oil, paying for holding reserve wells in readiness, making plans for sharp reductions in nonessential consumption, or in other ways. Measures such as these could provide insurance at a small fraction of the $ 3.5 billion a year the U.S. consumer is now paying.

" The political power of the oil industry, not national security, is the reason for the present subsidies to the industry. International disturbances simply offer a convenient excuse. "[57]

---

57. Not only did the activities of the Consortium hurt the American consumer and the American taxpayer ; they also had serious repercussions in underdeveloped countries and affected the international monetary situation.

The Consortium sold its oil from Venezuela, Colombia, Kuwait, Saudi Arabia, Irak, Iran, etc. exclusively in dollars and pounds sterling. (Even the internal operations of the members of the Consortium were carried out in dollars or in pounds.) As a result, the sales made in " oil dollars " and " oil sterling " swelled the treasuries of the United States and Great Britain, to the detriment of the currencies of the producing and consumer countries, in particular, and to the world financial situation in general.

This system contributed to the disequilibrium in the British balance of payments which led to the November, 1967 devaluation, and has forced the United States to take measures to protect the dollar. The financial difficulties besetting both countries today are symptoms of 20 years of abusive business practices, particularly in the marketing of raw commodities.

Indeed, the American oil industry enjoys extraordinary political power. When Kennedy entered the White House, the American fiscal system, and in particular the system of the depletion allowance, had enabled a few operators in the oil industry like H.L. Hunt to amass in only a few years the kind of fortune it had taken Rockefeller a half-century and a great deal of patience to accumulate.

If a person had enough capital, speculation in oil operations carried virtually no risk. He could take capital which normally would have been taxed at the rate of 90 % and invest it in new oil wells. A speculator with $ 900,000 in this tax bracket could drill nine wells (at an average cost of $ 10,000). The odds were that one well out of nine would be productive. The eight dry wells would have cost him $ 10,000 each, all tax-free, and the ninth would earn him a fortune. With a little perseverance, any speculator! could make a million.

Pools or joint ventures enabled citizens with more modest revenues, but whose income was still partly taxed in the 90 % bracket, to do the same thing. These persons would purchase fractional interests in an oil well. Some of them never even got to see " their " well, but every tax dollar they invested represented a gain of approximately 25 % on their capital. In the war and immediate post-war period, investment in the petroleum industry was one of the most obvious and attractive ways of reducing personal income tax liability. For the non-professionals this system was still, to a certain extent, a speculation, but the same was not true of the big companies, which employed experienced geologists and commanded unlimited capital.[58]

These special privileges constituted an international anomaly, and they cost the nation several billion dollars every year.[59] It has been estimated that the abolition of these favors would have enabled the government to avoid the 1951 tax increase that applied to taxpayers earning as little as $ 4,000 a year. The oilmen, conscious of the importance of these privileges, have always claimed that their abolition would hinder new explorations. But the fantastic number of wells drilled in the United States represents a waste of natural resources.

In 1963, the oilmen advanced other arguments.[60] They

noted that the market for American crude had grown from 1 billion barrels in 1930 to nearly 2 billion in 1950 and almost 3 billion in 1963, and they made known their " concern " about a future shortage. Their cautious and seemingly pessimistic prognostics, however, were not confirmed by more independent-minded experts. Professor A.I. Levorsen of Stanford University had declared in 1949 that world oil reserves were sufficient to cover the world's needs for the next five centuries, and other scientists estimated that only 1/1,000th of the surface of the earth and sea had been explored thus far.[61]

---

58. The Humble Oil and Refining Co. declared that in 40 years it had sunk $ 500 million (a figure which represents less than half of its present capital) in deep, dry wells. But although these dry wells cost it $ 62 million in 1957, the same wells cost the federal government more than half a million in lost revenues, and Humble Oil that year earned $ 175 million in profits.

59. In Britain, oil companies are not permitted to deduct their losses from unsuccessful explorations from their income from sources other than oil production. If the explorations are successful, the entire cost of the original installation can be written off, but may not be deducted as expenses, and there is no provision for a percentage depletion allowance deductible from revenue from current production.

60. In 1965 the oil industry claimed that American reserves were no more than 31 billion barrels. The Office of Oil and Gas of the Department of the Interior commented, however, that " Reserves so defined are probably on the conservative side " and added :

" A study compiled in late 1964 by the U.S. Geological Survey puts the amount of crude oil originally in place in known deposits as of January 1, 1964, at over 400 billion barrels. The study goes further to conclude that an additional 2 billion feet of exploratory drilling in favorable but as yet unexplored areas would yield an additional 600 billion barrels of crude oil in place. Of this, 73 billion had actually been withdrawn as of the end of 1963. On the basis of these cold figures, it would appear that the U.S. is in no danger of running out of oil for many years. "

Additionally, it is now possible to extract oil from deposits of bituminous shale (a ton of bituminous shale yields 30 gallons of oil). The bituminous shale reserves of the United States have been estimated by the U.N. at 320 billion tons.

61. The average depth of the wells drilled increased from 3,900 ft. in 1950 to 5,000 ft. in 1963 (an increase of 29 %).

The oilmen also complained that it was becoming harder and harder to find oil in sufficient quantity to make it as easily extractable and as profitable as in the past. Between 1956 and 1967, it took twice the number of new field wildcats to make one profitable discovery compared with 10 years earlier.

These arguments became the theme song of the National Petroleum Council, the only lobby representing private interests that enjoys official standing. The NPC was founded in 1946 and is composed of representatives of the front offices of the big companies. It elects its own President. In reality, it is the NPC that defines the oil policy of the federal government, in the spirit of John Jay's maxim : " The country should be governed by those who own it. "[62] The President of the United States has no business interfering.

A half-century ago, the oilmen lacked the influence in the White House that they had over Congress. They regarded the President with suspicion. For them, the country had been going to the dogs since McKinley. The power of the oil lobby was a concern to every President who entered the White House after the accession to power of Jersey Standard and its little brothers and sisters. In 1920 President Harding was elected with the massive backing of the oil industry. Two members of his Cabinet were oilmen (Hughes of Standard and Fall, an associate of Sinclair). Coolidge, and after him Hoover, did nothing to displease the oil magnates. On the day of Franklin D. Roosevelt's death, a San Antonio oilman threw a huge party to celebrate. Roosevelt, nevertheless, had not been particularly aggressive towards the oil industry. The prewar climate was hardly favorable, and the war, which was still going on at the time of his death, had brought a boom in the oil business.

In 1950 President Truman examined the depletion allowance system, and the oilmen learned that the President felt that an exoneration that withheld such amounts from the Treasury was not equitable. That same year Hubert H. Humphrey, then a political neophyte and regarded as a liberal, introduced an amendment to the tax bill that would reduce the depletion allowance. The amendment was rejected. It was re-introduced in 1951 but rejected again by a margin of 71 to 9. In 1952 President Truman turned again to the problem, but any decision he might make was at the mercy of

Congress, and Harry Truman liked the quiet life. Nevertheless, during his last days in office he adopted one of
Roosevelt's ideas and declared that the continental shelf (an
extension of the American coastline) was part of the national
reserves and should be placed under the control of the Department of Defense. The value of the oil beneath the sea had
been estimated at $ 250 billion, and Truman felt it would be
madness to let this oil, which was vital for national defense,
fall into private hands, obliging the government to buy it back
at high prices.

In 1952 Eisenhower received heavy financial backing from
the oil industry in his campaign against Adlai Stevenson. Ike
knew how say thanks. When Truman's bill came up before
Congress, the House rejected it in favor of a measure recognizing the property rights of the states over any oil discovered within ten and a half miles (twelve for Texas and
Florida) of their coastline. The federal government was left
with only a right of preemption over the resources of its
former territory. The bill was later voted into law by the
Senate.[63]

In 1954 Senator Humpthrey's timid offensive was taken up
by Senators Douglas (Illinois) and Williams (Delaware), both
of whom introduced amendments concerning the depletion
allowance. Senator Douglas noted that in 1953 one company

---

62. In 1948, the oil shortage revealed the need for a national
oil policy. The Secretary of the Interior, J.A. Krug, and his
successor, Chapman, wanted to preclude a future shortage by the
development of synthetic motor fuels, if necessary with government backing. The NPC opposed this plan. It assured the government that private industry would produce substitutes if the
need arose, but insisted that there was no need to constitue
stocks of synthetics for the present. The plan was dropped, and
protests about the waste engendered by industry production
method were stifled.

63. The states of Rhode Island and Alabama contested the
validity of this law in the Supreme Court, claiming that Congress
had no right to hand over a part of the national wealth to a few
privileged states without their consent. They lost the case.

In the meantime, Senator Butler (Nebraska) was already preparing a bill that would recognize state ownership of the bituminous shale deposits in the Rockies.

with a net income of $ 4 million had paid only $ 404 in taxes, that another had paid nothing on a revenue of $ 5 million, and that a third company with profits of $ 12 million had received a $ 500,000 subsidy. The amendments were rejected.

On March 27, 1957, Senator Williams again introduced an amendment that would reduce the depletion allowance from 27.5 % to 20 %. He explained to Congress that this privilege had been instated during the First World War, when it amounted to only 5 %. Later it had been increased to 12.5 %, then to 25 %, and finally to 27.5 %. Originally it had been a discovery depletion, permitting the recovery of the investment, " but the present 27.5 % oil depletion rate obviously gives a special tax advantage to the oil industry above that enjoyed by other taxpayers. " He added that when the present rate of 27.5 % had been adopted in 1926, the corporate tax rate had been approximately 14 %. The depletion allowance therefore did not represent a huge sum of money. But in 1957, " with our present corporation rate, this 27.5 % gross sales deduc-

---

64. " The tax laws since 1926 have authorized an oil or gas company to deduct 27.5 % from the gross income from any property producing oil or gas. This 27.5 % depletion allowance or deduction is computed as a percentage of the investment or of the amount of prior depletion deductions. One saving condition was attached, namely : In no case may the deduction exceed 50 % of the net income from the property — something that I do not believe happens very often.

" Obviously, over the life of an oil or gas-producing property the depletion allowance will not only exceed the investment or cost, but it will go on and on and possibly exceed the value on date of discovery.

" The committee can, no doubt, secure accurate up-to-date figures from the Treasury Department on what the 27.5 % depletion allowance means to every company or individual taking this on tax returns. However, there is in existence some few pieces of information denoting its tremendous size. Recently I tried to secure from Standard & Poor's Corp. reports the amount of Federal income-tax paid by Amerada Petroleum Corp., but I find this item is buried in a classification reading : ' Operational, general expenses, taxes, etc. It is quite obvious that Amerada pays little, if any, Federal income taxes, though in the year 1952 this company made net profits of $ 16,296,652. In the January 1946 issue of *Fortune* magazine there appeared a long article on Amerada Petroleum Corp., which is a crude-oil producing com-tion, or depletion allowance, represents a tremendous tax-free bonanza.[64]

" The importance of percentage depletion is more glaringly emphasized in connection with the operations of foreign companies, " he continued. " The Treasury Department has submitted three examples as to how this works. Corporation A with total earnings of approximately $ 200 million reported a United States tax liability of $ 103,887,000. They paid foreign taxes which are deductible from United States taxes in the

---

pany. The article stated in part, ' Amerada's tax situation is a businessman's dream. The corporation quite literally does not have to pay any Federal income tax it does not want to. This is due to the highly reasonable provisions of the internal revenue law designed for producers of crude oil. Amerada pays so little in Federal income taxes that it does not even segregate the tax item in its annual reports. In wartime, though Amerada's profits soared, it made no provison for excess-profits taxes, and from 1943 until 1944 its normal Federal income tax actually declined. In 1944, on a gross of $ 26 million, a gross profit of $ 17 million, and a net after all charges of $ 5 million, Amerada's allowance for its Federal income tax was only $ 200,000.'

" It is among these strictly producing companies that one can get an idea of the magnitude of the twin subsidy of depletion and writeoff of drilling and development costs. The major integrated companies benefit to the degree that they produce oil and gas, though they have other operations upon which taxes are paid.

" In addition to Amerada Petroleum Corp. referred to above, here are a few other examples of companies producing oil and gas :

" Argo Oil Corp. for the year 1952 made net profits after taxes of $ 3,496,477 and paid Federal income taxes of $ 91,660.

" Kerr-McGee Oil Industries, Inc. for the year ended June 30, 1952 had net income after taxes of $ 2,234,688 and paid Federal income taxes of $ 78,032. For that same period the 27.5 % depletion allowance for this one company amounted to $ 607,611. For the year ended June 30, 1953, this company had net income after taxes of $ 3,072,723. But in Standard & Poor's there is just a line where the amount of tax is usually indicated, so I do not know what Federal income taxes this company paid for that period. During this latter year its depletion allowance was $ 858,795.

" The Superior Oil Co. (California) for the year ended August 31, 1952 had net income of $ 11,900,165 and paid Federal income taxes of $ 200,000."

amount of $ 103,323,000, leaving a United States tax liability of $ 564,000. This company has a total allowable depletion allowance of $ 91,879,000.

" Corporation B reported an income of approximately $ 150 million. Their total allowable depletion was $ 123,977,000, and they reported a United States tax liability of $ 78,961,000. The taxes reported as paid to foreign countries by Company B amounted to $ 98,319,000, and the credit allowed for foreign taxes paid was $ 77,087,000, leaving a United States tax liability after foreign tax credit of $ 1,874,000. Corporation C reported an income of approximately $ 33 million. The total allowable depletion of Corporation C was $ 44,895,000. The United States tax liability of this company was $ 17,325,000, and foreign taxes paid were of the same amount, with credit being given for the full total, leaving Company C with no United States tax liability. "

Senator Williams cited and inserted in the Congressional Record the testimony of Mr. Paul E. Hadlick, general counsel of the National Oil Marketers Association, to the Senate Finance Committee. Mr. Hadlick had prepared a list of the incomes and taxes paid by the 23 largest oil companies. His figures indicated that Humble Oil had paid $ 30 million in federal income taxes on a net income of $ 145 million, that Socony Vacuum Oil had paid $ 51 million on a net income of $ 171 million, that Standard Oil of California had paid $ 40 million on an income of $ 174 million, and that the Texas Company had paid $ 47 million in taxes on an income of $ 181 million.

Senator Barrett (Wyoming) retorted that " *the depletion allowance is based upon the great risk involved in drilling and discovering oil* ", and he drew Senator Williams' attention to the fact that " *our first line of defence will rest in air power, but the planes will not be able to deliver the bombs without high octane gasoline and plenty of it, I might say.* "[65] Senator Carlson (Kansas) declared : " *Those of us who are familiar with the reserves in the stripper well are in a position to know that the producers must have the 27.5 % depletion allowance and any other encouragement they can get, or the United States will lose millions of barrels of oil, which will never come out of the ground.* ". Senators Monroney (Oklahoma) and Martin (Pennsylvania) joined in the chorus. Senator Williams quoted a statement by the Secretary of the Treasury in 1937 : " This is the most glaring loophole in our present revenue law. " Nevertheless, he noted, depletion had not been discussed during the 1937 hearings, and the committee had made no recommendation in its report on the subject " because of lack of time. "

" Mr. President ", Senator Williams continued, " today we hear the same argument : lack of time. " Senator Williams spoke for another 15 minutes and then called for a vote. Senator Johnson (Texas) suggested the absence of a quorum. But there was a quorum, the vote was held, and the amendment was rejected.

Senator Douglas of Illinois then introduced his amendment, which maintained the percentage of 27.5 % on revenues not exceeding $ 1 million, but lowered it to 21 % for revenues of between $ 1 and $ 5 million, and to 15 % for revenues exceeding $ 5 million. Senator Aiken (Vermont) supported the Douglas amendment. " I believe that when these enormous depletion allowances are given to one segment of our economy, it means that other people must dig into their pockets to make up for them ", he said, adding that in 1955 " the total depletion deductions were approximately $ 2,800,000,000. Since the corporate tax would have been 52 %, this resulted in a tax saving of $ 1,500,000,000 to the oil companies. " My amendment ", he continued, " would save approximately $ 700 million for the Treasury. I wish to emphasize again that it would not hit the small driller. The weight would fall almost entirely upon the big companies. " He went on to cite examples of oil companies that didn't pay a cent of taxes (on $ 7 million in income), or 1 % of taxes (on $ 1,800,000 in income), or 6 % (on $ 95 million in income), while in other industries companies were taxed at the rate of 52 %.

The parade of lobbyists for the oil industry began. Senator Long (Louisiana) declared : " *I must oppose this amendment. I submit that in many respects it works out to be the absolute*

---

65. In 1963 the Department of Defense purchased 278 million barrels of oil (1963 production equalled 2.75 billion barrels).

epitome of unfairness and injustice. This is an amendment which proposes to say : Oilman Rich can earn and receive $ 1 million a year and still retain the 27.5 % depletion allowance. On the other hand, Grandma Jones who does not have the importance or prominence of an independent oil and gas man owns $ 200 worth of stock in an oil company, and she receives an income of $ 20 a year from that ownership... I would like to protect Grandma Jones' little $ 20 dividend. "

Senator Johnson (Texas) again suggested the absence of a quorum. The legislative clerk called the roll. Eighty-seven Senators were present. There was a quorum. Senator Douglas then asked for the yeas and nays, but his request was not sufficiently seconded. The yeas and the nays were not ordered, and the amendment was rejected. The Senate turned to the examination of an amendment concerning transportation taxes, which were considered too high for the Western states.

The following year, on August 11, 1958, Senator Williams introduced his amendment once again. He was obliged to wait for four hours until there were enough Senators present. He reminded them of what Senator La Follette had said in 1942 : " In my opinion this percentage depletion is one of the worst features of the bill, and now it is being extended. We are vesting interests which will come back to plague us. If we are to include all these things, why do we not put in sand and gravel ; why do we not provide for the depletion the farmer suffers through erosion of the soil of his farm ? "

Senator Taft had followed up Senator La Follette's remark with one of his own : " I think with the Senator from Wisconsin that the percentage depletion is to a large extent a gift... a special privilege beyond what anyone else can get. " Senator Dirksen (Illinois) made a long speech declaring that the problem of national defense needs and the precarity of oil supplies in the Middle East. *" is worth infinitely more than a question of whether the oil companies get a few million dollars more or a few million dollars less... the oil companies "*, he added, *" which have given their best to the country. "*

Senator Williams acknowledged that " it is always popular to defend the little fellow, but what is small about a man with a million dollar income ? " He noted that in 1955 depletion deductions for all corporations had totalled $ 2,805,500,000, and that 67 % of these deductions had benefited companies with net assets of more than $ 100 million. He asked why the deduction for oil depletion wasn't the same as that for metal (15 %) or coal (5 %). He concluded : " One of the really major loopholes in the tax code is the method by which capital gains may be applied to oil and gas properties ", and he produced a document which explained exactly why the leaders of the oil and natural gas industry were opposed to a reduction in the tax rate for the highest income brackets.[66] Such a reduction, which was supported by the majority of the nation's corporations and taxpayers, would mean a *decrease* in the incomes of the oilmen.

Senator Williams' amendment was put to a vote and defeated by a margin of 63 to 26. A similar but less liberal amendment introduced by Senator Proxmire (Wisconsin) was also defeated, this time by a majority of 58 to 43. Senator John Kennedy (Massachusetts) voted against the Williams

---

66. This was a paper written by Paul Haber, J.D., Ph. D. entitled " Writeoffs, Cost Depletion and Percentage Depletion — an Appraisal ". It said in part :

" Our Federal tax system is supposed to be based on the principle of progressive taxation or ' ability to pay ' — the higher the net income, the higher the rate of tax. In the case of taxpayers who engage in the business of crude oil, however, this principle is made to work in reverse — the higher the net income from the production and sale of crude oil, the lower the rate of tax...

" Drilling for oil is like playing dice with the Treasury : ' Heads I win, tails you lose', with the Treasury always on the losing end. As a matter of fact, high tax rates are a boon to the crude oil industry rather than a burden, because the higher the rate of tax the lower the net cost (the after-tax cost) of the drilling operation. This explains why the American Petroleum Institute does not support the National Association of Manufacturers in its fight to reduce the top tax bracket from 90 percent to 40 percent. If the rate were reduced to 40 percent, the search for crude oil would fall off tremendously, because the taxpayer's share of the cost of the search would have been increased from 10 percent (100 percent less 90 percent) to 60 percent (100 percent less 40 percent). As a matter of fact, the phenomenal growth of the crude oil industry dates back to the year 1940, the year in which the wartime rates were first brought into the statute. "

amendment and in favor of Senator Proxmire's amendment. When the vote on the second amendment was announced, Senator Johnson (Texas) remarked, " *Mr. President, I do not think we should ask the Senate to stay any later this evening.* "

The oilmen and their representatives in the Senate were all the more concerned about these amendments because 1957 had been a record year for oil production in the Middle East, and everything indicated that the expansion would continue. (In fact, Middle East production rose from 6 billion barrels in 1958 to 9.7 billion barrels in 1963). In 1959 President Eisenhower imposed import quotas on foreign oil. The sales price of domestic American oil, which had been steadily rising since the end of the Depression and had dropped in 1959, held steady in 1960.[67]

On June 18, 1960 Senator Douglas re-introduced his amendment. He noted that the total depletion allowances taken could amount to $ 4 billion that year. He presented his Congressional colleagues with 20 pages of documents, remarking that if the other Senators were unable to hear him (for there were only three other people on the floor), they could perhaps read them. The following day, June 20, his audience was larger. Senator Douglas described his amendment as " a very moderate attempt to reduce the greatest tax racket in the entire American revenue system. It is probably safe to say, " he continued, " that the depletion allowances given to the gas and oil industry now amount to well over $ 2.5 billion a year. I have put into the Record time and time again the records of 28 oil companies — which I do not name, and which I identify only by letter, but which I could name — that show that there was one company which in 5 years had net profits of $ 65 million and not only paid no taxes, but received $ 145,000 back from the Government. There are many other corporations which have a similar favored record.

" My proposal is a modest one. I do not propose to abolish the depletion allowance. I do not propose to reduce it across the board. I merely propose to introduce a moderate, graduated reduction. On the first $ 1 million of gross revenue there would be no reduction whatsoever. That would remain at 27.5 %. On gross income from $ 1 million to $ 5 million, the depletion allowance would be 21 percent. On gross income in excess of $ 5 million, the depletion allowance would be 15 percent. This is a very moderate proposal.

" Mr. President, this issue has faced the Senate and the Nation for at least a decade. It is now before us again. We must make our decision as to what we shall do. It is time that we put our fiscal system in order. In our fiscal system some people pay too much because others pay too little. The time has come when we should deal with this issue. The depletion allowance can continue without any time limit. It occurs after depreciation has been allowed and fully taken account of. As long as the oil and the gas run, the depletion allowance can continue to be taken. There are cases in which the amount of the depletion is many, many times the total original cost, which bear in mind has already been deducted under the depreciation practice. I think the Senators are aware of the issues at stake. I wish to say to thé gas and oil industry, which has been fighting this amendment for years, that if they are once again successful in beating this amendment, as they may well be, there is likely to arise in the country a storm of indignation. "

But indignation is not a common emotion in the Senate. Senator Douglas' amendment would have resulted in a $ 350,000,000 loss to the oil industry. A vote was held, and the amendment was defeated by 56 to 30.[68] Senator John

---

67. It dropped again during President Kennedy's last year in office. The evolution of domestic prices (per barrel) was as follows :

1958 : $ 3.07
1959, 1960, 1961 and 1962 : $ 2.97
1963 : $ 2.93

(A barrel of oil cost $ 1.02 in 1939, $ 1.37 in 1946, $ 1.90 in 1947, and $ 2.57 in 1948).

68. The vote was as follows :

Yeas — 30	Nays — 56		Not\Voting — 14
Aiken	Allott	Hill	Bridges
Carroll	Anderson	Holland	Church
Case (N.J.)	Bartlett	Hruska	Eastland
Clark	Beall	Johnson (Tex.)	Goldwater
Dodd	Bennett	Johnson (S.C.)	Green
Douglas	Bible	Jordan	Hartke

Kennedy (Massachusetts) voted in favor of it.[69]

At the 1960 Democratic Convention, the representatives of the oil states, headed by Sam Rayburn, supported the candidacy of Lyndon Johnson, but Kennedy won the nomination. In the spring of 1961, Mr. Morgan Davis[70] remarked during a private luncheon, " It's impossible to get along with that man. "

As a Senator, John Kennedy had not been popular with the oilmen, but they weren't afraid of him. They knew that his father Joseph had invested a large part of his fortune in the oil business, and they couldn't conceive that his son, even if he were to become President, would dare take a position that would go against his own and his family's financial interests.[71] H.L. Hunt expressed the same opinion when he confided to *Playboy* in 1966, " Catholics are known for being anti-Communist, and I had never seen any evidence of fiscal irresponsibility in the Kennedy family. "

The oilmen were wrong. The new President decided to

Yeas — 30	*Nays — 56*		*Not Voting — 14*
Ervin	Brunsdale	Kerr	Hennings
Gore	Bush	Kuchel	Humphrey
Hart	Butler	Long (La.)	Kefauver
Jackson	Byrd (W.Va.)	McClellan	Lusk
Javits	Byrd (Va.)	McGee	Magnuson
Keating	Cannon	Mansfield	Murray
Kennedy	Capehart	Martin	O'Mahoney
Lausche	Carlson	Monroney	Sparkman
Long (Hawaii)	Case (S.Dak.)	Morton	
McCarthy	Chavez	Mundt	
McNamara	Cooper	Randolph	
Morse	Cotton	Robertson	
Muskie	Curtis	Saltonstall	
Pastore	Dirksen	Schoeppel	
Prouty	Dworshak	Scott	
Proxmire	Ellender	Stennis	
Russell	Engle	Talmadge	
Smathers	Fong	Thurmond	
Smith	Frear	Williams (N.J.)	
Symington	Fulbright	Yarborough	
Wiley	Gruening	Young (N.Dak.)	
Williams (Del.)	Hayden		
Young (Ohio)	Hickenlooper		

broach the issue. Although he didn't go as far as John Ise[72], he felt, like Roosevelt, that the control of the national economy should not be allowed to continue in the hands of the few, but should be enlarged to include millions of citizens or be taken over by the government, which in a democracy is responsible to the people. But he knew also that any re-examination of the principles of profit-making and free enterprise from the moral, social or even national point of view would be rejected not only by the oilmen, but also by a good many other citizens as an attack on the American way of life. In the past, such attacks by the administration and the Justice Department had been defeated.[73]

---

69. In 1964 the depletion allowance issue came up before the Senate again. On February 3 Senator Lausche (Ohio) offered an amendment that would diminish the depletion allowance privileges by $ 850 million, which sum could be used to compensate the revenues lost to the government by a tax credit granted to needy families with children in college proposed by Senator Ribicoff (New York). But Senator Lausche's amendment was considered not germane.

On February 6, Senator Williams re-introduced his traditional amendment and was defeated again (by 61 to 33). As Senator Javits was to remark, " This is the sacred cow of sacred cows. "

70. Chairman of the Board of Directors of Humble Oil and Refining Co. (1961-63), Director of the First National City Bank of Houston, member of the National Petroleum Council and the American Petroleum Institute.

71. In January, 1968, Senators Robert F. Kennedy (New York) and Edward M. Kennedy (Massachusetts) joined with several other Congressmen in urging that import limits be eased for home-heating oil. They were concerned about a threatened shortage and high prices.

72. John Ise, a professor of economics at the University of Kansas and author of *The United States Oil Policy*, recommended in 1929 the nationalization of all natural resources, including oil. " Private property has undoubtedly brought about more unfortunate consequences in the case of oil and natural gas than in any other domain. It has resulted in overproduction, instability, incessant price fluctuations, a waste of natural resources, capital, and labor, speculation, fraud, foolish extravagances and flagrant social injustice, and, finally, in the establishment of a monopoly ", he wrote.

73. Since the Clayton Antitrust Act of 1914 (which outlawed price discrimination and exclusive contracts between wholesaler

The only chance for a modification of the structures of the Oil Empire lay in a major crisis, internal or external — an economic crisis or a war. But President Kennedy was working for peace and economic expansion, and he knew that his objectives could not be attained unless the principles of the American autarchy were re-examined and their destructive action brought progressively to a halt.

A year after he entered the White House, in 1962, the new President studied the reports of his advisers and decided to act. He had reacted with violence to the dictates of the steel industry ; in the case of oil, he laid his plans more cautiously. On October 16, 1962, a law known as the Kennedy Act removed the distinction between repatriated profits and profits re-invested abroad in the case of American companies with overseas operations. Both were henceforth subject to American taxation. The law also sought to distinguish between " good " earnings resulting from normal commercial operations, and " suspicious " revenues siphoned off at some point in the commercial circuit by subsidiary companies located in tax havens abroad.

This measure was aimed at American industry as a whole, but it particularly affected the oil companies, which had the largest and most diversified overseas activities.[74] At the end of 1962, the oilmen were estimating that their earnings on

---

and retailer) and the National Recovery Act of 1933 (which eliminated unfair trade practices and destructive price cutting nd established fair codes of competition), the Justice Department had tried unsuccessfully on several occasions to break down the oil monopoly by halting mergers and opposing exclusive contracts, price, fixing, and production restrictions. Congress, and on occasion the Supreme Court, had defeated all its attempts.

74. Previously, while the profits earned abroad by American firms were subject to American taxation, the profits of subsidiary companies which were subject to local taxation (except in the tax havens) were only taxed in the United States when their dividends were distributed to the head companies in the United States. The Kennedy Act abolished this regime for the subsidiaries registered in tax haven countries, which were henceforth subject to American taxation whether or not their dividends were distributed to the head companies in the United States.

foreign invested capital, which in 1955 had equalled 30 %, would fall to 15 % as result of these measures.

But Kennedy's second measure was far more important and infinitely more dangerous. It affected not only the companies with overseas investments, but all companies which, in one way or another, benefited from the privileged status of the oil industry. It called into question both the principle and the rates of the fiscal privileges, the improper use of tax dollars, and the depletion allowance. If adopted, it would undermine the entire system upon which the Oil Empire was based.

On January 24, 1963, in presenting his bill to Congress, President Kennedy declared, " Now is the time to act. We cannot afford to be timid or slow. " For him, the fact that it was going to be difficult made it all the more necessary to act. But the Oil Empire wasn't the steel industry. Its leaders were of a different mettle. Ludwell Denny had said, " We fight for oil " By tangling with the oilmen, Kennedy was commencing the last year of his life. He considered his fiscal measures as the first step in a vast national reform.

As George Washington said to Henry Lee on October 31, 1786, " Precedents are dangerous things. " The oilmen thought so too. " Think " is the motto of the businessman. Once they had determined what had to be done, they set about choosing their battleground and meticulously laying their plans.

11

Texans

The myth of the indispensable man must be broken if our country is to survive.

HAROLDSON LAFAYETTE HUNT

The Panhandle State owes more to oil than it does to the Alamo. Texas didn't really come into its own until oil gushed forth from the swamps of Beaumont on January 10, 1901. Fed by more than 100,000 barrels a day from the Spindletop well[1], a lake of oil formed which was soon consumed by fire. Spindletop set off a second Gold Rush. The area was overrun by prospectors, the oil field was plundered, and the price of oil fluctuated wildly. At first, Rockefeller ignored the Texas strike.

---

1. Discovered by the Dalmatian engineer Luchich. His associates Galey and Guffey eased him out and formed a partnership with the richest man in Western Pennsylvania, Andrew W. Mellon. Other petroleum properties near Spindletop were ceded to certain Texas politicians in exchange for their support, in particular to former Governor Jim Hogg. This concession gave birth to the Texas Company. Spindletop was also the birthplace of American Shell. After a time, Andrew Mellon eased out Guffey and reorganized his company under the name of Gulf Oil.

But after Standard Oil of New Jersey was broken up in 1911, Standard Oil of Indiana bought up Humble, thereby becoming the largest producer in Texas, while Socony took over Magnolia. By 1930, the American oil empire was controlled by 20 big companies which seemed destined for eternal prosperity.

But on October 9, 1930, a stubborn prospector named " Dad " Joiner struck oil. at 3,000 feet in Est Texas. He had discovered the richest oil field in the United States. Forty miles long and 2 to 5 miles wide, its reserves have been estimated at one and a half billion tons. By the time Standard and the other big companies arrived on the scene, thousands of prospectors were drilling away on tens of thousands of rural and urban plots. It was the most ruinous waste in the history of oil, and just at the start of the Depression the bottom dropped out of the market.

Standard, Gulf, Texaco and Shell managed to regain control with the help of the federal government. Laws were voted by the states, concessions were closed down by force, and the Connally law on " black oil " put a stop to illegal production in East Texas. When the basin had been pumped dry, production quotas were established and order prevailed. Some independent producers managed to survive, but they were obliged to comply with the rules set by the Big Four, who tolerated them because their greater production costs enabled the larger comanies to keep prices high and increase profits.

Thirty years later, in 1963, Texas accounted for half the proven oil reserves on American soil. With 95,000 active oil wells owned by 6,500 oil companies (of the 12,325 in the United States), it constituted a key position for the big corporations, for it controlled production in the neighboring states of Louisiana and Oklahoma (65 % of the American total), and therefore prices.

Six companies control 80 % of Texas oil production. Humble produces 15 % and refines 30 % of this total. These giants command not only the oil, but also the sulphur and

---

2. WASHINGTON, Jan. 9, 1968 (UPI) — President Johnson's home state of Texas, which only a few years ago ranked seventh among states getting prime defense contracts, now has nosed out New York for no. 2 spot, Pentagon figures showed today.

natural gas markets, and consequently real estate, transportation facilities, power, water, and banks throughout the state.

Even without oil, Texas would be one of the richest states in
the Union. One hundred times larger than Delaware, five
times larger than New York, four times larger than Missouri,
three times larger than Minnesota, twice as large as Montana,
it covers 100,000 square miles more than the state of California, and each of its 254 counties is bigger than the state of
Rhode Island. There are 227,000 ranches in Texas, and the
King Ranch covers more territory than Switzerland. Texas
raises 10 million head of cattle and provides one-quarter of
the rice, one-third of the cotton, and half of all the synthetic
rubber consumed in the United States. In 1963 the state had a
population of 10,228,000, including one million Negroes and
one million Wetbacks.

The Second World War turned Texas into an industrial
state. Thanks to the Cold War, its industries expanded five
times faster than those of the rest of the nation. This industrial expansion reached a climax in 1963, when General
Dynamics of Fort Worth was awarded the TFX fighter plane
contract. The fantastic development of smaller firms such as
Texas Instruments is directly linked to the war in Vietnam.[2]

Texas offers these industries lower taxes, cheap labor (poor
whites, Negroes and Wetbacks), restrictive labor legislation

California still holds along lead in first place, but its percentage of total contract awards during the fiscal year that ended
last June 30 has now slipped to 17.9. Texas got 9.5 percent of
the contracts and New York 8.7 percent.

During fiscal 1966, the percentages were : California 18.3,
New York 8.9, and Texas 7.2. And as recently as 1962, the
percentages for the three were : California 23.9, New York 10.7,
and Texas 4.0, with Massachusetts, Connecticut, New Jersey and
Ohio ahead of Texas that year.

But Texas has moved up steadily since Mr. Johnson moved
into the White House, thanks in large part to the controversial
F-111 fighter-bomber (formerly the TFX).

Nearly a third of the contracts Texas received during fiscal
1967 — just under $ 1.2 billion worth — were for the F-111,
which is being produced by General Dynamics Corp. at Fort
Worth.

(the union shop is prohibited by state law), and its outstanding natural resources in oil, natural gas, and sulphur.[3] The federal government is one of the state's principal benefactors. Texas ranks second in the nation in terms of federal aid, with $ 3.9 billion in 1960-61, or 20.1 % of the total state revenue.[4] The wealthiest of the wealthy states, Texas in 1960 had 53 % more federal employees and received 65 % more federal aid than the average American state.[5] Washington's favors touched every sector of the economy. Texas, with the most extensive highway system (constructed with federal funds) in the country[6], received the largest amount of federal aid for paralyzed children, and the highest subsidies for flood prevention.

But not all the inhabitants of Texas share in this munificence. In 1963, the state of Texas spent only $ 282.46 per person on social welfare (education, health, hospitals, public welfare), as compared to the national average of $ 343.64 per inhabitant (a difference of 18 %). In the field of education, Texas ranked third in the nation in terms of federal aid per inhabitant, and 31st in terms of expenditures. It ranked first in terms of federal aid for child welfare, and 44th in terms of expenditures. It was second in the nation in terms of federal aid for the aged, and 40th in terms of expenditures. Nor does Texas neglect only its people. In 1963 it received more federal aid for experimental agricultural stations than any other state in the union, but ranked 47th in terms of the amount spent on improvements in cattle breeding.

There is little indication that the people of Texas merit such favoritism. Their state is first in the nation in terms of murder

---

3. Texas is the fifth state in the nation in terms of population (after New York, California, Pennsylvania, and Ilinois), but it is by far the richest in terms of natural ressources. In 1963, the mineral production of Texas totalled $ 4,413,084,000. Texas accounts for 35 % of the crude oil and 42 % of the natural gas produced in the United States.

Louisiana, whose petroleum resources are exploited in large part by companies based in Texas, produced $ 2,662,061,000 worth of mineral products. The combined oil production of Texas and Louisiana equals 35 % of the national total.

and armed robbery, and second for rape. Texas is the realm of intolerance. It calls itself Democratic, but for the past 25 years it has elected Republicans or would-be Democrats. It claims to be progressive, but only 15 % of its 2.5 million non-agricultural workers are unionized, and since 1954 a fine of $ 20,000 and 20 years in prison punishes membership in the Communist Party. In 1952, Governor Allan Shrivers even tried to obtain the death penalty for this " crime. "

Texas sees nothing wrong with prescribing the death penalty for a political opinion, but it protects the right to commit homicide. It is the paradise of murder, and even of murder

---

4. This percentage was only 12.7 % for the state of New York, and 10.1 % for the state of Illinois, despite their poorer natural resources.

5. Texas (10,228,000 inhabitants and a revenue of $ 21,451 billion in 1963) had in 1964 121,376 federal employees, 24 times more than the state of Wyoming (339,000 inhabitants and a revenue of $ 834 million, and 5,175 federal employees), and 17 times more than the state of Nevada (389,000 inhabitants, $ 1,246 million in revenue, and 7,039 federal employees). Ohio, with a population and revenue comparable to Texas (10,000,000 inhabitants and $ 25,164 billion) had only 88,785 federal employees. As for Delaware (480,000 inhabitants), it had only 3,624 federal employees, more than 40 times fewer than Texas, for there is a certain minimum of personnel required by any administrative infrastructure.

Statistics concerning the increase in federal employees per state since 1939 provide a further illustration of the favoritism shown the state of Texas :

Total federal employees

1939 :   967,765
1960 : 2,372,580

Texas   1939 : 29,818
               1960 : 112,647 (increase of 380 %)
Wyoming   1939 :   3,335
               1960 :   4,695 (increase of 140 %)
Nevada   1939 :   3,053
               1960 :   5,842 (increase of 190 %)
New York   1939 :   97,155
               1960 : 179,784 (increase of 190 %)

6. 17,744 miles. California has 9,653 miles of highways, New York 10,700, Illinois 10,995.

for thrills. The name " Texas " comes from the Indian " Tejas ",
meaning "Friendship", which is also the state motto. In
1879 *Harper's Bazaar wrote,* " In the past 12 years there
have been 300 murders in Texas, and only 11 death sentences. " Since then, Texans have done even better. In 1960
there were 1,080 murders in Texas, and 5 death sentences.

Moreover, Texas has its own definition of murder. Only 3
of the 254 counties in Texas require a coroner's examination
in the case of sudden or suspicious death. The 251 others
leave it to the Justice of the Peace[7] to determine the cause of
death. A verdict of death due to natural causes has been
known to coincide with the discovery of a bullet in the body
of the deceased. The FBI estimates that the number of murders
actually committed in Texas is several times the official
figure. Between 5,000 and 10,000 deaths occur every year in
Texas because of brutality, greed, or just because.[8]

One hundred and thirty-two counties in Texas are pro-
hibitonist, another form of intolerance that satisfies the puritanism of its inhabitants and the interests of the business
community. One out of every 12 Texans — 800,000 in all
— is illiterate, the highest percentage in the nation. Texas
delivers fewer high school diplomas than the poorest state in
the union, Mississippi.[9] It ranks third in the nation in terms
of the number of registered automobiles, but only 36th in
terms of insurance coverage.

Backwards, intolerant, and irresponsible, Texas lifts its soul
only towards God, if one is to judge from the number of its
churches. There are more than 1,000 churches in Dallas
alone. Waco (100,000 inhabitants) has 122, Midland (68,000
inhabitants) 82, and Tyler (50,000 inhabitants) 94.[10] Evangelist Billy Graham is popular in Texas, and playboys are
frowned upon.

Texans never tire of looking at money. The center of attrac-
tion at the Dallas Petroleum Club is a long ebony table inlaid
with coins from all over the world. The homes of Highland
Park, University Park, and River Oak are decorated with
Cezannes and Renoirs (many of them fakes), but they rarely
contain books. Texas don't read, with the possible exception
of the Sunday papers. Unlike other American cities, Texas

cities don't have bookstores. There is a second-hand bookstore in Dallas, but it is in the suburbs. The other bookstores are run by the churches. On the other hand, Dallas has an opera, a Museum of Contemporary Art, and 700 garden clubs. Texans like flowers.

Texas has 1,128 banks, more than any other state in the Union[11], but despite its wealth, the total income of the inhabitants of Texas falls well below that of many other states.[12] An oligarchic state if there ever was one, Texas is nevertheless first in the nation in terms of the number of personal incomes exceeding $ 1 million a year. Four-fifths of these millionaires are oilmen.

In this state of nabobs and beggers, where whole regions are still without electricity and where hundreds of thousands of people sleep out of doors, corruption is an institution, professional witnesses are a dime a dozen, and if you dial a certain number you can hear a recorded antisemitic diatribe.

Such a privileged state has to have influence in Washington. It has had, since before Roosevelt. In 1947, Harry Truman

---

7. In Texas, the Justice of the Peace is an elected magistrate, and not, as in the East, a minor functionary.

8. In the city of Dallas alone, there were 120 " official " murders in 1960, and 810 " accidents ".

9. Texas ranks 39th in the nation in terms of the amount spent on education.
High school graduates in 1963 : Texas — 0.8 % ; Mississippi — 1 %
High school students in 1964 : Texas — 6 % ; Mississippi — 10 %.

10. The population of Texas is 80 % Protestant, 19 % Catholic, and 1 % Jewish.

11. The state of Illinois has 1,030 banks, New York 479, and California 200.

12.

Incomes	Texas ranks in the nation
less than $ 2,000	13th
$ 2,000 to $ 3,000	17th
$ 3,000 to $ 4,000	17th
$ 4,000 to $ 5,000	30th
$ 5,000 to $ 6,000	38th
$ 6,000 to $ 7,000	34th
$ 7,000 to $ 9,000	33rd
$ 10,000 and over	30th

modified the law providing for the succession to the Presidency in favor of Texan Sam Rayburn, making the House
Majority Leader the third most important person in the country. Eisenhower, born in Tyler, Texas, faced a Congress led
by House Majority Leader Rayburn, a Texan, and Senate
majority Leader Lyndon Johnson, another Texan. But despite
the special favors, all the federal aid, and the federal employees paid by Washington, the state treasury has often
verged on bankruptcy. In 1959, Texas even paid its employees with rubber checks. Once again, the federal government was obliged to bail out the richest state in the union. In
1961, while it was still young and naive, the Kennedy Administration tried to enforce the payment of the federal tax on
business transactions in Texas. No Texan could remember
this law ever having been enforced. Texas, the state that
fortune smiled upon, lay outside the frontiers of America.
What did it want with the New Frontier ?

Texas is a separate way of life. The oil industry controls
the government, the politics, and the social life the state.[13]
Its contribution to the economy is so important, and its
influence so widespread, that it can make or break a project.
The independent producers wield as much, if not more, power
than the Presidents of the major oil companies, and because
their fortunes are generally the result of personal success and
their base of operations less far-flung, they are also more
aggressive. They are thus far more vulnerable to any attack on
the privileges of the oil industry, and in particular to any
change in the laws that govern it.

It has been estimated that there are more than 500 mil-
lionaires living in Houston, and probably as many in Dallas.
The income of the twenty richest independent oil producers
put together would be enough to cover the state budget.

Texas, which doesn't know the meaning of income tax, has
no more idea of what a constitution should be. The Texas
Constitution dates back to 1876. Consequently, the state
government has no power to deal with the abuses of its
inhabitants. The state legislature meets only once every two
years. Its members are paid $ 10 a day for a period of 120
days. If the session is prolonged beyond that limit, their pay is
halved. As a result, most state congressmen are either lawyers
representing their clients at Austin or students glad for a

chance to make a little extra money. For that matter, poor students and teachers interested in politics are especially well regarded by the real proprietors of the state. The oilmen finance the studies of a certain number of gifted and deserving students, and if they are elected to the state legislature they are rewarded with land leases, stocks, and allowances enabling them to devote themselves to the service of their country. The oilmen have little difficulty in getting their candidates elected to office — they control the press, radio and television. Their influence over the police and judicial authorities is such that only the most insignificant criminal and civil cases, and those in which they have no interests at stake, are ever bought to court.

One of the most eminent figures in Texas and the oil industry appeared one day in the Cokesbury Bookstore, a Methodist bookshop in Dallas, to autograph a book that he had published himself. This man rates only seven lines in *Who's Who*: " Haroldson Lafayette Hunt, oil producer ; Vandalia, Ill. ; ed. pub. schs ; m. Lynda Bunker (died May 7, 1955) ; married 2nd Ruth Ray Weight, December, 1957. Oil producer, Hunt Oil Co. Established Facts Forum, a foundation producing radio and TV programs relating to nat. issues. Democrat. Address : 4009 W. Lawther Dr., Dallas. "

Seven lines isn't much for a man who was, in 1963, and probably will be until he dies, the richest man in the world[14], with a fortune conservatively estimated at $ 4 billion. When you get into those kind of figures, you are no longer talking about wealth, but about power.

The book that the richest man in the world had come to autograph was called *Alpaca*, undoubtedly after the llama-like

---

13. Nevertheless, there is a strong opposition to the oil interests in Texas. It is made up of people who are more interested in the good of their country than the state of their pocketbooks, and who are more American than Texan, together with a certain number of progressive labor leaders. But this opposition comprises only one-third of the voters.

14. Contrary to the statistics published by *Fortune* in March, 1968, which place John Paul Getty and Howard Hughes at the top of the list.

South American ruminant of the same name so noted for its resistance. *Alpaca* is Hunt's Bible. It describes a mythical new nation where income taxes are limited to 25 %, and where every citizen is accorded a number of votes in direct proportion to his income-tax bracket.[15]

Hunt was accompanied by his second wife and his two step-daughters, and the little girls — Helen, 11, and Sewannee, 10 — sang a little song :

> *How much is that book in the window ?*
> *The one that says all the smart things.*
> *How much is that book in the window ?*
> *I do hope to learn all it brings.*
>
> *How much is that book in the window ?*
> *The one which my Popsy wrote.*
> *How much is that book in the window ?*
> *You can buy it without signing a note.*
>
> *Alpaca ! Fifty cents !*[16]

Hunt is a hard man to figure out. Few journalists have even tried. The real personality of this Puritan who was 74 in 1963 lies hidden behind a few cautious descriptions :

" As rich as Croesus, as shrewd as a river boat gambler, as tight as a new pair of shoes... "

" He thinks communism started in this country when the government took over distribution of the mail... "

" If he had more flair and imagination, if he were not basically such a damned hick, he could be one of the most dangerous men in America. "

For gifted psychologist Hugh Hefner, Hunt is " an irritating enigma ". " No one, not even his own family, professes to understand him ; no one, not even the partners he's made rich, seems to have any idea what drove him to amass his vast fortune ; and no one, not even Hunt himself, seems able to explain just what he is trying to accomplish in the political arena. "[17]

Hunt is the incarnation of Texas, but he was born into a prosperous family in Illinois. He left home a 15 with a pack on his back and worked for a time as a lumberjack. At 22, he took his inheritance of a few thousand dollars and set out for

Arkansas, where in 1912 he bought plantation land that hadn't overflowed for 35 years. That year and the next, it overflowed. The following year World War I broke out and the price of cotton dropped to 5 cents a pound. Hunt was ruined.

1918 brought a big land boom, and Hunt sold his plantation and bought more land. Three years later, he headed for an oil strike in El Dorado, Arkansas and began trading in leases. He drilled a few wells in the West Smackover fields and soon owned a hundred wells in Louisiana, Arkansas, and Oklahoma. In 1930 he went to East Texas and bought the famous Dad Joiner well, the Number One Daisy Bradford, which the big oil companies had disregarded. Before the Second World War, Hunt had made his first billion, mostly in oil, and re-invested it not only in oil and natural gas, but also in a multitude of other undertakings integrated vertically or horizontally, or completely diversified.

Hunt is the nation's biggest farmer. His business interests cover five continents and run from drugs to real estate, cotton, cattle, and timber. It has been estimated that " the Hunt assets are equal to those of such corporate complexes as General Electric. "[18] Hunt owns and controls companies the names of which have never been associated with his.[19] His name does not appear on the list of the 500 largest international corporations, although he is probably among the top five. The Hunt Oil Company (incorporated in Delaware in 1934) owns producing properties in Texas, Louisiana, North Dakota, and 9 more states, as well as undeveloped acreage in

---

15. Hunt has written three other books of the same type : *Fabians Fight Freedom, Why Not Speak ?*, and *Hunt for Truth.* He also writes a daily and weekly newspaper column.

16. Bainbridge, *The Super-Americans.*

17. *Playboy,* 1966.

18. The assets of General Electric, the fourth largest American corporation, equalled $ 4,851,718,000 in 1966, or one-third of the assets of Standard Oil of New Jersey, the largest corporation in the world, more than Standard Oil of California, and half again as much as American Shell or Standard of Indiana.

19. The man who is probably the richest oil producer after Hunt, Roy Cullen of Quintana Petroleum, has only about a million dollars.

18 other states, including Alaska. Hunt is behind a multitude of independent oil companies such as Placid Oil, the Hunt Petroleum Corp., and Placid International Oil, Ltd. (incorporated in 1958 in Delaware), with offices and activities in Australia, the Netherlands, Lebanon, England, and 17 other countries.

Haroldson Lafayette Hunt has neither stockholders nor board of directors. He owns 85 to 90 % of the shares in all of his companies[20] (his family owns the rest). This 200 lb. six-footer is a latecomer to politics. Until he was 60, he occupied himself with drilling his wells and building his empire. He likes to describe himself as " a registered Democrat who often votes Republican. " The last President of whom he approved was Calvin Coolidge. He calls Franklin D. Roosevelt " the first President to institute the struggle of class against class. " Roosevelt also recognized the Soviet Union, thus bearing, in his view, the responsibility for " the surrender of hundreds of millions of people into Communist domination. " He violently attacks the " myth of the indispensable man " created by Franklin D. Roosevelt and reclaimed by Kennedy. " This myth must be broken if our country is to survive ", he has been quoted as saying. For him, the principal arms of the " Indispensable Man " of the Sixties were " Communism " and " taxes ". Communism and taxes, it must be said, are the keys to the mind and activities of Haroldson Lafayette Hunt.

" The United States have been in charge of the world since World War Two, during which time the Communists have taken into domination one third of the world's population. "

" Communist activities in the United States are criminal and can be spoken of along with other criminal offenses. "

" All services to the public should be abolished in favor of personal enterprise where they can be more efficiently and economically performed. "

Hunt condemns the " strange persons with a twisted education who would prefer to be defeated. " He also attacks federal welfare programs for " harming the general public and giving some persons and groups an advantage over others. " He dismisses Social Security as " thousands of frivolous projects. " He declares, " People who have wealth should use it wisely, in a way that will do society the most good. They should be careful that in making supposedly charitable gifts, their money will not be used to destroy or impair the American system and promote atheism. "

For Hunt, Kennedy's assault on the tax privileges enjoyed by the oil industry were " criminal offenses " against " the American system. Depletion allowances are necessary for irreplaceable resources. The increased net income for the Government from their elimination would finance the Government 3 or 4 days per year... ", he declares, adding, " We are losing the right to keep a fair share of the money we earn and a fair share of the profits we make. "

Hunt's letterhead describes him as an " operator "[21] He considers himself one of the best poker players in the country, and he probably is. He has always placed his reliance on competent technicians. His personal bodyguard is made up of former FBI agents. Years ago he acquired the habit of acting through intermediaries. He has his own intelligence network, and his decisions are carried out by a powerful general staff. His business interests are so extensive that he subsidizes (along with other important oilmen) most of the influential men in Congress, men like Lyndon Johnson. Hunt was one of the financial backers of Senator Joseph McCarthy, whose deputy Roy Cohn attracted his attention and has since worked for him on several occasions.

Hunt is the most powerful American propagandist of the Far Right. In 1951 he financed " Facts Forum ", a series of radio and television programs which was later replaced by " Life Line ", a one-sided series of 15-minute radio broadcasts carried daily on 409 stations throughout the country. His propaganda campaign costs him $ 2 million a year and is

---

20. The Dallas headquarters of Placid Oil are located at 2500 First National Bank Building. H.L.H. Products are located at 700 Mercantile Bank Building, but most of Hunt's businesses are grouped at 1401 Elm Street : Hunt Oil Co., Hunt Petroleum Corp., Hunt Caroline Trust Estate, Hunt H.L., Hunt H. L. Jr., Hunt Hassie Trust, Hunt International Petroleum Company, Hunt Lamar, Hunt Lamar Trust Estate, Hunt Margaret Trust Estate, Hunt N.B., Hunt Nelson Bunker, Hunt W.H., Hunt William Herbert Trust Estate, etc.

21. Described by the Internal Revenue Service as a person " who holds the management and exploitation rights and is responsible for production costs. "

financed by companies that he owns, or on which he is in a position to exert pressure.[22]

Hunt's brand of anti-Communism has found support in the military camp. In 1952, Hunt supported the " MacArthur for President " campaign, and he has called MacArthur " truly the man of this century. " He was also impressed by the MacArthur-trained group of strategists.[23] He once declared, " We should do whatever our generals advise us to do. " Beginning in 1952, several influential military men, flattered by Hunt's attention and conscious of his power, acquired the habit of consulting and confiding in him. Thus General George C. Kenney (born in 1889), former Commanding General of the Strategic Air Command, who retired from the Air Force in 1951, told him of his personal plan for knocking out Russia's nuclear capacity, based on the strategy of a preventive strike. General Albert C. Wedemeyer (born in 1897), author of the " Wedemeyer Reports " and an active member of the John Birch Society[24], retired from the Army in 1951[25], and Admiral James Van Fleet (born in 1892 and retired from the Navy in 1953)[26] were among the specialists consulted by Hunt, who shared their passion for strategy and extermination. The advent of Kennedy and McNamara created a stir among the military, and there were many retirements and dismissals.

The leader of this warrior clan was General Edwin A. Walker (born in 1909), a Texan who returned to Dallas after leaving the Army and contacted H.L. Hunt. Then, with the support of the John Birchers[27], the Minutemen, and several of his former subordinates in the U.S. forces in Germany, he launched an extremist and militarist campaign. Robert A. Surrey, Walker's " associate ", had the financial backing of Hunt's companies. In 1962 ex-General Walker ran for Governor of Texas but was defeated by John Connally, whereupon he plunged headlong into a campaign of politico-economic action. By the winter of 1962-63, plans were being made for a preventive strike.

Hunt is the Big Man in Texas, the Giant, the richest and the stingiest[28], the most powerful and the most solitary of the oilmen. He has always shied away from the other Texas and Louisiana oil producers, men like Michel Halbouty, Ray Hubbard, R.E. Smith, Algur H. Meadows, Jake Hamon, Kay

Kimbell, O.C. Harper, C.V. Lyman, J.P. Gibbins, Ted Wiener, Thomas W. Blake, John W. Mecom, Billy Byars and Morgan Davis, but they have interests in common. Only the solidarity of the oil industry and, in some cases, fear kept certain habitués of the Fort Worth Petroleum Club, the Bayou and International Clubs in Houston, the Club Imperial, the Cipango Club and the Public Affairs Luncheon Club of Dallas from talking in the months and weeks preceding November 22. Instead, they let matters take their course.

The opinions and the aversions of obstinate old men often lead to excesses. Embittered puritan potentates frightened to see their lives drawing to an end are an even greater danger. Representatives Bruce Alger and Joe Pool stopped up their ears. In the streets of Texas, " Knock Out the Kennedys " stickers were already appearing on bumpers and windshields.

Hunt liked to say, " It is through weakness — not strength — that we lose esteem in the world. "

At 12 :23 on November 22, from his office on the 7th floor of the Mercantile Building, Haroldson Lafayette Hunt watched John Kennedy ride towards Dealey Plaza, where fate awaited him at 12 :30. A few minutes later, escorted by six men in two cars, Hunt left the center of Dallas without even stopping by his house.

---

22. Not only the Placid Oil Corp. of Shreveport, but Baker Oil Tools (Dallas and California), the Harry W. Bass Drilling Co. (Dallas), the Empire Drilling Co. (Dallas), the Mid-Continent Supply Co., United Tools, the Hudson Engineering Corp., the Nation and Geophysical Co., the New Seven Falls Co., and the First City National Bank of Dallas.

23. Which included former Generals like Courtney Whitney and Bonner Fellows, and also certain of their disciples, such as the brilliant Lawrence Bunker.

24. Texas had as many as ten John Birch Society chapters, mainly in Dallas and Houston.

25. Commander of the China Theater (1944-46), Chief of Staff of Generalissimo Chiang Kai Shek, then Deputy Chief of Staff for Plans and Combat Operations (1947-48).

26. Commander of the U.S. Naval Forces in Korea (1948-50)

27. Of which he, like General Wedemeyer, was a member.

28. Hunt lives modestly, buys ready-made suits, drives his own standard-make cars, dislikes private planes, cuts his own hair, and carries his lunch to work in a brown paper bag.

At that very moment ; General Walker was in a plane between New Orleans and Shreveport. He joined Mr. Hunt in one of his secret hideaways across the Mexican border. There they remained for a month, protected by personal guards, under the impassive eyes of the FBI. It was not until Christmas that Hunt, Walker and their party returned to Dallas.

In February, 1964, Elgin E. Crull, Dallas City Manager, declared, " *The vast majority of people in Dallas were affected by the murder of the President as they would have been by a sudden, violent death in their own family.* " But he added, " When life resumed its regular rhythm, there was general agreement that the actions of two maverick gunmen — the alleged assassin and his slayer — would not impede the dynamic growth of Big D. "

PART III

DESTINY

This generation of Americans, your generation of Americans, has a rendezvous with destiny . . .

FRANKLIN DELANO ROOSEVELT
JOHN FITZGERALD KENNEDY

12

Condemnation

I think we will see a very changing world in 1964...

JOHN FITZGERALD KENNEDY

" We are setting out upon a voyage in 1961 no less hazardous than that undertaken by the Arbella in 1630 ", President-Elect Kennedy told the Massachusetts State Legislature on January 9, 1961. " For of those whom much is given, much is required. And when at some future date the high court of history sits in judgment on each of us, recording whether in our brief span of service, we fulfilled our responsibilities to the state, our success or failure, in whatever office we hold, will be measured by the answers to four questions :

" First, were we truly men of courage, with the courage to stand up to one's enemies, and the courage to stand up, when necessary, to one's associates, the courage to resist public pressure as well as private greed ?
" Second, were we truly men of judgment, with perceptive judgment of the future as well as the past, of our own mistakes as well as the mistakes of others, with enough wisdom

to know what we did not know, and enough candor to admit it ?

" Third, were we truly men of integrity, men who never ran out on either the principles in which we believed or the people who believed in us, men whom neither financial gain nor political ambition could ever divert from the fulfillment of our sacred trust ?

" Finally, were we truly men of dedication, with an honor mortgaged not to a single individual or group, and compromised by no private obligation or aim, but devoted solely to serving the public good and the national interest ?

" Courage, judgment, integrity, dedication — these are the historic qualities of the Bay Colony and the Bay State, the qualities which this state has consistently sent to Beacon Hill here in Boston and to Capital Hill back in Washington. And these are the qualities which, with God's help, this son of Massachusetts hopes will characterize our government's conduct in the four stormy years that lie ahead. Humbly I ask His help in this undertaking ; but aware that on earth His will is worked by men, I ask for your help and your prayers as I embark on this new and solemn journey. "

Less than two years later, the final year of this " hazardous voyage " began. On January 14, 1963, President Kennedy sent his last State of the Union Message to Congress :

" I can report to you that the state of this old but youthful Union, in the 175th year of its life, is good... At home the recession is behind us... There may now be a temptation to relax. For the road has been long, the burden heavy, and the pace consistently urgent. But we cannot be satisfied to rest here. This is the side of the hill, not the top. The mere absence of recession is not growth. We have made a beginning — but we have only begun. Now the time has come to make the most of our gains — to translate the renewal of our national strength into the achievement of our national purpose...

" Tax reduction alone, however, is not enough to strengthen our society, to provide opportunities for the four million Americans who are born every year, to improve the lives of 32 million Americans who live on the outskirts of poverty. The quality of American life must keep pace with the quantity of American goods. This country cannot afford to be materially rich and spiritually poor.

" Therefore, by holding down the budgetary cost of existing programs to keep within the limitations I have set, it is both possible and imperative to adopt other new measures that we cannot afford to postpone. These measures are based on a series of fundamental premises, grouped under four related headings :

" First, we need to strengthen our Nation by investing in our youth...

" Second, we need to strengthen our Nation by safeguarding its health...

" Third, we need to strengthen our Nation by protecting the basic rights of its citizens...

" Fourth, we need to strengthen our Nation by making the best and the most economical use of its resources and facilities...

" We are not lulled by the momentary calm of the sea or the somewhat clearer skies above. We know the turbulence that lies below, and the storms that are beyond the horizon this year. But now the winds of change appear to be blowing more strongly than ever, in the world of communism as well as our own. For 175 years we have sailed with those winds at our back, and with the tides of human freedom in our favor. We steer our ship with hope, as Thomas Jefferson said ' leaving Fear astern. ' "

On January 15 he wrote : " Our ' bet ' is that the future will be a world community of independent nations, with a diversity of economic, political and religious systems, united by a common respect for the rights of others... But history is what men make of it — and we would be foolish to think that we can realize our own vision of a free and diverse future without unceasing vigilance, discipline and labor...

" Above all, we must both demonstrate and develop the affirmative power of the democratic ideal — remembering always that nations are great, not for what they are against, but what they are' for '. "

On the 16th, he offered a toast : " It reminds me of a story of Abraham Lincoln. After he was elected President, someone said, ' What are you going to do with your enemies, Mr. President ? ' Lincoln said, ' I am going to destroy them. I am going to make them my friends. ' "

On the 18th he celebrated the second anniversary of his inauguration : " I said the other day in the State of the Union that we were not on the top of the hill, but on the side of the hill. I don't think in this administration or in our generation or time will this country be at the top of the hill, but some day it will be, and I hope when it is that they will think we have done our part... "

On the 29th addressed Congress once again :
" Education is the keystone in the arch of freedom and progress... For the individual, the doors to the schoolhouse, to the library and to the college lead to the richest treasures of our open society : to the power of knowledge — to the training and skills necessary for productive employment — to the wisdom, the ideals, and the culture which enrich life — and to the creative, self-disciplined understanding of society needed for good citizenship in today's changing and challenging world. "

On February 5 he sent a 10,000 word message to Congress on the subject of mental illness and mental retardation. On the 7th he admonished his countrymen : " Each morning and evening, let us remember the advice of my fellow Bostonian, the Reverend Phillips Brooks : ' Do not pray for easy lives. Pray to be stronger men ! Do not pray for tasks equal to your powers. Pray for powers equal to your tasks. "

On the 8th he devoted another 8,000 words to the problem of improving the nation's health, on the 14th 8,000 words to the nation's youth, and on the 21st 12,000 words to the needs of the nation's senior citizens. On March 5, he told a delegation representing the American Indians : " I know that when I first took this office, one of the things which concerned me most was the fact that there were nearly 5,000 Indian boys and girls who had no school to go to. Now we built classrooms for about 7,000 in the last 2 years. "[1]

On March 11 he declared " Manpower is the basic resource. It is the indispensable means of converting other
resources to mankind's use and benefit. How well we develop
and employ human skills is fundamental in deciding how
much we will accomplish as a nation. "

On the 13th he remarked : " In front of the Archives building
there is a statue and under it it says, ' The past is prologue '
Not necessarily, and it is because we do not wish to regard
the past as necessarily a prologue in the 1960's that we have
attemped to put forward our proposals... ' The great advantage of Americans, wrote de Tocqueville in 1835, ' consists in
their being able to commit faults which they may afterwards
repair. To this I would add the fact that the great advantage of hindsight consists of our applying its lessons by
way of foresight. If this Nation can apply the lesson and
repair the faults of the last 5 years, if we can stick to the
facts, and cast out those things which really don't apply to the
situation, then surely this country can reach its goals... "

And on the 20th he told his audience at the University of
Costa Rica in San José : " What Franklin Roosevelt said to
the American people in the 1930's I say to you now : This
generation of Americans, your generation of Americans, has a
rendez-vous with destiny... We are committed to four basic
principles in this hemisphere in the Alliance for Progress. The
first is the right of every nation to govern itself, to be free
from outside dictation and coercion, to mold its own economy
and society in any fashion consistent with the will of the
people. Second is the right of every individual citizen to
political liberty, the right to speak his own views, to worship

---

1. On September 14, 1963 at Bismarck, North Dakota, Bob
Kennedy acknowledged before the Congress of American Indians
that Indian children received insufficient education, that the
Indians were poorly housed, often out of work, and that their
sanitary conditions were the poorest of any racial group in the
United States. He called their situation " tragically ironic " in
view of the fact that they were the only group in the
country who had the right to call themselves " the first
Americans. "

God in his own way, to select the government which rules him, and to reject it when it no longer serves the need of a nation. And Third, is the right to social justice, the right of every citizen to participate in the progress of his nation. This means land for the landless, and education for those who are denied their education today in this hemisphere. It means that ancient institutions which perpetuate privilege must give way. It means that rich and poor alike must bear the burden and the opportunity of building a nation... "

On the 23rd he told another audience, this time at Chicago, " Twenty-five hundred years ago the Greek poet Alcaeus laid down the principle which best sums up the greatness of Chicago : ' Not houses firmly roofed ', he wrote, ' or the stones of walls well builded, nay nor canals and dockyards, make the city — but men able to use their opportunities. ' "

On March 25 he welcomed twelve visiting French Gene-rals : " ...So we welcome you, coming as you do from a martial and distinguished race who have shown a mastery in the use of arms for a thousand years... "[2]

On April 2 he told the Congress : " ' Peace hath her victories no less renowned than war ', wrote Milton... This, for the American people, is a time for vision, for patience, for work, and for wisdom. For better or worse, we are the pacesetters. Freedom's leader cannot flag of falter, or another runner will set the pace. We have dared to label the Sixties the Decade of Development. But it is not the eloquence of our slogans, but the quality of our endurance, which will determine whether this generation of Americans deserves the leadership which history has thrust upon us. "

On the 11th he remarked at the White House : " This admin-istration is watching closely the possibilities of a general across the board increase in steel. I opposed such an increase last year. I oppose such an increase now... What it needs is more business at competitive prices, not less business at higher prices... I urge similar restraint on the steel workers union. With over 100,000 steel workers still unemployed, their need is for more jobs with job security, not fewer jobs at higher wages. "

On May 9, he spoke at Arlington National Cemetery : " It is no accident that men of genius in music like Paderewski or Chopin should also have been great patriots. You have to be a free man to be a great artist. "

On the 18th, he declared in Alabama : " ' At the Olympic Games', Aristotle wrote, ' it is not the finest and the strongest men who are crowned, but they who enter the lists — for out of these the prize-men are elected. ' So too, in life, of the honorable and the good, it is they who act who rightly win the prizes... I have read much of George Norris from Nebraska, and his favorite phrase, recurring throughout all of his speeches, was his reference, and his dedication, to ' generations yet unborn. ' The first of those generations is now enjoying the fruits of his labor, as will others for decades to come. So let us all, whether we are public officials or private citizens, northerners or southerners, easterners or westerners, farmers or city dwellers, live up to the ideals and ideas of George Norris, and resolve that we, too, in our time, 30 years later, will ourselves build a better Nation for ' generations yet unborn. ' "

On the 23rd, speaking at the Waldorf Astoria Hotel in New York, he remarked : " I think it is because the two political parties in our history have always been divided, as Emerson said, into the party of hope and into the party of memory. From the time of Jefferson, I think we have been the party of Hope. And therefore it is natural that artists, men and women who work in the theater and all the other related arts, should find themselves most at home in the party of hope. Up the way in this corridor tonight, the steel industry is presenting to my distinguished predecessor its annual award, to President

---

2. On February 14, President Kennedy had been asked at his press conference to comment on the attitude of the French government : " It would seem like, in a way, that President De Gaulle's intention to develop France's own nuclear capability and his recent pact with Chancellor Adenauer would meet in perhaps a rather perverse way, and certainly not as you envisaged it, our desire to begin withdrawing from Europe and having Western Europe assume more of its own defense. "

Eisenhower, as the man who has done most for the steel industry this year. Last year I won the award and they came to Washington to present it to me, but the Secret Service just wouldn't let them in. "

President Kennedy sometimes showed signs of bitterness, but that same morning he had seemed listless and pensive. Did he somehow know that his last trip was halfway over, that he had less than six months to live ? That noon, in New York's Battery Park, he recited an old Breton fisherman's prayer :
  " *O God, the sea is so great and my boat is so small...* "

On June 5 he was in Texas : " I am glad to leave Washington, D.C. and come to the Pass of the North, El Paso, a part of the Old West, but also a part of a new America... "

He had so little time left...

The following day he spoke at San Diego State College : " No country can possibly move ahead, no free society can possibly be sustained, unless it has an educated citizenry whose qualities of mind and heart permit it to take part in the complicated and increasingly sophisticated decisions that pour not only upon the President and upon the Congress, but upon all the citizens who exercice the ultimate power. "

On June 10 he gave the commencement address at American University in Washington :
  " What kind of peace do we seek ? Not a Pax Americana enforced on the world by American weapons of war. Not the peace of the grave or the security of the slave. I am talking about genuine peace, the kind of peace that makes life on earth worth living, the kind that enables men and nations to grow and to hope and to build a better life for their children — not merely peace for Americans but peace for all men and women — not merely peace in our time but peace for all time... ' When a man's way please the Lord ', the Scriptures tell us, ' he maketh even his enemies to be at peace with him. ' ... The United States, as the world knows, will never start a war. We do not want a war. We do not now expect a war. This generation of Americans has already had enough — more than enough — of war and hate and oppression. We

shall be prepared if others wish it. We shall be alert to try to stop it. But we shall also do our part to build a world of peace where the weak are safe and the strong are just. We are not helpless before that task or hopeless of its success. Confident and unafraid, we labor on — not toward a strategy of annihilation but toward a strategy of peace. "

On June 11 he addressed the American people from his office :
" This Nation was founded by men of many nations and backgrounds. It was founded on the principle that all men are created equal, and that the rights of every man are diminished when the rights of one man are threatened ... One hundred years of delay have passed since President Lincoln freed the slaves, yet their heirs, their grandsons are not fully free. They are not yet freed from the bonds of injustice. They are not yet freed from social and economic oppression. And this Nation, for all its hopes and all its boasts, will not be fully free until all its citizen are free.
" We preach freedom around the world, and we mean it, and we cherish our freedom here at home, but are we to say to the world, and much more importantly, to each other that this is a land of the free except for the Negroes ; that we have no second-class citizens except Negroes ; that we have no class or cast system, no ghettoes, no master race except with respect to Negroes ?
" Now the time has come for this Nation to fulfill its promise... We face, therefore, a moral crisis as a country and as a people. It cannot be met by repressive police action. It cannot be left to increased demonstrations in the streets. It cannot be quieted by token moves or talk. It is a time to act in the Congress, in your State and local legislative bodies, and above all, in all of our daily lives... Next week I shall ask the Congress of the United States to act, to make a commitment it has not fully made in this century to the proposition that race has no place in American life or law... "

On June 19 he asked the Congress to act : " I therefore ask every member of Congress to set aside sectional and political ties, and to look at this issue from the viewpoint of the Nation. I ask you to look into your hearts — not in search of charity, for the Negro neither wants nor needs condescension — but for the one plain, proud and priceless quality that unites us all as Americans : a sense of Justice. In this year of the Emancipation Centennial, justice requires us to insure the blessings of liberty for all Americans and their posterity — not merely for reasons of economic efficiency, world diplomacy and domestic tranquility — but, above all, because it is right. " He also asked Congress to establish an Advisory Council on the Arts : " An education needs schools so art needs museums, actors and playwrights need theatres, and composers and musicians need opera companies and orchestras... The concept of the public welfare should reflect cultural as well as economic considerations. We have agencies of the Government which are concerned with the welfare and advancement of science and technology, of education, recreation, and health. We should now begin to give similar attention to the arts. I am particularly interested in the opportunities for young people to develop their gifts... "

At Frankfurt on June 25 he remarked : " But Goethe tells us in his greatest poem that Faust lost the liberty of his soul when he said to the passing moment, ' Stay, thou art so fair. ' And our liberty, too, is endangered if we pause for the passing moment, if we rest on our achievements, if we resist the pace of progress. For time and the world do not stand still. Change is the law of life. And those who look only to the past or the present are certain to miss the future...

" So we are all idealists. We are all visionaries. Let it not be said of this Atlantic generation that we left ideals and visions to the past, nor purpose and determination to our adversaries. We have come too far, we have sacrificed too much, to disdain the future now. And we shall ever remember what Goethe told us — that the ' highest wisdom, the best that mankind ever knew ' was the realization that ' he only earns his freedom and existence who daily conquers them anew. ' "

At Dublin on June 28 he declared : " The problems of the world cannot possibly be solved by skeptics or cynics, whose horizons are limited by the obvious realities. We need men

who can dream of things that never were, and ask why
not... "

On June 29, as he left his beloved Ireland, he read a poem :

> *Tis it is the Shannon's brightly glancing stream,*
> *Brightly gleaming, silent in the morning beam*
> *Oh, the sight entrancing,*
> *Thus returns from travels long,*
> *Years of exile, years of pain,*
> *To see old Shannon's face again,*
> *O'er the waters dancing.*

" Well, I am going to come back and see old Shannon's
face again and I am taking, as I go back to America, all of
you with me... "

On July 17 he declared : " The United States has to move
very fast to even stand still... We are going to have to find in
the next decade 22 million jobs to take care of those coming
into the labor market and those who are eliminated by
technological gains... "

On July 26 he told American people : " Yesterday a shaft
of light cut into the darkness. Negations were concluded in
Moscow on a treaty to ban all nuclear tests in the atmosphere,
in outer space, and under water...

" This treaty is for all of us. It is particularly for our
children and our grandchildren, and they have no lobby here
in Washington... (But now), for the first time in many years,
the path of peace may be open. No one can be certain what
the future will bring. No one can say whether the time has
come for an easing of the struggle. But history and our own
conscience will judge us harsher if we do not now make every
effort to test our hopes by action, and this is the place to
begin. According to the Ancient Chinese proverb, ' A journey
of a thousand miles must begin with a single step. ' My fellow
Americans, let us take that first step. Let us, if we can, step
back from the shadows of war and seek out the way of peace.
And if that journey is a thousand miles, or even more, let

history record that we, in this land, at this time, took the first step... "[3]

On August 1 he remarked : " I think we will see a very changing world in 1964... " And that same day he warned : " The end of this summer of 1963 will be an especially critical time for 400,000 young Americans who, according to the experience of earlier years, will not return to school when the summer is ended. Moreover, without a special effort to reverse this trend, another 700,000 students will return to school in September, but will fail to complete the school year... "

And, turning to another subject : " I think there has been a common recognition that there is the necessity for revolution in Latin America, and it is either going to be peaceful or bloody. But there must be progress, there must be revolution... "

On August 27 he remarked, " ... To govern is to choose... "
On September 2, " I don't think that unless a greater effort is made by the Government (of South Vietnam) to win popular support that the war can be won out there. In the final analysis it is their war. They are the ones who have to win it or lose it. We can help them, we can give them equipment, we can send our men out there as advisers. but they have to win it, the people of Vietnam against the Communists. We are prepared to continue to assist them, but I don't think that the war can be won unless the people support the effort and, in my opinion, in the last two months, the government has gotten out of touch with the people. "[4]

On September 20, he addressed the United Nations General Assembly :
" The world has not escaped from the darkness. The long shadows of conflict and crisis envelop us still... My presence here today is not a sign of crisis, but of confidence... we believe that all the world — in Eastern Europe as well as Western, in Southern Africa as well as Northern, in old nations as well as new — the people must be free to choose their own future, without discrimination or dictation, without coercion or subversion... Why should the United States and

the Soviet Union, in preparing for such... expeditions, become involved in immense duplications of research, construction, and expenditure ? Surely we should explore whether the scientists and astronauts of our two countries — indeed of all the world — cannot work together in the conquest of space, sending some day in this decade to the moon not the representatives of a single nation, but the representatives of all our countries... The contest will continue — the contest between those who see a monolithic world and those who believe in diversity — but it should be a contest in leadership and responsibility instead of destruction, a contest in achievement instead of intimidation. Speaking for the United States of America, I welcome such a contest. For we believe that truth is stronger than error — and that freedom is more enduring than coercion. And in the contest for a better life, all the world can be a winner... Never before has man had such capacity to control his own environment, to end thirst and hunger, to conquer poverty and disease. to banish illiteracy and massive human misery. We have the power to make this the best generation of mankind in the history of the world — or to make it the last... For as the world renounces the competition of weapons, competition in ideas must flourish — and that competition must be as full and as fair as possible.

---

3. The Nuclear Test Ban Treaty was signed on October 7, 1963.

4. August 24 marked the beginning of the repressions against the Buddhists in South Vietnam. At the beginning of September, President Kennedy dispatched a new information mission to Saigon. A General and a diplomat made an inspection tour of the countryside and reported back to the National Security Council. General Krulack declared that the South Vietnamese troops were fighting magnificently, that the Diem government was popular with the people, and that there was no reason for concern. The diplomat, J. Mendenhall, reported that the country was in a desperate situation, that the Diem regime was on the brink of collapse, and recommended that Nehru be removed from power. Whereupon President Kennedy asked them if they were sure they had both visited the same country.

Diem and Nhu were assassinated on November 1, 1963.

On November 14, 1963 President Kennedy announced that some of the 16,000 American troops in Vietnam would be repatriated before the end of the year.

What the United Nations has done in the past in less important than the tasks for the future...

" My fellow inhabitants of this planet : let us take our
stand here in this assembly of nations. And let us see if we, in
our own time, can move the world to a just and lasting peace. "

On September 23 he wrote : " The American Presidency is a
formidable, exposed, and somewhat mysterious institution. It
is formidable because it represents the point of ultimate
decision in the American political system. It is exposed
because decision cannot take place in a vacuum : the Presidency is the center of the play of pressure, interest, and idea
in the Nation ; and the Presidential office is the vortex into
which all the elements of national decision are irresistibly
drawn. And it is mysterious because the essence of ultimate
decision remains impenetrable to the observer — often,
indeed, to the decider himself.

" Yet if the process of presidential decision is obscure, the
necessity for it is all too plain. To govern, as wise men have
said, is to choose. Lincoln observed that we cannot escape
history. It is equally true that we cannot escape choice : and
for an American President, choice is charged with a peculiar
and daunting responsibility for the safety and welfare of the
Nation. A President must choose among men, among measures, among methods. His choice helps determine the issues of
his Presidency, their priority in the national life, and the mode
and success of their execution. The heart of the Presidency is
therefore informed, prudent and resolute choice — and the
secret of the presidential enterprise is to be found in an
examination of the way presidential choices are made... "

The following day he left to tour the West. " We are
reaching the limits of our fundamental needs — of water to
drink, of fresh air to breathe, of open space to enjoy, of
abundant sources of energy to make life easier... Have we
ever thought why such a small proportion of our beaches
should be available for public use, how it is that so many of
our great cities have been developed without parks or
playgrounds, why so many of our rivers are so polluted, why
the air we breathe is so impure, or why the erosion of our
land was permitted to run so large as it has in this state
(Pennsylvania), and in Ohio, and all the way to the West

Coast... I don't know why it should be that 6 or 7 percent only of the whole Atlantic Coast should be in the public sphere and the rest owned by private citizens and denied to many millions of our fellow citizens. "

On September 25 he declared : " We must today prepare for those who are our heirs. The steps we take in conservation and reclamation will have very little effect upon all of us here immediately, and in this decade. What we are doing in the real sense is preparing for those who come after us... "

On the 26th he added : " I urge this generation of Americans who are the fathers and mothers of 350 million Americans who will live in this country in the year 2000, and I want those Americans who live in 2000 to feel that those of us who had positions of responsibility in the Sixties did our part... "

And the same day he revealed the key to his thinking : " If this nation is to survive and succeed in the real world of today, we must acknowledge the realities of the world ; and it is those realities that I mention now.

" We must first of all recognize that we cannot remake the world simply by our own command. When we cannot even bring all of our own people into full citizenship without acts of violence, we can understand how much harder it is to control events beyond our borders. " Every nation has its own traditions, its own values, its own aspirations. Our assistance from time to time can help other nations preserve their independence and advance their growth, but we cannot remake them in our own image. We cannot enact their laws, nor can we operate their governments or dictate our policies.

" Second, we must recognize that every nation determines its policies in terms of its own interests. ' No nation ', George Washington wrote, ' is to be trusted further than it is bound by its interest ; and no prudent statesman or politician will depart from it. ' National interest is more powerful than ideology, and the recent developments within the Communist empire show this very clearly. Friendship, as Palmerston said, may rise or wane, but interests endure.

" The United States has rightly determined, in the years since 1945 under three different administrations, that our interest, our national security, the interest of the United States of America, is best served by preserving and protecting a world of diversity in which no one power or no one combination of powers can threaten the security of the United States. The reason that we moved so far into the world was our fear that at the end of the war, and particularly when China became Communist, that Japan and Germany would collapse, and these two countries which had so long served as a barrier to the Soviet advance, and the Russian advance before that, would open up a wave of conquest of all Europe and all of Asia, and then the balance of power turning against us, we would finally be isolated and ultimately destroyed. That is what we have been engaged in for 18 years, to prevent that happening, to prevent any one monolithic power having sufficient force to destroy the United States.

" And third, we must recognize that foreign policy in the modern world does not lend itself to easy, simple black and white solution. If we were to have diplomatic relations only with those countries whose principles we approved of, we would have relations with very few countries in a very short time. If were to withdraw our assistance from all governments who are run differently from our own, we would relinquish half the world immediately to our adversaries. If we were to treat foreign policy as merely a medium for delivering self-righteous sermons to supposedly inferior people, we would give up all thought of world influence or world leadership.

" For the purpose of foreign policy is not to provide an outlet for our own sentiments of hope or indignation ; it is to shape real events in a real world. We cannot adopt a policy which says that if something does not happen, or others do not do exactly what we wish, we will return to ' Fortress America. ' That is the policy in this changing world of retreat, not of strength...

" The position of the United States, I believe, is happier and safer when history is going for us rather than when it is going against us. And we have history going for us today, but history is what men make it. The future is what men make it... "[5]

On the 27th he mused, " ... what green grass will they see... "

On September 28 he learned that there were 190 million Americans. On October 9 he told the press that he had consented to the sale by private dealers of surplus American wheat or wheat flour to the Soviet Union. He also remarked : " We are opposed to military coups, and it is the reason that we have broken off our relations with the Dominican Republic and Honduras... we are opposed to coups, because we think that they are defeating, self-defeating, and defeating for the hemisphere... "

On October 12 he noted : " That is always true, the first voyages are the hard ones and they require the perseverance and character. And I think that is a good lesson for all of us today as we attempt new things. The first voyages, as all of us know, are the more difficult, whether it is going into space, going to the bottom of the ocean, building a better country here, building a more prosperous country. The first voyage through our history has always been the most difficult... "

On October 18 he told a group of visitors from New Haven : " New Haven is typical of many cities faced by complex, interwoven problems. Ours is an age of great mobility. Each year thousands of families move from rural areas to urban slums. They come seeking better lives, but often find only new, unexpected barriers. These people find themselves in strange alien surroundings. Many have the added problem of racial discrimination. Much of the housing available to them is substandard. Most of them come without skills, seeking jobs, at a time when modern technology is rapidly making skilled training essential to employment. Their children enter already overcrowded schools, and often believe their studies bear little relation to the realities of their lives. Many of them drop out of school, only to become part of the growing army of unemployed youth. Health and recreational facilities for these young people are inadequate, and they are surrounded by crime, illiteracy, illegitimacy, and human despair. Finding

5. This passage is taken from a speech given by the President at the Mormon Tabernacle in Salt Lake City. Some commentators attacked it as " communistic. "

no work and little hope, too many of them turn to juvenile crime to obtain the material goods they think the society has denied them. Others turn to drink and narcotics addiction. And soon the cycle repeats itself, as this dispossessed generation bears children little better equipped than their parents to cope with urban life... "

That same day he reminded his listeners of that poem by Edna St. Vincent Millay :

Safe upon the solid rock the ugly houses stand
Come see my shining palace. It is built upon the sand.

On October 24 he concerned himself with the problem of retarded children. On the 26th, at Amherst College, he honored poet Robert Frost : " With privileges goes responsibility. Robert Frost said :

The roads diverged in a wood, and I-
I took the one less traveled by,
And that has made all the difference.

" In America, our heroes have customarily run to men of large accomplishments. But today this college and country honors a man whose contribution was not to our size but to our spirit, not to our political beliefs but to our insight, not to our self-esteem, but to our self-comprehension. In honoring Robert Frost, we therefore can pay honor to the deepest sources of our national strength. That strength takes many forms, and the most obvious forms are not always the most significant. The men who create power make an indispensable contribution to the Nation's greatness, but the men who question power make a contribution just as indispensable, especially when that questioning is disinterested, for they determine whether we use power or power uses us... When power narrows the areas of man's concern, poetry reminds him of the richness and diversity of his existence. When power corrupts, poetry cleanses...
" I see little of more importance to the future of our country and our civilization than full recognition of the place of the artist. If art is to nourish the roots of our culture,

society must set the artist free to follow his vision wherever it takes him. We must never forget that art is not a form of propanga ; it is a form of truth... Robert Frost was often skeptical about projects for human improvement, yet I do not think he would disdain this (American and world) hope. As he wrote during the uncertain days of the Second War :

Take human nature altogether since time began
And it must be a little more in favor of man,
Say a fraction of one percent at the very least...
Our hold on the planet wouldn't have so increased...

On the 30th he spoke at Philadelphia :
" ... May I repeat the words with which I summarized my view of America three years ago : ' I believe in an America that is on the march, an America respected by all nations, friends and foes alike, an America that is moving, doing, working, trying, a strong America in a world of peace. ' That was my credo then and that is my credo now...

" In the words which concluded an historic address to our party by the great American Claude Bowers, some 35 years ago, in the 28 campaign :

Now has come the time for action.
Clear away all thought of faction
Out from vacillating shame, every man no lie contain
Let him answer to his name.
Call the roll. "

The following day, President Kennedy signed a bill providing for the construction of mental retardation facilities and community mental health centers.

November 5 was Thanksgiving Day, and it marked his 1,019th day in office. " Yet, as our power has grown, so has our peril. Today we give our thanks, most of all, for the ideals of honor and faith we inherit from our forefathers — for the decency of purpose, steadfastness of resolve and strength of will, for the courage and the humility, which they possessed and which we must seek every day to emulate. As we express our gratitude, we must never forget that the highest appreciation is not to utter words but to live by them. Let us therefore proclaim our gratitude to Providence for manifold blessings — let us be humbly thankful for inherited ideals — and let us resolve to share those blessings and those ideals with our fellow human beings throughout the world... On that day let us gather in sanctuaries dedicated to worship and in homes blessed by family affection to express our gratitude for the glorious gifts of God ; and let us earnestly and humbly pray that He will continue to guide and sustain us in the great unfinished tasks of achieving peace, justice and understanding among all men and nations and of ending misery and suffering wherever they exist... "

On the 1,022nd day he declared : " The Family of Man is more than three billion strong. It lives in more than 100 nations. Most of its members are not white. Most of them are not Christians. Most of them know nothing about free enterprise or due process of law or the Australian ballot. If our society is to promote the Family of Man, let us realize the magnitude of our task. This is a sobering assignment. For the Family of Man in the world of today is not faring very well...

" Even little wars are dangerous in this nuclear world... The Korean conflict alone, forgetting for a moment the thousands of Americans who lost their lives, cost four times as much as our total world-wide aid budget for the current year...

" I do not want it said of us what T.S. Eliot said of others some years ago : ' These were a decent people. Their only monuments : the asphalt road and a thousand lost golf balls... '

" The struggle is by no means over. It is essential that we not only maintain our effort, but that we persevere ; that we not only endure, in Mr. Faulkner's words, but also prevail. It is essential, in short, that the word go forth from the United States to all who are concerned about the future of the Family of Man that we are not weary in well-doing. And we shall, I am confident, if we maintain the pace, we shall in due season reap the kind of world we deserve and deserve the kind of world we still have. "

In the days that followed he welcomed the members of the Black Watch regiment, met for the last time with the members of the press, turned once more to the problems of the children and the aged, and told this story to the delegates to the AFL-CIO Convention : " Marshal Lyautey, the great French Marshal, went out to his gardener and asked him to plant a tree. The gardener said, ' Why plant it ? It won't flower for 100 years. ' ' In that case, ' the Marshal said, ' plant it this afternoon. ' "

On the 1,032nd day, a Monday, he predicted that the month of April would bring " the longest and strongest peacetime economic expansion in our Nation's entire history. " And he added : " The steady conquest of the surely yielding enemies of misery and hopelessness, hunger, and injustice is the central task for the Americas in our time... ' Nothing is true except a man or men adhere to it — to live for it, to spend themselves on it, to die for it '... " Time was slipping through his hands...

On the 1,033rd day, a Tuesday, he remarked : " I realize once again in a very personal way what a tremendous flood of children are coming into our schools... "

On the 1,034th day, a Wednesday, he spoke of " a peace system worldwide in scope. "

On the 1,035th day, a Thursday, he reminisced : " Frank O'Connor, the Irish writer, tells in one of his books how, as a boy, he and his friends would make their way across the countryside, and when they came to an orchard wall that seemed too high and too doubtful to permit their voyage to continue, they took off their hats and tossed them over the wall — and then they had no choice but to follow them... " And he predicted, " When some meet here in 1990 they will look back on what we did and say that we made the right and wise decisions. ' Your old men shall dream dreams, your young men shall see visions', the Bible tells us, and ' where there is no vision, the people perish. ' "

On the 1,036th day at Fort Worth, he spoke again of

peace : " ... to that great cause, Texas and the United States are committed. "

" Committed " was his last word.

The 1,037th day never came.

13

Committee

Nothing is more prejudicial to the success of a plot than to try to carry it out on the basis of safety. Security requires more men, more time, more favorable circumstances, increasing the chances of discovery.

FRANCESCO GUICCIARDINI.

President Kennedy's assassination was the work of magicians. It was a stage trick, complete with accessories and false mirrors, and when the curtain fell the actors, and even the scenery, disappeared.

But the magicians were not illusionists but professionals, artists in their way. Abraham Lincoln too had been murdered by artists. Lincoln's election to the Presidency by the abolitionists had been the signal for the start of the Civil War. He was the first President to proclaim a government of the people, by the people, and for the people. Like Kennedy, he read Shakespeare, and he took long rides in the country, where he could dream far from the sounds of men. To a passing stranger he said, " If you have no friend, I will be your friend. " Even Karl Marx eulogized him.

Before the outbreak of the Civil War, there was a plot to kill Lincoln in Baltimore. He was warned by Pinkerton,

however, and saved his life by crossing the town at night.
Afterwards, the *New York Times* wrote : " This plot was
hatched by politicians, backed by bankers, and it was to be
carried out by a group of adventurers. "

On January 31, 1865, slavery was abolished. On April 14,
Lincoln was assassinated at Ford's Theatre in Washington.
The " assassin ", John Wilkes Booth, was trapped and shot in
a barn. Colonel Baker tore 18 pages out of a notebook he
was carrying. Nevertheless, there was a trial, and the prosecu-
tor, Bingham, proved that Jefferson Davis, the President of
the Confederacy, was behind the assassination. Eight accomplices were condemned, and four of them were hanged. Jacob
Thompson, the representative of the Confederacy in Canada,
had deposited a large sum of money in Booth's account at the
Bank of Ontario in Montreal. But Booth and his accomplices
were only the executants. The men behind the plot went free.
Lincoln was succeeded by Vice President Andrew Johnson,
who, on Christmas Day, 1886, proclaimed an amnesty and
complete pardon.

The war that Lincoln had tried to avoid was over before
his death. He was killed out of vengeance. But it was an era
when men killed for spite and made little attempt to hide it.
An Alabama newspaper had taken up a collection to cover
the cost of the assassination, and a Confederate officer had
volunteered for the job. In those days of the Old Frontier,
there were volunteers for all sorts of causes. Men then
were driven by their emotions.

Today's killers have less emotions and stronger motives.
William Manchester remarks that " some motives lie beyond
the rules of evidence. Like the shadow, they are elusive. "
These motives, nevertheless, were strong enough to persuade
Chief Justice Earl Warren to place " the good of the country "
ahead of justice. " The good of the country " is always
invoked with regard to an act contrary to the laws and justice
of the nation. The report to which Mr. Warren lent his name
may represent a political necessity designed to preserve the
national unity, but was it the place of the Chief Justice to
accept a responsibility so inconsistent with his vocation ? Was
it his place to disclose the testimony of witnesses before they
had even appeared ?[1] Was it his place, when Jack Ruby
begged to be brought to Washington to testify, to reply,

" Many things are at stake in this affair, Mr. Ruby ", and let him meet his fate without ever having heard him ?

History is filled with judges who, having attained the highest position and with nothing left to prove, with the exception perhaps of the magnitude of their responsibilities, have allowed their weakness or their senility to compromise their entire career. Would Joseph Warren have approved of Earl Warren ?[2]

The Warren Commission was christened *The President's Commission on the Assassination of President Kennedy*, and its report, dated September 24, 1964 and addressed to President Johnson, begins with the words : " Dear Mr. President : Your commission... " Could Earl Warren be hiding behind a syntax ?

The plotters were correct when they guessed that their crime would be concealed by shadows and silences, that it would be blamed on a " madman " and negligence.

A madman... a committee... negligence... Now, really.

We believe William Manchester when he says that he filled eighteen volumes of transcribed interviews and twenty-seven portfolios of documents with the understanding that they " would be made available to qualified· scholars after the death of all direct descendents of John F. Kennedy who were living at the time of his assassination. "[3] Was Mr. Manchester afraid that his files might reveal something that contradicted his thesis ? Did this " qualified historian " stoop to the worst vices of journalism under the guise of history ?

We believe him when he says, " I crawled over the roof of the Texas Book Depository and sat in Oswald's sixth floor perch. I rode his Dallas bus, watch in hand. Before taxi driver Bill Whaley died in Dallas he picked me up at the spot where he had picked up Oswald, drove me over the same route in the same taxi at the same speed, and dropped me off at the same curb... I went over the stretch of Elm Street where the President laid down his life. In Washington, Hyannis Port and

---

1. Marina Oswald's declarations of February 3 to 6, 1964.
2. General Joseph Warren, killed at Bunker Hill during the Revolutionary War.
3. *Death of a President,* page 11.

elsewhere, I studied each pertinent office, embassy and home — over a hundred of them — right down to the attic mentioned on the last page of the epilogue... I even had the damaged Dallas-to-Bethesda coffin uncrated for inspection. "[4]

But we admire him somewhat less when a careful examination of his sources[5] reveals that he claims to have interviewed eight different people in a single day, September 25, 1964, at Dallas, five of whom — Dallas oilman H.L. Hunt, General E.A. Walker, Dallas Police Chief J.F. Curry, J.W. Fritz, Chief of the Dallas Homicide Squad, and E.M. Dealey, publisher of the Dallas *Morning News* — were crucial witnesses. In addition, Mr. Manchester claims to have seen two newspaper editors[6] and funeral director Vernon B. Oneal, all of whom were capable of providing enough interesting details to justify his spending more than a few minutes with them. How much time did he have left for the others ? Did they refuse to answer his questions ? Apparently not, since he states that " only one, the assassin's widow, refused to respond to my request... "[7] Whatever the reason, Mr. Manchester spent little time in Dallas. Instead, he returned to his favorite haunts, where he interviewed John Metzler, Superintendent of Arlington National Cemetery, four times, and Mary Gallagher, Mrs. Kennedy's personal secretary, six.

Is Mr. Manchester afraid to tell what he knows ? To whom was Senator Fulbright referring when he spoke of the " responsibility for the national heritage of Pharisaism and puritanism and the tradition of the vigilantes, those citizens who take the law into their own hands " ?[8]

For commodity's sake, modern decisions in the domain of politics or organized crime must be group decisions, particularly when the subject is a political crime. Sixteen people had met at Hyannis Port on October 28, 1959 to plan the most scientific electoral campaign ever organized. Nothing was left to chance. Kennedy's Brain Trust relied on unemotional computers and public opinion polls. They analyzed living standards region by region and made detailed studies of local problems. They assembled statistics and established hypotheses. They weighed, they evaluated, they double-checked.

The men who organized the assassination, henceforth referred to as " The Committee ", were not as brilliant, but their task was simpler, for it is easier to kill a President than to get him elected. Later, we shall see why.

It is impossible to keep an assassination plot a secret. The decisions reached at the top secret meetings of such government bodies as the National Security Council are always known to at least 100 people within a few days. " Nothing is more prejudicial to the success of a plot than to try to carry it out on the basis of safety. Security requires more men, more time, more favorable circumstances, increasing the chances of discovery ", wrote Francesco Guicciardini. The Committee's plot required the participation of several dozen people, and the number of people who knew what was going to happen on November 22 was probably much higher than that.

Hitherto, we have attempted to pinpoint the reasons that impelled the Committee to act. Later, we shall see how the atmosphere of the moment and the cooperation of certain individuals and organizations contributed to its success.

Nearly all of the active members of the Committee came from either Texas or Louisiana, but they had technical advisers from New York, California and Washington. The multiple problems involved were discussed at technical conferences in New Orleans, Shreveport, Houston and Chicago.

" The southern states settle their internal problems themselves ", said Senator William Howard Taft, but since his time the old opposition between the industrial North and the romantic South has been replaced by a multiplicity of conflicting interests that are geographically more dispersed. Most of the Americans who felt threatened by Kennedy's policies, the big corporations for example, and even the big oil companies, were unwilling to be directly implicated in the assassination. They left the plotting to the Titans and to the professionals in their hire.

---

4. *Ibid,* page 12.

5. *Ibid,* " Sources ", page 741.

6. A.C. Greene, editor of the Dallas *Times-Herald* editorial page, and Joe Dealey, editor of the Dallas *Morning News.*

7. *Death of a President,* page 13.

8. Manchester failed to interview such eminent businessmen as Edgar R. Crissey, Nelson Bunker Hunt, and H.R. Bright, nor did he question Joseph P. Grinnan, head of the Dallas branch of the John Birch Society, nor Robert A. Surrey.

The only force that can bring the South and certain Americans to their knees is a President who is not only determined to act, but who also has the time. In the spring of 1963, Kennedy's re-election in November, 1964 was almost a certainty. Only 49.7 % of the voters had favored him in 1960, but his popularity, aided by a program that his adversaries attacked as " demagogic ", continued to grow. In June, 1963, a Gallup poll found that 59 % of the population approved of him.

Since the turn of the century, only two Presidents had been defeated for re-election — Taft in 1912 (after the Bull Moose split from the Republicans), and Hoover in 1932, as a result of the Depression. Kennedy still had a few weak points on the electoral map[9], but the Republican Party, already certain of defeat, had no strong candidate to oppose him.

In December, 1963, a few weeks after the assassination, 65 % of the people declared themselves in favor of Kennedy. This post-mortem enthusiasm was undoubtedly influenced by sentiment, but Kennedy probably would have gotten nearly as many votes as Johnson's 61 % against Goldwater in 1964. It was no secret among the young President's friends and advisers that once he had a solid majority behind him, he intended to lead a frontal attack on the ills and problems of the nation. A new America would emerge in the years to come.

During his second term, Kennedy would be rid of all party obligations, the compromises required by a close election, and the perspective of a second campaign. Owing no one anything, having no reason to humor anyone, he could go right to the heart of the problem. And his actions would be irreversible, as irreversible as the abolition of the monarchy, the enactment of free public education, or the creation of a state monopoly. " We've seen what he can do and what he has done with Congress on his back. Imagine how far he'll go in 1965 ! ", said Roy Cohn.[10]

What would be the advantages and the consequences of Kennedy's disappearance ? General Walker answered that question after the assassination when he declared, " Even if they aren't noticeable immediately, there will be considerable changes "[11] and Robert Kennedy remarked, " People just don't realize how conservative Lyndon really is. There are going to be a lot of changes. "

Once the decision had been made to eliminate the President, the members of the Committee turned their attention to political camouflage and technical arrangements. Secret operations in wartime, and even propaganda campaigns, employ techniques that to all appearances are illogical. They had to find a way to divert public anger. They needed a scapegoat, a " madman. "

History has often made use of a " madman " to shift the blame for a perfectly rational act. A " mad " assassin, captured immediately, would act as a magnet for public resentment. He would absorb the embarrassing questions and serve as a cover for the obvious accomplices. Quickly removed from the scene, he would leave behind him only the hatred inspired by solitary killers and the respect of the public for famous men now dead.

But the madman was only a detail. The Committee knew from its legal counselors that the assassination of a President is not a federal crime, and that the local authorities are legally competent to conduct an investigation. They would make sure it went wide of its mark.[12]

The collaboration on which the Committee was dependent, and the cooperation of those who did nothing to stop it, turned the assassination into a national conspiracy in which not only the local police and certain judicial officers, but also the FBI through its negligence and the CIA through its double agents and its operational units, the Army with its dissident

---

9. In addition to the South, Kennedy was concerned about Pennsylvania, New Jersey, Kentucky, Illinois, Michigan, Virginia, Missouri, and Oklahoma.

10. At the Stork Club in 1963.

11. Quoted in *U.S. News and World Report.* Another military man as interested and active as General Walker, Colonel Laurence E. Bunker, General MacArthur's staff aide, declared, " It's Kennedy or death. "

12. In 1963, there was no difference, in the eyes of the law, between the assassination of the President and the murder of a drunk in a bar. The Dallas assassination was covered only by Texas state law. Unless it could prove he was part of a conspiracy, the FBI had no legal right to arrest the assassin. It was a federal crime to threaten the President, but not to kill him. This loophole has since been mended.

generals, Congress and its corruption, and the entire economic system through its ideals and certain members of the Committee were implicated. A plot on this level is equivalent to a revolt. Kennedy's assassins were the arms of a counter-revolution.

The scandal would be suppressed. The United States isn't a banana republic, where a government can be overthrown by conspirators. Aided by the silence of the old regime, the new national leaders would dispel the unhealthy rumors, disguise the evidence, and camouflage the doubts. There was still a certain amount of risk, however, and the Committee was undoubtedly prepared to see certain compartments collapse under the pressure. But it also knew that America is not a romantic nation — that it buries its dead and then turns its attention to the living, and that its primary concern is for domestic tranquillity. There would be talk of negligence, but life would go on without Kennedy.

The Committee took a chance and won. On December 9, 1963, Vermont Royster, editor of the *Wall Street Journal,* washed the hands of the nation :

" In the shock of these past few days it is understandable that Americans should find their grief mingled with some shame that these events should happen in their country. We all stand a little less tall than we did last Friday morning.

" Yet, for our own part, we find past understanding the remarks of some otherwise thoughtful men who, in their moment of shock, would indict a whole nation with a collective guilt. It seems to us that they themselves have yielded to the hysteria they would charge to others, and, in so doing, show that their own country is past their understanding.

" Anyone who has been reading the newspapers, listening to the radio or watching television has heard these men — they include public commentators, members of our Congress and men of God. And the substance of what they charge is that the whole of the American people — and, by inclusion, the ways of the American society — are wrapped in a collective guilt for the murder of a President and the murder of a murderer.

" A Senator said that the responsibility lay ' on the people of Dallas ' because this is where the events took place. A

spokesman for one group of our people said the nation was
' reaping the whirlwind of hatred. ' One of our highest judges
said the President's murder was stimulated by the ' hatred and
malevolence' that are ' eating their way into the bloodstream
of American life ' A newspaper of great renown passed
judgment that ' none of us can escape a share of the fault for
the spiral of violence. ' And these were but a few among
many.

" Such statements can only come from men who have not
been abroad in the land, neither paused to reflect how the
events came about nor observed in what manner the whole
American people have responded to tragedy.

" A President lies dead because he moved freely among the
people. He did so because he was beloved by many people,
respected by all, and because everywhere people turned out in
great numbers to pay him honor. In a society of tyranny the
heads of state move in constant fear of murder, cordoned
behind an army of policemen. It is the fundamental order-
liness of the American society that leads Presidents to move
exposed to all the people, making possible the act of a
madman.

" In the tragedy there is blame, surely, for negligence. In
retrospect, perhaps, it was negligent of a President himself not
to be aware that there are ever madmen in the world, yet it is
a negligence born of courage and confidence. It was negligent
of the police authorities not to search and cover every corner,
every window, which might shield a madman, yet it was
negligence born of years of proven trust in the crowds of
Americans through which Presidents have safely moved.

" It was most certainly a terrible negligence on the part of
the local police authorities which permitted one man to take
vengeance into his own hands. It was an outrageous breach of
responsibility for them to have moved a man accused of so
heinous a crime in so careless a fashion. It was outrageous
precisely because all the American people were themselves so
outraged by the crime of assassination that anyone who knew
these people ought to have known that one among them
might be deranged enough to do exactly what was done.

" Yet the opportunity for negligence came because here the
accused was being treated as any other accused, his detention
in the hands of the local police, the procedures those followed

for the ordinary of murders. In another land he would have been efficiently buried by a secret police in a Lubyanka Prison, never again to be seen or heard of until his execution.

" One might say, we suppose, that some of this negligence could be laid to all of us. It is, after all, the eager interest of the people in the persons of their leaders that brings them into open caravans, and it is the desire of the people to follow the normal ways even in murders of state that left the accused to bungling local police.

" In sum, there is in all of this — let there be no mistake — much to grieve, to regret, to blame. We can't escape remorse that there are madmen in our midst, that a President is dead, that we have been denied the right to show in open court the virtue of a free society. Now we pay the price of all sorts of negligence.

" But this is something different from the charge in the indictment. It is more than nonsense to say that the good people of Dallas, crowding the streets to honor a President, share a murderous guilt ; or that the tragic acts of madmen cast a shadow on the whole of America. Such an indictment is vicious.

" Of reasons for shame we have enough this day without adding to them shameful injustice to a mourning people. "

The word " negligence " appears seven times, the word " people " ten. When a writer isn't used to certain words, he repeats them over and over again. For the Committee, this " negligence " was nothing but obstacles to avoid and accomplices to pay.

14

Secret Service

If they are to conquer, prophets must have at-
tentive partisans to protect them from the tumult.

MOHAMMED

The decision had been made, the money raised. The political
visionaries made way for the politicians.[1] It was time to
make plans.

It isn't enough to want to kill the President. There is also
the Secret Service to think about. The Presidential assistants
were prepared to affront political obstacles, but their " grace
and their airy flanerie "[2] had shielded them from the brutal
side of American life. Innocent of violence and ignorant of
hate, they failed to see the danger. Only Daniel P. Moynihan,
a former longshoreman, had some idea of such things. Of all
the Cabinet officials, only Bob Kennedy knew the risks of the
Presidency. But he couldn't be behind his brother every

---

1. We estimate the cost of the preparation, the assassination
itself and the post-assassination clean-up at between $ 5 and
$ 10 million. Contributions varied between $ 10.000 and
$ 500,000, and there were about 100 beneficiaries.
2. Manchester, *Death of a President*.

minute of the day.

Kennedy himself did little to discourage them. He was tolerant, he liked people, and he had a firm belief in his destiny. His boisterous or sophisticated cronies were barely conscious of the feelings aroused by the President's revolutionary action, and they paid little heed to his protection. Ken O'Donnell, who was in charge of the White House staff, had authority not only over the personnel, but also over the Secret Service. He could transfer or fire anyone he wanted, and he had the power to introduce reforms. He was also in charge of the President's trips.

O'Donnell is the soul of integrity, and, as he liked to say, he would have given his life for the President. He would have done better to protect him. It is surprising to realize that this man, chosen by Kennedy for his intellectual ability, acted without thinking. As he said one day to Jerry Behn, in his mind " politics and protection don't mix. " He was mistaken. It is a difficult and dangerous combination, but it is possible.

O'Donnell, though an excellent administrator, was a weak man, and he was unsure of himself. This became evident after the President's death at Parkland Hospital when, as the highest-ranking White House official present with the exception of President Johnson, he proved himself incapable of doing anything more than " standing off to one side and eyeing the medical examiner icily " when the latter opposed the removal of President Kennedy's body. It became all the more evident when, after behaving rudely towards the new President during the plane trip back to Washington (which was perhaps his right), he agreed to serve on his staff. It was he who kicked up such a fuss, only the day after the assassination, about a Boston funeral, proving once and for all that John Kennedy was for him more a friend than a President. He was so happy to have such a man as a friend that he gave too little thought to his enemies. We know how much these words may hurt Ken O'Donnell, and how unjust they may appear, but we imagine that O'Donnell must be blaming himself.

The 56 Secret Service agents assigned to the White House detail were under the authority of the Treasury Department, but the responsible official, Assistant Treasury Secretary Robert Wallace, left the everyday direction of the Service to

James Rowley, a mediocre civil servant. Gerald Behn, head of the White House Secret Service detail, lacked the necessary intelligence and qualifications for the job.

Three Presidents before Kennedy had been assassinated (Lincoln, Garfield, and McKinley), and four others (Jackson, Theodore and Franklin Roosevelt and Truman) had escaped assassination. This record, unequalled in any other stable republic, should have inspired the Secret Service to extra vigilance. Margaret Truman's overzealous bodyguards caused trouble in Sweden, which has some of the toughest policemen in the world. Eisenhower's trips abroad were meticulously organized. But since the advent of television, the protection of the President on American soil had become a difficult job. So that the public could see the President, his bodyguards were banished from the running-boards of the Presidential car. At first they ran alongside it ; later they rode on the back bumper. But nobody tried to kill Eisenhower during his two terms in office, and the Secret Service relaxed. Its relaxation was doubly dangerous, for the illusion remained that the President was well-protected.

It is difficult, of course, to protect an active President, and it is impossible to protect him completely during his public appearances. But there are ways to reduce the risk, and there are certain rules which are applied by Presidential security forces throughout the world, be it in France, the USSR, or Bolivia. The protection of the President within the United States[3] presents a special problem. The Secret Service is obliged to cooperate with the local police, which are sometimes incompetent or unreliable, and can even, as in Dallas, be dangerous.[4] But a Presidential security force should be able to rise to the challenge. The guerilla warfare specialists who organized the Dallas ambush were amazed to discover that Kennedy's Secret Service worked like a troop of boy scouts.

Since its creation following the assassination of McKinley

---

3. When the President travels abroad, the police of the host country are responsible for his security. In general, they take greater precautions than those taken in the United States.

4. The California and New York police are considered relatively reliable.

in 1901, the Secret Service had degenerated into a myth and a sinecure. In the first place, it wasn't secret. O'Donnell used Secret Service agents as errand boys, and at airport stops they handed out souvenirs to the crowds.[5] They all dressed alike in blue suits with white shirts and striped ties, and during Presidential trips they each wore an identical badge. The insignia for the Texas trip was known three weeks in advance : double white bars on a red background.

Several members of the White House detail were not qualified for their jobs. Their average age was 40, and as in the Senate the highest positions were awarded on the basis of seniority. Bill Greer, the driver of the Presidential Lincoln, was 54 and had 35 years' experience, enough to lull anybody's reflexes. After O'Donnell and perhaps Kellerman (the agent who rode in the front of the President's car in Dallas), Greer bears a heavy responsibility for the success of the assassination. We shall explain why a little later.

Finally, the Secret Service lacked direction. A security force must follow certain procedures and apply certain regulations without exception. The White House agents had no real leader. During Roosevelt's term in office, Frank J. Wilson ruled with authority, but the Secret Service chiefs who succeeded him were nothing but mediocre bureaucrats.

The White House agents had two sessions a year on a Washington firing range, but they practiced only target shooting like any amateur. Their reflexes were never tested. At any rate, a security agent's gun is of secondary importance. Generally, he has no time to shoot. His job is to anticipate an attempt on the President's life. Soviet security agents, for instance, have narrowly-defined responsibilities. In official motorcades, one agent watches the windows on the first floor, another those on the second, another the spectators in the front row, still another the people standing alone, another the local policemen and a sixth the soldiers lining the road. Every time a Soviet official travels, his security agents run down a check list of security precautions. No detail is omitted, and there are no exceptions. The same is true in France for the protection of President De Gaulle.[6]

Lawson, the Secret Service advance man in Dallas, let the local authorities show him around the city, and his report reached the White House only the day before the President's departure. A secretary whose married boss is planning an amorous weekend in Miami takes more precautions than Ken O'Donnell did for John Kennedy in Texas. Dealey Plaza on November 22, 1963 was about as heavily guarded as the Grand Cayon on a winter day, and Robert Kennedy's bodyguards showed little more vigilance on June 5, 1968. Of course, as the Warren Commission Report points out, " the limited effectives of the Secret Service make it impossible to watch hundreds of buildings and thousands of windows. " That, however, is not the problem.

There is a standard procedure for assuring the security of a motorcade traversing a city. As Superintendent Ducret, the man responsible for President De Gaulle's security, describes it : " Of course, it is impossible to watch everything and

---

5. Secret Service agents are less qualified on the average than FBI agents. They earn between $ 600 and $ 1,000 a month, considerably less (even with overtime pay) than J. Edgar Hoover's men.

6. The security officers charged with the protection of President De Gaulle even take the precaution of photographing the V.I.P.'s received by him or who are in contact with him, for example at the V.I.P. Waiting Room at Örly Airport. The crowds lining the streets during a parade are also photographed at vital spots before he passes, and if De Gaulle stops and approaches the crowd, a camera follows his every move. Later, these photographs are carefully studied.

Whenever De Gaulle travels by car, he is protected by 47 motorcycle policemen spread out in rows. Several police cars precede and follow the Presidential vehicle, and the car immediately following the President contains a sharpshooter and a photographer equiped with an automatic Japanese camera similar to a Robot. When de Gaulle makes shorter, routine trips, he is protected by a smaller force of 8 motorcycle policemen who surround the car.

There were only 4 motorcycle policemen at Dallas and all were following President Kennedy's car, making them totally ineffective. The role of a motorcycle policeman in this case is (1) to make it difficult to fire at the President from a crowd, and (2) to stop anyone who tries from approaching the car. During a parade along the Champs Elysées in Paris, a woman somehow managed to climb over the barriers and started towards De Gaulle's car. She was carrying a bouquet of flowers and was completely harmless, but the policeman who was supposed to be watching the barriers at that point lost his job.

occupy everything along the President's route. But it can be assumed that occupied office or apartment buildings are relatively safe. A potential assassin might, of course, try to enter one of these buildings, but he would be at the mercy of a witness. Serious conspirators will rarely take such a risk.

" On the other hand, all unoccupied buildings, administrative buildings outside of working hours, warehouses, building sites, and naturally all bridges, walls, and vacant lots that would be ideal for an ambush must not only be watched, but actually occupied by forces placed directly under the supervision of the Presidential security division. "

Surrounded by five buildings[7] and a great deal of open ground, Dealy Plaza was the most dangerous spot on President Kennedy's route, but a few men would have sufficed to guard it effectively.

A representative of the Committee followed the President's trips at the end of September through Wisconsin, North Dakota, Wyoming, Montana, Washington, Utah, Oregon, Nevada and California. Apparently the Committee planned to assassinate Kennedy, first in Chicago and then in Florida the week before his trip to Texas, but both times the Secret Service was alerted. The Chicago trip was cancelled, and special precautions were taken in Miami (the President used a helicopter). The Committee would have preferred to act in Florida, but it had its doubts about the reliability of the Florida state police and the Tampa and Miami police departments, and the operation was postponed until Dallas on November 22.[8]

On November 21, the two men in charge of the ambush observed the Kennedy motorcade in Houston. In Texas, as in Utah, the Secret Service was entirely dependent upon the local police. Not only did the agents behave on these trips as if they were members of the party ; they were always one step ahead. At 12 :30 p.m., seconds before the assassination, agent Emory Roberts jotted in his shift report," 12.35 p.m., the President arrived at the Trade Mart... " The Secret Service was already thinking ahead to tomorrow, when Kennedy was to visit Lyndon Johnson on his ranch.

Every time the President travels, the Protective Research Section[9] makes a security check of the area. The PRS had reservations about the Florida trip because of the large number of Cuban refugees and the rumors of an assassination attempt, but it issued no warning about Texas. The Secret Service, therefore, took no special precautions. The security measures taken in Dallas were the same as those in effect in New York, Palm Beach, Tampa, Miami, Houston and Fort Worth. The Secret Service could count on the reinforcement of its 28 agents in Texas, including 5 based in Dallas. Eight agents were assigned to guard the Trade Mart, but there were none at all at Dealey Plaza. The Secret Service was so unconcerned about the Texas trip that it even left its chief behind. At the time of the assassination, Jerry Behn was dining in a Washington restaurant. Roy Kellerman, who took his place at Dallas, proved so incompetent that at Parkland Hospital his men started taking orders from agent Emory Roberts. Later, during the flight back to Washington, Rufus Younglood took over. These men had traveled 200,000 miles with the President. Somewhere along the line, they had neglected the first rule of security : they had lost their reflexes.

When the first shot rang out at Dealey Plaza, agent Clint Hill, who was later decorated, was the first to move, and it took him 7 or 8 seconds to react. In eight seconds, the average sprinter can cover 80 yards. Yet " Halfback ", the back-up car in which Hill was riding, was almost touching the Presidential limousine, and neither vehicule was traveling more than 12 miles an hour.[10]

---

7. The Texas School Book Depository, the Dal Tex Building, the Dallas County Records Building, the Criminal Courts, and the Old Court House.

8. The Committee was also probably trying to throw the Secret Service off the scent.

9. The Protective Research Section, headed by Robert I. Bouck, had 65 offices across the country and 50,000 files on people who had threatened the President. Between November, 1961 and November, 1963, it investigated 34 Texas residents and opened 115 other files on Texans. On November 8, 1963, the PRS spent ten minutes inspecting Dallas.

10. Clint Hill reached the back of the President's car 2.6 seconds after the final shot. The shooting lasted about 7 seconds. At least twelve seconds elapsed between the first shot and the instant when Hill was in a position to cover the President's body. Vice-President Johnson was covered by agent Youngblood in less than three seconds.

Kennedy's Secret Service agents apparently had no idea of the importance of a second in an assassination attempt. Agent Hickey, riding in Halfback, had an AR-15 automatic rifle on his lap, but it took him two seconds to load it and get ready to fire. In two seconds a modern bullet travels more than a mile.

The organizers of the ambush knew, of course, that the Secret Service was inefficient, but they had never imagined that their reflexes were that slow, and they had laid their plans in the assumption that Kennedy's agents would react immediately. The tactical and ballistic aspects of the operation, which we shall examine later, were based on a hypothetical operating time of three seconds. This was the estimated reaction time of Kennedy's bodyguards. But the President's driver could have reduced it even more. The President's car was a Lincoln with a souped-up engine specially designed for rapid accelerations, and we shall see later how speed affects the accuracy of a gunman.

On November 18 in Tampa, the President ordered the two Secret Service agents off the back bumper of his car. The men from the Committee noted this change, which persisted at Fort Worth, San Antonio and Houston, but they maintained their original plan, which took into account the possibility of instantaneous intervention by the bodyguards.

The blame must be laid not so much on the Secret Service agents as on their chiefs, and on the White House assistant responsible for the President's security. We have cited only their most glaring errors, but there were others — less impor-

---

11. Several Secret Service agents were notorious alcoholics. The regulations stipulate that any Secret Service agent found drinking on duty will be fired forthwith, and when the President is traveling, his agents are on duty 24 hours a day.

But they were so little concerned about Texas that four of them in the President's party sat and drank in a Fort Worth bar until the wee hours of the morning on the day of the assassination.

A century earlier, President Lincoln's bodyguard had sneaked off for a drink when Booth entered the Presidential box at Ford's Theatre.

12. In 1967, Mr. Bolden was being held at the federal medical center in Springfield, Mo.

tant perhaps, but characteristic of their lack of discipline, such as their drinking on duty.[11] Abraham Bolden, the only Negro in the Presidential bodyguard, asked to testify before the Warren Commission on the subject of some of these accusations, but the Committee refused to hear him. Later, he was fired from the Secret Service on grounds of professional incompetence.[12]

The Secret Service was guilty of negligence, as the highly-respected *Wall Street Journal* commented. But its agents were professionals, and they recognized the work of other professionals. They were the first in the President's entourage to realize that the assassination was a well-organized plot. They discussed it among themselves at Parkland Hospital and later during the plane ride back to Washington. They mentioned it in their personal reports to Secret Service Chief James Rowley that night. Ten hours after the assassination, Rowley knew that there had been three gunmen, and perhaps four, at Dallas that day, and later on the telephone Jerry Behn remarked to Forrest Sorrels (head of the Dallas Secret Service), " It's a plot. " " Of course ", was Sorrel's reply. Robert Kennedy, who had already interrogated Kellerman, learned that evening from Rowley that the Secret Service believed the President had been the victim of a powerful organization.

President Kennedy was dead, but the Secret Service was never officially inculpated. There were several staff changes in the White House detail, but two agents, Youngblood and Hill, were decorated. Because it reinforced its thesis, the Warren Commission blamed the Presidential guards, but a soldier is worth no more than his commanding officer, and the heads of the Secret Service were not worth much.

As for Ken O'Donnell, ex-captain of the Harvard rugby team, at Dallas he was up against a team that played rough.

15

Spies

I never had any thought... when I set up the CIA, that it would be injected into peacetime cloak-and-dagger operations. Some of the complications and embarrassment that I think we have experienced are in a part attributable to the fact that this quiet intelligence arm of the President has been so removed from its intended role...

HARRY TRUMAN

Everywhere — and the United States is no exception — there are criminals who will do anything for money. But it is one thing to murder a creditor, a Senator or a jealous husband, and quite another to assassinate the President of the United States.

Hired killers are rarely employed by a parapolitical or paramilitary group. They are much too dangerous. Their connections, their morals, and their insatiable avarice pose too many problems for a responsible organization. On the other hand, a number of individuals active in groups like the John Birch Society, the Patrick Henry Association, and the Christian Crusaders would be only too happy to volunteer for an ideological crime. But, although successful assassinations have on occasion been the work of fanatics, serious-minded conspirators would prefer not to rely on idealists. History tells us why.

The Tsar's Prime Minister, Stolypin, was shot to death in 1911 during a performance of Rimsky-Korsakov's " Tsar Saltan " at the Kiev Opera.[1] The assassin, a lawyer named Dimitri Bogrov, was convinced he had acted in the cause of freedom, and many others before him had sacrificed themselves in the struggle against the Tsars. But fanatics like Bogrov who are prepared to die for a cause are few indeed, and the nihilists lost more men than the imperial families.

Today, professional soldiers and guerilla warriors have taken up where the nihilists left off. They are just as courageous, but often less successful. In Germany, in 12 years of Nazism and 5 years of war, despite the Kreisau Circle and the numerous groups that claimed in 1946 to have belonged to the underground, despite the work of the Allied intelligence services and the plots hatched by several high-ranking officers of the Wehrmacht and the OKW, Hitler was never assassinated. Two officers, however, tried.

The first planted a bomb on one of Hitler's aides, claiming it was a bottle of cognac. The bomb was due to go off in the plane carrying the Fuhrer to the eastern front, but it failed to explode. The assassination attempt was never discovered. It was publicized later by its author, who meanwhile had recovered his " bottle of cognac. "

The second, more serious attempt was the work of Colonel Klaus Von Stauffenberg. His failure dealt a deathblow to the plot of July 20, 1944. Stauffenberg either didn't dare or didn't care to shoot Hitler.[2] Instead, he placed his briefcase, containing the equivalent of a pound of TNT[3], under the conference table where Hitler was sitting and left the room, claming he had to make a phone call. The TNT was set off by a detonator a few minutes later.

But Colonel Von Stauffenberg, while a brilliant cavalryman, was a poor saboteur. His bomb would have killed Hitler, and probably most of the other officers present, if the conference had been held, as was usually the case at Rastenburg, in the casemate of a cement blockhouse. The closed quarters would have magnified the compression, and the explosion would have proved fatal. On that hot July day, however, the conference was held instead in a wooden barracks with the windows open. Hitler was only knocked to the floor and slightly wounded by the explosion.

Colonel Von Stauffenberg was mistaken in his choice of an explosive. TNT is excellent for blowing up railroad lines and bridges, but for this type of operation Von Stauffenberg should have used a defensive grenade of the type used by the German Army, along with a phosphorous grenade and, as an additional precaution, a bottle containing about a pint of gasoline. The explosive power of the blasting agent would have been amplified by bits of flying steel and the heat from the phosphorus and the gasoline. Regardless of where the meeting was held, the explosion would have done its work. Those officers who weren't killed immediately would have been burned alive. But despite their small chance of survival, it would nevertheless have been wise to verify the success of the operation before giving the signal for a revolt that resulted in hundreds of executions, including that of Von Stauffenberg, about whom any biographer is forced to conclude that he was a total failure as an assassin. His technical incompetence caused the collapse of the German resistance and probably cost the Allies several more months of war.

Another Colonel, the Frenchman Bastien Thiry, attempted in 1962 to avenge the honor of the French Army by assassinating General De Gaulle. He set up an ambush using submachine guns at an intersection in the suburbs of Paris

---

1. He succeeded in his attempt even though he himself had warned the police that someone would try to kill Stolypin that night. As a sign of their gratitude, the police sent him an invitation to the opera. Bogrov was hung two months later, still attired in evening dress.

2. He declared before and after the assassination attempt that he was willing to take the risk, but that he considered himself indispensable to the conspiracy, the members of which were waiting for him in Berlin. Despite a radio signal announcing the success of the operation sent with the help of General Fellgiebel, Chief of Signals, who was also mixed up in the plot, the General Staff in Berlin postponed the insurrection until Von Stauffenberg's return to Berlin. The success of the conspiracy depended on a single man, who tried to do too much and blundered.

3. Trinitrotoluene, a stable and very powerful explosive.

one evening when the General's car was due to pass on the way to the airport. The car, an ordinary Citroen, was going about 40 miles an hour. On a signal from the Colonel (a brandished newspaper), the gunmen fired more than 100 rounds, but neither the General nor his wife nor the driver nor the security agent accompanying them was hit. The tires were shot out, but the driver accelerated immediately, and the General disappeared over the horizon.

Colonel Thiry was a graduate of the foremost scientific school in France, the Ecole Polytechnique, the students of which are renowned for their reasoning power. Moreover, he was a leading aeronautical specialist and, like Von Stauffenberg, a disinterested patriot. But, as far as assassinations were concerned, he too was a failure.[4] Like Von Stauffenberg, he was executed, and from a technical point of view his failure is understandable. He was an amateur, and assassinations are not for amateurs. His plan was of interest to the men at Dallas because its target was a moving vehicule. An attack on a moving target presents special problems which we shall examine later. In any case, these are problems that can only be solved by a specialist.

The Committee needed professionals who were accustomed to planning clandestine and risky operations, and who had the proper mentality — in other words, professionals who had not lost their amateur standing. The men best qualified for this type of job are undoubtedly the specialists of the intelligence services like the Soviet KGB and the CIA, which have a special section for assassinations. It is safe to assume that nothing is impossible or surprising in the world of espionnage, in the widest sense of the term. Obstacles that would hamper organized criminals or conscientious conspirators can be overcome or avoided more easily by those who are known as " spies. "

Spies ! The spy trade has come a long way since A. Curtis Roth wrote in the *Saturday Evening Post* in 1917 :

" Scientific spying knows no ethics, owns no friendships and enjoys no code of honor. It delights to operate through degenerates, international highbinders and licentious women. It shrinks before no meanness or blackguardism to attain its ends, even callously conducting official houses of prostitution for the entrapment of the unwary. "

Twenty-five years later, Winston Churchill described it as
" plot and counterplot, deceit and treachery, double-dealing
and triple dealing, real agents, fake agents, gold and steel, the
bomb and the dagger. "

Today, the cloak and the dagger have been replaced by
scientific administration. Intelligence organizations, be they
American or Russian, direct activities that run from routine
murders to full-scale revolutions. The necessary technicians
are trained and available. They can be used for official ends,
but they may also be corrupted and their abilities exploited
for more questionable purposes. Once we step into the world
of these organizations and the individuals who work for them,
it is no longer possible, as we have done in preceding chapters, to set out and analyze the facts in logical order. Espionage activities know no logic, nor is it possible to learn the
entire truth. If the Warren Commission devoted several thousand pages to Oswald, it did so not only to conceal the nature
and the origins of the plot, but also because Oswald, im-
mersed in the muddy waters of the intelligence world, had
anything but a simple life. The object of this book is not to
study his short and picturesque history, which in the end has
little significance, nor to provide a detailed description of the
organization and activities of the CIA in the period between
1960 and 1963.[5] But it is necessary to know something about
the CIA in order to understand the Oswald affair, and to

---

4. Thiry's assassination plot failed because :
- the site was a poor choice (a straight road that enabled the car
to move too fast)
- the firing was badly synchronized, and failed to take account
of the speed of the objective
- the signal used (a brandished newspaper) was ridiculous at
nightfall
- no radical means of stopping the car (an explosion, a herse,
some sort of obstacle) was planned
- the gunmen were placed along a line nearly perpendicular to the
car, which reduced their angle of fire and increased the dispersion.
5. We advise our readers who are especially interested in this
subject to consult the two books written by David Wise and
Thomas B. Ross, *The Invisible Government* and *The Espionage
Establishment.*

draw together all the threads that lead to the 22nd of November.

The CIA celebrated its twentieth anniversary in September, 1967. It was created on September 8, 1947 by the same law that instituted a unified Defense Department and established the National Security Council.[6] Its mission was the coordination and evaluation of intelligence information, but it immediately branched out into special operations, which took on such importance that the Plans Division was organized in 1961 to plan and carry them out.[7] In 1949 a law was passed exempting the CIA from disclosing its activities, the names and official titles of its personnel, their salaries, and the number of persons it employed. The Director of the CIA was authorized to spend his entire budget[8] on the strength of his signature, without ever having to account for the way in which it was spent.

This provision enabled the CIA to become, during the Fifties, a sort of " invisible government " which expanded its authority when Allen Welsh Dulles became Assistant Director in 1951, then Director on February 10, 1953.[9] Six months later, in August, 1953, the CIA proved to the world just how powerful it had become when General Fazollah Zahedi replaced Mossadegh as Prime Minister of Iran. In 1951, Mossadegh had nationalized the Anglo-Iranian Oil Company and confiscated the Abadan refinery with the support of Tudeh, the Iranian Communist Party. The CIA succeeded in having Mossadegh arrested, and the leaders of Tudeh were executed. A consortium of the major oil companies thereby signed a 25-year agreement with Iran granting 40 % of the shares in the former Anglo-Iranian to Standard Oil of New Jersey, Gulf Oil, Standard Oil of California, Socony Mobil and Texaco. A few months later, in April, 1955, nine other independent American companies were given a share in the operations. The CIA man who directed the operation was Kermit Roosevelt[10], a State Department consultant for Middle Eastern and Communist affairs since 1947. When " Kim " Roosevelt left the CIA in 1958, he was hired by Gulf Oil as its " director for governmental relations ". He became vice-president of Gulf in 1960 (he is also a consultant for Socony Mobil).

Its Iranian success consolidated the power of the CIA,

which in the years that followed multiplied its interventions and carried off some brilliant operations, the best-known of which took place in Guatemala and behind the Iron Curtain, where the CIA attempted to split up the Communist Bloc. It was the West German intelligence service, a step-child of the CIA, that set off the East German revolt of June 17, 1953 that was checked by Soviet intervention and caused 2,000 dead or wounded in East Berlin alone. In 1956, the CIA was behind the Hungarian uprising, which proved even more costly to the Hungarian people.

The CIA established several intelligence rings in the USSR and multiplied its special missions. Between 1956 and 1960, its U2 spy planes furnished valuable intelligence on airfields, the locations of planes and missiles, rocket experiments, special ammunitions dumps, submarine production and atomic installations.[11] In Egypt the CIA, under the cover of Ambassador Jefferson Caffrey, who was acting on instructions from

---

6. Its predecessors were the Office of Coordinator of Information and the Office of Strategic Services (OSS), created on June 13, 1942 and directed by General Donovan, followed by the Central Intelligence Group, created on January 22, 1946 and directed at first by Rear Admiral Sidney W. Souers and then by Rear Admiral Roscoe H. Hillenkoeter, who became the first Director of the CIA.

7. The Plans Division has sole control over secret operations of all kinds (Iran in 1953, Guatemala in 1954, the U2 flights, the Bay of Pigs, the Congo revolt in 1964, etc.)

8. Which in 1963 amounted to nearly $ 2 billion. In 1967, total U.S. intelligence expenditures amounted to $ 4 billion annually.

9. His brother, John Foster Dulles, was Secretary of State at the time and the most influential figure in the Eisenhower administration. The reign of the Dulles brothers lasted until the death of John Foster Dulles in 1959.

The Eisenhower Administration, it will be remembered, lasted from 1952 until 1960.

10. Theodore Roosevelt's grandson and a cousin of Franklin Delano Roosevelt.

11. The Soviets reponded to the U2's by launching military observation satellites, which were used to photograph American strategic bases. Between October, 1957 and October, 1967, the Russians launched about 100 of these Cosmos " scientific " satellites from their bases at Tyuratam and Plesetsk. The satellites

John Foster Dulles, played an important role in the 1952 overthrow of King Farouk and the seizure of power by Colonel Neguib, and later in the latter's overthrow by Colonel Nasser.

In 1954 the CIA overthrew the Guatemalan regime of President Jacob Arbenz Guzman because of his " Communist leanings " 'and replaced him with one of their puppets, Colonel Castillo-Armas, who immediately denied illiterates (who made up 70 % of the population) the right to vote and returned to Frutera[12] the 225,000 acres of land that President Arbenz had confiscated. One million acres which had already been distributed to the peasants were taken back, and a committee was created to fight communism in the country.[13]

The CIA also suffered failures — in Indonesia against Sukarno in 1958, in Laos with Phoumi in 1960, in South Vietnam with Ngo Diem between 1956 and 1963[14], or partial successes, as in West Germany.[15]

Nor did the CIA confine its activities to the hotspots of the

---

remained in orbit from 3 to 8 days before being brought back to earth.

During the same period, the United States launched about 200 secret military satellites. At the end of 1967, there were 254 American and 54 Russian satellites in orbit.

12. A subsidiary of United Fruit.

13. President Eisenhower described Guatemala that year as " a beautiful land of Central America whose mountains and moderate climate make it one of the garden spots of the hemisphere "

14. In these three countries, Kennedy's foreign policy was in direct opposition to that of the CIA, which was forced, officially at least, to fall into line. But the CIA continued to operate in the shadows, often against the instructions of the federal government.

15. The Bundesnachrichtendienst, better known as the Federal Intelligence Agency or FIA, is largely dependent on the CIA, which subsidizes and controls it. It is directed by Gerhard Wessel, a former lieutenant Colonel in the Wehrmacht. Wessel in 1967 replaced Reinhard Gehlen, a former ex-Nazi Colonel " recuperated " in August, 1945 by Allen Dulles, who at the time headed the OSS in Switserland and was in charge of American intelligence activities in occupied Germany.

Gehlen, who had conceived the idea of the " Vlassov Army " (Russian anti-Communist troops), was given the responsibility for the underground that continued to operate behind Communist

world — the Middle East, Southeast Asia, the Central and Latin American " protectorates ", and the Iron Curtain countries. The CIA was naturally strongly established in the socialist countries such as Yugoslavia, and in neutral states like Austria and Switzerland, but it was also active, for economic and political reasons, in zones of international tension throughout the world. In some cases, for example in Algeria, these reasons were directly opposed.[16] In 1955,

---

lines until 1950. In Poland, Gehlen's guerillas on March 28, 1947 murdered General Karol Swierczenski, Vice-Minister of Defense who, under the name of Walter, had commanded the 14th International Brigade in Spain, and who served as the model for one of the characters in Hemingway's *For Whom the Bell Tolls*.

Gehlen developed his network under the cover of a firm known as the " Economic Association for the Development of South Germany. " He employed former members of the Gestapo such as Boemel-Burg, his intelligence chief in Berlin, and Franz Alfred Six, former SS General and one of Eichmann's subordinates, who was put in charge of Gehlen's contacts in Western Europe.

With the aid of other highly-qualified specialists, Gehlen successfully infiltrated East Germany and the Eastern European states, uncovered Soviet intelligence rings, planted agents among groups of expatriate workers, and took charge of the refugee organizations.

But he also suffered failures. In 1954 Dr. Otto John, the head of a rival West German intelligence organization backed by the British, disappeared in Berlin and fled to the USSR. In 1961 the CIA learned that three of Gehlen's agents, Heinz Felfe, Hans Clemens, and Erwin Tiebel, had been passing information to the Russians since 1950. A short time before they were uncovered, the three double agents had been honored by their chiefs (Gehlen and Shelepin, chief of the KGB). As a result, the CIA grew wary of West German intelligence and has since treated it with caution.

16. Under Eisenhower, financial agreements, particularly in the domain of oil, were under discussion between American firms and the Provisional Government of the Algerian Republic (GPRA). Contact had been made between representatives of Aramco (which was interested in the Sahara) and Ben Bella a short time before a plane carrying the Algerian nationalist leader from Morocco to Tunisia was intercepted on the orders of French Minister Robert Lacoste.

But at the same time the CIA was active in anti-Communist

the CIA intervened in Costa Rica, one of the most stable and democratic of the Latin American nations, where it tried to overthrow the moderate socialist government of President Jose Figueres.

Thus, endowed with complete autonomy, a virtually unlimited budget, and a *de facto* co-directorship under the Eisenhower administration, the CIA in the period between 1953 and 1960 developed into a world power.[17] The CIA was represented in 108 different countries, commanded submarines and jet planes, and controlled 30,000 agents under the cover of diplomatic, commercial, industrial, journalistic, military, technical, labor, university and secret activities.

The CIA, of course had competition. The Soviet KGB has been described by Allen Dulles as a " multipurpose, clandestine arm of power, more than a secret police organization, more than an intelligence and counterintelligence organization. It is an instrument for subversion, manipulation and violence, for secret intervention in the affairs of other countries " (a definition that seems equally applicable to the CIA). Apparently, the budget of the KGB is about the same as that of the CIA, which means that it employs many more agents, since a Russian costs far less than an American[18]. Most of the agents employed by both organizations are " legal ", which means that they have a diplomatic cover job abroad. According to Colonel Oleg Penkovsky, who was executed by the Russians in 1963 for espionage activities in favor of the United States, three-quarters of all Soviet diplomats abroad, and all of the consular personnel, are members of the KGB.

This percentage is far lower in the United States ; about one-third of all American embassy and consular personnel

---

and anti-Gaullist movements, and it backed preparations for the 1961 French Generals' putsch. Richard M. Bissell, Director of the Plans Division of the CIA, met on Dcember 7, 1960 with Jacques Soustelle, a French political figure who was planning a previous coup that failed.

17. The influence and activities of the CIA are beyond the scope of the imagination. It has been involved in nearly all the major international events of the past 15 years. It played an important role in Israeli intelligence activities during the 1967

belongs to the CIA, although the figure varies widely from country to country.[19] When Kennedy became President, an American Ambassador had no more authority over the CIA "Station Chief" in his embassy than a Soviet Ambassador had over the KGB "resident."

The CIA had infiltrated all the international organizations of which the United States was a member, even UNESCO and the FAO, and its agents operated in all the NATO centers in Europe. In 1961 the CIA was represented in every country in the world, even Iceland (where it had 28 agents and two offices, one at the U.S. Embassy at Reyjkavik and the other at the military base at Keplavik), Uganda, Surinam, the Ryukyu Islands, and Sierra Leone. Photographs and reports from its agents poured in from all over the world to Langley[20], where they were analyzed by photo-interpretation experts and fed into Walnut, the CIA's electronic computer.

In addition, the CIA controlled the most colossal propaganda apparatus of all times, concealed behind the names of more than 600 different companies. Hundreds of organizations were financed wholly or in part by the CIA.[21] The CIA

---

six-day war, and it was involved in the Greek military coup that originated in 1965 as a result of the Aspida plot, and which brought General George Papadopoulos, a CIA man, to power. In the South Pacific the CIA runs a large-scale training center for guerillas and saboteurs on Saipan Island, one of the Mariannas group. In 1961 the Saipan school had already furnished 6 to 700 guerilla warfare experts to Chiang Kai Shek to be used to stir up subversion on the Chinese mainland.

18. The First Directorate, or department in charge of foreign intelligence, is not the sole activity of the KGB. The Second Directorate is responsible for keeping the Soviet people in order, and there are other departments which constitute technical support sections.

19. On July 14, 1966, Senator Fulbright declared, "The operations of the CIA have grown today to exceed the Department of State in both number of personnel and budget."

20. Langley, Virginia, 10 miles outside Washington, where CIA headquarters are located.

21. The African American Institute, American Council for International Commission of Jurists, American Federation of State, County and Municipal Employees, American Friends of the Middle East, American Newspaper Guild, American Society

controlled, directly or through subsidies, radio stations, newspapers, and publishing houses in the United States and throughout the world.[22] Some, like Praeger, Doubleday, and Van Nostrand, agreed to publish propaganda works such as *Why Vietnam* ? Its influence even extended to television and the motion picture industry. Until 1956, it controlled the Near East Broadcasting Station, with the most powerful transmitter (located on Cyprus) in the Middle East, and a newspaper chain in Beirut run by a double agent for the CIA and the British Secret Service, Kamel Mrowa, that published the dailies *Al .Hayat* and *Daily Star*. In 1958 it installed seven clandestine radio stations based in Aden, Jordan, Lebanon and Kenya to counter Radio Cairo and defend the " independence " of Irak (sixth largest producer of oil in the world, and the only Arab state that is a member of the pro-Western Bagdad Pact). In North America, the CIA operated a short-wave radio station, WRUL, used to broadcast coded messages to its agents, and it had an interest in the gigantic Voice of America transmitting complex located at Greenville, North Carolina, the most powerful radio station in the world. In Europe, Radio Liberty (transmitters at Lampertheim in West Germany and Pals in Spain) employed 12.000 persons in its offices in Paris, Munich and Rome, and Radio Free Europe

---

of African Culture, Asia Foundation, Association of Hungarian Students in North America, Committee for Self-Determination, Committee of Correspondence, Committee on International Relations. Fund for International Social and Economic Education, Independent Research Service, Institute of International Labor Research, International Development Foundation, International Marketing Institute, National Council of Churches, National Education Association, Paderewski Foundation, Pan American Foundation, Synod of Bishops of the Russian Church Outside Russia, United States Youth Council, and the Philadelphia Education Fund for the Nordic Arts.

Conduits for CIA money included': the Andrew Hamilton Fund, Beacon Fund, Benjamin Rosenthal Foundation, Borden Trust, Broad-High Foundation, Catherwood Foundation, Chesapeake Foundation, David, Joseph and Winfield Baird Foundation, Dodge Foundation, Edsel Fund, Florence Foundation, Gothan Fund, Heights Fund, Independence Foundation, J. Frederick Brown Foundation, J.M. Kaplan Foundation, Jones-O'Donnell, Kentfield Fund, Littauer Foundation, Marshall Foun-

had 28 transmitting stations in West Germany (at Frankfurt
and Munich) and in Portugal. The principal radio stations
operated by the CIA in the Far East were located at Taipeh,
Formosa, Seoul, Korea, and at three places along the coast of
Japan. It also controlled stations in Australia and in the
French-owned islands of the Pacific.

Beginning in 1955, the CIA extended its intelligence networks on the continent of Africa, which up till then, with the
exception of Egypt and Libya, had been considered of secon-

---

dation, McGregor Fund, Michigan Fund, Monroe Fund, Norman
Fund, Pappas Charitable Trust, Price Fund, Robert E. Smith
Fund, San Miguel Fund, Sydney and Esther Rabb Charitable
Foundation, Tower Fund, Vernon Fund, Warden Trust, Williford-
Telford Fund.

The CIA subsidized the following international organizations :
the Inter-America Federation of Newspapermen's Organizations,
International Federation of Free Journalists, International Journalists, International Student Conference, Public Services International World Assembly of Youth, World Confederation of Organizations of the Teaching Profession. Overseas, the CIA is the
benefactor of *Africa Forum, Africa Report, Berliner Verein,*
Center of Studies and Documentation (Mexico), Congress for
Cultural Freedom (Paris) which supports the publications *Preuves*
in France, *Encounter* in Britain, *Forum* in Austria and *Hiwar* in
Lebanon, Frente Departemental de Capesinos de Puno, Foreign
News Service, Inc., Institute of Political Education (Costa Rica),
etc.

As of December 31, 1967, the CIA no longer contributes
financially — in theory at least — to American private or
cultural organizations abroad. However, the State Department
specifies that " in certain cases " certain cultural organizations
may continue to receive official subsidies on a temporary basis
to enable them to overcome financial difficulties, and that the
government of the United States will continue to study the
possibility of granting public funds to certain cultural organizations with activities abroad in so far as these activities are
considered to promote the national interest.

22. These activities may not be considered normal, but they
are nevertheless logical. They have been copied by the Russians,
which in 1958 created Section D (for Disinformation and De-
composition) of the KGB. Section D, directed by Ivan Ivano-
vitch Agayants, employs new post-Stalin techniques borrowed
from the Americans which are far more sophisticated than those
generally ascribed to the Soviets. Section D's new approach
consists of using agents of Western appearance and Western

dary importance. It established itself solidly in Algeria, the Republic of South Africa, the ex-Belgian Congo, French West Africa and the Portuguese African colonies. Latin America and the Caribbean were controlled by its American Division.

When Kennedy entered the White House, preparations were already underway for an invasion of Cuba. The project had originated with an executive order signed by President Eisenhower on March 17, 1960 authorizing the clandestine training and arming of Cuban refugees. The operation was directed by Richard Mervin Bissell, Jr., a brilliant graduate of the London School of Economics and former professor of economics at Yale who had joined the CIA in 1954 and, as director of its Plans Division, had supervised the U2 project. Bissell's original plan included the organization of guerilla troops in Cuba itself, but the shortage of qualified volunteers and the lack of support among the Cuban population and Castro's army rendered this impossible. Instead, Allen Dulles decided on a military invasion of the island by Cuban exile forces.

The CIA immediately began looking for a suitable training site. At the beginning of April, 1960, Robert Kendall Davis, First Secretary of the American Embassy in Guatemala and the local CIA Station Chief, visited Guatemala President Ydigoras at his official residence, situated out of precaution on the grounds of the Guatemalan military school.[23] Ydigoras, who had no sympathy for Castro and who was also faced with a mounting budget, agreed to allow the CIA to train " special forces " on a base in Guatemala. The CIA chose the " Helvetia " coffee plantation at Retalhuleu, which covered 5,000 acres, was easy to guard, and offered 50 miles of private roads. There it established a training center for saboteurs and combat forces equipped with barracks and a swimming pool.

At the end of May, 1960, the CIA met with representatives

---

manners who are as un-Bolshevik as possible — journalists, writers, economists, professors, and Soviet citizens who reside or travel abroad. These agents even go so far as to criticize Soviet society. They are in constant contact with influential Western officials. The old dialectic has been replaced by persuasion. In this area, as in the domain of pure intelligence, the KGB is superior to the CIA.

of the five Cuban exile groups, which joined in a common front, the Cuban Revolutionary Council, for which the CIA opened bank accounts in New York, New Orleans, and Miami. The majority of the Cuban exiles lived in Florida or Louisiana. Word spread quickly that something big was in the wind and that there was no lack of funds. Volunteers poured in, and a first contingent of men described as " geometrical engineers " departed for Guatemala at the end of May; 1960.

The CIA provided military specialists and foreign technicians, mainly German and Japanese contractuals, to train the Cubans as radio operators, paratroopers, frogmen, saboteurs, and in the techniques of BOA.[24] In August, an airstrip was constructed, and the first planes, camouflaged as civilian aircraft, landed at Retalhuleu.[25] An airlift was established between the CIA bases in the United States and the base at Guatemala. The volunteers who applied to the recruitment offices camouflaged behind the nanes of various associations in New Orleans and Miami were interrogated, their background was checked, and they were tested in the training camps run by the CIA in the Everglades near Miami and on Lake Ponchartrain in Louisiana before being flown from a clandestine airport, Opa Locka or R2, to Retalhuleu.

All of these activities were conducted in that special atmosphere of mystery and secrecy so dear to intelligence people, with false identity papers, planes without lights, post office box addresses, fake licence plates, security checks, " advice ",

---

In 1967, for example, Section D launched a campaign to discredit Svetlana Stalin's book of memoirs, the publication of which is credited to the CIA. In 1968 it launched " Operation Philby " with the object of discrediting Her Majesty's Secret Service and bringing about a reduction in its budget through the publication of the memoirs of the former British counter-espionage chief.

23. Ydigoras' predecessor, President Carlos Castillo Armas, who had seized power in 1954 in a coup d'état organized by the CIA, had been assassinated in the Presidential Palace.

24. Techniques for the recuperation and reception of personnel and supplies parachuted into an area.

25. The Guatemalan government explained to foreign diplomats that these were private planes used to transport fruit and shrimp.

and informers — official or otherwise. Anti-Castro fanatics of bourgeois background rubbed shoulders with unemployed or hungry Cuban refugees, Castroist agents, mercenary pilots, U.S. Marine Corps instructors, mail collectors, Japanese karate specialists, arms dealers,[26] soldiers of fortune, Army Colonels, and extremist orators. Under the scrutiny of the FBI they milled about and crossed each others' paths, play-acted, pretended not to know one another, flew, fought, talked of their island home or drugged themselves in hotel rooms, apartments, or bungalows rented by the CIA using the names of tourists or non-existant companies. From time to time, top CIA men from privileged backgrounds, exuding Anglophilia and a gentlemanly attitude, came to inspect their troops.

Across the water in Cuba, these events were followed attentively by Ramiro Valdes, chief of the Cuban Intelligence Service, and Sergei M. Kudryatsev, Soviet Ambassador to Cuba and a veteran KBG agent. The CIA knew, of course, that they knew, but the preparations dragged on. Dulles requested Bissell to speed up the training. He wanted the invasion carried out before the November, 1960 Presidential elections. But there were delays in the recruiting and training of the Cuban pilots needed to parachute supplies and carry out bombing raids.

In September, 1960, despite all the extra efforts, the overtime and the bonuses, the invasion force still wasn't ready. Then bad weather intervened. The CIA realized that it would have to postpone the operation until the spring of 1961. The extra time was used for additional training and to strengthen the logistics of the operation.

On October 20th, 1960, towards the end of his electoral campaign, Kennedy declared that the United States should " attempt to strengthen the non-Batista democratic anti-Castro forces in exile, and in Cuba itself, who offer eventual hope of overthrowing Castro. " This campaign position, which probably contributed to Kennedy's victory, reassured the CIA, but it placed Kennedy in an uncomfortable position when he was confronted with the impending invasion the following spring (he had been partially informed of the plan in his capacity as President-elect by Allen Dulles in November, 1960).

The invasion was a disaster. The remnants of the Cuban

exile brigade were captured in Cuba. The CIA had lost the first round. The second was won a year later, in October, 1962, by Kennedy, when he persuaded the Soviets to dismantle their Cuban missile bases. On December 24, 1962, 1,113 captured survivors of the invasion brigade were traded for a large quantity of medicine and drugs.[27] On December 29th, Kennedy paid hommage to their courage in Miami. In January, 1963, 450 of these men, including 200 officers, were retrieved by the CIA, which had begun to organize another invasion force. Once again they were sent to camps in Florida and Louisiana, where they were trained until the spring of 1963.[28]

But the CIA did not go unpunished for its failure. Kennedy had decided to take the intelligence agency in hand. He

---

26. Although it possessed enormous stocks of arms itself and had all of the weapons of the U.S. Army at its disposal, the CIA was continually buying weapons, particularly foreign-made weapons : Israeli machineguns, Swiss pistols, Belgian rifles, and even out-of-date weapons from the Second and First World Wars, which it supplied to its confederates and " protectorate " states. It even purchased Vampire jets from Canada. It used well-known firms such as Interarmco, as well as fly-by-night arms dealers, which it protected and paid in either cash or drugs (the latter imported by the CIA from the Far East).

27. The last shipment of medicine reached Havana on July 3, 1963. Castro had set a price per head for the invaders. He demanded $ 500,000 for Manuel Artime Buesa, the leader of the expeditionary force, and $ 63 million for the 1,200 others. Their ransom was paid mainly by the federal government, which obtained the drugs from pharmaceutical companies at wholesale prices.

28. Dozens of commercial enterprises in Florida and Louisiana are actually covers for the CIA. These include shipping concerns like the Gibraltar Steamship Corporation, airlines like Southern Air Transport, advertising agencies such as Evergreen Advertising, employment agencies such as Workers, Inc., import-export firms like Sherman Export, and, naturally, radio stations such as Radio Swan which, after its cover was blown, became Radio Americas.

The contacts between these cover agencies are made rarely by telephone, but person-to-person, through post office box addresses, and by innocent-sounding personal advertisements broadcast over commercial radio stations in Florida and Louisiana.

blamed it not only for the Cuban fiasco, but for activities in Central and South America and the Far East which ran counter to his foreign policy.[29] After relying during the first months of his administration on the experts, Kennedy had ordered a member of his staff, McGeorge Bundy, to represent him in Special Group 54/12.[30] But he was dissatisfied with the results. Dulles was condemned. He was allowed a few months of respite to save his face, but on November 29, 1961 he was replaced by John McCone.

The Kennedy's choice of McCone was surprising. McCone was a good Republican, but he was hardly as pure as Douglas Dillon. His entire career had been spent in the oil industry. In 1937, at the age of 35, he had been one of the founders of the Bechtel McCone Parson's Corporation of Los Angeles, which specialized in the construction of petroleum refineries and electrical power plants in the United States, Latin America and the Middle East. During the Second World War, McCone's California Shipbuilding Company[31] had earned huge profits. Later he took over Panama Pacific Tankers, a .

---

29. President Kennedy had been informed of the Bay of Pigs invasion, but not of the CIA's plan to contaminate a shipment of Cuban sugar in Puerto Rico in August, 1962. This shipment was headed for the Soviet Union. In its defense, the CIA declared that it was only following the instructions of the Special Group, which had enjoined it to sabotage the Cuban economy wherever possible. The President informed the CIA that in this instance it had exceeded its powers.

30. The Eisenhower Administration had sought to solve the problem of the CIA by exercising a greater measure of control. In December, 1954, the National Security Council had created a high-level coordinating body called the Special Group (or Group 54/12) consisting of the CIA Director, the President's adviser on national security affairs, the Deputy Secretary of Defense, and the Undersecretary of State for Political Affairs or his deputy. The Special Group was supposed to authorize all " black " operations and any expenditure of more than $ 10,000 that might have embarrassing political repercussions.

In point of fact, the CIA managed in large measure to escape the control of the Special Group.

During the period between Dulles' disgrace and McCone's arrival, and at the instigation of the Pentagon's inter-services study group, which was anxious to take advantage of the temporary eclipse of the CIA, the Defense Intelligence Agency (DIA)

fleet of oil tankers. In 1961 he owned a million dollars worth of stock in Standard Oil of California.[32] After his appointment, he offered to sell them[33], but the Senate Armed Services Committee concluded that this was unnecessary, although Senator Clark of Pennsylvania protested that the American oil industry, like the CIA, was deeply involved in the politics of the Middle East.

What was the reason behind Kennedy's choice ? It has been suggested that " with a conservative Republican at the head of the invisible government, the President clearly thought the political fire would be somewhat diverted ".[34] The

---

was created on October 1, 1961, with the announced intention of remedying the (presumed) American inferiority in missile technoogy. Actually, the DIA brought together the intelligence divisions of the three branches of the armed services, the Army, the Air Force, and the Navy, to the benefit of the Pentagon. Lieutenant General Joseph F. Carroll, who had begun his career in the FBI and served as one of J. Edgar Hoover's deputies in 1947, when Hoover, in his capacity as an expert, had created a section for investigation and counter-espionage for the Air Force in which he left a certain number of " correspondents ", was named Director of the DIA.

John McCone, who at the time was head of the Atomic Energy Commission, favored the establishment of the DIA, but it would have been difficult for him to do otherwise, and he changed his mind seven weeks later when he was named Director of the CIA and saw how quickly its young rival was developing. By 1963 the DIA had more than 2,000 employees and controlled all military intelligence.

McCone installed a new team at the CIA. Between January and May, 1962, General Marshall Sylvester Carter was named Deputy Director, Lyman Kirkpatrick, an OSS and CIA veteran, was appointed Executive Director, Ray S. Cline became Deputy Director for Intelligence (DDI), and Richard M. Helms was named Deputy Director for Plans (DDP).

31. Ralph E. Casey of the General Accounting Office testified that in 1946 McCone and his associates had earned $ 44 million on a $ 100,000 investment (mainly on defense contracts).

32. Senate Armed Services Committee Hearing on the Appointment of John McCone, January 18, 1962.

33. As John Kennedy had done with all his stocks when he became President. (He transformed them into U.S. Savings Bonds).

34. A more likely explanation was that Kennedy was a magnaninous President who was more interested in a person's abili-

fact is that the world of intelligence was repugnant to President Kennedy, although he was well aware of its power.[35] He put off this problem until later, considering it of only secondary importance. It was not resolved until after his death.[36]

In the spring of 1963, the anti-Castro invaders were killing time in Florida and Louisiana. Many of them had been surprised and disillusioned when the Air Force and Navy planes had failed to come to their rescue in 1961 at the Bay of Pigs. Their resentment had been aggravated by their captivity in Cuba, and their CIA superiors did nothing to calm them.

In the first months of 1963, President Kennedy couldn't hold a press conference without being asked about the " 16,000 or 17,000 " Soviet technicians reported to be in Cuba. The President was concentrating on an end to the Cold War, which meant peaceful coexistence with the USSR and the maintenance of the status quo with Castro. But the CIA failed to take the diplomatic thaw seriously, and word never reached the lower echelons. Everything proceeded as before. In the training camps hope, money and ammunition continued to be dispensed. Preparations were speeded up, and security precautions were multiplied. The techniques of secret warfare, the post office boxes, the clandestine airstrips, the meetings in the Turkish baths and the encounters in the railroad stations,

---

ties and experience than in his political color or his personal opinions. In August, 1963 he appointed Henry Cabot Lodge, who had been his opponent in the Massachusetts Senatorial race and again in 1956 in the Vice-Presidential campaign, as Ambassador to Vietnam to succeed Ambassador Frederick Nolting (a close friend of Madame Nhu).

35. On April 23, three days after he announced the Bay of Pigs disaster to the nation, Kennedy appointed a board of inquiry composed of Robert Kennedy, General Maxwell Taylor, Allen Dulles and Admiral Burke. On May 4 he revived the Foreign Intelligence Advisory Board presided by James R. Killian, to which he appointed Robert Murphy, William Langer, and General Jimmie Doolittle. Killian was succeeded by Clark Clifford in 1963. The Killian Committee was ordered to make a thorough investigation of the organization of the American intelligence community.

the messages in the toilets, the passwords, the pseudonyms and the smuggling flourished, all the more so since the CIA had grown suspicious of the federal government and distrustful of the DIA. Meanwhile, the FBI carefully noted every encroachment of the CIA on its territory.[37]

On October 17, 1962 in New York, the FBI uncovered and seized a cache of arms and ammunition belonging to Castroist Cubans and arrested three men, including Robert Santiesteban Casanova, an attaché at the Cuban United Na-

---

36. In 1965 President Johnson, who is known for his distrust of cultivated Easterners, appointed a Texan, retired Vice Admiral William F. Raborn, Jr., to succeed McCone. David Wise and Thomas B. Ross wrote in *The Espionage Establishment* that " The CIA professionals feared that, perhaps, the choice of Raborn merely reflected the President's disinterest in the more intellectual aspects of intelligence. " Helms' promotion as CIA Director in 1966 was a triumph for the OSS Ivy League types. The CIA was back in the hands of the Establishment.

37. Their rivalry was a result not of the discrepancy in their power on the international scale, but of the evolution of their activities. Counterespionage in the United States is the exclusive responsibility of the FBI, and more particularly of its secret Division (domestic intelligence), which in 1963 was headed by William C. Sullivan.

This division is in charge of espionage, sabotage, and subversion. It handles more than 100,000 cases a year, and it is responsible for most of the successes (both known and unknown) in the United States in the field of counter-espionage in the past 20 years. It was the FBI that exposed the National Security Agency employees (Martin Mitchell, Petersen, and Sergeant Dunlap) who were working for the Soviet Union.

The FBI had known for some time that the CIA was behind several " illegal acts " committed on its territory, and the CIA was aware that the FBI was behind several official denunciations that impeded its operations. The FBI bragged that its reports were more accurate and less hysterical than those of the CIA, while the CIA considered the FBI a bunch of choir boys.

When the CIA (which is prohibited by law from operating within the United States) extended its activities on American soil, setting up reception centers and training bases in several states, the resulting confusion and risk of infiltration led to encounters, protests, and finally to blows. Soon the two intelligence powers were setting traps for one another and organizing reprisals.

tions Mission. This was only one of the many episodes in the quiet but growing conflict between the CIA and the FBI over the limits of their respective jurisdictions. Their struggle for power grew steadily more serious.

To the anger of the exiles, the impatience of the CIA, and the investigations of the FBI, something else was added : the training officers who belonged to the Minutemen and other extremist organizations remained in contact with the leaders of these movements, and in particular with disgruntled military officers like General Walker.

One of the CIA men in New Orleans was named Guy Bannister. A former FBI agent and member of the Minutemen, he had worked for the CIA since 1958. His office was located at 544 Camp Street. His deputy, Hugh Ward, also belonged to the Minutemen and to an organization called the " Caribbean Anticommunism League ", which had been used as a CIA cover group since the Guatemalan operation in 1954. One of the people who frequented 544 Camp Street was a young man named Lee Harvey Oswald.

16

William Bobo

American spies must lead difficult lives. The most honest of them, and even their superiors, don't always know whom they're working for.

VLADIMIR Y. SEMICHASTNY, HEAD OF THE KGB

Many American families named Oswald have petitioned the courts to change their name to Smith or Jones. What they read here will surprise them. The skeptics will complain that we don't know anything, or at least don't tell anything, about " the Oswald affair ". If we were to expand on the subject, if we were to take his life apart piece by piece as the Warren Commission tried to do, we would only be attributing to Oswald a role far more important than the part he was destined to play in the Kennedy assassination. To do so would be to divert public attention, as the Warren Commission, has done, from the essential matter at hand, the plot.

The Oswald story has been twisted out of all proportion. We have established the truth about the most important aspects of the affair. We have cut out or simplified the parts that seemed to us superfluous. Espionage affairs and conspiracies always have their share of romantic detail, but this is better left aside when the object is to get at the truth. Oswald was nothing more than a bit actor in a play with far wider implications, a pawn who was manipulated by the conspirators. Once he had outlived his usefulness, he was murdered and his body tossed to the crowd.[1] The public, after all, had to be told *something*.

Senator Millard L. Simpson (Wyoming) has described Oswald as " a Communist with an insane urge to kill. " William Manchester wrote that Oswald and Ruby " both were misfits with twisted personalities, outcasts who craved attention, nursed grudges, were prey to wild impulses and fits of murderous temper, couldn't relate to other people — women especially — and were indifferent to public affairs. " Manchester also describes Oswald as an " arrogant, weedy malcontent " and speaks of his " monumental stupidity. "[2]

Dr. Lewis Robbins claims that Oswald was suffering from " advanced paranoia ".[3] Manchester agrees, adding, " We now know what kindled the firestorm in Lee Harvey Oswald. It was the disintegration of his marriage. We also know when the wave overwhelmed him. It fell on the evening of Thursday, November 21, 1963. " We are asked to believe that Oswald assassinated the President of the United States because his Russian wife made fun of him and left him for a Lesbian ![4] (which doesn't prevent Mr. Manchester from suggesting in another part of the book that Oswald, like Ferrie and Ruby, had homosexual tendencies.)

Who was he, really, this " two-gun Pete " whose body was so hastily shoved in the ground on November 25, 1963 in a

---

1. With the exception of a few scholary works such as Mark Lane's *Rush to Judgment,* most of the 50-odd books devoted to the Kennedy assassination have little more foundation than the detective story published in Paris in 1931 by an author who used the bizarre and premonitory pseudonym " Oswald Dallas " (*Le Capitaine Fragalle,* Collection Le Masque).

2. Explaining Oswald's behavior, Manchester writes : " Kennedy was all-powerful. Oswald was impotent. Kennedy was cheered. Oswald ignored. Kennedy was noble, Oswald ignoble. Kennedy was beloved, Oswald despised. Kennedy was a hero ; Oswald was a victim. One man had almost everything, the other had nothing. Kennedy, for example, was spectacularly handsome. Oswald... was already balding, and he had the physique of a ferret. "

Fort Worth cemetery ? Who was he, really, the man who was
buried as " William Bobo " ?

Despite an unhappy childhood and a modest education,
Oswald was a bright[5] and well-organized young man[6] who
wrote well and expressed himself with ease. He was impres-
sible, gentle, polite and reserved. His father (who was neither
a gangster nor a good-for-nothing, but an insurance salesman)
died before he was born, and Lee was placed in an orphanage
for a time and deprived of parental affection. His I.Q. was
118, which according to Dr. Irving Sokolow is well above
average. He dropped out of high school in New Orleans at the
age of 16 and, like his older brother and his step-brother,
joined the Marine Corps when he was 17, in 1956.[7]

Oswald was a good soldier. He was promoted to Private
First Class and sent to Japan, where he was trained as a radio
operator. An American who knew him in Tokyo[8] says, " He
was a proud kid, full of the Marine Corps spirit. He didn't
talk much, but he really swallowed the Communist line. "

At that time, the CIA was developing its U2 program,[9]
and it needed radar specialists. It recruited its personnel from

---

3. Because Oswald, according to Dr. Robbins, deliberately left
clues behind him.

4. Mrs. Paine, Marina Oswald's " friend " with whom she was
staying at the time of the assassination, was President of the
East-West Contacts Committee, an association promoting literary
contacts with the Soviet Union.

5. The counselor at the Dallas Employment Office was impressed by Oswald's vocabulary and his aptitudes, and remarked
that he expressed himself extremely well.

One of the officials at the U.S. Consulate in Moscou, Richard
E. Snyder, calls him " intelligent. "

William Stuckley of radio station WDSU in New Orleans
describes him as " intelligent and very logical " and adds that
Oswald reminded him of a " young attorney. "

6. He took notes on everything he read.

7. The Marine Corps has a high percentage of orphans.
Perhaps it offers them the warmth and companionship that they
never knew at home.

8. Richard N. Savitt.

9. The first squadron of U2's, consisting of three planes, was
formed in January, 1956 at Watertown Strip in Nevada. Other
squadrons were based at Lakenheath Air Force Base in Great

the ranks of the Army, or preferably from the Marine Corps. Oswald was one of those contacted at the Atsugi base in Japan[10], and he accepted the CIA's offer. At 19, he received his diploma as a radar specialist. His technical training was rounded out by the general courses (" spy training ") given to all CIA trainees, and by language classes (Spanish and Russian) and courses in Marxist dialectic. The CIA provided him with a " funny "[11] and opened a file on him which contained a report on his Marxist opinions and another stating that he had been court-martialled for carrying a personal weapon and insulting an officer. In 1958 he was sent to Santa Ana, California, where he received detailed instruction on the U2. He had been discharged from the Marine Corps and no longer had regular sessions on the firing range. In addition to his technical abilities, he showed a real aptitude for languages. Moreover, he was reserved and discreet, essential characteristics for a secret agent.

In 1959, the U 2 missions were intensified. The CIA was expanding its intelligence rings in China and especially in the Soviet Union. We do not know the nature of Oswald's CIA assignment, but we do know that he left New Orleans on September 20, 1959 for the Soviet Union via Finland.[12] The President of the United States, however, is sometimes no better informed. Eisenhower declared on May 11, 1960, speaking of the U 2 affair, that " these activities have their own rules and methods of concealment which seek to mislead and

---

Britain, Wiesbaden, Germany, Adana, Turkey, and Atsugi, Japan. The planes were sometimes flown from other secret bases located on Formosa, in Korea, and possibly elsewhere.

10. The CIA maintained an office at Atsugi, which was used as a fuelling stop for flights from the United States which operated over the Soviet Union and China.

11. A faked document in CIA jargon.

12. It was probably around then, or perhaps a month later, that the FBI opened a file on Oswald, as it does for all the CIA agents that it manages to identify. This file was kept up to date regularly.

13. It will be recalled that the Warren Commission described Oswald as a penniless soldier who defected to the Soviet Union because he believed in Communism and who tried to renounce his American citizenship in order to live like a Marxist.

obscure. " The fact that he remained in the Soviet Union for 30 months[13] indicates that it was probably a long-term assignment, and he may not have been given any specific duties for the first few years. He was immediately placed under surveillance by the Soviet GRU, which among other things seeks to obtain information about the enemy by studying its intelligence techniques (the goal of every counter-espionnage unit is to infiltrate the enemy's intelligence services in order to learn its real intentions, and even to take part in its activities).

In the past [14] a spy, once uncovered, was immediately placed under arrest and most probably executed. Intelligence services today prefer to locate an enemy agent and keep him under surveillance to see what they can learn, or try to recruit him as a double agent. Spies who are arrested are no longer shot ; instead, they are exchanged.[15] By allowing an identified

---

14. In his book *The Craft of Intelligence,* Allen W. Dulles cites one of his predecessors, a Fifth Century Chinese named Sun Tzu, who classified spies according to category. Things have not changed a great deal since then. Sun Tzu distinguished between : 1) classical agents, introduced from the outside ; 2) converted agents, who have been captured and sent back to the enemy ; 3) condemned agents, used to transmit false information to the enemy in order to get rid of them ; and 4) surviving agents, who have infiltrated the enemy and managed to get out alive.

Dulles adds that all four categories are necessary to an intelligence organization, and that an agent may change categories several times in the course of his career.

15. Two fliers from an Air Force RB 47 shot down on July 1, 1960, Captain Olmsted and Captain McKone, were exchanged in 1960 for two GRU agents, Igor Melekh and Willie Hirsch, arrested by the FBI on October 27, 1960. " The return of the RB 47 fliers and President Kennedy's release of Willie Hirsch and Igor Melekh was the first cautious groping of both sides toward what rapidly became standard procedure. As unthinkable as it might have been in the previous decade. nations began publicly trading their spies in the 1960's " (Wise and Ross, *The Espionage Establishment).* "

On February 10, 1962, Soviet Colonel Rudolf Abel, who was serving a 30-year prison sentence at the Atlanta Federal Penitentiary, was exchanged on a Berlin bridge for U2 pilot Francis Gary Powers.

The recuperation of important captured agents has become

agent to remain in the Soviet Union, the Russians may have hoped to learn more about Oswald's mission.

Oswald was permitted to settle in Minsk, a closed city where a school for spying and sabotage, the existence of which the CIA was naturally aware of, is located. He was hired by a local factory as an electrician. In order to be able to watch him day and night, the KGB sent Marina Prusakova, officially a pharmacist at the same factory, onto the scene, and the CIA obtained pictures of the " couple. "

Six months after Oswald's arrival in the Soviet Union, Gary Power's U 2 plane was shot down by an S A 2 rocket over Sverdlosk in the Urals. The diplomatic reverberations from this incident resulted in the cancellation of the Paris summit conference. The CIA suspended the U 2 flights over the Soviet Union, and with it the activities of some of its agents.[16] Oswald, however (who had probably planned on a longer stay), married Miss Prusakova, whom he had taken a liking to and thought might prove useful.

In 1962 the CIA resumed its aerial espionage activity using Midas and Samos satellites (launched by Thor Delta rockets) which overflew Soviet territory at an altitude of 300 miles every 72 hours and required no assistance from the ground. Soon afterwards, Oswald obtained an exit visa and returned to the United States, taking his wife and child with him. The Oswald couple was nothing less than a rather picturesque case of Funkspiel.[17]

With Marina Prusakova, the FBI faced a problem similar to that which Oswald had presented to the KGB almost three years before. When Mr. and Mrs. Oswald landed in the

---

customary, and it has sometimes led to the arrest of tourists. To recuperate one of their agents, Igor Alexandrovitch Ivanov, arrested in New York in November, 1963, the KGB arrested Professor Frederick C. Barghoorn of Yale and three other American tourists, Wortham, Gilmour and Mott (Mott later committed suicide while being transferred to a forced labor camp). The KGB failed to obtain Ivanov's release, but Kennedy persuaded them to release Professor Barghoorn.

Spy trades are now practiced regularly by the Soviet Union and the Eastern European satellites (Gordon Lonsdale in England, Alfred Frenzel in West Germany, and Zvoboda in France).

United States in June, 1962, the FBI re-activated its file on Oswald and opened another on Marina Nikolaevna Prusakova. At the same time, the couple's activities were probably being closely scrutinized and carefully noted in the files of Zapiski.[18]

Oswald was recuperated by the CIA but was assigned to another program, probably because, with the exception of the reconnaissance flights over Cuba for which only limited personnel was required, the U 2 was seldom used anymore. " Promotions " in intelligence work don't follow the same rules as promotions in the civil service. An agent is obliged to remain inactive for as long as his superiors deem necessary. The CIA, moreover, had reason to suspect Oswald, as it does any operative returning from enemy territory who may have been turned into a double agent. Thus, Oswald was placed under CIA surveillance and was even tested and interrogated by an expert employed by both the CIA and Texas oil circles, a man known as George S. de Mohrenschildt and nicknamed " The Chinese ".[19]

---

16. Oswald was in regular contact with the CIA through its Moscow Station at the American Embassy. As a U2 specialist, he may have used a special radio transmitter broadcasting on a 30 inch wave length, which is indetectable on the ground but can be picked up at 70,000 feet by a U2, which is equipped with an ultra-high frequency recording system (5,000 words in 7 seconds). The discovery in the wreakage of the U2 of the special tape recorder used by Powers probably enabled the Soviets to neutralize this ingenious system of communications.

17. " Funkspiel " consists of infiltrating the enemy intelligence service and feeding the enemy a certain amount of false information, using double agents or what their employers believe are double agents. It is a tricky and subtle game that can be played in a number of different ways. There were some extraordinary cases during the Second World War. More recently, there was Kim Philby, the head of the Soviet Department of British intelligence and a Soviet agent. If Oswald fell into this category, he was no more than an elementary case.

18. Zapiski, the central files department of the KGB, where more than 400 persons are employed.

19. The Chinese claimed to have been born in the Ukraine and to have served in the Polish cavalry. He was recruited by the OSS during the war and entered the University of Texas in 1944, where he obtained his degree in geological engineering

Oswald attended a training course at a Dallas firm specializing in the reproduction of maps and secret documents and which was run, naturally enough, by the CIA. But the FBI was also interested in Oswald. On June 26, 1962, two FBI agents, John W. Fain and Thomas Carter, made him an offer in line with his abilities. They wanted him to use his Marxist reputation to infiltrate several Communist groups, especially the Young Socialist Alliance, the Socialist Workers Party, and the newspaper *The Worker,* and to furnish information on the members of the Slavic immigrant community around Fort Worth to which Marina Prusakova, of course, belonged.[20]

In August, 1962 Oswald took out a subscription to *The Worker* and offered his services as a photographer.[21] In October and November, he also contacted the Socialist Labor Party and subscribed to its publication *The Militant.* Throughout the winter of 1962-63, Oswald corresponded with these leftist groups, helping them out from time to time. In October, 1962 the CIA, frightened by the Cuban missile crisis, called back those of its agents who were in training or on vacation. Oswald made several trips to New Orleans, where he received new instructions, changed his occupational disguise, and rented a post office box (P.O.B. 2915). In April, 1963, Oswald was told to move to New Orleans, where he continued to infiltrate Communist groups. It is highly probable that he was working simultaneously for the CIA and the FBI. He tried to join subversive groups like the Fair Play for Cuba Committee (FPCC), which was violently critical of American policy towards Castro. Oswald distributed Communist literature in the streets of New Orleans to win the approval of the FPCC

(specializing in petroleum geology). The CIA used him in Iran, Egypt, Indonesia, Panama, Guatemala, Haiti, Nicaragua, San Salvador, Honduras, Nigeria, Ghana and Togo. One of his covers was the International Cooperation Administration (ICA), but he also worked for Sinclair Oil.

Mohrenschildt was a distinguished and cultivated man, a member of The Establishment and the New York Social Register. His wife, a White Russian born in China, often worked with him. He belonged to the Dallas Petroleum Club, the Abilene Country Club and the Dallas Society of Petroleum Geologists

and make contact with the pro-Castro groups in Louisiana. Actually, he was working for the opposition group, the anti-Castro Cuban Democratic Revolutionary Front, which was controlled by the CIA. Oswald worked out of an office located at 544 Camp Street.[22]

In New Orleans Oswald encountered several other CIA men, including Bannister, Ward, and David Ferrie, all of whom belonged to the Minutemen. Ferrie was what is known as an adventurer. At 45 he was a licensed pilot and had flown for a time for an airline, but he had worked for the CIA since 1955 and had been employed in several Central American operations. Ferrie had worked for Castro in the days when he was an exiled idealist in Mexico and the CIA was behind him. He had parachuted weapons and explosives to Castro and Che Guevara when they were fighting in the Sierra Maestra. One of Ferrie's cargos had enabled the Castro guerillas to blow up a munitions train belonging to Batista. When Batista was overthrown by Castro, the CIA switched its allegiance to the ex-dictator, and Ferrie was assigned to work against the new Cuban regime.[23] Between 1960 and 1962 he was seen at CIA bases in San Antonio, Puerto Cabezas,

---

and had close connections with the oil industry, in particular with the presidents of McGee Oil, Kerr, Continental Oil, Cogwell Oil Equipment Co., Texas Eastern Corp., and with John Mecom of Houston.

20. Infiltrating the American and emigre socialist and Communist movements in the United States in order to obtain information about their activities is one of the major preoccupations of the FBI.

21. Colonel Abel's hobby was also photography, and he had a studio in Kelton Street. Oswald was hardly in the same class with Abel, but photography is a practical hobby which is popular with many intelligence agents.

22. The confusion that reigned in the CIA's operations in New Orleans at that time was such that this address appeared on some of the Communist literature that Oswald was given·to hand out on the streets. The slip came to someone's attention, however, and the Camp Street address was replaced by 4907 Magazine Street.

23. One of his " clients " during this period, Eladio del Valle, was killed in Miami the same day Ferrie was found dead in New Orleans. The Cuban's murder has never been explained.

Nicaragua, and on Swan Island off Honduras, and he had
been one of the instructors at the coffee plantation at Retalhuleu. In Miami he worked for Alex Carlson.[24] In New Orleans,
he was regarded as a tough guy. Like Bannister and Ward, he
belonged to the Minutemen. He knew Oswald, whom he had
met in 1959 shortly before his departure for the U.S.S.R.

All of these men, regardless of their past or their political
affiliations, were in the pay of the CIA, and they were hard at
work when, in July, 1963, the training, the simulated raids,
and even the airlifts were called off. President Kennedy had
just ordered the CIA to abandon its plans for the invasion and
the harassment of Cuba. John McCone argued against this
decision, but in the end he was forced to yield. It proved
more difficult, however, to convince the men in the lower
echelons of the agency.

On July 31, 1963, acting on orders from Washington, the
FBI surrounded the CIA training centers and most of the
other establishments connected with the Cuban operation and
closed them down.[25] The following day, August 1, President Kennedy announced the conclusion of a nuclear test
ban treaty and the installation of a direct telephone line
between the White House and the Kremlin. Once again he
stated, ". Our goal is not war, but peace".

A few days later, Ferrie was contacted by Clay Shaw, a
New Orleans businessman and Director of the International

---

24. Alex E. Carlson, a Spanish-speaking lawyer from Miami
Springs who fought in the Philippines and Okinawa, is President
of the Double-Chek Corporation, a brokerage firm that serves as
a CIA cover for the recruitment of pilots employed in Central
American and the Caribbean. He uses post office box addresses
for his contacts.

Among the other picturesque figures in this milieu were :

David F. Green, a former Marine Corps Lieutenant who
served in Korea and was recruited by the CIA in Tokyo. He was
used in Laos and then in South Vietnam, and served as a rifle
instructor at the Pontchartrain base.

Kurt Schmitt, a former non-commissioned officer with the
28th Panzer Division of the Wehrmacht, who emigrated to the
United States in 1947 and became a naturalized American citizen
in 1953. He was recruited by the CIA in 1955 to serve as a radio
instructor.

Trade Mart in New Orleans since 1947, who was acting as a front man for another businessman.[26] The Committee needed both a commando and a scapegoat. The commando was recruited from among the CIA Minutemen, and Oswald and the anti-Castro men were chosen for the other role. In September he introduced him to Clay Shaw and General Walker.

Oswald was probably told that he had been chosen to participate in a new anti-Communist operation together with Ferrie and several other agents. The plan consisted of influencing public opinion by simulating an attack against President Kennedy, whose policy of coexistence with the Communists

---

25. More methodical and often more discreet than their CIA counterparts, Mr. Hoover's agents were remarkably well-informed about what was going on in Florida, New Orleans, Texas, and California, and also (we shall see why later) about the CIA's activities abroad.

The FBI kept a file on every identified agent of the CIA, whether he be a temporary, a correspondent, or a contractual, and after the assassination it had little difficulty in determining whom to question. Its reports were so detailed, and were submitted to the Warren Commission so promptly, that even the professional investigators employed by the Commission were surprised. Some of these secret reports are now deposited in the National Archives. Others, more confidential, are still in the hands of the FBI.

FBI agents Regis Kennedy and Warren de Brueys knew David Ferrie well. De Brueys was based in New Orleans, where he was involved in the CIA's anti-Castro activities. After the assassination, the FBI interrogated David Ferrie and Gordon Novel. Novel was a buddy of Ferrie's who had been with the CIA since 1959. He worked through the Double Chek Corporation and the Evergreen Advertising Agency. He had carried out several missions in the Caribbean, was involved in arms purchases, and knew both Ruby and Oswald. The FBI questioned him on five separate occasions, but Novel didn't scare easily, and he didn't talk.

In 1967 New Orleans District Attorney Jim Garrison subpoened him, but he left Louisiana for Ohio, and Garrison never succeeded in obtaining his extradition.

26. Clay Shaw was indicted by District Attorney Garrison for participating in a plot to assassinate President Kennedy and released on $ 10,000 bail. But Shaw only acted as an intermediary for the Committee. His trial was repeatedly postponed, and in May, 1968, a federal court blocked the case.

deserved a reprimand. Another assassination attempt, also
designed to arouse public feeling, had been simulated on
April 10 against General Walker.[27]

Oswald was arrested by the New Orleans police on August
9, but was later freed at the request of FBI agent John L.
Quigley. Contrary to the FBI, the upper spheres of the CIA
were certainly not informed of the preparations for the assassination.[28] The activities of the CIA are highly compartmental-
ized. The team that operated at Dallas included specialists
who had worked for the CIA's DCA.[29] Several of them
belonged to the Minutemen, which was thus able to keep
the upper hand in the situation.[30]

Oswald had no special reason to suspect this new mission.
In four years he had seen and done worse, and he was so
psychologically involved in intelligence work that at times
he would confuse his assignments for the CIA and the FBI,
and his " Marxist " and " anti-Marxist " activities. Furthermore, he was not in the habit of asking questions. There is no
doubt that he considered himself well-covered on November
22.

Time passed... Meticulous as always, Oswald closed the
new post office box (P.O. Box 30061) that he had rented in
New Orleans on June 3. He arrived in Dallas on October 2
and rented a room. That same day, Governor Connally
held a meeting at the Hotel Adolphus. The principal subject

---

27. After his death, Oswald was also blamed for this incident.
It seems highly improbable that he played a major role in it.
Specialists are hired to deliberately miss someone as well as to
kill him, and Oswald was not an expert marksman.

28. The CIA makes it a rule never to admit or claim responsibility for its operations, even when they are successful, as was
the case in Guatemala and Iran. As Allen Dulles once remarked, " We are not journalists. " Nevertheless, it has deposited
51 Top Secret documents in the National Archives, including
several disclosing that Oswald was one of its agents :

Document CD 392, " Reproduction of Official CIA Dossier
on Oswald. "

Document CD 698, " Reports on Travel and Activities of
Oswald. "

Document CD 931, " Oswald's Access to Information about
U2."

The public will be allowed to read them in the year 2 038.

of discussion was the President's trip, but the Governor was not kept informed of all of the plans. On October 3 the Texas Congressional delegation met at the Capitol in Washington, and the following day Governor Connally went to the White House to go over the details of the trip with Ken O'Donnell. October 5, a Saturday, was the final day of a three-day celebration in Houston. Sandra Smith, daughter of Lloyd Hilton Smith, Vice-President of Humble Oil, was wed to a New York broker. Under a tent set up in the garden, the young socialites of Houston and Dallas danced the night away. The two daughters of Henry Ford II whirled in the arms of Ivy League students, and Mr. Morgan Davis was one of the guests.

---

29. The DCA, or Department of Covert Activity, is responsible for sabotages, kidnappings and " liquidations ". It is the equivalent of the Soviet KRO.

The first person to mention CIA involvement in the assassination was Gary Underhill, a former OSS agent who occasionally carried out an assignment for the CIA. On November 28, 1963, he told friends in New Jersey that he knew who was responsible for the President's murder. Soon afterwards he was found dead in his Washington apartment with a bullet in his brain.

30. The Minutemen were also in charge of planting evidence against Oswald, removing or destroying other damaging evidence, and killing Patrolman Tippit, but they made several mistakes. The " evidence of premeditation " at a gun shop, a firing range and a used car lot involving a man who resembled Oswald was so obviously fabricated that not even the Warren Commission dared invoke it. Officer Tippit was to be killed by two Minutemen to give other Minutemen on the Dallas police force an excuse to shoot Oswald, but the latter, realizing that this was no simulated assassination but the real thing, had probably grown suspicious. He went to the appointed meeting place at the Texas Theatre, where he was fortunate enough — for the moment at least — to be arrested by a police patrol which, as he didn't resist, did not shoot him as planned. Two days later Jack Ruby, another employee of the Committee, killed Oswald (with the cooperation of the Dallas police). Ruby was later liquidated in prison by a slower but no less radical means. (Oswald was not killed instantly, but by attempting artificial respiration a Dallas police inspector managed to aggravate his internal hemorraging. Another accomplice was planted at Parkland Hospital where Oswald was taken, and it appears that his intervention hastened Oswald's death.

Between October 7 and 10, Ferrie and six other men arrived in Dallas. On October 14, the Committee arranged to have Oswald hired (at the minimum wage of $ 1.25 an hour) at the Texas School Book Depository. On October 15, Oswald visited the warehouse, and on October 16 he began taking inventory and moving boxes of books. The other employees were quick to notice that he didn't talk much.

One week later, President Kennedy drove beneath the windows of the Depository. Then the leaves began to fall, and soon the traces disappeared. Policemen, journalists, a taxi driver, women, and a number of other people died suddenly. Even the CIA suffered losses. In 1964 Bannister died of a " heart attack ", and Ward was killed in a " plane crash. " Ferrie was tougher, but he died in 1967 of a " cerebral hemorrage. "

These, at least, were listed as the official causes of death.

17

Police

" *The art of the police consists of not seeing what there is no use seeing.* "

NAPOLEON

Like an ambush in time of war, a political assassination depends on the nature of the terrain and the competence of the men who occupy it. The Committee had the means to recruit a team of high-qualified men, but the choice of a terrain depended on the enemy.

The spring of 1963 was filled with meetings at which nothing was decided. Several contingency plans were prepared. One consisted of attacking the President in his car on a Virginia highway. Another was to shoot him in Chicago. There was also a suggestion for blowing up the President's Boeing, Air Force One. These plans were rejected, for they required accomplices among the President's staff. It was to risky. They had to be sure of killing Kennedy.

On Thursday, June 6, there was news. The President would meet his assassins on their own territory, the state of Texas.[1] The Committee, however, awaited confirmation of the

---

1. On June 5, at the Hotel Cortez in El Paso, President Kennedy informed Governor Connally that he would make an

Texas trip, and the final decision was not made until July.
Plans got underway in mid-September.[2] It was a complicated
plan with many separate parts, but it had one major advantage : the cooperation of the local police.

Well before the assassination, Max Lerner had written :

" In addition to its slums every city has its vice area and its
crime problem. Whenever some vice inquiry has caught national attention or a newspaper puts on pressure or a city
reform administration gets to power, the police force develops
a spurt of energy. At such times, there are ' round-ups ' of
petty criminals, prostitutes, or even the usual lodging-house
population, and sometimes the more scabrous criminals also
are kept moving and forced to seek other hunting grounds.
But reform administrations are short-lived, and the ties between vice and politics, and between ' rackets ' and the respectable business elements of the city, are too close to be easily
broken. In many cities the dynasty of political bosses started
with the saloonkeeper who knew the weaknesses and tragedies
of the slum people and built his political empire on the
exchange of loyalty for favors. At a later stage in the dynasty,
the boss may have become a contractor, dealing by a Pro-
vidential coincidence with the very materials the city needed
for its public works. There is scarcely a big American city
whose administration is not at least marginally involved in
this trinity of crime, political corruption, and business favors. "[3]

Colonel Kane, chief of the Baltimore police when Lincoln
was assassinated in 1865, was in the pay of the assassins. At
Phenix City, Alabama, in 1954, a warrant was issued for the
arrest of former District Attorney Silas Garrett, accused of
murdering Albert Patterson, who had just been elected to

---

official trip to Texas before the end of the year. The following
day, several influential Texans were advised.

2. Information about the President's trip to Dallas appeared
in Texas newspapers for the first time on September 13, but
his visit was not officially announced by the Dallas *Morning
News* until September 26. The Committee, however, wasn't
relying on the newspapers. It knew for certain on Monday,
September 16 that the President was coming to Dallas.

3. *America as a Civilization*, p. 168.

succeed him. In 1958, Albert Patterson's son John was elected Governor of Alabama (with the support of Robert Shelton, Grand Dragon of the Ku Klux Klan), but not before the Mayor of Phenix City had been arrested and the municipal police force stripped of its powers.

In Texas, similar cases occurred every day, but the Grand Jury inquests never revealed anything. Nonetheless, several officials in Jefferson County, Beaumont and Port Arthur were indicted in 1962. County Sheriff Charles Meyer admitted receiving $ 85,581 in campaign contributions, although no one had dared run against him. The Chief of Police of Port Arthur had received $ 65,000 for the same reason, although he was appointed rather than elected to office. Beaumont Police Chief J. H. Mulligan, whose official salary was $ 735 a month, had $ 40,000 in the bank and owned $ 73,000 worth of property. District Attorney Ramie Griffin charged between $ 5,000 and $ 10,000 to fix a relatively unimportant case. At that time, the municipal budget of Beaumont showed a $ 1,475,000 deficit.

Dallas (" Big D " to its residents) was in an even worse situation. The city had grown rapidly : from 42.3 square miles in 1942 to 288 in 1963. In 1940, it had placed 31st among American cities. By 1963, it had climbed to 13th place. Its leaders were acutely conscious of the need to protect their city's interests. Dallas was an orderly town. The Crime Confederation, which prospered in other cities, had never succeeded in implanting itself openly in Dallas. Aaron Kohn, who came to New Orleans in 1963 to head the Metropolitan Crime Commission, was puzzled at first. In Chicago, where he came from, there were two kinds of people : those who were honest, and those who were not. In Texas and Louisiana, there was apparently no distinction between the two.

Dallas was careful about appearances. It was a clean town. There was no more gambling, murder, rackets, or prostitution than in any other American city of comparable size. Dallas was too wealthy for such common vices. Organized crime was overpowered in Dallas. " The most virtuous and best-governed city in the United States " had been ruled since 1937 by a Hanseatic oligarchy dominated by seven key leaders. Below them were sixty " level leaders ", the Citizens' Council and the Citizens' Charter Association (its political arm). These bodies were consulted and kept informed, but they didn't know everything, and only the Seven had the power to make decisions.

Nothing, with the exception of a natural calamity, could happen in Dallas without the approval of this Holy Synod, which controlled all elective and appointive offices. This included the police. Citing the lawyers for the Warren Commission, Manchester has written (but without expanding on the idea), " If we write what we really think (of the Dallas police), nobody will believe anything else we say. "

Despite the opulence of its inhabitants, the Dallas municipal budget was very small — only half that of Boston. City officials were therefore dependent on the incentives awarded for their obedience and their silence. The Dallas police were paid by the city leaders to carry out their orders, and that covered a lot of territory. The District Attorney's office and the municipal judges were equally corrupt. Considering the importance of the issues at stake, these men were fairly inexpensive. They were paid by the year, with occasional bonuses for good behavior. Sergeants, patrolmen, city clerks and new arrivals were added to the payroll only after a probationary period. If they were unable to adjust to the situation, they were obliged to seek employment elsewhere. There is nothing worse for a cop than to be quarantined by his fellow policemen.

Every one of the Dallas police officials — Chief Curry, Assistant Chief Charles Batchelor and Deputy Chief N.T. Fisher, J.W. Fritz, Chief of the Homicide and Robbery Bureau, Captain W.P. Gannaway of the Special Division, Captain P.W. Lawrence of the Traffic Division, Captain Glen D. King, Curry's administrative assistant, Chief Investigator Lieutenant J.C. Day of the Identification Bureau, Lieutenant Wells of Homicide, Lieutenant Revill, Inspector Sawyer, and 15 others — was on the special payroll. The Committee had nothing to fear. The policemen in the lower grades either received bonuses or were afraid. But they kept their mouths shut.

For his good work on November 22, the Citizens' Council voted a motion of confidence in Police Chief Curry. Curry, a great admirer of J. Edgar Hoover, whom he resembles somewhat, has since resigned from the police force for " medical reasons. " Apparently he has no financial worries.

Curry and his deputies were accustomed to covering minor offenses, but the assassination of a President was in a class by itself. The plan didn't shock them. The rewards were especially attractive, and so many of their superiors were involved that they had little to fear. But their subordinates presented a problem. Many Dallas policemen were admirers of Kennedy. Many others were cowards. The plot did not extend beyond the official hierarchy. The rank of a Dallas policeman was in direct proportion to his degree of corruption.

Several policemen who belonged to the Minutemen were in charge of coordinating the activities of the police and the Committee. In addition to this internal surveillance, those policemen whom Curry and the Minutemen considered unreliable were carefully removed from the scene. The Dallas police force numbers 1,175 men. On November 22, 400 of them were assigned to Love Field, 200 to the Trade Mart, and the rest were scattered along the parade route between the airport and the end of Main Street.[4]

It may be assumed that all of the Dallas police realized afterwards what had happened. Few protested, but a handful muttered their disapproval. Three of them were murdered, and the others were obliged to flee from Dallas.[5] The Warren Commission even refused to hear their testimony.

The fact that Curry couldn't count on all of his men complicated matters. The secrecy imposed by the Committee resulted in a certain number of misunderstandings and conflicting testimony by the policemen assigned to the Texas School Book Depository, police headquarters, the railroad overpass, and the Texas Theatre. Like all military organizations, a police department has certain standard operating procedures [6],

---

4. And not 365 and 60, respectively, as Manchester writes.

5. See the evidence produced by Mark Lane and District Attorney James Garrison.

6. Curry had several meetings with the organizers of the ambush. A dozen reliable policemen both in and out of uniform were responsible for the security of the assassins themselves. They were supposed to keep the crowd out of Dealey Plaza and watch for journalists and suspicious individuals (a news photo-

and even the Dallas police force has a semblance of administrative organization. As a result, there were a few slip-ups which the Warren Commission was obliged to gloss over. In the minutes following the assassination, several men, including, it would seem, two of the gunmen and a radio operator, were arrested.

The Sheriff of Dallas County, J.E. Decker, was another problem. Neither he nor his principal lieutenants, Eugene Boone, Roger Craig, and Luke Mooney, were considered reliable by Curry and the Committee. It was not that the Sheriff was any less corrupt than the police. But, like Wyatt Earp, he was a loner.

On November 22 the lead car in the Presidential motorcade was driven by Curry. Sheriff Decker, Forrest Sorrels, chief of the Dallas Secret Service, and Winston G. Lawson, the Secret Service advance man' from Washington[7], were assigned to ride in it. At least two of these men could be dangerous. To minimize the risk of a chance regard upwards, the car used was a closed sedan.

The lead car in a parade is generally a convertible, so as to give its occupants the widest possible view. This was the rule even at Dallas, where open cars were always used in good weather. November 22 was a beautiful day, and the bubble top was removed from the President's convertible.

---

grapher was asked to leave the railroad overpass). It was also decided that no clear instructions would be issued as to who was allowed into the railroad yard, Dealey Plaza, and the neighboring buildings. They had to make sure that an uninformed and over-zealous policemen didn't arrest or shoot one of the assassins.

The reliable policemen facing the gunmen later declared that they had been instructed by Captain Lawrence to watch only the traffic and any " unusual movements " in the crowd. They claimed they had never even glanced at the buildings.

The gunmens' escape was even simpler. Tney were evacuated by the police, in official cars.

7. Lawson's name appears 15 times in *Death of a President,* but Manchester apparently didn't consider it worthwhile interviewing him. His time was probably taken up by interviews with Harry Martin, a Houston caterer, and Peter Saccu, chief caterer of a Forth Worth hotel.

8. Manchester dismisses this incident as a stuck microphone button.

Forrest Sorrels told the Warren Commission that he was unable to get a good view from the car. As for Lawson, he declared that he saw nothing. Was Curry also instructed to distract the other occupants of the car ? Sorrels recalled after the assassination that he had never seen the Chief so nervous and talkative. Sheriff Decker realized that the shots came from the direction of the parking lot, and he declared afterwards that he had radiod his men to close in on the railroad yard. But on Curry's orders the police radio was temporarily out of commission.[8]

The Warren Commission refused to hear the testimony of Sheriff Decker's deputies. The plot died in the silence in which it was born.

There was one leak. Rose Cheramie, whom Ruby dispatched to Miami on November 18, was the victim of an automobile accident near Eunice, Louisiana. She was taken to East Louisiana Hospital in Jackson. On November 19, as she was coming out of a coma, she revealed that the President was to be assassinated three days later. She repeated her story on November 20, but the doctors concluded that she was hysterical and put her under sedation. She recovered and returned to Texas, where she was killed in a hit-and-run accident in a Dallas suburb.

18

Slaughter

Hail to the Chief who in Triumph advances!
Honor'd and bless'd be the evergreen pine... "

Secret Service advance man Lawson met with Police Chief
Curry in Dallas on November 13. Together they visited the
Trade Mart, where Curry suggested the November 22 banquet be held.[1] Lawson forwarded a favorable report to Washington, and the next day, November 14, O'Donnell confirmed his choice.

That same day, Curry held a meeting with his deputies,
Batchelor and Fisher, Lawson, and Sorrels to study the problems raised by the President's visit. The meeting continued
into the next day, November 15, with the participation of
members of the local host committee. Sorrels and Lawson
were preoccupied with security problems in and around the

---

1. There were five possible locations for the Dallas luncheon,
but the Sheraton-Dallas Hotel and Memorial Auditorium refused
on various pretenses to play host to the President, the Market
Hall was occupied by a bottlers' convention, and the Womens'
Building was vetoed by local authorities as being too drab and
impractical for serving a luncheon. That left the Trade Mart.
At Curry's urging, Sorrels approved the choice of the Trade
Mart on November 4 and advised Behn at the White House.

Trade Mart, and Curry promised massive reinforcements.

That weekend, or Monday morning at the latest, J. Edgar Hoover received a TWX (inter-office telegram) from special agent James W. Bookhout of the FBI's Dallas office. The Warren Commission was never informed of the existence of this message. On Monday, November 18, Lawson and Sorrels drove over the motorcade route from Love Field to the Trade Mart for the first time. Curry stressed the fact that it could be covered in 45 minutes, and even suggested that a short section along the Central Express-way be eliminated because of the security risks it offered. After they had driven through the center of the city and reached Dealey Plaza, Curry pointed down Main Street past the railroad overpass and said, " And afterwards there's only the freeway. " But instead of turning right into Houston Street in the direction of Elm Street, as the motorcade did on November 22, Curry turned left in front of the Old Court-house (see map p. 356-357), and neither Lawson nor Sorrels followed the parade route past that point, where they would have been obliged to make a 90 degree right turn into Houston Street, followed 70 yards later by a 120 degree turn to the left into Elm Street. Had they done so, it might have occurred to them that the big Presidential Lincoln would be obliged to slow down almost to a stop in order to make that second turn.[2] This type of double turn is contrary to Secret Service regulations, which specify that when a Presidential motorcade has to slow down to make a turn, " the entire intersection must be

---

2. The Warren commission claimed that all motorists are obliged to make this inconvenient detour in order to reach Stemmons Freeway (which leads to the Trade Mart), but the Commission acknowledged that it would have been possible for the motorcade to continue straight down Main Street through the underpass and make a 100 degree turn around a concrete barrier onto the freeway approach. The Commission declared, however, that " a sign located on this barrier instructs Main Street traffic not to make any turns. " We do not mean to criticize the Dallas traffic laws, but on November 22 all the streets had been cleared to make way for the motorcade, and it would have been normal to follow the easiest, the quickest, and the safest (because it involved only one turn) route onto the freeway.

examined in advance, searched and inspected from top to bottom. " Curry, however, brought the reconnaissance to an end at the very point where it became unacceptable (as well as unusual) from the point of view of security.[3]

On Tuesday, November 19, the *Times Herald* and the *Morning News* of Dallas ran stories about Friday's motorcade, but neither of these papers published a map, which would have brought the curious hairpin turn coming at the end of a long straight route to the attention of even a non-observant person like Lawson. That same day, Kennedy asked his secretary, " Where are those clowns ? " The " clowns " were O'Donnell, O'Brien, and Powers, who were resting at home that morning after their trip to Florida with the President. At any rate, O'Donnell's presence at the White House that day wouldn't have made any difference. He was only interested in the political aspects of the motorcade — how many people would be there, and where. On the other hand, Kennedy's perspicacious press secretary, Pierre Salinger, might have noticed the curious hairpin turn had he seen it in one of the newspapers, but it didn't appear in the Dallas papers, and Salinger left that same morning for Honolulu.

The hairpin turn was as ideal a set-up for an ambush as any potential assassin could hope for.[4] The Committee was not going to let a chance like this go by. The attack was to be carried out by a team of ten men, including four gunmen, each seconded by an assistant who would be responsible for their protection, evacuation, and radio liaison, and who would retrieve the shells. The ninth man would serve as a central radio operator, and the tenth was to create a last-minute

---

3. The route followed by the motorcade that day surprised even Senator Yarborough, a Texan, who may have remembered continuing straight down Main Street onto Stemmons Freeway despite the no turn sign on some other occasion.

4. Reinhard Heydrich, head of the S.S. Security Service and deputy chief of the Gestapo, was ambushed in similar circumstances on May 29, 1942. Heydrich was driving his open Mercedes towards Prague when, in a hairpin turn, two members of the free Czechoslovak army who had been parachuted by the R.A.F. tossed a bomb into his car and fled under the cover of a smoke screen. The Gestapo executed 1,331 Czechs (including 201 women) and 3,000 Jews in reprisal.

diversion to enable the gunmen to get into position.[5]

The lay-out of the site (see map p. 338-339) determined an optimum firing zone within which the shots would have to be concentrated, but a target riding in a moving vehicle raised a number of special problems. The first concerned the speed of the vehicle. The Presidential car was watched and timed during Kennedy's trips in September, and its minimum speed was estimated at 10 miles an hour. The sharp turn into Elm Street was expected to slow it down even more, but as Dealey Plaza marked the end of the motorcade and the approach to the freeway, the driver would probably accelerate as he came out of the turn. The estimate was therefore cautiously revised to 15 miles an hour.[6]

Fifteen miles an hour is the equivalent of approximately 22 feet per second. That is extremely slow for a car, but extremely fast for a gunman, particularly if he placed in a perpendicular or even a lateral position. The positions of the gunmen were determined with this in mind. The best possible position for an ambush of this sort (when neither explosives nor bazookas or other powerful weapons are used) is in front of and perpendicular to the car. The lay-out of Dealey Plaza offered several possibilities. The gunman in position no. 1 would have the car coming straight towards him, on a level with him, as it came out of the turn 400 feet away. This position offered a wide firing angle and the possibility of shooting at the President up to a very close range (approximately 100 feet). It seemed so ideal that it was decided to station another gunman, no. 2, beyond no. 1 and close to the railroad overpass. Both would be firing from approximately the same angle. The other two gunmen, 3 and 4, occupied less favorable positions. They could not fire at the President and hope to hit him until a precise instant determined by a number of different factors.

The first was the obstacle presented by the two Secret Service men who habitually rode on the back bumper of the President's car [7]. The second was the fact that the shots of the four gunmen must be carefully synchronized. After studying these factors and others (distances and angles), the organizers delimited an exact firing zone 60 feet long which took into account the distance of each gunman from his target and the trajectory of his bullet, and which offered the maximum chances for success (see map p. 338-339).

Accuracy was, of course, essential. The gunmen were chosen for their marksmanship, and they were provided with excellent weapons. [8] But they had to aim at the President's head, and they had to be sure to kill him.[9] No plans were made for a second round of fire. It was assumed that the first shots would set off instantaneous reactions. Roy Kellerman, in the front seat of the President's car, would throw himself over Kennedy. The President himself might collapse or drop to the floor of the car. In a fraction of a second the driver could accelerate and the car would roar out of sight.

But the reaction on November 22 was one of total surprise. Not only did Kellerman and the driver fail to move (they turned to look at the President), but when agent John Ready wanted to jump off the running board of the backup car[10], agent Emory Roberts ordered him back. It would seem, then,

---

5. A few minutes before the arrival of the motorcade, a man wearing green army fatigues had a sudden fit of epilepsy in Elm Street. The attack lasted less than a minute and was over as suddenly as it had begun, but it drew the attention of the people standing around him. The police took the " epileptic " away.

6. The Warren Commission estimated the speed of the car at 11 miles per hour.

7. The President himself had ordered them off week before at Tampa. The person in charge of the ambush noted in Miami, and later at San Antonio and Houston, that the " human shield " had not been reinstated, but he preferred to take it into account just in case, and the original plan was maintained.

8. Robert Kennedy was killed with an Iver Johnson 22 pistol, one of the best weapons that exists for close-range firing in a crowd.

9. The Committee was worried less about killing John Connally, who was in almost the same line of fire as the President, than about accidentally killing a federal agent, which would have transformed the assassination into a federal rather than a state crime.

This was one of the reasons why a plan for killing driver Bill Greer was dropped, the others being that a dead or wounded driver might press down on the accelerator and send the car hurtling forward, and third that they didn't want to waste their bullets on a secondary target.

10. Manchester, *Death of a President,* p. 191.

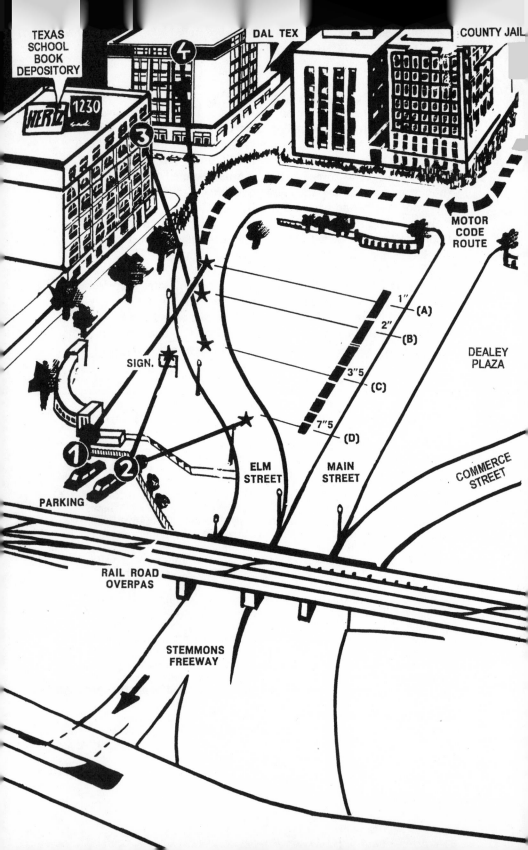

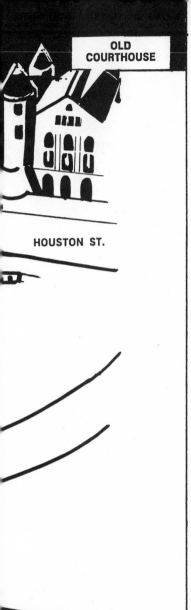

OLD COURTHOUSE

HOUSTON ST.

THE ASSASSINATION

November 22, 1963

Second by second

A. (Gunman 1)
The President is hit in the throat.

B. (Gunman 4)
The President is hit in the shoulder.

C. (Gunman 3)
Governor Connally is hit in the back.

D. (Gunman 2)
The President is hit in the head.

that some Secret Service agents did have the impulse to jump, but that they felt obliged to ask permission !

What had been planned as a salvo wasn't really a salvo. The first shot was clearly distinct, and the second narrowly preceded the third and fourth, which blended into one. The four shots thus formed three distinct detonations, but the acoustical phenomena at Dealey Plaza led many witnesses to believe that they had heard only two shots.[11] The first shot, fired in the open, was muffled, and the second and third, separated by only 2 seconds, had the effect of an echo.

The first bullet came from no. 1 and struck the President in the throat. The second apparently came from no. 4 and hit the President in the back. No. 3 hit Connally, and no. 2's bullet went through a traffic sign between him and the car.

Then, as Youngblood covered Johnson and spectators began to scream, there was a pause. Four seconds after they opened fire, the gunmen must have been dumbfounded. When the first shot strangled the President, no one moved. At the sound of the second, Governor Connally turned around and was wounded, but the driver still didn't budge, and Kellerman barely turned his head. The final shots awakened the agents in the back-up car, but Kellerman was still lost in his dreams, and Greer failed to react even to the whine of Halfback's siren. Four shots had been fired, and the car was still moving at the same speed. Despite the careful preparations and the

---

11. People who knew guns, however, and those in the rear of the motorcade who had not yet reached Dealey Plaza, were not fooled. UPI correspondent Merriman Smith reported a " burst " of gunfire, and in Main Street General Clifton and General McHugh mistook the three distinct reports for a salute.

12. Apparently 3 and 4 also took second shots, but missed. They may have been shaken by the general inertia ; at any rate, their shots were much more difficult.

13. A study of ballistics makes it clear why, despite the fact that he is so poorly protected, it takes a highly-organized plot and expert gunmen (except on the off-chance) to kill the President of the United States when he is riding in a moving car. Gunmen 3 and 4, stationed in the rear, had difficult shots. They hit the President only once (in the back), and one of their shots also struck Connally. Their other shots probably bounced off the car or hit the ground.

skillful marksmanship, not only was the President alive, but he was not mortally wounded. His life depended literally on Greer's reflexes, but the old driver was drugged by 35 years on the job.

The gunmen weren't dreaming, however. They were professionals. The car continued towards 1 and 2. It was 2 who hit the President, and from very close range (see the map on p. 338-339).[12] John Fitzgerald Kennedy, strangled by the first shot and knocked forward by the second, was thrust backwards. The bullet pierced his temple and penetrated his brain, and his skull literally exploded.[13]

There were two principal reasons why they missed. In the first place, the average spread of an accurate rifle is about 2 inches to either side for every 100 yards. In the second place, in the instant between the time the gunman presses the trigger and the impact of the bullet, a moving target shifts position. For the fastest rifles, such as the Winchester 284 or the Colt AR 15 223, this interval is approximately 1/11th of a second at a distance of 100 yards. In 1/11th of a second, a car moving 10 or 11 miles an hour advances about a foot and a half. The angle at which they were placed (15 or 20 degrees) reduced this displacement somewhat, but it still amounted to several inches, which was easily doubled by their reflex time. A few inches is enough to miss a target the size of a head. Moreover, it is one thing to shoot on a firing range and quite another to fire from a rooftop or a window overlooking a public park amidst the noises of the crowd.

The feat attributed to Oswald at Dallas was impossible for any but a world champion marksman using a high-precision semi-automatic rifle mounted on a carriage and equipped with an aim corrector, and who had practiced on moving targets in similar set-ups.

The rifles used for the assassination were Mausers without scopes. An optical scope has the advantage of bringing the target 3 or 4 times closer, but it needs frequent adjustment and must be handled with care. Furthermore, it is unnecessary for a target 300 feet away.

There was some question as to whether heavy rifles with large-caliber bullets or lighter weapons making it easier to follow a moving target should be used. An example of the latter-type weapon is the Colt AR 15.223 mentioned by Manchester, who notes (p. 167) that there was one on the back seat of Halfback, the back-up car, between Secret Service agents George Hickey and Glen Bennett. Manchester states that this rifle has a muzzle

It would never have happened if the bubble-top had been used that day.[14] The plexiglas would not have stopped the bullets, but it would have deflected them, interfering with the gunmen's aim. But on the morning of November 22, Ken O'Donnell glanced up at the sky at Fort Worth and noted with satisfaction that " It was going to be a day with a halo around it, a glittering lacuna of a day. There would be no bubbletop ".[15] He was right. The sun was shining in Dallas.

In 30 years on the job, J. Edgar Hoover has developed an intelligence system which nothing — no racket, and certainly no conspiracy — can escape. Through its extensive network of informers, the FBI knows everything worth knowing that goes on in the United States, even in areas that lie outside its legal jurisdiction [16]. The Dallas conspiracy was born and took root in places where the FBI was well represented. Its informers included former FBI agent James Rowley, chief of the Secret Service, Dallas District Attorney Henry Wade, CIA agent Guy Bannister, also a member of the Minutemen, and Lee Harvey Oswald. H.L. Hunt used former FBI agents as bodyguards, and Dallas Police Chief Curry was in contact with several FBI men and was under surveillance by the FBI, which had no fewer than 75 agents in Dallas.

By mid-October, Hoover had been informed of the existence of a plot and was familiar with many of the details. The FBI often launches an investigation on the strength of a rumor, and the information it received that fall from Boston, Chicago and Dallas was based on far more than hearsay. These reports were checked out and verified. The week before the President's departure for Texas, Hoover knew exactly what was going to happen. Why did the FBI fail to intervene ?

It is true that the FBI bore no responsibility for the security

---

velocity so powerful that should a bullet strike a man's chest, it would blow his head off (sic), thereby showing (though elsewhere in the book he describes himself as an expert marksman who, " like Oswald ", was trained in the Marine Corps at Parris Island) how little he knows about firearms. The .223 caliber 21 barrel Colt AR 15 Sporter is a powerful weapon, with the same shock power as the NATO 7.62 at a distance of 300 feet, but it

of the President. It is also true that every year dozens of investigations are made of threats against the life of the President. Moreover, the FBI is an investigative agency, not a national police force. Nevertheless, a section of the FBI Manual issued to each agent stipulates that :

" *Investigation of threats against the President of the United States, members of his immediate family, the President-Elect, and the Vice-President is within the exclusive jurisdiction of the U.S. Secret Service. Any information indicating the possibility of an attempt against the person or safety of the President, members of the immediate family of the President, the President-Elect or the Vice-President must be referred immediately by the most expeditious means of communication to the nearest office of the U.S. Secret Service. Advise the Bureau at the same time of the information so furnished to the Secret Service and the fact that it has been so disseminated. The above action should be taken without delay in order to attempt to verify the information, and no evaluation of the information should be attempted. When the threat is in the form of a written communication, give a copy to the local Secret Service and forward the original to the Bureau where it*

---

has never been known to strike a man's chest and knock his head off. The principal advantages of the AR 15 (known to the military as the M 16) are its light weight (8 lbs.), rate of fire (900 to 1,000 shots per minute), initial speed (3,000 feet per second), range (8,000 yards) and flat trajectory at close range.

The bullets used were frangible bullets specially cast from a lead and silver alloy with no jacket, so that they would disintegrate on impact. The bullet that killed Robert Kennedy was also a frangible bullet.

14. If it had rained that day, the Lincoln would have been covered with its plexiglas " bubble-top ", which according to V.E. Baughman, former chief of the Secret Service, is not bulletproof. The British and the French, however, not to speak of the Russians, use transparent plastic tops that, while heavier, are capable of deflecting even large-caliber bullets fired at point-blank range.

15. Manchester, *Death of a President*, p. 154.

16. After the assassination, the FBI submitted 25,000 investigative reports. It went so far as to describe the dreams of some of the witnesses.

will be made available to the Secret Service headquarters in Washington. The referral of the copy to local Secret Service should not delay the immediate referral of the information by the fastest available means of communication to Secret Service locally. "

The regulations, however, were ignored.

Hoover, " the man who is almost a legend " (in the words of Rep. Gerald Ford) would probably not have agreed to cooperate with the Committee, but he did absolutely nothing to stop it. He may not have approved of the assassination, but he didn't disapprove of it either. Hoover preferred to stay out of other people's fights, especially when they involved business circles over which he exercised little control. Faced with a choice between his professional duty and his abhorrence of everything that President Kennedy represented, he chose the latter alternative. He also hoped that the affair would tarnish the reputation of the CIA and shatter his Attorney General.

After the assassination, the FBI pulled out its files and submitted its report. It laid the blame and designated the culprits. Texas got back at Hoover by declaring, on January 24, 1964, that Lee Oswald had been on the FBI payroll as an informer since 1962. Neither the FBI nor the CIA were ever called upon to clear themselves. The assassination was bigger than both of them. It was rooted in a system that had produced a Senator named Lyndon Johnson, and it was

---

17. Hoover has always denied this, claiming that the agency's activities abroad are confined to domestic law enforcement and related duties. He is not telling the truth. Since 1963, the FBI has expanded its overseas operations (it already had offices in London, Tokyo, Paris, Bonn, Buenos Aires, Rio de Janeiro, Mexico, and even Moscow.) It still has a long way to go to catch up with the CIA, but it is trying hard. It is firmly ensconced in the Dominican Republic, where its intelligence reports were so highly regarded by the White House that it was given the green light to operate in other countries. This does not mean that the CIA has abdicated or been relieved of its responsibilities, but that the FBI is concerning itself more and more with overseas intelligence.

suppressed by the same system, now presided over by the same Lyndon Johnson. In the belief that he was acting for the good of the country, Chief Justice Warren agreed to perjure himself.

Regardless of the cost to the country, the FBI's maneuverings paid off. Since 1963 it has been steadily shortening the CIA's lead in the intelligence race. It has reinforced its control in the field of counter-espionage and branched out into the overseas activities that were once the CIA's private preserve.[17]

But although he recognizes its technical compentence, President Johnson apparently doesn't trust the FBI with his life. On November 22, 1964, a board presided by Treasury Secretary Douglas Dillon and including Attorney General Nicholas de B. Katzenbach, White House assistant McGeorge Bundy, and CIA Director John McCone examined ways of strengthening Presidential security. It rejected the suggestion that the FBI be given overall responsibility for the protection of the President, including prevention and investigation, leaving the Secret Service with the limited responsibility for his physical protection.

Exactly one year earlier, the stern and hard-working Mr. Hoover had already had his lunch and been back at work for more than 30 minutes when the first news flash clattered over the UPI wires at 1 : 34 p.m. E.S.T. But does Mr. Hoover ever learn anything from the wire services ?

The following day, November 23, the White House received a package sent over by his remarkable bureau. In it was a piece of President Kennedy's skull.

PART IV

REVIVAL

It's the quality and not the length of a man's life that counts. If a man is assassinated while he is fighting to save the soul of the nation, his death contributes more than anything else to its redemption.

MARTIN LUTHER KING

19

Yesterday

" I don't think in this administration or in our generation or time will this country be at the top of the hill, but some day it will be, and I hope when it is that they will think we have done our part... "

JOHN FITZGERALD KENNEDY

Empires have always succumbed to the same disease. With each new conquest, Rome thrust forward her frontiers and retreated from her principles. The first Romans were simple people, wholly devoted to their land and their gods, But the pilgrims, the settlers and the sages were succeeded by a promiscuous mob that capitalized on the victories. The growing number of slaves and the afflux of the poor swelled the population. The patricians found their chances for survival considerably reduced as hordes of former slaves, freed and newly-wealthy, fought over their estates.

For the Romans, all things reflected their greatness — the victories of Marius, Pompey, and Caesar, but also the Empire, history, and the future of the Roman people. But there was neither justice in the courts nor honesty in the elections. Only one standard decided the merit of a candidate or the innocence of a defendent : gold.

The spectacles at the Circus served to distract the populace. The free wheat and olives distributed to the needy at the Forum served as a subterfuge for social reforms. The aristocracy purchased seats in the Senate. The magistracy of the empire and the spoils of victory went to the senators, the consuls, the praetors, the quaestors, the censors and their wives. Rome had become a corporation.

The government was in the hands of a few opulent families of the world of finance, supported by the military junta. These families knew how to protect their interests : they disguised them as national necessities. The preservation of Rome was identified with that of the ruling families. " The Roman people consisted of a small oligarchy of landowners, bankers, speculators, merchants, artisans, adventurers, and tatterdemalions, avid for pleasure, excitement, and sudden gain, proud, turbulent, corrupted by the life of the city, and placing their own interests ahead of even the most salutary reform... ".[1]

The national honor of the Roman Empire was nothing more than the caprices or the indignation of the rulers of the moment, its political institutions no more than the cupidity of its dignitaries and the indolence of its masses, its history nothing more than a series of petty larcenies and more important crimes.

And then the Gracchus brothers, nephews of Scipion the African, appeared on the scene. The elder brother, Tiberius (160-133 B.C.), the son of a consul and born a patrician, had been raised by Greek philosophers, Blossus of Cumes and Diophanes of Mytilene. He was a veteran of the Spanish campaign. He was elected a tribune. His fortitude, his temperance, his humanity, his passion for justice and his natural eloquence elicited the admiration of Cicero. It was evident that he would make his mark in politics.

Tiberius was as calm, as sober, and as moderate as his brother Gaius was vehement, impassioned, and impetuous. He worked for Italy, for the people, and for liberty. He would not be stopped by either threats or clamor.

On Rogation Day[2], he addressed the people massed around the tribune. A fragment of this speech, in which he evoked the misery and the helplessness of the people, the depopulation of Italy and the rapacity of the wealthy, has been preserved. " The landowners in mourning dress appeared on the Forum in the most wretched and humble condition in order to move the people whom they despoiled so mercilessly to pity. But they had little confidence in this demonstration, and they hired assassins to kill Tiberius...[3] "

Tiberius, nevertheless, proceeded with his reforms. One of his laws authorized the people to circulate freely on the roads and highways. Another stipulated that the treasure of Attala, who had made the Roman people his heir, would be distributed among the citizens. Other laws distributed lands, subsidized the cost of the first planting, decreased the length of military service, and reorganized the judiciary. Henceforth, no Roman citizen could own more than 750 acres of public land for himself and 375 for each of his sons. This law threatened the owners of the largest herds.

In his speeches Tiberius declared that the will of the people was the supreme authority of the state. This was too much. On the day of his re-election to the tribunate, which would have enabled Tiberius to complete his reforms, Scipion Nasicaa, one of the richest of the landowners, assembled all of the wealthy Romans. Followed by an army of slaves and clients, they climbed to the Capitol. One of Tiberius' colleagues, a tribune, dealt him the first blow. Other assassins finished the job. His body was profaned and thrown into the Tiber.

Rome, which had found senators to assassinate him, found no historian to stigmatize his assassins. After centuries of law and order, the Empire watched with stupefaction as the violence of a faction that had taken the law into its own hands not only went unpunished, but was admired.

Gaius (152-121 B.C.), eight years younger than his brother, appeared to accept his death and to be unaware of the identities of his assassins. He was appointed quaestor of Sardinia and, against the wishes of the Senate, he did not

---

1. Guglielmo Ferrero.
2. The day the laws were proposed to the people.
3. Leon Jouberti.

disappear from view. He lived the life of his soldiers and looked after their interests. He liked long marches and took long, lonely swims in the sea, and he remained chaste.

" The fate of his brother and his reforms had proved that it was vain to attempt to remedy the ills of Rome without first having destroyed, or at least humiliated, the large landowners and the usurpers of the public domain ; that the idea of transforming the poor people of Rome into a landowing class was too simple and, in reality, not very effective.

" But once the terror had disappeared, the little people of Rome began to seek a protector, and the victim's brother, who was known for his virtues and was already suspect to the wealthy, appeared to be just the person they needed.

" The persistent hatred of the nobility precipitated him into the fray, although he had no intention of taking up his brother's reforms. Boldly, Gaius ran for the office of tribune and was elected. He immediately proved that he was no ordinary man. He denounced his brother's assassins and punished them. He promulgated the laws that Tiberius would have wanted. He cited Tiberius incessantly in his speeches. He was re-elected a tribune. He reduced the authority of the Senate. He controlled everthing, organized everything, imparting his prodigious activity and his indefatigable energy to everyone.

" He was craftier than his brother. He had learned from him, and he had had time to meditate his revenge without beclouding his mind. For a long while, he retained the support of the wealthy by proposing laws that pleased the rich and others that suited the poor. But eventually he voiced the idea that he had so long meditated in silence : that all Italians should be given the rights of citizens. "

Rome would be the capital of a vast Italic nation. No longer would the Empire be founded on a municipal oligarchy allied with the corrupt merchants, but on rival classes working in partnership. The former centers of civilization and commerce, now destroyed or declined, would be restored, and the wealth and the multitudes that poured into Rome, threatening to choke the nerve-center of the Empire, would be distributed evenly throughout the different lands.

It was the historic task of Rome that Gaius had in mind,

but he thought he could accomplish alone what it was to take six generations to achieve. His grandiose ideas were too premature. His plan to accord the rights of a Roman citizen to all Italians pleased neither the nobility nor the little people.

The Senate decided that things had gone far enough. The Consul Lucien Opimius led the conspiracy. Pursued and about to be taken, Gaius killed himself in a wood dedicated to the Furies. Septimuleius cut off his head. Gaius in his turn was thrown into the Tiber, along with 3,000 of his followers.

The year of Gaius' death, the grape harvest was exceptionally good. The nobles, the wealthy, the big and the small landowners bought up all the slaves on the market.

The Gracchus brothers were the last true aristocrats of Rome. Licentiousness robbed the aristocracy of its traditional energy and its virtues. Most of their laws were abolished. The robber barons rid the Roman Empire of all the leaders who had dreamed of being generous, or simply of being just. Balbinus, Emilian, Valerian, Aurelius, and Maximus were assassinated in their turn. Probus lasted six years, Tacitus ten months, and Pertinax 97 days.

Sixteen centuries later, Machiavelli wrote that " men forget the death of their father more easily than the loss of their patrimony, and they hesitate less to harm a man who is loved than another who is feared. "

Later, after Honorius, the frontiers of the Empire were overrun by the barbarians. The Empire, invaded, was split asunder, and Rome faded into oblivion. The Gracchus brothers were not forgotten by the Roman people. Statues were erected in their memory, and a cult was founded in their honor.

20

Tomorrow

" *After centuries of oppression, may the revolution which has just taken place across the sea,
by offering to all the inhabitants of Europe an asyl-
um against fanaticism and tyranny, teach those
who govern men about the legitimate use of their
authority ! May those courageous Americans, who
preferred to see their wives assaulted, their children
butchered, their homes destroyed, their fields ravag-
ed, their towns burned, to spill their blood and to
die, rather than lose even a tiny portion of their
liberty, prevent the enormous growth and the un-
equal distribution of wealth, extravagance, indolence, and corruption, and guarantee the maintenance of their liberty and the duration of their government. May they defer, at least for several centuries, the judgment pronounced against all the
things of this world, the judgment which condemned
them to have their birth, their period of strength,
their decrepitude, and their end.*

" *Adversity employs great talents ; prosperity
renders them useless and carries the inept, the corrupted wealthy and the wicked to the top. May*

they bear in mind that virtue often contains the seeds of tyranny. May they bear in mind that it is neither gold nor even a multitude of arms that sustains a state, but its morals. May each of them keep in his house, in a corner of his field, next to his workbench, next to his plow, his gun, his sword and his bayonet. May they all be soldiers. May they bear in mind that in circumstances where deliberation is possible, the advice of old men is good, but that in moments of crisis youth is generally better informed than its elders.

DENIS DIDEROT,
APOSTROPHE TO THE INSURGENTS, 1782

Historical comparisons are dangerous things, but there is little doubt that Robert Kennedy would have taken up the torch so rudely wrested from his brother's hand. Because his first concern was for his mission, because he was already a statesman, he put off until later the punishment of his brother's assassins. For him, the unity of the nation came before sentiment.

He would certainly have been elected Thirty-Seventh President of the United States, and he would have guided his people towards the Frontier, towards that zone where men must confront the realities of this world, and no longer be content with borrowed images of it.

He would have gone further than his brother John, for five years had passed, and much time had been lost. Younger than John, Robert was more mature when he died, but sadder and lonelier. He lacked his brother's style, but he moved faster. He was the only American politician who was a man of his time... who was, in other words, ahead of his time. He liked to say, " I'm going to tell it like it is. "

Once he had been laid in the ground, the conspiracy of silence closed once more over the conspiracy of the crime. *Life* magazine headed its story, " The Kennedys, those princes destroyed by the gods. "

This book attempts not so much to describe a crime as to explain how it came about, and to disclose the motives that inspired it. The problems facing the United States today are fundamentally the same as those that it confronted in 1960, but they have grown more serious. Our analysis of the Kennedy years is, in fact, an autopsy of the Johnson administration.

The fortresses that John Kennedy prepared to attack are stronger today than ever before. The America of 1968 differs little from the America of the Eisenhower years.[1]

The death of Robert Kennedy, like that of his brother John, was neither an accident nor a misunderstanding. Both crimes bore the signature of frangible bullets. Both murders were the work of a few men desirous of maintaining the political, social and economic situations and philosophy of another era. Most of these men are still in power. Must the American people wait until the year 2038 to examine the files deposited in the National Archives, to hear the testimony of other witnesses ? Who can say what the America of 2038 will be like, whether she will take an interest in the dust of centuries past, in the heroes of her history and their assassins ?

Long before then, American children will learn in school that John Fitzgerald Kennedy ranks with a Lincoln and a Washington. True, he sometimes showed a lack of realism, too great a faith in the virtue of words. He was too trusting of men, and especially of those around him. He did not belong to that great family of emperors who, from Peter the Great to Frederick of Prussia to Charles De Gaulle, have always placed the interest of the state above sentiment — even when it caused their heart to suffer.

But it is not only for his generous heart that John Kennedy

---

1. Only the race problem has evolved. Calvin Lockridge, chief of the Black Consortium, has defined this evolution as follows :

" You thought we were ugly, stupid and lazy, and we believed you. All that is finished now. We've decided we're handsome, intelligent, efficient and artistic, and we're not about to change our minds. " And he adds, " There's no black problem here. Only a white problem. "

will be remembered. He was the first to have a prophetic conception of a new Society of Mankind.

Before the double tomb at Arlington, there are lessons to be learned. Ethel and Edward Kennedy made of Robert's funeral an occasion, not of sadness, but of hope. A man can be destroyed, but some men are never vanquished... not if the true meaning of their death is understood, and the significance of their struggle.

As this page is written, 200,515 young Americans, dead, wounded or missing in Vietnam, bear witness to the longest and most pointless war the United States has ever known. But the price paid by the Great Society is greater still. The decade of the Sixties opened, you will recall, in the blaze of a New America and the warmth of world affection for her President. As the same decade draws to a close, the one and the other are held in universal contempt.

" I know the look that people give to Americans today — to the tourists in the streets of Mexico, to the soldiers on leave in the Far East, to the businessmen passing through Italy or Sweden. It is the same look they give to your embassies, your warships, your exhibits throughout the world. It is a terrible look, for it makes no distinctions, no concessions. I know that look, because I an German, and I have felt it in the past. It is a mixture of distrust and resentment, of fear and envy, of hate and absolute contempt. It is the look they give to your President, who can no longer appear in public in any capital of the world ; but it is also the look they give to the little old lady in the plane between Delhi and Benares. "[2]

Within the frontiers and the souls of America, the cost is even higher. True, the national income is leaping to new heights. But is that enough ?

The United States came into being not as a result of nationalism, nor of ethnic or religious unity, but of a common faith in liberty. It was for freedom that millions of Europeans crossed the Atlantic in the Nineteenth Century. Today, what remains of this faith ?

Far from constituting an " American Challenge ", it seems to us that the Great Society is tolling its death-knell. True, the American way of life remains a model for the consumer society and the socialist republic alike. But if Europe is trying to close the technology gap, it is not with the object of adopting American civilization, but rather of protecting itself from the model, of preventing it from sterilizing its traditions and its particularisms, corrupting its peoples and subjugating its children to the idols of an alien society.

On February 7, 1968, the Chase Manhatten Bank predicted that the New Year would be " prosperous but uncomfortable. " Among the most important problems it listed the conduct of the war, firmness in the face of social disorders, inflation, the balance of payments problem, and the financial repercussions of all of these issues.

Richard Nixon, who is more of a realist, or at least more of a demagogue, declared on September 5, 1968 that " What happened in Chicago last week was not the agony of Chicago, and was not even the agony of the Democratic Party. It was the agony of America. "

On August 9, after his triumph in Miami, he had said, speaking of the " great " President that was Eisenhower, " This time we'll go on to win... It will be different... We have to win for Ike... We are going to win. It's time to have power go back from Washington, D.C. to the cities. Tonight, its the real voice of America. "

A few days later, Hubert H. Humphrey remarked at a Michigan caucus, " I want Richard Nixon to understand that he won't be President just because John F. Kennedy isn't here. "

It took the disappearance of two Kennedys to bring to the foreground two Vice-Presidents who had never been more than the shadows of other shadows.

For four years, Lyndon Johnson ran the country as his background and his obligations required, concealing his conservatism beneath minor racial and social reforms. John Kennedy had willed him a country that was almost ready to take the lead of the universe. Because he admired President Kennedy and because he was aware of his own limitations, few men were as badly shaken by the assassination as President Johnson. He understood who was behind it, and he knew that, his personal ambitions notwithstanding, he would always be the hostage of those to whom he owed his political career,

---

2. Hans Magnus Ensensberger.

of the men who had gone so far as to open that last door. He also knew how much separated him from John Kennedy.

The rich fragrances of four years in the White House were probably not enough to enable him to forget the odors of the backrooms where he had grown up. There is little doubt that he was weary when, on March 31, he handed in his final report.

Robert Kennedy's assassination pushed him down a little more. One June 6 he told his wife and a group of friends who urged him to return to the lead of the Democratic Party, " No, this is the end... the end... the end. "

It was a sad month of August and a gloomy September, and the country found itself confronted with one candidate who " ran like a scared candidate for Sheriff "[3] and another who couldn't even sell a used car.

" I'm jumping for joy ! ", shouted H.H.H., but he was the only person who was, and a little later he slipped into a bedroom and wept... " not just for the bloodied kids in the streets, but for his country, his party and himself. "[4]

As for the other candidate, Richard Nixon never cries.

One of these two men will be 37th President of the United States. Which is of little importance. The delegates to the Philadelphia Convention in 1787 were right to voice their fears that democracy would bring about an end to freedom. They drew up a Constitution that was a succession of compromises between big states and small. They hoped to protect the government from the pressures of the voters. The political system they created was appropriate for the time of Montesquieu and Locke, and it was well-suited to the type of men present at the Convention — men wealthy enough to be disinterested, experienced and intelligent enough to govern, and sufficiently idealistic to respect the principles on which the Republic was founded. Apprehending anarchy, distrusting the aristocracy, they gave birth to a synarchic regime. The political leaders of 1968 are twice as old as the founders of the Republic.[5]

Today, the United States is the only major western nation whose political institutions are completely out-of-date, the only democracy that denies its people a direct voice in the choice of its governors, the only great power whose President lacks the authority to institute a simple fiscal reform.

A national image is a very fragile thing. In a single night, the orders issued from the cold depths of the Communist Party destroyed 15 years of efforts and sacrificed the Soviet Union to the myth of the empire of the Tsars.

The USSR admits that it acted in Prague in order to stop a " legal counter-revolution ". The men who govern the United States are inspired by the same principles. The two nations that seek to divide up the world are both ruled by anachronisms.

At the heart of the conflict between modern Soviet society and the government of the Kremlin lies the question of freedom of speech. The central problem in today's America is the search for a new moral ethic. Only the young people will know how to find it.

The day after the Los Angeles assassination, Tom Wicker wrote : " A whole new generation — the children of affluence — has taken up the cause of the black and the poor, not so much out of class feeling or shared experience, perhaps as from recognition of a common enemy — the Establishment. It is the Establishment — the elders, the politicians, the military-industrial complex, the Administration, the press, the university trustees, the landlords, the system — that represses the black, exploits the poor, stultifies the students, vulgarizes American life. And it is the Establishment, of course, that wages the war in Vietnam... Never in history or in any country have such profound struggles as these been waged without blooshed and human tragedy. "

A nation cannot be built without its youth, let alone against its youth. The young people of today may be only real adults in the hesitant world of their fathers.

Robert Kennedy wrote :

" The young people of today reject a morality that measures everything by profit. They know that certain heads of large corporations conspire to fix prices, and that they meet in secret to steal a few pennies every month from the people.

---

3. *Newsweek.*
4. *Ibid.*
5. *Newsweek.*

They have seen us throw marajuana smokers into jail, but they also see us refuse to limit the sales and advertising of tobacco, which kills several thousand Americans every year. They have seen us hesitate to impose even the most elementary norms of safety on automobile manufacturers, to require department stores and loan companies to reveal the true rates of interest they apply. They have come to realize that organized crime, corruption, bribery and extortion flourish not only because of government tolerance, but also because of the complicity of labor, economic and political leaders...

" The gap that exists between the generations today will probably never be completely filled, but it must be straddled. It is vital that our young people be made to feel that an evolution is possible, that they be made to realize that this mad, cruel world can give way before their sacrifices... Each generation has its principal preoccupation. The youth of today seem to have chosen the dignity of man... "

It is you, the youth of the Seventies, who will build a New America.

There are only two alternatives : reform or revolution. The march that lies before you will not be easy. But others have shown you the way.[6] The Kennedy brothers left behind them not only " a legacy of zest and vigor "[7], but the

---

6. Nearly 35 years ago in China, the longest march began. Harassed by Chiang Kai-shek, Mao Tse-tung, with a following of 100,000 men and 300,000 women and children, set out on a stupendous 368-day journey. The pilgrims survived five extermination campaigns. Leaving south China, they crossed the Yunnan mountains, skirted Tibet, traversed the Lolos forest, immense swamps, and the Setchuan and Ken Si deserts, until they finally reached the loop of the Yellow River near the Great Wall. They scaled eighteen mountain ranges, five of them covered with snow, and forded 24 rivers. After 7,500 miles, their number had dwindled to 40,000. But they had faith in China, and in themselves. In a Promised Land reminiscent of the Yucatan Desert, the kind of land where corn can be grown between the stones, the most resistant among them survived and hardened. There they forged their doctrine, and they waited...

One day, their grandchildren or their great-grandchildren may live in a China that is worth the cost.

7. *Life*.

certainty of a Renaissance. History moves forward only through the genius and the audacity of a few great men. From the ashes of Ghandi, tossed into the Granges and sown from the skies, a modern India will someday arise. The remains of Che Guevara, scattered by the winds, will gradually cover over the last of the empires.

In the short decade of the Sixties, at the end of the Twentieth Century, two sons of Massachusetts certainly did their part. As the Twenty-First Century opens, it is you, the youth of America, who must take up the torch.

For it is " not houses firmly roofed, or the stones of walls well-builded, nay nor canals and dockyards which make the city, but men able to use their opportunities. "

Dare, and you will prevail.

That day, even Texas will blossom again.

That day, you will reach the top of the hill.

Appendixes

There are many files on the Kennedy assassination. The most accurate and the most complete are those of the C.I.A. and the F.B.I.

The American people are denied the right to consult these documents, as they are denied the right to examine the files deposited in the National Archives (see Appendix 1). In the same way, the sole irrefutable witness of the events in Dallas, Abraham Zapruder's 8 mm. color film of the assassination, has never been released to the public.

We were fortunate enough to obtain two copies of this film, from two different sources in the United States. One is a poor copy, the other of excellent quality. We have run through this film dozens of times. Certain of the photographs taken from it and published by leading magazines throughout the world have been retouched. Others were never published at all. These faked photographs and these cuts were the work of the photographic technicians of Time-Life, Inc., who were acting on official instructions.

The unedited version of this very moving film utterly demolishes the official version of the assassination of President Kennedy put out by the Warren Commission[1]. The Zapruder movie belongs to history and to men everywhere.

We challenge Time-Life to make this film available to the general public so that the people may see for themselves, in slow motion, the impact of the bullets and the reactions of the President, may hear ballistics experts point out the exact position of each of the gunmen, may watch John Kennedy's head explode in a cloud of red blood lasting nearly a second, may see how the President was thrust violently backwards by a bullet fired at point-blank range by a gunman situated in front of the car.

Appendix 2 contains a list of the documents from both European and American sources which we had the privilege to consult, and which helped us in the writing of this book.

---

1. A California resident, Mrs. Marjorie Field, has succeeded in reconstructing the real Warren Commission Report by putting the twenty-six volumes of evidence, the testimony of the witnesses and the times into logical order. This implacable demonstration, entitled *The Evidence*, is also being kept from the American people. At this writing, no publisher has accepted to publish it.

APPENDIX 1

NATIONAL ARCHIVES

CLASSIFIED DOCUMENTS PERTAINING TO

THE KENNEDY ASSASSINATION

Classified Documents in Archives. March, 1967

Abbreviations :

C	*Confidential*
S	*Secret*
TS	*Top Secret*
U	*? (see CD 1545)*

Guidelines :

1.	*Classified by statutory requirement for that Agency*
2.	*"National Security"*
3A	*Disclosure prejudicial to law enforcement*
3B	*Disclosure would reveal Confidential source of information*
3C	*Disclosure would embarrass innocent persons*

CD	Agency	Guideline	Subject	Date	Place
66	FBI	3C	Oswald	12-4-63	San Diego
76	FBI	3ABC	Hoaxes, False reports, irresponsible reporting	12-13-63	
78	FBI	2	Oswald Mexican trip	12-23-63	
89	FBI	?	Income tax returns of Ruby & associates	1-3-64	
90	FBI	?	Income tax returns of Oswald & relatives	1-6-64	
100	CIA	2	Analysis of world reaction to assassination	12-13-63	
101a	Treas.	1	Income tax info on Ruby, Oswald et al.	1-2-64	
101f	Treas.		Narcotics Bureau report re. Ruby	10-31-47	
114	FBI	3C	Oswald	12-5-63	Louisville
117	FBI	3C	Oswald	12-5-63	St. Louis
119	FBI	3C	Oswald	12-6-63	Albany
136	FBI	3C	Oswald	12-7-63	Tampa
153	FBI	3C	Oswald	12-10-63	Norfolk
181	FBI	2 ; 3B	Oswald	12-16-63	Cincinnati C
190	FBI	2 ; 3B	Oswald	12-18-63	Cincinnati C
212	FBI	2	Ruth Hyde Paine	12-17-63	Philadelphia C
218	FBI	2	Michael Ralph Paine	12-20-63	Los Angeles C
222	SS	3C	re Lloyd John Wilson & his implication in assass.	9-10-63	thru 1-10-64
227	FBI	2	Lee Harvey Oswald	12-20-63	Miami S
258	FBI	2	Michael Ralph Paine	12-20-63	Los Angeles C
271	FBI	3C	Assassination of President John Kennedy	12-4-63	El Paso
273	FBI	3B	Assassination of President John Kennedy	12-5-63	Charlotte
278 thru 287	State		Reports on various assassination attempts throughout the world		
299	FBI	?	Tax returns for Jack and Earl Ruby	1-20-64	

No.	Agency	Copy	Description	Date	Location	Class.
300	CIA	2	re recent Soviet statements of Oswald	1-21-64		
321	CIA	2	Chronology of Oswald in USSR	1-25-64	Wash. DC	S
322f	USIA		Foreign radio and press reaction to assassination	11-26-63		
322g	USIA		Public and propaganda Reactions to assass. in Poland	12-18-63		
347	CIA	2	Activity of Oswald in Mexico City	1-31-64		S
351	SIC		Lee Harvey Oswald (Subcommittee on Int Security)	1-28-64		
355	Just.		Witnesses interviewed re Ruby (Justice Dept.)	2-4-64		
361	CIA	2	Biographic info on Mrs. Oswald & relatives	1-31-64		
365	La. State		Compiled info of Lee Harvey Oswald (pps 31-41 withheld. Rest is CE 1413)	2-4-64	Baton Rouge	
367	FBI	?	Jack & Earl Ruby tax returns	2-7-64		
382	FBI	2	Medical Records of Fanny Rubenstein (CE 1281)			
384	CIA	2	Activity of Lee Harvey Oswald in Mexico City	2-19-64		
390	FBI	3B	Lee Harvey Oswald	1-16-64	Chicago	
425	IRS	1	Summary of tax returns	2-17-64	Wash.DC	
426	CIA	2	Interrogations of Silvia Duran & Husband in Mex. City	2-21-64		
432			Material sent by James H. Martin pertaining Marina O. "Mark Lane"			
433	FBI	2	Memorandum report : "Lee Harvey Oswald"	2-26-64	Wash. DC	
434	FBI	3A	Telegrams between State Dept. & US Embassy, Mex. C.	2-28-64		TS
442	State		National Guardian; Mark Lane	2-28-64	New York	S
445	FBI	2	Mohammed Reggab allegations re Marina Oswald	2-3-64		
448	CIA	2	re residence of Marina Oswald, James Martin	3-5-64		
449	FBI	3C	Yuri Ivanovich Nosenko interview	3-5-64		
451	FBI	3A	Lee Harvey Oswald	3-6-64		
469	FBI	3C	Lee Harvey Oswald	2-19-64	Oklahoma	
470	FBI	3C	Lee Harvey Oswald	2-22-64	Dallas	
471	FBI	3C	Lee Harvey Oswald	2-24-64	Cleveland	
478	FBI	3C	Memorandum : " Lee Harvey Oswald, also known as "	2-22-64	Dallas	
480	FBI	2	Marguerite Oswald in Boston	3-4-64	Boston	

ID	Agency	Code	Description	Date	Location	C/S
489	FBI	2	Mark Lane, Buffalo appearances	3-6-64	Buffalo	C
499	FBI	2	Deirdre Griswold; Robert Gwathmey	3-13-64	Wash. DC	C
504	thru		Sylvia Ludlow Hyde Hoke		Cincinnati	C
506	FBI	2		9. -56	NY; Seattle	C
508	FBI	2	Sylvia Ludlow Hyde Hoke	2-6-67	NY	C
527	IRS	1	Hyman Rubenstein tax returns	3-17-64		
528	CIA	2	re allegation Oswald interviewed by CIA in USSR	3-18-64		
530	FBI	2; 3B	George DeMohrenschildt	2-27-64	Wash. DC	C
540	FBI	2; 3B	George DeMohrenschildt	3-3-64	Wash. DC	C
548	FBI	2; 3C	George DeMohrenschildt	3-6-64	Wash. DC	C
557	FBI	3B	re Oswald's alleged suicide	3-4-64	Dallas	C
564	FBI	2	Lee Harvey Oswald	2-7-64	Wash. DC	C
565	FBI	2	Lee Harvey Oswald	2-19-64	Wash. DC	C
566	FBI	2	Lee Harvey Oswald	2-24-64	Wash. DC	C
597	FBI	3B	Bundesnachrichtendienst file	1-24-64	Wash. DC	C
599	FBI	3C	Vada Oswald statements	3-15-64	Denton	C
600	thru	2	George Lyman Paine, Jr.	nearly all		C
629	FBI	2	Frances Drake Paine	pre assass L..		
631	CIA	2	re CIA dissemination of info on Oswald	3-24-64		
653	FBI	3B	Lee Harvey Oswald	3-13-64	Chicago	C
663	FBI	2	Lee Harvey Oswald	3-6-64	Wash. DC	C
664	FBI	2; 3B	Lee Harvey Oswald	3-9-64	Wash. DC	C
665	FBI	2	Lee Harvey Oswald	3-10-64	Wash. DC	C
669	FBI	1	Lee Harvey Oswald	3-13-64	Dallas	S
674	CIA	2	Info given to the SS but not yet the WC.	3-24-64	Wash. DC	C
677	SS	3C	Memo from Chief Rowley to Mr. Belin	3-19-64		S
680	CIA	2	Appendix to CD 321	3-25-64		
681	IRS	1	Tax returns: Carroll, Ruby, Meyers, Volpert	11-30-62		
687	SS	3B; 3C	Ruth Paine - Naushon Island Cottages	3-11-64	Boston	S

No.	Agency	Code	Description	Date	Location	
688	IRS	1	Numerous tax returns	3-26-64		
691	CIA	2	Appendix A to CD 321	3-6-64		
692	CIA	2	Reproduction of CIA official dossier on Oswald	3-27-64		
694	FBI	2	Various Mark Lane appearances			
698	CIA	2	Reports of travel & activities LHO & Marina			
700	HEW	1	Various social security records; Ruby associates	3-31-64		
702	FBI	3A	FBI criteria for giving info to the SS	3-31-64		
703	IRS	1	IRS info on those mentioned in CD 681	3-19-64		
708	CIA	2	Reply to questions posed by State Dept.	4-6-64		
710	CIA	2	re: Richard Thomas Gibson	4-3-64		
713	FBI	2	Tax returns, Michael & Ruth Paine	4-2-64		
720	FBI	?	(r) thru (cc) : Photos Ruby strippers			
721	FBI	2	Oswald's trip to Mexico	4-6-64	Wash. DC	C
726	CIA	2	Actions of Silvia Duran after 1st interrogn.	4-7-64	Wash. DC	S
729	FBI	2	Allegation Oswald in Montreal, summer 1963	3-26-64	Wash. DC	C
751	FBI	2	Oswald: re Mexican trip	2-27-64	Wash. DC	C
763	FBI	2; 3B	Mark Lane appearances	4-2-64	L.A.	C
785	FBI	2	Oswald in Mexico. 7 photos attached	4-7-64	Wash. DC	C
788	FBI	3B; 3C	Memorandum on Eugene B. Dinkin	4-9-64	Chicago	S
794	FBI	2	"Lee Harvey Oswald" re Elizabeth Catlett Mora	4-10-64	Dallas	
795	SS	3B; 3C	Control 1366: Harry McCormick. Dal Mor News	4-1-64	Wash. DC	
798	HEW	1	Social security info on Karen Bennett et al.	4-16-64	Chicago	
801	FBI	3B	Jeanne DeMohrenschildt	4-1-64	Cincinnati	
808	FBI	3B; 3C	Lee Harvey Oswald	3-25-64	Miami	
812	FBI	2	Lee Harvey Oswald	4-4-64	Wash. DC	S
817	CIA	2	Allegations concerning Anton Erdlinger	4-20-64	Wash. DC	S
818	CIA	2	Revisions of CD 321	4-21-64	Wash. DC	S
811	CIA	2	re Lydia Dimytruk. Russian acquaintance Marina	4-24-64	Wash. DC	S
818	FBI	1	Michael & Ruth Paine tax returns '56-'58	4-24-64	Wash. DC	

No.	Agency	Codes	Description	Date	Location	Class.
853	SS	1; 3B; 3C	re; Manuel Rodriguez; 5310 Columbia, Dallas	4-24-64	Wash. DC	S
	SS		Reaction of Cuban exile community to Pres.		Miami	S
			Kennedy's death		Dallas	S
854	SS	3B; 3C	Control no. 1426 : Odio, McChann, Leopoldo, J. Martin	4-24-64	Miami	S
871	CIA	2	Photos of Oswald in Russia	4-29-64	Wash. DC	C
872	FBI	2	Oswald's travel in Mexico	3-31-64	Wash. DC	C
873	FBI	2	Oswald's travel in Mexico	4-20-64	Wash. DC	C
874	FBI	2	Oswald's travel in Mexico	4-24-64	Wash. DC	S
880	FBI	3B	re Oswald safe deposit box in Laredo, Houston	4-30-64	Wash. DC	
894	FBI	1	re Detroit branch of the FPCC	4-9-64	Detroit	C
895	FBI	1	re Reva and Joseph Bernstein	4-10-64	Wash. DC	S
896	FBI	2	Letterhead memorandum : " Lee Harvey Oswald "	4-13-64	Wash. DC	C
902	CIA	2	Criteria for giving info to the SS.	5-6-64	Wash. DC	S
908	FBI	3B	Oswald trust fund	5-4-64	Dallas	
910	FBI	2	Inquiry into Oswald's Mexican trip	4-28-64	Wash. DC	C
911	CIA	2	Marina Oswald's notebook	5-28-64	Wash. DC	S
928	CIA	2	Lev Setyayev & LHO contact with USSR citizens	5-6-64	Wash. DC	S
931	CIA	2	Oswald's access to info about the U-2	5-13-64	Wash. DC	S
933	FBI	3C	Investigation of Paul V. Carroll	5-1-64	El Paso	TS
935	CIA	2 `	Role of Cuba Intcll. Serv. in processing visa appl.	5-15-64	Wash. DC	C
941	FBI	2	Telephone nos. on 47th page of O's address book	5-6-64	Wash. DC	C
943	CIA	2	Allegations of PFC Eugene Dinkin re assass. plot	5-19-64	Wash. DC	S
944	CIA	2	Work hours at Soviet & Cuban consulates	5-19-64	Wash. DC	S
945	SS	3A; 3B; 3C	Interview of Rev Walter McChann on April 30th	5-5-64	Wash. DC	S
955	FBI	3C	Lee Harvey Oswald	5-6-64	Los Angeles	
959	FBI	2	Arnold Louis Kessler	5-4-64	Wash. DC	C
971	CIA	2	Tel call to US embassy, Canberra re planned assass.	5-22-64	Wash. DC	S
977	FBI	3C	Interview with Abraham Bolden	5-25-64	Chicago	
983	FBI	2	re claims of Manuel Santamarina Mendez	5-7-64	Wash. DS	C

aka: Luis Fernandez Gonzalez

ID	Agency	Code	Description	Date	Location	Class
988	FBI	3C	Info concerning General Edwin Walker	5-21-64	Boston	
990	CIA	2	Khrushchev & Drew Pearson discussion re Oswald	5-27-64	Wash. DC	S
991	FBI	3C	Letter to Atty. Genl. from Norman P. Michaud	4-23-64	Bureau Prisons	
992	FBI	3C	re: Norman P. Michaud; threat against LBJ.	1-31-64	Phoenix	
1000	CIA	2	Mexican interrogation of Gilberto Alvarado	6-1-64	Wash. DC	S
1005	FBI	3B; 3C	Interview of Mrs. Lucille Labonte, Sudburry, Ontario	5-26-64	Wash. DC	C
1006	FBI	2	re Charles Small, aka Smolikoff, (Mexican trip)	5-21-64	Wash. DC	C
1007	FBI	2	Oswald's Mexican trip; entry & departure	5-21-64	Wash. DC	C
1008	FBI	2	Oswald's Mexican trip; hotel registration	5-21-64	Wash. DC	C
1012	CIA	2	George and Jeanne DeMohrenschildt	6-3-64	Wash. DC	S
1014	SS	3B; 3C	Memo Soddels to Chief Rowley re Zapruder film	1-22-64	Dallas	C
1029	FBI	2	Oswald Mexican trip	5-12-64	Wash. DC	S
1030	FBI	1; 3B	Statements of Reva Frank Bernstein	5-13-64	Wash. DC	C
1037	FBI	2	Mexican aspects of Oswald investigation	5-25-64	Wash. DC	C
1038	FBI	2	Mexican aspects of Oswald investigation	5-28-64	Wash. DC	C
1039	FBI	3C	re Charles William Deaton	5-21-64	New York	
1041	CIA	2	Allegations re intell Training School in Minsk	6-5-64	Wash. DC	S
1054	CIA	2	Information on Jack Ruby and associates	6-10-64	Wash. DC	S
1080	FBI	3C	Information on Harold R. Isaacs	5-22-64	Boston	
1084	FBI	2	Lee Harvey Oswald; Luis Fernandez Gonzalez	6-10-64	Wash. DC	S
1085	FBI	2; 3A; 3B; 3C	Cuban exile Groups and individuals (xeroxed)	6-11-64	Wash. DC	S
1089	CIA	2	Letter re assass. sent to Costa Rican embassy	6-12-64	Wash. DC	S
1096	CIA	2	Fascists and Nazis today. Paris, Albin Michel	6-9-64		
1098	FBI	2; 3B	Interviews of Capt. Voltz & Capt. Stutts	6-9-64	San Francisco	C
1126	FBI	3B	Jack Ruby: Long distance phone calls.	6-15-64	Wash. DC	
1131	CIA	2	"Soviet Brainwashing techniques"	6-19-64	Wash. DC	
1133	FBI	3B	Toll charges incurred by Seth Kantor	6-17-64	Dallas	
1138	FBI	3B	Various Ruby phone calls. (Evan Grant; Vegas club)	6-12-64	Dallas	

No.	Agency	Cat.	Description	Date	Location	Class.
1149	FBI	3B	Investigations re Ruby, Paul, Senator, Breck Wall	6-16-64	Dallas	
1171	FBI	2	Lee Harvey Oswald - Internal Security-R-Cuba	6-11-64	Miami	S
1173	FBI	3B; 3C	Letter to Tulsa Tribune by Nick Krochmal, Cleveland	6-12-64	Cleveland	C
1180	FBI	2	Mexican aspects of the investigation	6-26-64	Wash. DC	S
1188	CIA	2	Allegation Oswald was in Tangier, Morocco	6-29-64	Wash. DC	S
1206	FBI	2; 3B	Lee Harvey Oswald - Internal Security-R-Cuba	6-18-64	San Francisco	
1212	FBI	3B	Lee Harvey Oswald re checks	6-23-64	New York	
1216	CIA	2	Memo from Helms entitled " Lee Harvey Oswald "	7-2-64	Wash. DC	S
1220	FBI	2	Oswald; re: Guests at Hotel Del Conmercio	6-26-64	Wash. DC	C
1222	CIA	2	Statements by DeMohrenschildt re assass & LHO	7-6-64	Wash. DC	S
1262	FBI	3C	Jack Ruby: investigation relating to Paul R. Jones	6-29-64	Charlotte	
1268	FBI	3B	Re-interview of Jess Willard Lynch	7-16-64	Phoenix	
1269	FBI	3B; 3C	Location of photos of a bone specimen - CIA	7-14-64	Dallas	
1273	CIA	2	Memo from Helms re apparent inconsistencies from	7-22-64	Wash. DC	S
1287	CIA	2	re Oswald and affidavit concerning cropped picture	7-23-64	Wash. DC	S
1345			Dulles memo re help given O by Mme Yekaterina	7-23-64		
1353	FBI	2	Oswald - Internal Security-R-Cuba	7-27-64	Baltimore	S
1356	CIA	2	Soviet Hunting Societies	8-7-64	Wash. DC	S
1358	CIA	2	Time required for Soviet visa in Helsinki 1964	7-31-64	Wash. DC	TS
1359	FBI	2	re Castro statements on assassination	6-17-64	Wash. DC	
1373	SS	3B; 3C	re Waldemar Boris Kara Patnitsky	8-5-64	New York	
1378	State	2?	Various embassy (Moscow) conversations	7-31-64	Moscow	
1380	FBI	?	Mark Lane	8-4-64	New York	C
1394	FBI	2; 3C	Info furnished by Katherine M. Halle re A.I. Kinchuk	8-7-64	Wash. DC	C
1404	FBI	3B	Records of Dall police Phone calls to Ft Worth	8-11-64	Dallas	
1409	FBI	2	Results of invest to locate Carlos Camorgo	7-29-64	Wash. DC	C
1413	FBI	3C	Interview with Richard D. Walker	8-11-64	Dallas	
1414	FBI	3C	Copy of slip of paper Ruby left at Graphic Studio		Dallas	
1424	FBI	?	Earl Ruby letter to the Commission	7-14-64	Dallas	

No.	Agency	Code	Description	Date	Location	Class.
1425	FBI	2	re American GI Forum	8-25-64	Wash. DC	C
1427	FBI	2	re maintaining contact w Albert Alexander Osborne	5-7-64	Wash. DC	C
1437	FBI	3C	re Sidney Joseph Whiteside	8-17-64	Houston	S
1443	CIA	2	re Konstantin Petrovich Sergievsky	8-28-64	Wash. DC	C
1452	SS	?	re Nancy M. Dowell aka Tami True	8-25-64	Dallas	
1457	FBI	2	Mark Lane and his trip to Europe	8-17-64	Wash. DC	C
1470	FBI	3B	Long distance calls of Harry Olsen	8-11-64	Dallas	
1479	CIA	2	republication of documents furnished the Commiss.	9-11-64	Wash. DC	S
1482	IRS	1	Tax returns Robert B. Baker, Bruce Carlin et al.	9-10-64	Wash. DC	
1486	FBI	2; 3B	Oswald - Internal Security-R-Cuba	9-2-64	Miami	S
1487	FBI	2	Memo entitled Mark Lane James Delaney Garst	8-31-64	Wash. DC	S
1490	State		re permission for WC to publish certain State Docs	9-14-64	Wash. DC	
1504	FBI	3B	Bruce Ray Carlin toll charges	9-14-64	Dallas	
1510	FBI	2	Translations of FBI items D-244 to D-248 & 250	9-15-64	Wash. DC	C
1522	FBI	2; 3A	Mark Lane	9-22-64		C
1523	FBI	3B; 3C	Statement from Omaha re Warren Egbert Hefflon	9-18-64		
1528	FBI	3C	re William Wayne Howe's interest providing home	9-15-64		
1532	CIA	2	Documents seized at end WWII re Joachim Joesten	10-1-64		
1539	FBI	2; 3C	Orest Pena	9-18-64	New Orléans	C
1543	FBI	2	German newspaper article	6-26-64	Wash. DC	S
1544	FBI	3B	Report from a confidential source pertaining to a document from West Germany			C
1545	CIA	2	Activity of Lee Harvey Oswald in Mexico City	6-4-64	Wash. DC	U
1551	CIA	2	Conversations between Cuban President & ambass.	5-22-64		TS
1552	CIA	2	Soviet use of Kidnapping & assass; Sov. press reaction	2-28-64		S

APPENDIX 2

LIST OF DOCUMENTS

REPORTS, MEMORANDA AND DOSSIERS

— Schlumberger Organization in Central America
— Schlumberger Organigram
— Hunt Organization - subsidiary companies - associated companies
— Sinclair Oil Company
— Activities of General Electric, 1955-1966
— General Dynamics - Dossier F 111 (TFX)
    idem   - Laos - Singapore
— Activities of Air America
— American Friends of the Middle East
— Sherman Export Company
— International Cooperation Administration, Washington
— B.R. Report on Molden and Co.
— Organigram of Security Section, United States Embassy, Paris

— Ferguson Trips (Houston, Dallas, New Orleans, London)

— Morgan Davis (testimony on)

— J. Edgar Hoover - Report 7
    - Report M. 1.
    - Copies of photographs

— Dossier Richard M. Helms

— Dossier Richard M. Bissell, Jr.

— George de Mohrenschildt - Alexis Lichine Report
    - Mohrenschilt in Haiti
    - Travels and Contacts in France
    - Recordings of Mohrenschildt and F.D.
    - Mohrenschildt-Schlumberger Connections
    - Identity (Polish, Belgian and Russian testimony)
    - Mohrenschildt Travels in Africa (Lagos Report)

— Richard E. Snyder in Moscow
    idem   - Frankfurt film

— Listening post Panam Building

— PL 26100

— Dossier Lawrence Bunker - B.F.C. Report, 1954 (O.S.)
    - Washington Report, 1963
    - Bank Inquiry, New York

— Mexico Interrogations - Joaquin, Manuel. Recording Maria-Isabel. Testimony P.F. (3-12-64)

— Gary Powers Trial - Persons Present - U2 Dossier

— Gilquen Message

— Mormon Photo - Laboratory Analysis

— Dossier Ray - Montreal and Washington Reports.

— Dossier E.N.I. Mattei Accident.

— Brussels Information - God. (1967)

— Wiesbaden 1963 - Listening Reports

— Dossier General Edwin Anderson Walker

— Corporations Registered in Delaware

— NOR Report, Laos

— Royal Dutch Shell - Iran Report - Nigeria Report

— Roy Cohn - First Testimony
     - Second Testimony
     - Reconstitution of R.C. Activities, 1962-1963
     - Dossier A.G.

— John McCone

— David Green Interrogation

— John Austin - First Testimony
     - Second Testimony (New York, New Orleans)
     - Ranch in California

— FBI Activities in the Caribbean

— FBI Activities in Berlin

— Cuban Intelligence Report on Interrogation of Special Agent G.D.

— Cuban Intelligence Report on Interrogations (April 1964 and September 1966)

— Robert Depugh - Report on Organization of Urban Guerilla Units

— Ballistics Report - Cercottes Firing Tests
     idem   - B.W. Firing Tests

— Copies of photographs 11 - 17

— Photographic Documents 12-38-309-367-G4-G5

Index